STRONG VOICES
the story of the women's chorus movement

Rita M. Kissen

Cover Design by Lisa Brodsky

Published and edited by Lynette McClain and Allen Peacock
McClain Productions
Longmont, Colorado
mcclainproductions.com

In memory of my singing sisters,
Anine Burgess, Betsy Tiemann, and Bobbie Jordan

And of all the lovers and friends
kept from gathering

*"Let's have a song here for me and for you
and the love that we cannot hide."*
--John Calvi, "The Ones Who Aren't Here"

Photo Credits

Cover photo: Anna Crusis Women's Choir and MUSE
        Women's Choir performing at the 2010 Sister
        Singers Festival. Photo by Kat Fitzgerald.

p. 139: Images from Sister Singers Network Archive, 1981-
        2003, Sophia Smith Collection, Smith College,
        Northampton, Massachusetts. Used by Permission.

p. 140: Poster courtesy of Marte Parham.
        Photo courtesy of Womansong of Asheville

p. 141: Posters courtesy of Common Woman Chorus,
        Durham, NC and San Diego Women's Chorus

All Sister Singers festival photos by Kat Fitzgerald, Mystic
        Images, www.mysticimagesphotography.com

p. 144: Posters courtesy of Voices Rising, Sister Singers Network, and
        Amasong Lesbian/Feminist Chorus of Champaign-Urbana

p. 145: Posters courtesy of PFLAG Juneau Pride Chorus
        and The New Mexico Women's Chorus

p. 146: Posters courtesy of the San Diego Women's Chorus, Rainbow
        Women's Chorus of San Jose, and MUSE Women's Choir of Cincinnati

p. 147: Women in Harmony photo by Dylan Verner;
        Women in Harmony poster by Joshua Boley

p. 349: Author photo by Norm Rasulis

Acknowledgements

Most writers thank their spouses or significant others at the end of their acknowledgements, after they have expressed their gratitude to editors, agents, colleagues, and friends. I too have a long list of people who helped make this book a reality, but my greatest thanks go to my husband, Norm Rasulis. For more than 30 years, Norm and I have shared a life rich with parenting and grandparenting, gardening and social action, and adventures that have taken us from an island in Maine to the Front Range of the Rocky Mountains. During the long incubation of this book, Norm has been my faithful reader, editor, literary critic, and moral supporter. In a very real sense, *Strong Voices* belongs to him as much as it does to me and the women who speak in these pages.

Strong Voices had its genesis during my years as a second soprano in Portland Maine's Women in Harmony, where I discovered the magic of choral singing and the power of women's voices. No matter where I live or where I sing, Kitty Beller-McKenna, Deana Ingraham Gurney, and the members of Women in Harmony will always be my sisters in song. Singing alongside them, the members of the Maine Gay Men's Chorus have enhanced LGBT choral pride in Maine and honored me by performing several of my compositions.

The women's choruses of the Sister Singers Network and the members of the Sister Singers Steering Committee have kept our network alive and well through hard times and good times, and are a constant inspiration to all of us who sing for social justice. My thanks to all the singers, composers and directors who shared their stories with me and to Marte Parham and DeDe Shelton, who welcomed me to their home and their city of Houston with a memorable HeartSong reunion. I am also inspired by the choruses of GALA, North America's LGBT premier choral association, who have fostered visibility and pride and brought beautiful music to audiences all over the world. Closer to home, the members of the Silvertones Senior Choir have offered me a new singing community in Fort Collins, Colorado.

My editor, Lynette McClain, has been my political collaborator and valued friend from the time I first moved to Colorado; it has been a joy to work together as she transformed *Strong Voices* from a document to a finished book.

My parents, Goldie and Isidore Kissen, first taught me about social justice and social activism as they shared their stories of Popular Front marches, of seeing Billie Holiday sing "Strange Fruit" to a transfixed audience at Café Society, and of walks around the lake at Camp Nitgadaiget, where my father proposed to my mother. Their memories live in every page of this book.

Finally, I celebrate the members of my blended and extended family: my children and stepchildren, Michelle Brodsky, Andrew Brodsky, Mich Rasulis, and Andre Rasulis, and their spouses, Lisa Brodsky and Tiffany Marra—and most of all, my five wonderful grandchildren: Benjamin, Julian, Nina, Conrad, and Lilah. You remind me every day why we struggle and why we sing.

Introduction

One summer afternoon in 1980, a small group of women gathered at a women's music festival in Western Michigan with a pad of yellow lined paper and the hope of starting a women's chorus network. They were members of the choruses that were appearing in the wake of the second wave of the feminist movement, the Civil Rights movement, and the women's music movement that had brought lesbian/feminist singer-songwriters to concert stages and women's bookstores. The story of how that handwritten list grew into a national network of women's choruses singing for social justice is a story about the power of music to transform the lives of the women who sing together, the communities they build, and the world around them.

In recent years more and more Americans have discovered the benefits and pleasures of choral singing. A 2008 study of choral singers by Chorus America found that over 32 million adults regularly sing in 270,000 independent, school-related and religious choirs nationwide.[1] The benefits of choral singing, which have been well documented by researchers, literally begin at the cellular level, since singing with others increases levels of the hormones that fight disease and promote trust and lowers levels of cortisol, the "stress hormone."[2] Because singing begins with the breath and demands slower than normal respiration, it fosters vocal and respiratory health and aids cardiovascular function.[3] Music therapists employ singing to treat those affected by strokes, Parkinson's Disease, Alzheimer's, autism, and various forms of brain damage; feminist music therapists have used women's music to help women suffering from chronic pain and abuse to heal. Lynn O'Brien, a board-certified music therapist and singer-songwriter in Minneapolis, calls music "an incredible language that touches us in places that words can't."[4]

Singing together transforms choral communities as well as individual singers. Studies show that choral singers synchronize their heart rates and that singing with others promotes social bonding and combats isolation.[5] "Singers don't just join choruses; they belong to choruses," writes Don Lee of Chorus America. "In that unique, ritualized setting, people of divergent backgrounds gather in order to make music, and by making music together, they form a community. Choral singers experience the truth in the cliché that the whole is greater than the sum of its parts."[6]

Some contemporary choral communities have formed to lend emotional and physical support for singers in stressful life situations, like the Military Wives Choirs of Great Britain, which help women in the military community survive the frequent moves and the uncertainty of their loved ones' long deployments.[7] Other choruses have reached out to foster coalitions in places where politics have not succeeded: the YMCA Jerusalem Youth Chorus provides a space for Israeli and Palestinian high school students from East and West Jerusalem "to grow together in song and dialogue."[8] One of the fastest growing segments of the choral community is the network of senior choruses, which counteract the physical challenges of aging and the mental and emotional isolation that often besets older people. Young@ Heart in Northampton, Massachusetts has been singing and performing since 1982 and was featured in a 2007 documentary that included numbers by Jimi Hendrix, Coldplay, and Sonic Youth, among others. In 2014, the chorus launched the Young@ Heart Prison Project, bringing the chorus to sing with inmates at three local jails and inspiring a live album featuring chorus members and inmates singing together.[9] Encore Creativity for Older Adults, a national network of twenty-one senior chorales with over 1200 singers, began as a study by Dr. Gene Cohen, Director for the Center on Aging, Health and Humanities at George Washington University, investigating the impact of cultural programs on the mental, physical, and social well-being of older adults. By 2018, the organization was running "summer camps" for senior singers, a Canadian concert tour, and a full schedule of concerts by individual and combined chorales.[10]

One of the largest of the senior choruses that have proliferated around the country is the Silvertones of Fort Collins, Colorado, with over 150 singing members. Founded in 2012 under the auspices of Fort Collins's classical concert choir, the Larimer Chorale, the Silvertones chorus was partly inspired by Young@ Heart; however, after founder Wendy White, who also served as Executive Director of the Larimer Chorale, attended a Young@ Heart concert in Boulder, Colorado, she asked herself, "Okay, how are we different? ... Young@Heart is much smaller and they cover rock songs." The Silvertones included many seniors with serious choral experience: "When they could be singing four part harmonies of classic music, why should they be singing 'Born to be Wild'?"[11] Nevertheless, the Silvertones remains an inclusive chorus, with members ranging from choral novices to experienced professionals. Director Michael Todd Krueger, who also directs the Larimer Chorale, tells singers in the Silvertones, "We have to take some chances. We have to trust each other. We have to trust ourselves. Then you can take chances in other parts of your life."[12]

Feminist Choruses: "There is Something Different"

All choral singers, whether they are high school students, community singers, or the Sweet Adelines, share the physical and social bonds of making music together. Similarly, political activists working toward a common goal share a dedication to their cause, from worker solidarity to lesbian and gay visibility. Women's groups, from quilters to soccer teams, work together for a common purpose and often create relationships that radiate into the rest of their lives. But feminist choruses bring all these elements together to create something new. Estelle Phillips, a long-time singer with the Charlottesville Women's Choir, spoke for many when she said, "There is something different—the sense of joy that comes from singing the music and hearing the music and the group effort and working through problems that, say, my tennis group doesn't involve and my book group doesn't involve."[13]

Thirty years ago women's choruses were among the few places where lesbians felt free to be themselves—in the words of one singer who had just come out in her school district, "the place to breathe." Though LGBT people have become more visible in American society, women continue to find their authentic voices in feminist choruses. Women whose high school chorus directors told them just to mouth the words discover that they can sing. Survivors of emotional or physical abuse—many of whom had literally lost their voices—find the courage to speak and to sing. Many women describe their experiences in spiritual terms; they speak of the connection to the other singers and to the chorus as a whole, to the audience, and to the Divine (however they chose to name or define it). Along with this sense of connection, they often describe feelings of "deep and quiet joy," "peace and joy," "happiness and wholeness."[14] Janice Scalza, who sings with the Grand Rapids Women's Chorus, believes that women's choruses "have a mission that's different from the Sweet Adelines, that's different from the church chorus. It's about what you're doing as a group and what you're saying when you're up there. [It's] the joy of the actual singing, the joy of the music itself, the joy of the beauty of the music combined with the purpose of the connection of the women within your group, and then knowing you're connected to women across the world."[15]

The story of women's choruses is also a story of how a coalition of singers that began as a mostly separatist musical home for the lesbian community grew into an inclusive network welcoming women of all sexual and gender orientations and singing for social justice in the wider world. As identity politics yielded to coalition-building, and as essentialism gave way to intersectionality—the concept of overlapping biological, social, and cultural identities —women's choruses have become a vital part of the LGBT choral movement, with a mission expressed in the words of Gary Miller, founding director of the New York City Gay Men's Chorus: "If you want to sing, join a chorus. If you want to change the world, join a gay chorus."[16]

My Story: Women's Studies and Women in Harmony

My own relationship to women's choruses began when I joined Women in Harmony, a women's chorus in Portland,

Maine, shortly after retiring from thirty-five years of teaching English, women's studies, and teacher education. Though I had not sung in a choir since eighth grade, singing had always been part of my life, and I already knew many WIH members through my political work in the women's and LGBT communities.

By the time I joined, Women in Harmony had been singing for twelve years and had evolved from a small group of lesbians to a fifty-five-member chorus with a paid director and accompanist, a performance schedule of two yearly concerts, and a membership composed about equally of lesbians and straight women. Lesbians were out and visible in the chorus, but by 2005 solidarity had long since replaced separatism. It was only much later that I learned of the identity conflicts that had once threatened the life of the chorus.

As a long-time member of the women's studies faculty at my university, and as a researcher who had interviewed dozens of lesbian and gay teachers for my first book, *The Last Closet: The Real Lives of Lesbian and Gay Teachers*, I had been immersed in the world of feminist theory for much of my career. I had also co-founded a local chapter of the Gay, Lesbian and Straight Education Network (GLSEN), and the first Maine chapter of Parents, Families and Friends of Lesbians and Gays (PFLAG), and had served as a media spokesperson for a successful campaign to add sexual orientation to the Portland Human Rights Ordinance. I was proud to consider myself a scholar/ activist (a self-definition that did not always sit well with tenure committees), working simultaneously in academia and civic life.

Teaching and writing connected me to a community of academic feminists; political advocacy gave me a home in the lesbian and gay community. But from the moment I joined the second sopranos in the communal backrub that began every Women in Harmony rehearsal, I realized there was something about this community that was different from any other group I had ever belonged to. When I discovered that we were part of a larger network that shared our mission of singing together for social justice, the scholar/researcher in me wondered how and why these two hours every week could foster a community unlike any other, while my activist side wanted to understand the place of this unique choral network in the feminist and LGBT movements of which I was a part.

Studying contemporary feminist choruses led me back to earlier women's choral communities, ranging from the anonymous drummers depicted on ancient terra cottas to Miriam in the Hebrew Bible; from the *partheneia* (girls' choruses) of ancient Greece to the medieval nuns singing under the leadership of Hildegard of Bingen; and from the orphan girls of the eighteenth century Venetian *Pietà*, for whom Antonio Vivaldi composed some of his most glorious choral music, to Johannes Brahms's *Frauenchor* in 1850s Hamburg. Feminist singer/activists still debate the nature and degree of the power enjoyed by these women. Some argue that women working together in groups have greater opportunities for enhanced status than women without such ties, and that the religious function of women's choral singing in the ancient world exerted a form of social control. Others remind us that no matter how transformative choral singing may have been for individual singers or choruses, their power did not translate into the wider world of patriarchal societies or effect the transformation of these societies from patriarchy to something else. Queer theorists, who view musical composition and performance through the lens of gender and sexuality, have redefined the relations between composer and performer and between performer and audience.

Moving to more recent history, Chapter 2 explores choral singing in nineteenth and twentieth century immigrant, labor, and Civil Rights struggles, and the part women played in those choruses and those movements. Along with this history, "The People's Music" continues the exploration begun in Chapter 1 of the relationship between music and power and the role of singing in social and political change. Finally, Chapter 3 describes the rise and significance of the women's music movement of the 1970s and 1980s—the musical expression of second wave feminism that gave birth to feminist choruses, the main focus of this book.

Part II traces the women's chorus movement from its origins in the lesbian communities and women's music festivals of the 1980s to the formation of Sister Singers, a national network uniting women's choruses all over the country. Chapters 5 and 6 consider the challenges of creating musical communities that embody lesbian/feminist values while pursuing musical excellence and dealing with the legal, financial and logistical challenges of running an organization. Part II also explores the deeper limitations faced by mostly White choruses seeking to reach across boundaries of race and ethnicity—a question that still troubles many feminist choruses despite the examples of a few successes.

Part III begins with the shift from separatism to solidarity, precipitated in part by the AIDS crisis that brought gay men and lesbians together in the choral world as well as in the world at large. As the crisis receded, women's choruses continued to pursue partnerships with their gay fellow-singers. While Sister Singers remained the primary network for feminist choruses, some also joined GALA, the Gay and Lesbian Association of Choruses, whose membership included men's, women's, mixed, and eventually, youth and trans choruses. The final chapters of *Strong Voices* carry the story into the present, as women's choruses continue to sing for LGBT equality and for social justice in the wider world. In 2014, Sister Singers celebrated the thirtieth anniversary of the first National Women's Chorus Festival, when seven choruses came to Kansas City to join together in song. Though much has changed since that first gathering, feminist choruses remain true to the mission statement of the Network's oldest chorus, Anna Crusis: "We sing to celebrate the diversity of women's lives and culture; to find communion; to nurture and sustain; to comfort and to heal; to open hearts and minds; and to struggle together for a just and compassionate world."[17]

A Note About Terminology

In writing about sex and gender identification, I have generally echoed the terminology of the particular historical moments described in this book. The acronym LGBTQ (Lesbian, Gay, Bisexual, Transgender and Queer) is a twenty-first century umbrella term frequently employed by members of those communities and their allies. I have used it in my narrative, particularly when describing people and events of the late 1990s and early 2000s. In the early days of the gay liberation movement, men and women who were not heterosexual generally referred to themselves as "gay" or "lesbian" (with "gay" occasionally used to cover both sexes), and so I use those terms when quoting or referencing specific people or movements of those eras. The term "queer" arose among non-heterosexuals in the late 1980s, and though there is still debate over the use of the term by heterosexual allies, I have used it in the sense that people who identify as queer use it—that is, to suggest that sexual identities are fluid and not necessarily binary. These shifting terminologies reflect our shifting understandings of sex and gender identity, a phenomenon which I have tried to honor and acknowledge in my story.

Table of Contents

Part I

Foremothers

1

Miriam's Daughters:
A Historical Perspective

Women have been singing together since the beginning of recorded history, and undoubtedly long before that. Terracottas depicting female figures with disc-shaped objects presumed to be frame drums and dating back as far as the third century B.C.E. have been found at various sites in Mesopotamia, the Mediterranean, and Egypt, along with carvings and sacred texts depicting women with frame drums singing and dancing.[1] Women's dancing, drumming, and singing were associated with temple rituals in Egypt, with victory celebrations in ancient Israel, and with Dionysian rites in Greece, where *maenads* (Dionysian women) performed "frenzied dances" and ran screaming through the woods during midwinter nights.[2] The late Layne Redmond, herself a celebrated performer and promoter of the frame drum, asserted that "the drum was the primary trance-inducing instrument in transition rites" and that "the drumming priestess was the intermediary between divine and human realms."[3]

Redmond based many of her assumptions on the evidence of Çatalhöyük, in present day Turkey, one of the largest known Neolithic sites, which was occupied continuously from 7,200 to 5,500 B.C.E. Çatalhöyük was first excavated in the 1960s by James Mellaart, an assistant director of the British Institute of Archaeology at Ankara. Mellaart discovered what may be the oldest representation of the frame drum, a wall painting of human figures, one of whom holds a frame drum, surrounding a giant bull.[4] His elaborate theory of Mother Goddess worship at Çatalhöyük was challenged by many other archaeologists, some of whom accused him of fabricating some of the supposed mythological evidence on which he based his theories; the furor led the Turkish government to expel Mellaart and close the site, which did not reopen until a new team of archeologists began exploring it again in the mid-1990s.

This debacle notwithstanding, the idea of a female-dominated past built on goddess worship attracted a good deal of passionate energy from second-wave feminists like Marija Gimbutas, Riane Eisler, and Merlin Stone,[5] and an equally passionate response from scholars like theologian Rita Gross, who asserts that the existence of female forms in the archaeological record of prehistoric societies and of powerful goddesses in mythological literature "[does] not prove that women were equal, in the modern sense of the term, which seems quite unlikely, or that they lived lives with which modern women could be satisfied."[6]

Sarah Pomeroy, in the 1995 edition of her groundbreaking work on Greek and Roman women's roles, *Goddesses, Whores, Wives and Slaves*, chose to retain the text of the original 1975 edition but declared herself "even less willing to entertain the possibility of a prehistoric society in the Greek world in which women enjoyed a higher status than men or were equal to them. ...As later, well-documented historical periods show, a queen may rule in a patriarchal society."[7]

Although the debate over goddess theology has receded from feminist scholarship, the concept remains alive in popular culture and still inspires many women, including those in some feminist choruses, who find that woman-identified songs and chants foster solidarity and transcendence. I will return to this topic in my discussion of repertoire in Chapter 8.

Sophie Drinker: Women's Musical History

Originally published in 1948, Sophie Drinker's landmark account of women singing together, *Music & Women*, documented the universality of women's choral singing and of patriarchal attempts to silence women's voices across the globe. Drinker asserted, "The earliest forms of human society seem to have resembled those of the tribes that today have the least developed cultures."[8] She linked motherhood and heterosexuality to women's musical power and lamented patriarchal society's "deep denial" of women's inner life— "a deep and intuitive wisdom, a kind of at-oneness with all the processes of growth and decay, birth and rebirth, in the universe."[9] Drinker's final chapter, "Artemis Rising," celebrated women's increasing musical prominence at mid-century and looked forward to greater female leadership in religion, healing, and music, the arenas for which she believed women were innately gifted.

Although Drinker's essentialism, her view of "primitive" societies, and her readiness to draw conclusions about eras for which we have no written record may trouble a modern reader, the questions she raised still resonate for contemporary feminists. As Ruth Solie points out in her Afterword to the 1995 edition, Drinker manifested "a vividly clear understanding of the systematic ways in which social institutions had deprived women of [their] birthright" and of the ways that patriarchal culture has sought to silence women's voices.[10]

Miriam's Song

The earliest record of women's choral singing in the Judeo-Christian tradition is the story of Miriam in the Hebrew Bible. She first appears by name in Exodus 15:20-21, where she leads the women in song and dance after the crossing of the Red Sea: "And Miriam the prophetess, the sister of Aaron, took a timbrel in her hand; and all the women went after her with timbrels and with dances. And Miriam sang to them: 'Sing to God, for He has triumphed gloriously, the horse and his rider He has thrown into the sea.'"[11]

These brief verses have inspired much speculation among Biblical scholars and historians, as well as contemporary feminists seeking alternatives to the patriarchal messages of the

Hebrew Bible. Carol Meyers connects them to ancient images and accounts of women drumming, dancing and singing, pointing out that the Hebrew word *tof* probably refers to a hand drum, rather than its usual translation as a tambourine, which Meyers contends was not invented until the Roman period.[12] Meyers and many other modern scholars agree with Frank M. Cross, Jr. and David Noel Freedman, who first suggested that Miriam's Song is among the oldest verses in the Torah and was originally part of a longer song (now lost) celebrating the Israelites' victory over Pharaoh's pursuing forces. Others conclude that these verses were originally attached to Moses's much longer victory song immediately preceding Miriam's verses.[13] Whatever the provenance of Miriam's song, she is unquestionably unique. She is the only woman in the Torah to be introduced as a prophetess, and although the Torah contains no examples of Miriam actually prophesying, other Biblical accounts frequently associate musical performances with prophecy.[14]

Though the absence of archeological evidence and contemporary literary and historical references has convinced many scholars that neither Miriam nor Moses was a historical figure, her importance for this study lies in the legends that have grown up around her as a leader of women. In addition to leading women's drumming, singing, and dancing, Miriam is associated throughout the Bible with water, the element of life. Although she is referred to by name for the first time in Exodus 15, her identity as the sister of Aaron has led commentators to assume that she is Moses's unnamed sister in Exodus 2:4, where she stands nearby after Moses's mother Jochebed has put the basket holding the baby Moses in the river, hoping to save him from Pharaoh's edict condemning all first-born Hebrew boys. When Pharaoh's daughter finds the basket, Miriam steps forward and offers to find a woman to nurse the baby. She brings baby Moses back to Jochebed, his natural mother, to be cared for until he is weaned.

Numbers 20:1 describes Miriam's death, after which "there was no water for the congregation" (20:2). From this brief reference has developed a Midrash (commentary) describing a well that followed Miriam and the people through the desert during their wanderings and sustained the people until her death.

Finally, the story of Miriam, whether historical or apocryphal, raises significant questions about women's singing and women's power. Carol Meyers believes that women's dance-drumming-song performances "would have exerted social control because of the intrinsic aesthetic appeal of the event and also because of its political and religious function." Further, she argues that "women who have formal social ties with other women—who work with them in groups—have much greater opportunities for enhanced status than women without such ties."[15]

Meyers's emphasis on the power enjoyed by women singers raises an important question: what kind of power? Feminists have distinguished between the (mostly male) "power over" and the female/feminist concept of "power with." Does the power experienced by women who create communities of singers and enact religious rituals translate into other kinds of power in a patriarchal society?

Some writers point out that women in liminal situations—environments where old structures have been overthrown and new ones not yet created—may experience a heightened degree of independence and cite the moments after the crossing of the Red Sea as one of those liminal times, when the old structures of Egyptian slavery had been destroyed and the Israelites did not yet know what awaited them in the desert. In such times, "some gender roles among the colonized are temporarily suspended. ... Women and men are both victims of imperialism; they fight to reclaim their human rights together."[16]

Early Classical Choruses: *The Partheneia*

In 1851, French Egyptologist August Mariette discovered a ruin at Saqqara, a vast ancient burial ground nineteen miles south of present day Cairo. Inside lay a fantastic trove of statues, tablets, and papyri, including a papyrus with a fragment comprising a *partheneion* (Greek lyric poem) by the seventh century B.C. Spartan poet Alcman, unearthed four years later.

The poem was meant to be sung by two choirs of young women under the direction of a choir leader named Hagesichora (meaning, literally, "she who leads the chorus"), and a second leader, Agido ("a girl belonging to the family of the Agiads," one of the two Spartan royal houses). Both legend and written and iconographic evidence suggest that the female *choregos* was probably a slightly older or more mature young woman, and was distinguished from her sister-singers by her beauty, celebrated in great detail in the *partheneia*. These generic names suggest that the *partheneion* was not a piece of occasional poetry composed for a single occasion and for a specific group of girls, but that "the chorus represented the polis as such and the poem was, so to speak, timeless."[17]

Though little is known about Alcman, his papyri provide a window into the choral world of young Greek women and the role of choral singing in their education, their adult lives, and the life of the community. Music was an essential part of both boys' and girls' education in ancient Greece, and since girls did not attend school (unlike their male counterparts), choral singing was the primary mode of their education.

Claude Calame, author of the definitive study of young women's choruses in ancient Greece, places the *partheneia* in the context of tribal initiation rites marking the transition from youth to adulthood, creating "a complete system of reproduction of the community, particularly in the domain of the social relationships of sex." For Greek adolescent girls, "the recitation of mythical legends was an introduction to the mythical and religious patrimony upon which the city's institutions were founded."[18]

Unlike Calame, Eva Stehle believes that the *partheneia* were performed in a public ceremony rather than as a private initiation rite but she agrees that "the performance was directed at the community at large, combining a celebration of the harvest season with the presentation of the young women."[19]

For adolescent girls in ancient Greece, entering womanhood meant entering an adult society where gender roles were strictly delineated and women had few or no legal or economic rights. Marriages were arranged by men on the basis of economic and political considerations, with the primary purpose of procreation. Women were excluded from the law courts and although they did participate in some economic activity, most of their work took place at home, such as wool working, spinning, baking and selling bread, nursing, and midwifery. Athenian women's primary responsibility was the maintenance of the *oikos*, or household establishment, following the dictates of Aristotle as summarized by Eva Cantarella: "The *oikos* (the central element of his political theory) is arranged around a head, and 'although there may be exceptions to the order of nature, the male is by nature fitter to command than the female.'"[20]

The one arena of civic life in which Greek women played a significant public role was religion. In addition to the rituals enacted in the *partheneia*, adult women's choruses celebrated Aphrodite and Hera, goddesses associated with adult female sexuality and marriage. In addition, choruses of married women reenacted the Bacchic frenzy of the *Maenads*, the mythical followers of Dionysus—one of the few occasions when the line separating women of different social classes temporarily disappeared. Women also had an important role in wedding and mourning rituals. In her study of the "choreography of women's speech," Josine Blok writes that "women were considered the true lamenters because they were thought both by men and by themselves to be the ones who suffered the greatest pain, indeed, as the ones who knew the truth of fate and grief."[21]

Despite their importance in communal religious observances, Athenian women had no part in writing, performing or judging the Greek dramas that formed part of the religious life of Athens, including the most important theatrical event, the annual *Dionysia*. While there is conflicting evidence about whether women actually attended the *Dionysia*, we do know that there were female choruses in more than half of the extant comedies and tragedies. Mary deForest states that female choruses served as "an embarrassment. Terrible acts of violence are witnessed by fifteen people who do nothing to prevent it." deForest also claims that the female chorus "reinforced the Athenian stereotype of women as an alien subculture — the race of women." She points out that some female choruses "look weird: blood-sucking *Erinyes*; dark-skinned *Danaids*; *Oceanids* on winged chariots; *Bacchants* dressed in deer skins. Even choruses made up of ordinary women are often foreign—captives or tourists." [22]

Although women in Greek society were expected to fulfill assigned roles of wives and mothers, conditions for Spartan women were somewhat different from those of their Athenian counterparts. Unlike Athenian women, who married at fourteen, Spartan women did not marry or bear children until they turned eighteen. While this custom was meant to ensure that Spartan women gave birth to healthy boys who would become strong Spartan warriors, it undoubtedly contributed to the greater well-being of Spartan mothers. Spartans were the only Greek women who were well fed and drank wine, and they had more social and political freedom than their Athenian sisters. Pomeroy speculates that the greater social freedom enjoyed by Spartan women also led to more same-sex relationships.[23] The most famous Spartan woman poet, Sappho of Lesbos, was only one of a number of women with a circle of young followers. Yet, as Kay O'Pry points out, "A Spartan woman was still a means for producing children for the state. A Spartan woman's role in politics was much like that of all other women in Greece. They could not take active part in it."[24]

Given the subordination of Athenian women (and to a lesser extent, of their Spartan sisters), the rituals suggested in Alcman's *partheneia* and documented elsewhere are in striking contrast to the lives these young singers would live as adult women. In Alcman's poem, Hagesichora's choir and the Pleiades compete against each other in the dedication of a new plough just before sunrise, probably on the night of a full moon. The dedication takes place before Aotis, a goddess roughly identified with the Greek goddess Artemis. The choral song praises the beauty of Hagesichora and Agido, comparing them to powerful stallions. Most striking is the sensuous praise for Hagesichora expressed by all the choral singers as erotic longing: "It is Hagesichora who makes me waste away."[25] The chorus's overtly erotic language contrasts sharply with the standards of sexual modesty for young women in ancient

Greece, providing "another example of the *parrhesia* [the right of free speech accorded to men in ancient Greece] extended to choruses of young women on specific, ritual occasions."[26] The choral structure itself contributed to the special character of the *partheneia*: in contrast to the singers in tragic choruses, who were grouped in a rectangle, lyric choruses were generally arranged in a circle with the *choregos* serving as both chorus leader and chorus member. Particularly in Sparta, the homoeroticism of the choral culture united each chorus member to the *choregos* as the leader expressed her love for all the members through her love for one of them.[27]

Modern commentators recognize the importance of the *partheneia* in creating bonds among young women and in marking their transition from childhood to womanhood. However, they disagree on the degree to which the young women singing in these choruses were bound by male ideology or were able to subvert or defy it. André Lardinois believes that the *partheneia* "represent an implicit acknowledgement by ancient Greek men that women have a distinctive and valid perspective on life, especially when it came to what they considered feminine issues like motherhood, marriage, and love. Greek men—on occasion!—allowed their women to express this perspective in public and were willing to listen to it.[28]

James William Smith takes a similarly essentialist view of female performance in ancient Greece, alluding to "the power that comes from a specific moment in the female life cycle [when] the *parthenoi* are at their most fertile and their most beautiful, with Hagesichora and Agido serving as prime examples." According to Smith, this makes the *parthenoi* "desirable, fertile, politically important, and economically valuable." Though a young woman might feel "nostalgic" at leaving the "social, political, and economic status of a *parthenos*" behind, Smith assures us, she could look forward to the "prospect of motherhood and wedded life, [which] doubtless provided some women with a great deal of pleasure."[29]

Most of Smith's analysis focuses on Spartan women, who did have more social freedom than Athenian women. But as Eva Cantarella observes, even Spartan women "still had only one function, that of producing sons for the city. ...For the male, the achievement of citizenship was marked by a series of stages; for the woman. the end state was marriage, and only one stage preceded it—virginity."[30]

Medieval Cloisters and Hildegard of Bingen

Turning from ancient to medieval times in Europe, we find that the majority of women's choral performances took place among cloistered nuns under the patriarchal authority of the church. Life during the High Middle Ages (approximately 1000 to 1300) offered few choices for women; noblewomen were betrothed by their parents, often in infancy, and married in their teens, while peasant women married later and had somewhat more freedom in their choice of mates. In all cases, women were subject to the rule of their husbands as sanctioned by the Bible, and pregnancy and childbirth were dangerous and often fatal. The only other choice open to medieval women was to enter a nunnery, although the dowry system that prevailed in most convents meant that most nuns came from families of means. Some women took religious orders out of piety or to escape arranged marriages; others were promised to the Church by parents with too many daughters, for political advantage, or as a measure of their own piety.

In the year 1106, an eight-year-old girl named Hildegard, the tenth and last child of a family of the lower nobility, was enclosed at Disibodenberg, a Benedictine monastery in the southwestern part of what is now Germany. Her companion and mentor was Jutta, an anchoress several years her senior (sources differ on whether Jutta was an adolescent or a young woman), who taught Hildegard to write and to chant the psalms of the Benedictine liturgy.

Hildegard's entry into Disibodenberg marks the beginning of one of the most remarkable stories of the High Middle Ages. As Barbara Newman, one of her most prolific biographers, points out, Hildegard was the only woman of her age accepted as an authoritative voice on Christian doctrine and allowed to preach openly before mixed audiences of clergy and laity; the author of the first known morality play; a widely-respected authority on botany and biology; a medical authority and herbalist; and the first saint whose official biography includes a first-person memoir. Most remarkable of all, Hildegard was the composer of dozens of chants and choral songs, the only composer of her era known both by name and by a surviving body of choral music.[31]

Hildegard's theology—and her spiritual authority—came from what she called the "living light," the source of spiritual visions throughout her life. At the age of three, she later wrote, "I saw an immense light that shook my soul [but] when I became exhausted I tried to find out from my nurse if she saw anything at all other than the usual external objects. And she answered 'Nothing,' because she saw nothing like I did. Then I was seized with a great fear and did not dare to reveal this to anyone."[32] For the rest of her life Hildegard experienced visions, which she described as "an extremely strong, sparkling, fiery light coming from the open heavens. It pierced my brain, my heart and my breast through and through like a flame which did not burn; however, it warmed me. It heated me up very much like the sun warms an object on which it is pouring out rays."[33]

In the year 1136, when Hildegard was thirty, her mentor Jutta died and Hildegard was appointed abbess of the nuns' community at Disibodenberg. (Because her women's community was neither a women's house nor a double monastery, Hildegard was given the title *magistra*, or prioress; however, she and others commonly referred to her as "abbess.") Jutta's death and Hildegard's promotion marked the beginning of a lifetime of creativity that included *Scivias*, three great volumes of visionary theology; one of the largest bodies of letters (nearly 400) to survive from the Middle ages, addressed to correspondents ranging from popes to emperors to abbots and abbesses and including records of many of the sermons she preached in the 1160s and 1170s; two volumes of natural medicine, *Physica* and *Causae et Curae*; an invented language called the *lingua ignota* ("unknown language"); and various minor works. Most significant for music historians is Hildegard's *Symphonia armonie celestium revelationum* (Symphony of the Harmony of Heavenly Revelations), which consists of sixty-nine chants divided into eight sections, including "Songs to God the Father and Son," "Songs to the Virgin Mary," "Songs to the Holy Spirit," "Songs for the Celestial Choirs," "Songs for Patron Saints," "Songs for Virgins, Widows and Innocents," and "Songs for the Church" (*Eclesia*).[34] Though the texts followed the received repertoire of liturgical chant, the musical settings that Hildegard composed were decidedly original. Margot Fassler speculates that Hildegard "probably composed her liturgical texts as she sang, in the way the twentieth century composer Igor Stravinsky wrote music at the piano or Charlie Parker improvised compositions on his saxophone."[35]

Benedictine life revolved around music and prayer, inextricably linked together. The Rule of St. Benedict specified eight separate Offices, beginning with Matins at 2 a.m. and ending with Compline at bedtime. The Cistercian Reform of the twelfth century attempted to bring all monastic music into line with the ascetic properties of Cistercian monastic life, declaring, "It befits men to sing with a manly voice, and not in a womanish manner ... with tinkling, or, as it is said in the vernacular, with 'false' voices, as if imitating the wantonness of minstrels."[36] There is no record of whether Hildegard knew of this edict, but her melodies represent an entirely different approach to chant. Bruce Holsinger, whose studies of medieval music argue for what he calls "the corporeality of musical culture and musical experience in the European Middle Ages," notes that Hildegard exceeded the proper melodic range for twelfth-century plainchant.[37] Others have noted Hildegard's "freely spun melodic lines with their irregular, unpredictable gestures" in which "musical stability arises from melodic unity, rather than from external factors such as strophic form or regular poetic meter." Her melodies made serious demands on the nuns who sang them, often encompassing a range of two or more octaves, and in some cases nearly three octaves.[38] The best way to appreciate the particular qualities of Hildegard's music in the *Symphonia* is to listen: since the 1990s numerous recordings of her music have appeared on CD.[39]

Musical composition was only one of the ways in which Hildegard defied conventional expectations. Soon after her appointment as abbess, she began writing music for her nuns to sing as part of the Divine Office. Then, in 1141, she experienced a vision that convinced her to write about the inner life that she had kept hidden from the rest of the world. Recalling this vision in *Scivias*, she wrote:

> I saw a great splendor in which resounded a voice from Heaven saying to me, "O fragile human, ashes of ashes and filth of filth! Say and write what you see and hear. But since you are timid in speaking, and simple in expounding, and untaught in writing, speak and write these things not by a human mouth, and not by the understanding of human invention, and not by the requirements of human composition, but as you see and hear them on high in the heavenly places as the wonders of God.... It happened that in the eleven hundred and forty-first year of the incarnation of the Son of God, Jesus Christ, when I was forty-two years and seven months old, Heaven was opened and a fiery light of exceeding brilliance came and permeated my whole brain and inflamed my whole heart and my whole breast, not like a burning but like a warming flame, as the sun warms anything its rays touch.[40]

In her account of this vision, as in most of her writing and preaching, Hildegard presents herself as "untaught" and "timid"; elsewhere in her writing she refers to herself as "a poor little figure of a woman."[41] Assuming the mantle of humility, Hildegard could associate herself with Christ's exaltation of the lowly, as well as with his mother, Mary. Hildegard always maintained that her visions came directly from God, whose authority superseded all human judgment. This assertion received papal sanction when various monks at Disibodenberg learned of her visions and reported then to Pope Eugene III. The Pope sent a delegation to Disibodenberg to meet with Hildegard and examine some of her writings in the *Scivias*, which they brought back for his perusal. After several more meetings and exchanges of letters, the Pope gave his approval for her writing, which Hildegard took to mean papal sanction for her visions as well.[42]

By 1140, word of Hildegard's community had spread and the number of nuns at Disibodenberg had grown from twelve to eighteen. Hildegard had learned of a ruined monastery at Rupertsberg, a small mountain near Bingen on the Rhine. After a particularly powerful vision, she determined to free herself from Disibodenberg and move her nuns to Rupertsberg, where she would be in full charge of the community. Not surprisingly, the monks at Disibodenberg denied this request, whereupon Hildegard fell into deep physical distress. At last Abbot Kuno entered her chamber and found her "sick and utterly paralyzed like a pile of stones."[43] Forced to conclude that the mandate to move to Rupertsberg had come directly from God, Kano and the monks reluctantly acceded to Hildegard's plan, and in 1150 Hildegard and her nuns moved to Rupertsberg along with Volmar, who served as Provost as well as Hildegard's confessor and scribe. The chapel to Rupert was rededicated on May 1, 1151 and Archbishop Henry of Mainz issued the house's founding document early in 1152.[44]

Once ensconced at Rupertsberg, Hildegard continued writing her scientific and theological texts, along with musical compositions for her nuns. Lorna Collingridge describes Hildegard's music as "transgressive singing," by which she means not only the way Hildegard exceeded the boundaries set by twelfth-century monastic authorities for liturgical chant, but "the sense of going beyond ... the boundaries set by ecclesiastical authorities concerning the dangers for women in unmediated experience of relationship with the Divine."[45] An example of this "transgressive" behavior appears in an exchange of letters between Hildegard and Abbess Tengswich (Tenxwind) between 1148-1150. The Abbess had written to question Hildegard about

> ...certain strange and irregular practices that you countenance. They say that on feast days your virgins stand in the church with unbound hair when singing the

psalms and that as part of their dress they wear white, silk veils, so long that they touch the floor.... And all this despite the express prohibition of the great Shepherd of the Church, who writes in admonition: Let women comport themselves with modesty, not with plaited hair, or gold, or pearls, or costly attire [Tim 2:9].[46]

Hildegard responded that the strictures applied to married women:

...do not apply to a virgin, for she stands in the unsullied purity of paradise, lovely and unwithering. ...Virgins are married with holiness in the Holy Spirit and in the bright dawn of virginity, and so it is proper that they come before the great High Priest as an oblation presented to God.[47]

At the heart of Hildegard's power was a fierce belief in the Living Light of her visions, which, as one historian puts it, "reached but did not overstep the bounds of traditional orthodoxy.... As long as this feminist doctrine remained at a metaphorical level, it was barely tolerable to the hierarchy of the church."[48] At the heart of this belief was the connection between women and music: in the section on childbirth in *Causae et Curae* she writes that women's bodies "are open like a wooden frame in which strings have been fastened for strumming."[49]

Near the end of her life, Hildegard experienced a crisis that prompted one of the most moving formulations of her belief in music and prayer. In 1178, when Hildegard was eighty years old, the Canons of Mainz placed an interdict (ban) on her Rupertsberg community, forbidding the abbess and her nuns to sing the Divine Office or celebrate mass. The ostensible reason was that Hildegard had permitted the burial of a man who had been excommunicated from the church. The Archbishop ordered that the corpse be exhumed and removed from the Rupertsberg graveyard; Hildegard not only refused to remove the corpse, but blessed the grave with her abbatial staff and wrote a scathing letter to the Bishop of Mainz in her defense.[50] Her letter clearly articulates her belief in the divine power of music to unite body and soul in praise of God and reveals the moral and spiritual strength of this remarkable woman:

> When that deceiver, the Devil, heard that man began to sing through the inspiration of God ... then even in the heart of the Church and wherever he was able, whether through dissension and scandal or unjust oppression, he continually disrupted the manifestation and beauty of the psalms and hymns.... It is always necessary to beware that in your judgment you are not possessed by Satan who took man away from the heavenly music and from the delights of paradise ... All of the arts are brought to life by that breath of life which God breathed into the body of man: and therefore it is just that God be praised in all things.[51]

Eventually Hildegard's clerical allies provided proof that the man in question had been absolved of sin and accepted back into the Church. The interdict was lifted and then renewed, and finally lifted for good in March, 1179. Hildegard died six months later.[52]

Hildegard and her music remained the province of academics and specialized choral ensembles until the 800th anniversary of her death in 1979 and the 900th anniversary of her birth in 1998 inspired a broad-based revival. While previous Hildegard devotees had mainly been religious or German nationalist figures, interest in her work began to arise in the literary and musical worlds, including scholars and performers influenced by late-twentieth century feminism, and from a renewed interest in mysticism popularized by New Age spirituality.[53]

Women's choruses were among those celebrating the rediscovery of Hildegard's works. In 1994 Joan Szymko, director of Portland, Oregon's Aurora Chorus, was inspired by a passage in Matthew Fox's book *Illuminations of Hildegard of Bingen*, in which Fox wrote:

One of the most wonderful concepts that Hildegard gifts us with is a term that I have never found in any other theologian. She made up the word *viriditas*, or greening power.... For Hildegard, the Holy Spirit is greening power in motion, making all things grow, expand, celebrate.[54]

Moved by Hildegard's images and Fox's words, Szymko wrote "Viriditas," a choral work that she premiered with her select ensemble of the same name. She also shared the work with Patricia Hennings and the Peninsula Women's Chorus, who performed it at a Hildegard festival in 1999.[55] More recently, Amasong founding director Kristina Boerger, who has sung Hildegard's music in concert and studied her work extensively, has been leading workshops with women's choruses focused on chanting and singing the work of this remarkable woman.

Vivaldi's Girls, Vivaldi's Women

With the dawn of the Renaissance in Europe, women's choral singing was no longer limited to the voices of cloistered nuns singing behind screens, but women singing in society were still constrained by the rule of men. The *Concerto delle Donne* (consort of women), founded by Alfonso II, Duke of Ferrara, in 1580, began as an amateur group of courtiers who performed for each other within the context of the Duke's informal *musica secreta* in the 1570s. It evolved into an all-female group of professional musicians, who presented formal concerts for members of the inner circle of the court and important visitors. Their signature style of florid, highly ornamented singing brought prestige to Ferrara and inspired composers of the time, but although they were celebrated and well paid, the women of the *Concerto* were still considered their husbands' property. A telling example quoted by Laura Macy in her essay on women's history and early music is that of Caterina Martinelli, a young Roman singer brought to Mantua to be housed with the composer Monteverdi and trained by his wife, a

Mantuan court singer. Before approving this arrangement, Duke Vincenzo I ordered an examination to confirm thirteen-year-old Caterina's virginity. Macy suggests that the Duke's request and the compliance of all concerned, including Caterina's father, confirms the status of female professionals and their association with prostitution—a connection often blurred in reality as well as in the public mind.[56]

In 1715 Antonio Vivaldi became *Maestro dei Concerti* of the *Ospedale della Pietà* in Venice, a haven for abandoned children. Thus began one of the most fascinating chapters in the history of women's choruses. The *Ospedale della Pietà* had been founded in 1346 as a haven for unwanted babies. Like the three other Venetian *ospedali*, it was not a convent, but a charity connected to a local church, with ex-pupils helping administer its day-to-day operation. Mothers who could not care for their babies, whether through poverty, difficulty in producing enough milk, or most often, illegitimacy and prostitution, could place them in a niche in the wall called the *scarffetta*, a revolving drawer just large enough for a basket with a baby inside. The desperate mother would ring a bell, and the *portinara* (gatekeeper) would retrieve the baby, examine it for disease or lice, and remove the clothes the baby had been wrapped in. Every baby was registered in the book known as the *Libro della Scaffetta*, with the date and hour of entry, a name given by the *scrivana*, (recorder), and a list of any physical abnormalities (often found in the children of prostitutes afflicted with syphilis.) Babies were then branded on the upper left arm with the sign of the "P," a practice meant to protect the baby from theft when he or she was taken to a wet nurse in Venice or out in the country for the first few years of life. Babies who died in infancy also had the place and date of their death recorded.[57]

Upon their return to the *Pietà*, the girls and boys were separated, with boys trained in manual skills and expected to leave at the age of sixteen, while girls became part of the *figlie di commun* (commoners), who received a general education, or the *figli di coro* (choristers and musicians), who received extensive training in *solfeggio*, singing and instrumental technique. These girls were known by names indicating their musical role, such as "*Pellegrina dal Violin*" and "*Apollonia dal Soprano.*" In 1703, Vivaldi became the *Maestro Di Violin* at the *Pietà* and in 1716 he was hired as *Maestro di Coro*, or Chorus Master, a post he retained, on and off, until 1740.

As contemporary travelers' accounts attest, the *Pietà* singers became famous all over Europe. The young women sang by candlelight behind a gauze curtain and a metal grating, so that they were only dimly visible, leading many contemporary visitors (most of whom were men) to compare their singing to the voices of angels. Yet male viewers were also surprised (and often amused) to see young women in the orchestra playing all the instruments that were traditionally male. "The sight of the orchestra still makes me smile," wrote William Beckford, who would later become Lord Mayor of London. "You know, I suppose, it is entirely of the feminine gender, and that nothing is more common than to see a delicate white hand journeying across an enormous double bass, or a pair of roseate cheeks puffing, with all their efforts, at a French horn. Some that are grown old and Amazonian, who have abandoned their fiddles and their lovers, take vigorously to the kettle-drum; and one poor limping lady, who had been crossed in love, now makes an admirable figure on the bassoon." (It should be noted that the women of the *Pietà* lived fairly secluded lives, and with a few rebellious exceptions, did not have male lovers.)[58]

Charles de Brosses, president of the Dijon Parliament, France, made a similar observation: "They sing like angels, and play violin, flute, organ, hautboy (oboe), violoncello, bassoon, in short, there is no instrument so large as to frighten them."[59] Most poignant, perhaps, is the account by Jean Jacques Rousseau, who managed to obtain an invitation to share a meal with the singers. "M. le Blond introduced me to one after another of those famous singers whose voices and names were all that were known to me. 'Come, Sophie,' – she was horrible. 'Come, Cattina,' – she was blind in one eye. 'Come, Bettina,' – the smallpox had disfigured her. Scarcely one was without some considerable blemish ... I was desolate." But by the end of the meal, he wrote, "my way of looking at them changed so much that I left nearly in love with all these ugly girls."[60]

Much of what we know about the musicians at the *Pietà* comes from the work of Micky White, the *Pietà's* resident archivist. White was a Wimbledon photographer when she read a biography of Vivaldi that changed her life. ("He was just like John McEnroe—an unconventional genius.") White moved to Venice and has devoted her life to translating the eighteenth-century record-books of the *Pietà*, where Vivaldi was employed for nearly forty years. She has unearthed registers dating back to the seventeenth century, still tied with the ribbons that had last bound them. From these *libri della scaffetta*, in which the circumstances of each infant's reception were meticulously entered, and the *registri dei morti*, or death records, along with records in other archives, White has reconstructed a detailed account of these girls' lives. She has also studied Vivaldi's relationship with the girls, which she asserts was compassionate and inclusive. "The more deeply one goes into the records," she says, "the more evident it becomes that … whether or not the governors were aware of it, they enabled *figlie di coro* to achieve through music a degree of personal fulfillment that in the early eighteenth century must have been rare for women of any background, let alone the most despised of all."[61]

The unusual presence of tenor and bass singers in Vivaldi's girls' chorus was a topic of debate among musicologists for years. In 1994, Michael Talbot identified four explanations that had gained the greatest currency, which Meredith Bowen, herself a women's chorus director, later titled "The Hidden Men," "Seen but Not Heard," "Sung at Pitch," and "Octave Transposition." Additionally, Bowen cited two other theories suggested by musical historian Robert Kendrick, which she called "Instrumental Substitution" and "Whole Score Transposition."[62]

The realities of life at the *Pietà* and the recorded testimonies of visitors who heard the singers make it virtually impossible to believe that men were present in the chorus, while the idea that some parts were written but not sung belies the importance of the lower parts in many of the compositions. Furthermore, many contemporary accounts attest to seventeenth and eighteenth century performances by women singing in the low registers.

In 1687, the news-sheet *Pallade veneta* described a singer at the *Mendicanti*, Maria Anna Ziani, as follows:

> [A]lthough a woman, she is endowed naturally with a male voice, but one that is so tender and full, and of such a sweet tone, that she sings baritone with enough grace to transport and captivate the minds of her listeners.

Similarly, in 1724 an amateur musician named Jan Alensoon described a performance by a nun at Santa Radegonda:

> She sang three or four cantatas, and accompanied herself at the harpsichord ... I was amazed when I heard that her voice could reach the highest *a* of the harpsichord, and descend to the second *d* below, two and a half octaves altogether; she sang a nice canto, alto, and tenor.[63]

Finally, a 1758 diary entry by the Venetian Pietro Gradenigo reported the death of the octogenarian Anna Cremona, "a distinguished bass singer." [64]

Considering vocal range through the lens of contemporary feminist awareness, Patricia O'Toole, former director of the Columbus Women's Chorus, calls it "a gendered aspect of choral practice [that is] seldom questioned." She points out that "directors teach men to explore the full extent of their range; they learn to sing falsetto as well as chest voices, and some men even specialize in the alto or countertenor voice. The profession has developed pedagogy to create a healthy upper range for men. The inverse is not true. For the most part, women are not encouraged to explore and use their lower ranges." Putting the whole issue in a cross-cultural context, O'Toole observes:

> Many women tenors and basses exist (and can be found in abundance in non-Western and nonclassical traditions), but admitting to their validity is somewhat of a professional taboo in Western choral practices.... Cultural notions of vocal production prevent women

from singing SATB music with the full scope of timbres that are produced by a mixed-voice or a men's choir [and] suggest that boys can be independent and experimental, while girls must remain dependent and acquiescent.[65]

More than three centuries after Vivaldi's tenure at the *Pietà*, Richard Vendome, director of the Oxford Girls Choir, was inspired by Micky White's research to recruit a group of young women reflecting the age range of Vivaldi's original singers, "with a distinct mission to demonstrate women's ability to sing all parts at pitch."

"I started looking round for women who could sing low," Vendome recalled. "I was sure that there were such people. We tried two or three people and then we met Margaret Jackson-Roberts, who's got a very deep and powerful voice."[66]

In 2005 the BBC invited Vendome and members of the Oxford Girls' Choir to participate in a documentary about Vivaldi's chorus, with women singing all parts, including tenor and bass, just as they did in Vivaldi's choir. The *Schola Pietatis Antonio Vivaldi* ("Vivaldi's Women") traveled to Venice, where they stayed at the *Casa per Ferie*, near where the orphans of the *Pietà* had lived, and sang at the Church of the *Pietà*. Rosie Dinot recalled,

> A kind of sympathetic magic gripped us all. Being in Venice and especially singing there is romantic enough, but there was the added *frisson* of treading in the steps of the original performers, for whom we felt a marked empathy across the years....One could almost imagine the spirit of Vivaldi benignly encouraging us.[67]

During their visit to the *Pietà*, the women of SPAV had the opportunity to meet with Micky White in person. In addition to showing them some of the registers where the lives of the *Pietà* singers were recorded, White confirmed Vendome's belief that the tenor and bass singers in Vivaldi's chorus were indeed women.

The clincher for us was Micky's research that the bass part was actually sung at pitch by one named person called Anna dal Basso.... After half an hour of singing with our choir in the *Pietà*, it seemed as if this is how it should be done and there's no reason to think that anyone should do it any other way.[68]

Margaret Jackson-Roberts agrees: "I enjoy singing bass. [It's] the foundation of the choir.... And giving the foundation to the harmony is very important.... It gives confidence to the rest of the choir." Jackson-Roberts and her sister-basses and tenors know that they represent a challenge to conventional gendered expectations for women musicians.

I've had it happen to me that people say, "You're a freak. Freak voice...." We're not men of course. We produce our own particular timbre ... It's something you have to rise to because it's such a new venture. You feel that you want to give more than your best, you want to surpass yourself.[69]

SPAV now has a Facebook page documenting their continuing activities. The chorus currently includes several past and present members of the Oxford Girls Choir and is still directed by Richard Vendome. Since filming the 2005 BBC video, the members of SPAV have sung in Antwerp, Utrecht, London and Bristol, as well as various locations in Britain, and have issued a CD and a DVD of Vivaldi's "Gloria."[70]

Brahms' *Frauenchor*

In 1856, Friedchen Wagner, the twenty-one-year-old daughter of a prosperous Hamburg family, asked her piano instructor, Johannes Brahms, to compose some folksongs for her and her two sisters. Gradually, other young women joined them and Brahms suggested that Friedchen and her friends organize a women's chorus. On June 6, 1859, twenty-eight young women gathered at the Wagners' home for the first rehearsal of the Hamburg *Frauenchor*.

Like many bourgeois families, the Wagners sang part songs, played instruments at home, and were on familiar terms with the important composers and performers of the day—part of a nineteenth-century choral movement sweeping Europe that had made Germany "the Mecca of musicians the world over."[71] For middle- and upper-class women, choral singing provided a unique social and artistic opportunity. Choral practice was an amateur endeavor, taking place in women's homes and allowing women to participate in a musical activity "without claiming an inappropriate professional ambition."[72] As Celia Applegate describes it, "With the warm-ups, the repetitions, the tea breaks with sweet cakes, the talking and exchanging of musical (and other) opinions and experiences, the coming together and leaving only to return again the next week, the choral rehearsal became a central experience of everyday life for hundreds of thousands throughout Europe and the Americas, made all the more memorable by the unconscious effects, so hard to measure, of the music itself."[73] Over ninety percent of women's chorus members were single and young, shifting their energies to their husbands and families when they married.[74]

However, although the *Frauenchor* resembled the women's choruses that sang in bourgeois drawing rooms in the nineteenth century, the relationship between the young singers and their director made the *Frauenchor* unique for its time and unique in the history of women's choruses.

Much of what we know about Brahms and the *Frauenchor* comes from Sophie Drinker's *Brahms and his Women's Choruses*, an account that she based on one of the singers' music books and the diary of Franziska Meier, a member of the chorus. Drinker's interest had been piqued while singing in a women's chorus that she and her husband Henry had organized in their home. "As I sang a second alto part in that compelling Romantic music," Drinker later wrote, "I used to wonder what those girls, who had first sung it, were like and what were the circumstances that had led Brahms to compose it."[75] The Drinkers eventually contacted the children of the original *Frauenchor* members, who gave them the music books and diaries that Drinker used to tell their story.

Johannes Brahms was not the only nineteenth century composer to write for women's choruses: Franz Schubert, Robert Schumann, Felix Mendelssohn, and Franz Liszt also composed sacred and secular women's choral music.[76] However, Brahms was the only one of his contemporaries with his own women's choir, and his musical relationship with them reveals a great deal about these young nineteenth century women, as well as about Brahms himself.

Brahms was twenty-six—only a few years older than his singers— and had already tried his hand at composing women's choral music in Göttingen when he began conducting the *Frauenchor*. From the beginning, the members of his young chorus were smitten with their handsome, charismatic young director and thrilled at the opportunity to sing together under his direction. Even before the first meeting, Franziska and some of her friends attended a concert at which Brahms's friend Joseph Joachim conducted a performance of Brahms's Serenade. After the concert Franziska wrote that she "spent an almost sleepless night during which I wrote in my diary, made poetry and drew sketches of Joachim and Brahms."[77] Shortly afterwards, Franziska and two of her friends, a trio who called themselves The Three Crows, wrote a letter to Brahms congratulating him on his Serenade Op. 11, which had been performed at the concert. The three girls went to the *Fuhlentwiete*, the street where Brahms lived, and bribed a little boy to deliver the letter. Franziska wrote in her diary: "All day I felt as though I had committed a murder. It is hard for me to try to fool my mother. At breakfast (a few days later) we confessed. Thank goodness that abyss has been crossed."[78] Months later, when the *Frauenchor* had already begun practicing, Franziska wrote the following:

Tilla and I sat down in the center of the second sopranos. We sang the Psalm by Schubert, two songs by Brahms, three by Schumann, and then "Poor Peter" by Gradener, for six-part women's chorus—terrifically difficult! It went very badly. I admired Brahms' patience. We practiced only the first two parts, then in conclusion, the Psalm over again. I like Brahms as a conductor exceedingly. He noticed us especially, and so he should! Once when he looked at me for so long, I tried to respond to his steady glance. Suddenly, it came into my mind: now he is thinking of the letter! And then I lost courage and willpower and had to look away.[79]

Franziska's descriptions of the *Frauenchor*'s infatuation with Brahms display all the ardor of an adolescent crush. Indeed, these young women in their twenties were kept in perpetual adolescence by the strict limits their society placed on female expression. Brahms, young and handsome and enjoying a growing musical reputation across Europe, was a safe target for feelings that their upbringing as proper young women would have otherwise demanded that they repress. On August 29, 1859, Franziska wrote, "Monday, August 29, at the Wagners. At a quarter to nine, we went to the Sthamer's. Of course, Tilla was not ready. Then we ran to the Brahmafest. On Diistern Street, I was possessed with the idea that I must look back. I saw Brahms behind us; also, he noticed us and the distance between us became less and less. Why did that make me so nervous? We arrived at the door at almost the same time as Brahms."[80]

On September 9, Franziska records a visit from Brahms to her home.

John brought in a card: "A gentleman is outside and asks if he might have his music." *Johannes Brahms*! I could hardly believe my eyes. I looked out and asked him to step inside for a moment. He entered the little room. I expressed my regrets that he had to take the trouble to come here. "Oh, that does not matter at all! Ave [Theodor Avé-Lallment, a music teacher and friend of Brahms] is also outside. You have the voice parts, don't you?" ... He hunted in the dark with me for the music on the piano, and then he hurried quickly away. But the goblets of bliss were spilled, the fair fruits scattered and night was darkening round about.[81]

Like Mimi and Rudolfo hunting for her lost key, the scene fairly trembles with repressed sexual energy—but unlike the Bohemians of *La Boheme*, Brahms and Franziska carefully followed the dictates of bourgeois propriety.

Brahms's correspondence reveals an equally idealized relationship with his young singers. In September, 1859, after his first summer directing the chorus, Brahms wrote to Clara Schumann from Detmold, where he was to conduct the castle choir during the fall:

But on Monday in the church, what a touching farewell it was! ... When I got home in the afternoon, I found a little box, and, in it, charmingly hidden among flowers, a silver inkstand inscribed with the words: "In memory of the summer of '59 from the girls' choir." What will next summer not bring in the form of Psalms and songs of joy! ....O, my dear girls, where are you? I shall certainly not stare about me when you are singing me the pretty things I have written for you; all forty of you shall stand before me and I shall see you and hear you in my mind's eye. I tell you that one of my most endearing memories is this ladies' choir.... I implore you to regard this as a rational letter in spite of its unpardonable sentimentalities regarding the forty girls![82]

Brahms's own sexual history affected his relationships with women all his life. According to Jan Swafford, one of Brahms's many biographers, Brahms's father sent him to earn extra money playing at Hamburg's seedy waterfront honky-tonks when the boy was only thirteen. Swafford writes: "As he approached puberty, Brahms was steeped in an atmosphere where the deepest intimacies between men and women were a matter of ceaseless and shameful transactions. That sense of human relations haunted him for life. He felt intimacy as a threat, female sexuality as a threat."[83] Although a few writers have debunked this story, it is certainly true that Brahms frequented prostitutes all his adult life but was unable to form intimate relationships with women of his own class, viewing all women though "the old poisonous dichotomy of virgin and whore." As Swafford points out, Brahms's sexual attitudes were "only exaggerated norms of his time and culture....Germany was misogynistic, the role of women circumscribed by *Kinder, Kirche, und Küche* (kids, church and kitchen)."[84] Brahms's fear of intimacy played out most poignantly in his long relationship with Clara Schumann, to whom he could never make a marriage commitment even after Robert Schumann's death. It also made him a safe object for the veneration of the *Frauenchor* singers; his idealization of them was a mirror image of their chaste but passionate infatuation with him.

Nevertheless, the *Frauenchor* was a serious musical experience for the singers, not merely an opportunity to idolize their conductor. Unlike many women's choruses of the time, where socializing was the main event, the *Frauenchor* girls were required to work hard on their singing. Early on, Brahms established a motto for the chorus: *immer rüstig vorwarts—* "forging energetically ahead."[85]

An entry from Franziska's diary in August, 1859, suggests the businesslike way that Brahms conducted rehearsals: "He is very precise at practice.... Brahms asked me whether it had been hard for me to follow. I answered, 'In the beginning, very.' Then he said, 'Ladies, next Monday, be here at five minutes before 9, at the latest.'"[86]

Brahms also insisted that the *Frauenchor* sing all four women's parts, from first soprano to second alto. Later in August, while preparing to sing at St. Peter's Church in Hamburg, Franziska noted that many women found it challenging to sing alto. "I said that on the whole, I believed alto was much more difficult than second soprano. Altos always have to sing the notes which are missing. Then he laughed: 'Certainly, alto is always difficult. If I let the ladies do as they pleased, not a single one would sing alto.

They would all sing second soprano. That is the favorite part.'"[87]

Occasionally even the *Frauenchor* could not or would not sing the lower parts: at the first performance of the *Marienlieder*, Op. 22, in 1859, tenors sang the second alto part.[88] Thinking back to Vivaldi's chorus at the *Pietà*, where girls sang not only second alto but even the tenor and bass lines, one is tempted to wonder to what extent the aversion—or presumed inability—to sing in the lower registers arose from nineteenth century conceptions of appropriate female behavior and gendered assumptions about women's voices.

Nevertheless, the *Frauenchor*'s excellence prompted an invitation from Clara Schumann to join her in a concert in Hamburg in January, 1861. The program included selections by Beethoven, Brahms, Robert Schumann, and Chopin, along with three of Brahms's songs performed by the *Frauenchor*. Sophie Drinker reminds us that in 1861, women's choral performances generally took place in one of three settings: a private home, before invited guests; a Conservatory building, as part of the activities of a music school; or a church, on the occasion of a wedding, christening, or funeral. "It was not until the 20th century that a women's chorus appeared in public on the concert stage on a par with a mixed chorus, an orchestra, or a soloist.... Clara's concert of January 15, 1861, therefore, was very important in the annals of women's choruses."[89]

In 1863, Brahms applied for the directorship of the Hamburg *Singakademie* and the philharmonic. When his application was refused, he left for Vienna, and though he returned to Hamburg the following summer, he never called the *Frauenchor* together again. Drinker speculates:

> It was not because some of the girls had married and moved away—they could have been replaced by others. It was not because he had lost interest in the women's voices. His contacts with different groups of women in Vienna dispose of that suspicion. The real reason was that his attitude toward his Hamburg friends had changed. He was deeply hurt that they had not offered him the leadership of the Singakademie and the Philharmonic

Orchestra when the opportunity to engage new directors arose. ...While the members of the *Frauenchor* were not themselves influential enough to have sponsored him, their families could probably have exerted pressure upon the managers of the Hamburg musical institutions. As it was, he felt too angry to continue his formal association with the Ladies' Choral Society.[90]

The members of the *Frauenchor* were deeply saddened by Brahms's departure. Friedchen Wagner later wrote:

During one of the last lessons before he left for Vienna, I asked him to write something for me as a souvenir and he promised me to do so. ...As I was very sad, I did not open the piano for some days, but when I did open it again, I found there the beautiful gift I had been promised: the marvelous chorale prelude to *Traurigkeit, Herzeleid*. My maid told me that Herr Brahms had put it in the piano himself.[91]

Though Brahms went on to conduct women's choruses in Vienna, his influence on the members of the *Frauenchor* did not end with the dissolution of the chorus. When Franziska Meier married and went to live in Cuxhaven, she was determined to start a women's chorus there. She and her sister Camilla wrote to Brahms asking for some of the music he had composed and arranged for the *Frauenchor*. Brahms's reply suggests that he was still bitter about his departure from Hamburg.

Dear Fraulein: Permit me to write you somewhat hastily and briefly that I do not begrudge you any of the things you wish, which you yourself can get together. I myself do not possess a single note and do not know who may have saved anything. Unfortunately, my unsettled life prevents me from guarding the memory of lovely musical and sociable pleasures....Give my regards to all of you.[92]

Undaunted, Franziska and Camilla made new copies of the *Stimmenhefte* and organized a choir, which she conducted herself. In a 1935 letter to Sophie Drinker, Franziska's daughter Anna described the Cuxhaven chorus:

> The members had little practice, and sang only for enthusiasm....[They] were not at all accustomed to read notes [and] had domestic duties. ... In the beginning, my mother had to write all the *Stimmenhefte* herself, until gradually the ladies learned to write them....Later, my mother had founded a second choir in the 80s, in which I and three sisters joined.[93]

Reprise

A complete history of women's choral singing would require a book unto itself; however, some important constants emerge even in this brief survey. Sophie Drinker's hypotheses of goddess-based religious practices and women's societal empowerment in prehistory notwithstanding, recorded history shows us that until the twentieth century, women's choral singing took place almost entirely under the control of men. The women in the Greek *parthenoi*, the cloistered nuns of the Middle Ages, the girls and women for whom Vivaldi and Brahms wrote their magnificent choral works, may have experienced personal transformation and even exerted a momentary power over their audiences, but they lived and sang in societies controlled by men.

It would be several generations before the first women's chorus organized by, with, and for women would take the stage. Meanwhile, a movement was growing in which singing would play a crucial role in the struggle for social justice and which would eventually nurture the revolutionary ideas of woman-identified music and feminist transformation through song.

2

The People's Music

In her essay on building community through choral singing, Celia Applegate calls the nineteenth century "the choral century par excellence....No other century in recorded human history was so rich in forms of choral activity, so diverse in venues and sizes and purposes of choral history."[1] The community choruses that proliferated in late nineteenth century America were focused primarily on bringing people together to sing, but a few reflected contemporary concerns with social justice that would inspire feminist choruses in the twentieth century. One of those was the People's Choral Union of New York City, founded in 1893 by Frank Damrosch.

The son of a prominent musical family, Damrosch had emigrated from Germany in 1871. After a brief career in business, he turned to music, his true calling, and became a music supervisor in the Denver Public Schools. In 1885, his father's death brought Damrosch back to New York City, where he conducted the Mendelssohn Glee Club and eventually became director of the Metropolitan Opera Chorus. He also served as organist at the Ethical Culture Society of New York, where he came to know the Society's founder, Felix Adler.

Adler's work with the poor immigrant communities of the Lower East Side introduced Damrosch to a population far removed from the Vanderbilts and Carnegies of his Metropolitan Opera world. In 1892, he was inspired to reach out to the people of the Lower East Side by offering singing classes at Cooper Union, the New York college that had become a mecca for young immigrant and working class people seeking to better themselves through its free education. Unlike many humanitarians of his era, Damrosch never patronized the people he served: he insisted that his students learn to read notes (what he called "the key to the storehouse") and after debating whether to offer the classes free of charge, he decided to charge ten cents per lesson—enough so that singers would not feel that they were being offered charity, but low enough for even poor people to afford. He announced his intentions in a flyer addressed to "the working people of New York"; it read:

> Recognizing the fact that music contributes more than any other art to brighten and beautify our lives, and that it is the art which can be practiced by the greatest number of people, since nature has furnished nearly every person with a correct ear and a singing voice, I have decided to open a course of lessons in reading music and choral singing. It is my purpose to teach everyone who desires to learn, to read music from notes, and I hope ultimately to form from the members of these classes a grand People's Chorus that shall be able to sing the greatest works of the greatest masters.[2]

By the time the People's Singing Classes disbanded in 1917, Damrosch had taught an estimated 50,000 people to sing. Stacey Horn writes that roofers and plasterers would often stop Damrosch in the street to thank him. "One man ran off to get his well-worn and much-marked Handel score to illustrate the story he proceeded to proudly tell. He was a school janitor and the father of six children, he said. Even though he was working a second job, he couldn't afford the music education he wanted his children to have. Then he heard about the Choral Union. Now he was taking classes and teaching his children what he'd learned."[3] A decade after his death, one of his former students wrote that Damrosch had opened the door to great music for thousands. "Dr. Frank is our own hero. He was our friend."[4]

Although the People's Choral Union enriched the lives of working people and their families, Frank Damrosch had no agenda beyond his deep belief in the power of music to "brighten and beautify" people's lives, and in this he certainly succeeded. Yet in making choral singing available to everyone regardless of race or economic class, Damrosch anticipated the people's music movements of the mid-twentieth century, the music of the Civil Rights Movement, and eventually, the women's music and women's choral movement of our own time—movements that would embrace choral singing as a vehicle for political, as well as personal change, and in which women would come to play an increasingly important role.

Suffrage, Temperance, and Songs of True Womanhood

Singing played a significant part in the two preeminent women's movements of the second half of the nineteenth century: temperance and suffrage. Between 1848, when participants in the Seneca Falls convention declared their intention to seek the vote, and 1920, when the ratification of the nineteenth amendment secured that right, suffragists and their allies published hundreds of songs and sang in venues ranging from small gatherings to massive parades. In her 1998 anthology, *Give the Ballot to the Mothers: Songs of the Suffragists; A History in Song*, Francie Wolff describes three types of suffrage songs: rally songs, songs of persuasion, and popular songs.[5] Many of these sought to frame suffrage within the Cult of True Womanhood— the American version of *Kinder, Kirche, und Küche* described in Chapter 1—which defined piousness, submissiveness, purity, and domesticity as the appropriate qualities for women.[6] One of the most popular suffrage songs of the early twentieth century declared, "She's Good Enough to be Your Baby's Mother and She's Good enough to Vote with You." (In 2016, nine singer-actors included the song in their two-act concert, "Forward Into the Light: The American Women's Suffrage Movement in New York State in Song and Story"; contemporary readers can see and hear the song on YouTube.[7]) Yet, as Sheryl Hurner points out, suffragist songs also challenged the Cult of True Womanhood, asserting, "I will speak my mind if I die for it!" and portraying women as "enslaved patriots" as they compared the women's rights movement to the nation's founding fight against tyranny and the struggles of the abolitionists.[8]

Like the suffragists, temperance activists used songs to promote their agenda and create solidarity. Frances Willard, long-time president of the Women's Christian Temperance Union, declared, "Song is a sentient maker and … every chorus rendered at a public entertainment ought to add new converts to the cause of Temperance.… We have not appreciated the magic power of song to win the hearts of those whom we may have supposed to be indifferent or opposed to Temperance work."[9] As the Temperance movement gathered strength, its songs heightened the focus on legislative reform while still maintaining their evangelical cast. One popular number urged citizens to "Vote as you pray, 'twill hasten the day/ When the rum fiend's work shall end."[10]

Women's Music Clubs

Middle- and upper-class women at the forefront of the women's suffrage movement and of philanthropic undertakings like the settlement movement, both reinforced and challenged the concept of separate spheres. Even as they moved beyond the realm of *Kinder Kirche Küche*, women still saw themselves as a collective moral conscience, bringing "feminine" values of care and nurturing to an often heartless (male dominated) society. One of the most important manifestations of this "social feminism" was the women's club movement, which began as a vehicle for socializing, but grew more political at the turn of the century, as women became more involved in campaigns for civic reform. Black women, excluded from White women's clubs, formed clubs of their own, which focused on a wide range of social, political, and economic reforms, as well as the anti-lynching campaign spearheaded by the pioneering journalist Ida B. Wells. In 1896, clubwomen came together to form the National Association of Colored Women, whose motto was "Lifting as We Climb."[11]

Among the societies that grew out of the women's club movement were women's music clubs, some of which sponsored vocal and orchestral performances in cities and towns; in others, the members themselves sang and performed. Like the rest of the women's club movement, music clubs saw their mission in moral terms, believing that listening to and performing music was the highest form of moral development, and considering music clubs an extension of their work for America's moral and cultural advancement as well as a means for their own self-improvement. The first women's music club in America, the Rossini Club of Portland, Maine, was organized in 1869 "for... mutual improvement in the art of Music."[12] Other clubs soon followed, as women across the country celebrated the values of sisterhood and moral uplift these clubs promoted. Anticipating the sentiments that would animate the women's choruses of the late twentieth century, a member of the Mozart Club of Dayton, Ohio wrote, "It has been a training in itself to learn to work together in a musical society, with kindness, forbearance, patience and in honor, preferring one another, especially when we remember that musical people are said to be the most sensitive in the world."[13]

In 1876, Fanny Raymond Ritter, herself an accomplished musician, joined the call for women to use their inborn inclinations toward beauty and moral uplift to promote the arts, especially music. In her essay "Woman as Musician: An Art-Historical Study," originally written for the1876 Centennial Congress of the Association for the Advancement of Women, Ritter urged women to "promote the formation of libraries of musical literature ...and of private societies for the home practice of music." Though not every woman "could boast a Gluck, a Handel, a Beethoven, a Michelangelo, a Tasso, among her everyday friends" or possessed "the wealth and power" of a Baroness Rothschild, Ritter asserted,

> every American lady who possesses the indispensable
> kindness of heart, refinement, generosity and culture, as
> well as influence—the wives of men of intellectual power,

inherited wealth, or great commercial prominence more especially—can accomplish a great deal in her own small circle.

Ritter's appeal to White middle- and upper-class women—an appeal that today we would label bourgeois feminism—was echoed by Fanny Morris Smith, who urged readers "tired out with economical housekeeping [and] weary of keeping up an artificial life of cruel etiquette" or "lonely because the opportunity for loving self-denial has been taken from you, and time hangs heavy on your hands" to "go into club life… Live an hour with Mozart or Beethoven or Liszt … Spend a day at the club music class and enter into the feelings of the working girls assembled there."[14]

Despite America's nineteenth century enthusiasm for community choruses, women's music clubs were not always welcomed by the musical establishment. *New York Tribune* music critic Henry Edward Krehbiel (who had written favorably of the People's Choral Union concerts) opined that "[a] female chorus cannot be a success, and if you should form one of angels from heaven, with Saint Cecilia as conductress, I would say the same." On April 18, 1890, Krehbiel reviewed a performance by the Rubinstein Club, declaring that it was "a pity that so much energy and money should be expended when the results can only be of the most superficial interest."[15]

The Rubenstein Club had been formed as New York's first all-female choir in 1886, when a group of women approached their former music teacher, William Chapman, who had just conducted a performance by a newly formed all-male choral society. The women begged Chapman to let them sing with him as well, and a year later, sixty women presented the choir's first concert. Krehbiel continued his attacks on the chorus, writing in a letter to Chapman, "I cannot be convinced that a female chorus has any reason to exist except it amuses itself and those who are willing to pay for it; surely it has no claim on artistic consideration."[16]

Nevertheless, the Rubinstein Club flourished and continued to perform for the next fifty years. At a celebration honoring Chapman on his retirement in 1911, he recalled, "We held our first meeting ... at the old Chickering Hall at Eighteenth Street and Fifth Avenue and were but a mere handful of music lovers. Today our work has grown to such proportions my wife and I received a telegram from President and Mrs. Taft wishing us good times at our dinner and expressing regret that they cannot be with us. Almost all of the famous singers and performers of the last twenty-five years and of the present day have been with us whenever they were in New York and we now meet as a real music-loving family to mutually enjoy our work at these club concerts."[17]

By 1919, more than 600 active women's music clubs, with a combined membership of approximately 200,000, were meeting regularly in the United States. Although some, like the Rubinstein Club of New York, catered to elite audiences, others included social welfare in their mission. Ella May Smith, a piano teacher, vocal coach, and instructor of harmony, theory, and composition, served as president of the 3,000-member Music Club of Columbus from 1903-1916 and spearheaded the creation of numerous community programs, including community music in settlement houses, a student club for boys and girls, and a system of scholarships to music students.[18] Others focused on bringing the music of classical composers to their home cities: the Rubenstein Club of Cleveland, organized in 1899, grew to an eighty-five-voice chorus and performed works by Bach and Schubert as well as local composers.[19]

The Mothersingers, organized in the late 1920s under the auspices of California PTA's, still survives as the California Women's Chorus, Inc., an umbrella organization with ten individual choruses and over 300 members. The CWC has expanded the Mothersingers' original mission to include fundraising for vocal scholarships; performing at senior residences, hospitals, and local service groups; and touring abroad.[20]

Women in Gospel: "Controlled Joy and Spiritual Fervor"

Like the women's club movement as a whole, women's music clubs were organized by and for White middle class women.

But the members of Chapman's "music loving family" were not the only American women forming music communities during the late nineteenth and early twentieth century. Consigned to second-class citizenship and low wage work by their race and their gender, Black women found a sense of self-worth in the Black church, which became their spiritual, social, and above all, musical home.

The Women's Convention, established in 1900 as an auxiliary to the National Baptist Convention, advocated for women's self-determination within the male dominated Baptist Church, the largest African American denomination in the country, and played a far more important role in women's advocacy than most historians have acknowledged.[21] In the Church of God in Christ, on the other hand, "the spiritual dimension of sacred music accorded women a level of musical authority for which women in secular fields often had to struggle."[22] Since music was regarded as "the manifestation of a divine gift," women who were officially banned from preaching in the Church of God were encouraged to sing. In addition, Jenna Jackson documents numerous accounts of female missionaries who ignored the official prohibition on preaching and "simply followed the dictates they received from the Holy Spirit."[23] One of them was Agnes Campbell, who grew up in the church and began singing at an early age. Campbell explained, "Sometimes when I was very young they used to say, 'The women don't preach, the men preach.' But now they say, 'the women teach and preach so don't worry about it.' I tell them, I just do what the Lord say, y'all can call it what you want to."[24]

Campbell's unapologetic assertion that her inspiration came directly from the Lord recalls the utter confidence with which Hildegard of Bingen described her visions and led her community of nuns. Though separated by a vast gulf of culture and history, both these women defined themselves through their direct spiritual experience and allied themselves with communities where they could assert their spiritual authority, whether among the nuns of Rupertsberg in the twelfth century or in the Church of God in Chicago, Illinois, in the twentieth century.

The music that nurtured Agnes Campbell and so many others was part of a tradition dating back to the spirituals that grew up among the slaves on southern plantations and even further back, to the African rhythms and melodies that most music historians now regard as the genesis of Black music in America.[25] In 1867, three northern abolitionists, William Francis Allen, Lucy McKim Garrison, and Charles Pickard Ware, published the first collection of African American spirituals in the U.S., *Slave Songs of the United States*. Four years later, the Fisk Jubilee Singers began a U.S. tour to raise money for Fisk University, founded six months after the end of the Civil War to educate freed slaves. At first, audiences were cool to the singers and many hotels refused them admittance. But as the tour went on, listeners warmed to their performances, especially of Negro spirituals, and midway through the tour director George L. White was moved to name them "the Jubilee Singers," after the "year of jubilee," or emancipation.[26]

As the Fisk Jubilee Singers' popularity grew, their success inspired at least a dozen imitators all over the south as well as numerous songbooks.[27] In 1914, they were invited to sing at the Convention of the National Woman Suffrage Association, where their performance helped relieve "the tension of the week."[28] Their success with White audiences was based at least in part on the style and arrangements of the songs they sang. A reporter for the *Peoria Journal* wrote in 1881 after a Fisk Jubilee Singers concert, "They have lost the wild rhythms, the barbaric melody, the passion.... They smack of the North."[29] In the words of gospel historian Robert Darden, the Jubilee Singers

> helped spawn a wonderful subgenre, the classically arranged spiritual, which provided the impetus for important careers ... for singers such as Paul Robeson and Marian Anderson. But what these singers performed were not spirituals.... In time, the distinctions between the words spiritual and jubilee would become blurred in the minds of many musicians. But to those who study and love African-American music, the distinctions are worth preserving.[30]

In contrast to the Jubilee Singers, members of Black churches were singing what would eventually develop into gospel music, in a very different style. The man responsible for much of this development was Rev. Charles A. Tindley, the son of slaves, who pastored a 10,000-member church in Philadelphia and wrote hymns reflecting his childhood familiarity with both spirituals and camp-meeting songs. Although the National Baptist Convention advocated restraint and respectability, Tindley's music "carried a camp-meeting intensity and fervor that would inspire the later development and crystallization of the black gospel style."[31] Among his compositions was "I'll Overcome Someday," which became the anthem of the Civil Rights movement as "We Shall Overcome."

Lucie Campbell, who became music director of the NBC, wrote hymns that "set a tone of and atmosphere of exuberant yet controlled joy and spiritual fervor."[32] As Pamela Palmer writes, "From the moment that Campbell joined the National Baptist Convention, gospel music became the voice of the masses of Black Christians as they sought to express their hopes and dreams, as well as their joys and sorrows on their Christian journey. If Thomas A. Dorsey is the 'Father of Gospel Music,' then certainly Lucie E. Campbell is the 'Mother of Gospel Music.'"[33]

Like Tindley and Campbell before him, Thomas A. Dorsey brought a more exuberant style to sanctified music; he also infused the gospel tradition with blues and jazz and embraced commercial music publishing. Dorsey's gospel chorus at Chicago's Pilgrim Baptist Church provoked the same controversies that had surrounded the Fisk Jubilee Singers and the Holiness choruses in the Church of Christ decades earlier. But despite some initial resistance by musical conservatives, Dorsey's brand of jazz-inflected gospel grew into a nationwide movement, which culminated in the National Convention of Gospel Choirs and Choruses in 1933. Dorsey served as director of the NCGCC for the next thirty years. In addition to directing mass choirs, he promoted the careers of a host of female gospel singers. George T. Nirenberg's 1982 film, *Say Amen, Somebody*, features several of them, including Willie Mae Ford Smith (known in the gospel community as Mother Smith); Sallie Martin; and the Barrett Sisters, DeLois Barrett Campbell, Billie Barrett GreenBey, and Rodessa Barrett Porter. Although the film focuses mainly on Dorsey and the gospel movement he led, it includes some telling revelations of gender politics within the movement. One of the most memorable scenes finds DeLois and her husband in the kitchen of their home, discussing a trip abroad that she is planning. "I'll be glad when our ministry can be together, as a husband and wife team, more than your sisters' team," he says. DeLois considers this for a long moment, then says "You want some eggs with your sausage?"[34]

Dorsey's most famous protégée was Mahalia Jackson, who became associated with his most famous hymn, "Take My Hand, Precious Lord," a song Dorsey wrote after his wife's death in childbirth and which is considered by many to be the greatest gospel song ever written. Gospel historian Robert Darden writes, "Like no song before it, 'Precious Lord' melded the 'sorrow songs,' spirituals, jubilee, and camp meeting songs into the intimate wail of the blues."[35] As a favorite of Dr. Martin Luther King, who often invited Mahalia Jackson to sing it at rallies, "Take My Hand, Precious Lord" became a musical link between the gospel tradition of the 1930s and the Civil Rights movement of the '50s and '60s, when the Black Baptist church became the spiritual and political home of the struggle for racial justice. Years later, Louis Armstrong told interviewer Studs Terkel, "Whatever song I'm singing, I'm in a spiritual feeling in the song.... There's something beyond the notes, 'cause you're feeling it in your heart."[36]

At Home in Utopia: Third Wave Immigrant Choruses

Between 1880 and 1920, more than twenty-three million immigrants entered the United States in the so-called third wave of American immigration. Initially, most immigrants came from northern and western Europe, but by the turn of the century, vast numbers were from southern and eastern

Europe, drawn by the promise of political and religious freedom and economic betterment.[37]

Among the earliest arrivals during this period were the Germans, who brought with them the choral traditions of their homeland. The first German American singing societies in the United States, the Philadelphia *Männerchor* and the Baltimore *Liederkranz*, organized the first U.S *Sängerfest*, or Song Festival, in 1837; the following year, the *Liederkranz* became the first singing society to accept women, forming a mixed voice chorus. During the latter half of the nineteenth century, German singing societies proliferated across the rural Midwest, along with choruses founded by Welsh immigrants in Pennsylvania and Ohio; Scandinavians in Minneapolis; Irish, Hungarian, Czech, and Italian immigrants in Cleveland; and Polish immigrants in Buffalo.[38]

Many of these choirs sang primarily to affirm their ethnic identity, but others brought a European tradition of workers' choruses dating back to the nineteenth century, when the labor movement had encouraged the development of proletarian choirs to inspire solidarity and educate singers and listeners.

By the turn of the century, southern and eastern European immigrants were settling in major American cities, bringing with them their own tradition of workers' music organizations. By this time, the list included Lithuanian, Yugoslavian, Finnish, Italian, and Ukrainian workers' orchestras and choruses.[39] Among the most notable were the Yiddish labor choruses and orchestras founded by Eastern European Jews who flocked to New York and other large cities during the early twentieth century, especially after a wave of pogroms that began in Kishniev on Easter Day, 1903, when forty-nine Jews were murdered and 1300 homes and businesses destroyed. These refugees brought with them a socialist consciousness and a tradition of Yiddishism—the promotion of Yiddish as the unifying force in the life of the Jewish people and the language of the proletariat (as opposed to Hebrew, considered the language of the elite).[40] Arriving in New York, Philadelphia, Boston, and Chicago, they found a world of crowded tenements, meager wages, and grueling working conditions in the garment factories of the newly industrialized ready-made clothing industry. Steeped in the social justice ethic of Jewish tradition and in the workers' movements they had already founded in Europe, they were "perhaps the most politically aware of all immigrant groups," founding socialist and Communist newspapers, working to unionize shops and factories, and organizing schools, theaters, and orchestras and choruses.[41]

Between 1926 and 1929, the United Workers Association, an organization composed mainly of secular Jewish needle-trade workers with Communist sympathies, built a cooperative colony on Allerton Avenue in the Bronx, where all members had an equal voice in management and were prohibited from selling apartments at a profit. The Coops, as the buildings came to be known, provided an alternative to the tenements of the Lower East Side and included classrooms, a library, youth clubs, a grocery store and a day care center, and eventually included a small number of Black families (Blacks and Whites did not live in the same building anywhere in New York at that time). The founders of the Coops may not have defined their mission in explicitly feminist terms, but their choices revealed a commitment to the needs of women and children as well as to racial equality.

In 1922, the United Workers Cooperative Association purchased 250 acres of land in Beacon, New York, and developed Camp Nitgadaiget ("No Worries"), one of over 300 left-wing summer camps for adults and children around the U.S. Camp Nitgadaiget was run as a nonprofit, with a pool formed by a man-made dam, hot and cold running showers, and a dining hall that seated 800.

Camp Nitgadaiget and camps like it were a refuge from the world of city and factory. The camp's proximity to the Hudson River provided an idyllic environment, offering freedom and fresh air with a strong dose of political solidarity. Yiddish theater and music, especially folk songs, were an essential part of camp life: people sang in the dining hall, on the camp grounds, and at the auditorium, where a thousand guests might gather on a weekend to sing along with Paul Robeson or Pete Seeger.

(Seeger eventually bought seventeen acres of land adjacent to the camp and built the home where he and his wife Toshi lived for the rest of their lives.) Camp visitors walking along the rustic paths might hear strains of the camp song:

> *In unzer kemp Nit Gedayget,*
> *Zaynen mir ale yatn un khaveyrim,*
> *Arbet un kamf hot farbridert,*
> *Zorg un noyt hot unz bafraynt.*
> In Our Camp Nitgadaiget
> We are all family and comrades
> Work and struggle has united us
> Worry and need has made us friends.[42]

Kol isha for *col isha*

Women played a key role in the labor movement and the cultural organizations that grew out of it. While girls in the old country were married off young, women in America worked in the garment factories and then continued to do piecework at home after they were married. [43] As a result, women like Rose Schneiderman and Clara Lemlich became prominent trade union organizers and sang in the dozens of Yiddish labor choruses that gave voice to the labor movement. Although workers' movements and labor choruses emphasized class solidarity above all else, the very presence of women in the Yiddish labor choruses represented a challenge to traditional gender norms. According to Jewish law, men and women were separated in almost every aspect of public and religious life. *Kol ish*a, the voice of a woman, was considered an illicit temptation and a distraction from men's study of the Torah; consequently, in the Old World mixed singing in public was forbidden.[44] Because the Bundists (members of the left-wing Jewish workers' movement) and other progressive Jews had established a defiant secular identity even before they came to the New World, singing in mixed choruses had "an extra 'edge,' a quality of subversiveness that helped feed its revolutionary underpinnings."[45] Many years later, the late singer-songwriter Debbie Friedman put forth an interpretation of *kol isha* that would probably have pleased her Yiddish foremothers:

> It was *kol isha* (the voice of women) for *col isha* (every woman) that inspired me to write inclusive music.... Ultimately, the voices of women, their sense of empowerment, can be borne from song, which can form the core of political, spiritual, and economic transformation. The more our voices are heard in song, the more we become our lyrics, our prayers, and our convictions. Then every woman will be heard, and every voice will be heard: *kol isha* for *col isha*.[46]

Women were prominent members of the most famous of the Yiddish choruses, the *Freiheit Gesang Ferein* (Freedom Singing Society), founded in Chicago in 1914 but officially established in New York City in 1923 with "seventy-five enthusiastic people" who sang at rallies, strikes, and public concerts for the labor left community.[47] In a 1923 photo, the chorus members face the camera, the women seated on the floor in front and the men standing behind them. Wearing long white dresses, the women face the camera straight-on, many of them smiling naturally.[48] Not far away, the Paterson (New Jersey) *Freiheit Gesang Ferein* was established by striking textile workers in 1915; in 1927, the two choruses appeared together at Carnegie Hall in a program highlighted by an oratorio titled "Twelve," derived from a poem about the Russian Revolution.[49]

The Yiddish press covered the choruses regularly, highlighting their importance in the Jewish left community and celebrating the accomplishments of everyday singers who devoted themselves to the highest artistic standards without concern for financial remuneration. "If you sang in that chorus, you were really somebody," recalled a woman whose mother sang with the New York *Freiheit Gesang Ferein* in its early days.[50]

Singing for Solidarity

The Yiddish choruses of the early 20th twentieth century celebrated the political, social and linguistic heritage they had brought with them from eastern Europe, but like the other workers' choruses of the period, they were part of a larger movement that grew and diversified during the first half of the twentieth century. In 1905, organizers meeting in Chicago under the leadership of William "Big Bill" Haywood declared themselves "the Continental Congress of the Working Class" and established the Industrial Workers of the World "to confederate the workers of this country into a working-class movement that shall have for its purpose the emancipation of the working class from the slave bondage of capitalism."[51]

Though it was only one of many Marxist and Socialist groups of the time, the IWW stood out in its effective use of songs to promote its message. Two of its earliest members, Joe Hill and Ralph Chaplin, are indelibly associated with IWW musical history. Joe Hill, a Swedish immigrant born Joel Emmanuel Hägglund, traveled the country organizing for the IWW and wrote some of its most important songs, including "The Preacher and the Slave" and "The Rebel Girl," which celebrates the heroine who "brings courage, pride and joy / To the fighting Rebel Boy" (despite the fact that it was written in tribute to Elizabeth Gurley Flynn, as daring a feminist activist as anyone in the IWW). Hill's execution in 1915, on a murder charge widely believed to be a frame-up, changed him from an organizer to a martyr; Alfred Hayes's 1930 tribute, later set to music by Earl Robinson, has become one of the staples of the folk music repertoire, sung and recorded by everyone from Pete Seeger to Joan Baez to Bruce Springsteen.

Ralph Chaplin, the other great IWW songwriter, was inspired by his work with striking coal miners in West Virginia to write the words to "Solidarity Forever," possibly the most famous labor anthem of all time. In its musical setting to the tune of "John Brown's Body," "Solidarity Forever" has been sung at union meetings and labor conferences across the English-speaking world, where women's groups and others have added verses to update the song and its message. In 1936, the song figured prominently in one of the great labor events of modern history, the sit-down strike at the Flint, Michigan, General Motors plant that won union recognition for the United Auto Workers. Women were crucial to the success of the strike, bringing food to their husbands, who had barricaded themselves inside the plant, breaking windows when police attacked the striking workers with tear gas, and defying plant authorities with marches and pickets. *With Babies and Banners: The Story of the Women's Emergency Brigade*, a 1979 film by Lorraine Gray, Anne Bohlen, and Lyn Goldfarb, uses archival footage and contemporary interviews to document this history, concluding with the fortieth anniversary celebration of the strike. Amid chants of "UAW Needs an ERA," Women's Brigade leader Genora Johnson Dollinger brings the crowd to their feet, demanding that the union include women's rights in its future agenda. Set against this speech, her recitation of the last verse of "Solidarity Forever" transforms Chaplin's labor hymn into a feminist anthem. The film's final credits appear over a background vocal by Hazel Dickens, singing "The Rebel Girl" with her own updated chorus:

> She's a Rebel Girl, a Rebel Girl!
> She's the working class,
> The strength of this world.
> From Maine to Georgia you'll see
> Her fighting for you and for me.
> Yes, she's there by your side
> With her courage and pride.
> She's unequaled anywhere.
> And, I'm proud to fight for freedom
> With a Rebel Girl.[52]

Singing for Bread and Roses

Though only twelve women were present at the IWW's inaugural convention, the One Big Union had many strong women leaders. Nevertheless, like the labor movements that preceded it, the IWW's commitment to worker solidarity emphasized class rather than gender. However, in 1912, women asserted their own demands as they marched in the famous Lawrence textile strike carrying signs that said, "We want bread and roses too."

The concept of bread and roses had originated in a speech to a group of wealthy women by union activist Rose Schneiderman that invoked both female solidarity and class consciousness. Schneiderman declared, "What the woman who labors wants is the right to live, not simply exist — the right to life as the rich woman has the right to life, and the sun and music and art. You have nothing that the humblest worker has not a right to have also. The worker must have bread, but she must have roses, too."[53]

"Bread and Roses" became a slogan for the women's labor movement. The Lawrence strike came to be known as the "Bread and Roses strike" and the poem of the same name by James Oppenheim, initially set to music by Martha Coleman and Caroline Kohlsaat, became a standard for modern folk singers and activists in the 1970s version by Mimi Farina.[54] "Bread and Roses" has been recorded by Judy Collins, Ani DeFranco, Utah Philips and John Denver, among many others, and is frequently performed by contemporary feminist choruses. In one unlikely but moving appearance, the song was featured in a 2014 film titled *Pride*, based on the true story of a group of LGBT activists who raised money to help families affected by the Welsh miners' strike of 1984. Documenting the struggle to build a coalition between the LGBT community and the striking miners, the film also highlights the role of women (including a splinter group called Lesbians Against Pit Closures). In one of the most memorable scenes, Bronwen Lewis begins singing the first verse of "Bread and Roses" during a gathering at the local union hall, where the leader of the lesbian and gay support group has just made a speech pledging to raise more money for the striking miners. As she sings the second and third verses, other women in the pub rise to join her; one by one, the camera focuses on each of them until the last verse, when some of the men rise to join in.[55]

Singing and the Popular Front

During the 1930s two major events—the Great Depression in America and the rise of Nazism and Fascism abroad—consumed the labor movement and its musical activists. Partly in response to these events, the Communist Party of the USA, which had been founded in 1919, drew idealists and activists who saw the Bolshevik Revolution in Russia as a harbinger of world revolution that would end capitalist oppression and bring about a workers' paradise. Inspired by the Russian model, workers' choruses organized mass singing, for as the CPUSA Manifesto declared:

> Every participant in revolutionary activity knows from his own experience that a good mass song is a powerful weapon in the class struggle. It creates solidarity and inspires action. No other form of collective art activity exerts so far-reaching and all-pervading an influence.[56]

In the words of novelist John Steinbeck, who vividly chronicled the plight of the victims of social and economic injustice, "The songs of working people have always been their sharpest statement and the one statement which cannot be destroyed. You can burn books.... but you cannot prevent singing."[57]

Under the auspices of the Workers Music League (later renamed the Peter Degeyter Club after the composer of the *Internationale*), a host of different "people's" and workers' choruses sprang up, mostly in urban centers.

In the mid-1930s, the Communist Party shifted from a hardline condemnation of all non-communist organizations to a call for a "popular front," a movement for political coalitions that now included New Deal Democrats, mainstream trade unions and left wing writers and musicians, many of whom found the Party line too confining and doctrinaire and joined organizations like the John Reed Clubs.

With the advent of the Popular Front came government-sponsored programs like the Federal Writers Project of the WPA, which was "designed to effect an increased political awareness of the plight of sharecroppers, migrants, and the American proletariat"—an increased awareness that would ideally lead to increased action.[58] Another WPA project, the Federal Music Project, promoted folk and classical music through recordings, radio broadcasts, school concerts and free or inexpensive live performances that drew thousands of people in Middle American towns and cities. Though it promoted far fewer women than either the Federal Writers Project or the Federal Theater Project, the FMP did include women musicians and a few female guest conductors (including Antonia Brico, who would go on to achieve worldwide renown as a conductor and concert pianist) and challenged prevailing notions of women's music inequality.[59] The Federal Music Project also gave Black musicians a unique opportunity for large-scale participation in the arts. One of the most successful choral enterprises under its auspices was Elmer Keeton's Oakland Colored Chorus, an *a cappella* ensemble that performed concert spirituals in the style of the Fisk Jubilee Singers.[60]

The 1930s also saw a strong interest in the "people's music" of rural America. In 1932, activist Myles Horton, educator Don West, and Methodist minister James Dombrowski founded the Highlander Folk School in Monteagle, Tennessee, with the goal of organizing unemployed and working people and training union organizers and leaders. Three years later, Myles married Zilphia Johnson, who became Highlander's music director, collecting more than 1,300 labor, topical and folk songs and helping to disseminate many of them through eleven songbooks put out by the school over the years. In 1946, Horton collected "We Shall Overcome" from striking members of the Food, Tobacco, Agricultural and Allied Workers Union, who sang it as a version of the gospel song, "I'll be All Right." Horton revised the lyrics and taught it to Pete Seeger, who published it in the *People's Songs Bulletin* as "We Shall Overcome."[61]

"Singing of Women"

Although Popular Front singer-activists continued to focus on worker solidarity and racial justice—and, as the decade wore on, on opposing totalitarianism abroad and at home—women played a significant role in Popular Front organizations. In 1951, People's Artists performed "Singing of Women," a musical review by Eve Merriam and Gerda Lerner that dramatized key moments in women's history, with Sojourner Truth asking, "Ain't I a Woman?" Union women struggling for better lives, and contemporary women demanding equal pay—as Flexner put it, "the history of American women dating back to the time when women were sold for 20 pounds of tobacco 'because they would make good workers and had a fine set of teeth.'"[62] Flexner's review of the production in the *Daily Worker* praised its portrayal of "the fight for women's rights and its integration with other progressive struggles such as Abolitionism and trade unionism."[63]

Another Popular Front activist whose work anticipated the tenets of second wave feminism was Mary Inman. Like Flexner and her collaborator Gerda Lerner, Inman argued that women's oppression was tied to gender as well as class; her 1940 book *In Woman's Defense* asserted that women constituted a class independent of racial or economic identity. This proved too much for hard-line Marxists, who expelled her from the Communist Party in 1943. Nevertheless, Inman continued writing and organizing until her death in 1985 at the age of 91.[64]

In 1933, John Lomax, a folk song enthusiast who had just lost his wife to illness and his job at the Republic Bank of Texas to the Depression, set off on a summer-long road trip with his son Alan and a 350-pound Presto recording machine built into the back seat of his car. During that trip and the dozens that followed, the Lomaxes recorded hundreds of thousands of songs by "poor people, farmers, laborers, convicts, old-age pensioners, relief workers, housewives, wandering guitar pickers."[65]

The singers recorded by Lomax and the Highlander School included many women, who sang of cruel lovers and hard times, marriage and childbirth, and the plight of miners, farmers and factory workers. Among them was Florence Reece, a coal miner's wife, who wrote "Which Side Are You On" during the 1931 Harlan County Strike; Aunt Molly Jackson, another Harlan County miner's wife, who wrote "I am a Union Woman" and "Poor Miner's Farewell"; and Aunt Molly Jackson's half-sister, Sarah Ogan Gunning, who wrote "I Am a Girl of Constant Sorrow," recorded in the 1960s and '70s by Peggy Seeger and Judy Collins, among others. Though they were embraced by the Lomaxes, and later by the folk song leaders of the 1940s and '50s, these women's contributions were subsumed under the heading of "folk music," "protest music," or "labor songs." Their lives had little connection with middle class femininity and it was not until many decades later that the songs they wrote and the experiences they wrote about were rediscovered by the founders of "women's music."

In the summer of 1937 the Lomaxes hired composer Ruth Crawford Seeger to transcribe the field recordings into standard western musical notation. It took Ruth, a classically trained composer, four years to produce a transcription and preface, and *Our Singing Country* was finally published in 1941, less than a month before the U.S. entered World War II.[66] In the years that followed, she put much of her classical training aside to join the political movement in which her husband, Charles Seeger, was to play a prominent role. Judith Tick, Ruth Crawford Seeger's biographer, describes Crawford Seeger as an enthusiastic convert to musical activism; yet Tick also describes a crisis at the end of Ruth's life. Finding herself unable to complete the symphonic sketches she had composed, she burned the score of her 1926 *Sonata for Violin and Piano*. Tick concludes: "Her dreams of a union between mother and music-maker that propelled her into marriage faded in the wake of a terrible inner crisis about which no further information survives."[67]

In her 2008 memoir, Bess Lomax Hawes recalls working with her brother and Ruth Crawford Seeger transcribing and researching the background of the songs her father and brother had collected in the field. The questions they asked themselves resonate for any folk music collector or performer, and are among the concerns that would preoccupy the directors and singers in women's choruses many years later:

> Whose criteria of organization should be followed: the people primarily interested in the music, the people primarily interested in the poetry, or the singers themselves? ... Which audience was most important: was it the general reader, the musical specialist, the academic specialist, the community song leader, the church choral director?[68]

"Pins and Needles"—Workers' Theater with "Feminist Energies"

In November, 1937, a group of amateur singers and dancers made theater and labor history when *Pins and Needles*, the only hit ever produced by a labor union, opened on Broadway. *Pins and Needles* was the brainchild of Louis Schaffer, the head of the drama division of the International Ladies Garment Workers Union (ILGWU), who wanted to produce a musical revue that would work as entertainment "not just because it is a labor theater."[69] The union hired Harold Rome, a left-wing songwriter and arranger, to write the lyrics for the show, which historian Michael Denning describes as "a song cycle about working-class romance, a gentle parody of 'moon songs and June songs' and their place in working class life."[70] *Pins and Needles* consisted of nineteen numbers performed by a cast of forty-four cutters, pressers, operators, and finishers who worked in the Seventh Avenue needle trades, "the symbolic center of Popular Front womanhood."[71] Ruth Rubenstein, one of the show's leading players, later remembered, "While at work I would keep peeping into my machine drawer where I kept the lines of the new skit or song, memorizing as the brassieres flowed out of the machine."[72]

What set *Pins and Needles* apart from its cultural counterparts in the labor movement was its realistic portrayal of women workers. Among the songs Rubenstein performed was "Chain Store Daisy," the satiric lament of a young woman who has gone from making daisy chains with her sister-coeds to working as a Macy's clerk:

Chain Store Daisy
They told me my fine education
Would help improve my situation.
So then I crammed and crammed
'til I was almost in a coma.
And CC's and exams
'til I got me a diploma.
Aha, they said, now comes admission
Into a very high position.
So out I went and looked around.
And Macy's was the place I found.
I used to be on the daisy chain
Now I'm a chain store daisy.[73]

Michael Denning points out that although women were a majority in the needle trades, the ILGWU was led by men. He adds:

Though the women of the ILGWU were unable to achieve representation in the union's leadership in these years ... they did achieve representation in *Pins and Needles*. Unlike most proletarian drama, it was largely a woman's show. This was not the intention of the men who wrote and directed the show: the archives and the oral histories suggest that the "political" sketches were the subject of more attention and controversy than the women's songs. Moreover, other ILGWU cultural events did not share the labor feminism of *Pins and Needles*.[74]

In 1962, Columbia records issued a twenty-fifth anniversary edition of *Pins and Needles* personally supervised by Harold Rome himself and starring Barbra Streisand in the role originally played by Ruth Rubenstein. The recording was re-released as a CD in 1993 and is still available online. A 2016 revival at

New York's Provincetown Playhouse commemorated the 105th anniversary of the Triangle Shirtwaist fire, the infamous disaster that claimed the lives of 146 women working in a garment factory where the doors to stairwells and exits had been locked, and which had spurred the growth of the nascent ILGWU.

"Strange Fruit" and Café Society

While John and Alan Lomax were collecting and transcribing songs by Black sharecroppers and archiving narratives of ex-slaves in the Library of Congress, Popular Front activists were marching under the CIO banner of "Black and White, Unite and Fight." But in the restaurants and nightclubs of New York City, Blacks were second-class citizens if they appeared at all, and in New York City there was not a single nightclub where Black and White musicians performed together. At Harlem's Cotton Club, African American employees were depicted as exotic savages or plantation residents, and despite the fact that most of the performers were Black, the Cotton Club admitted White patrons only, except for prominent Black entertainers.[75]

In 1938, Barney Josephson, a former shoe salesman from Trenton, New Jersey, opened a different kind of nightclub on Sheridan Square in Greenwich Village. Working with producer John Hammond, Josephson named his new club Café Society in a dig at the city's upscale nightclubs, and adopted the slogan "the wrong place for the Right people." Doormen at Café Society wore rags and ragged white gloves; bartenders were reputedly veterans of the Abraham Lincoln Brigade, the Americans who had fought against fascism in Spain. Black patrons were given the best tables, while anyone in evening clothes would be placed behind a pillar or near the kitchen.[76]

Not long afterwards, Josephson recruited a young Black singer named Billie Holiday to perform "Strange Fruit," a graphic portrayal of a lynching written by Lewis Allen—a pen name for Abel Meeropol, a New York schoolteacher who, with his wife Anne, would later adopt the orphaned sons of Ethel and Julius Rosenberg.

Café Society audiences found "Strange Fruit" overwhelming and it became Holiday's signature song. Years later, Café Society veterans remembered every detail of her performance. "Strange Fruit" was always the last song of each of her three sets.

Before she began, all service stopped. Waiters, cashiers, busboys were all immobilized. The room went completely dark, save for a pin spot on Holiday's face. When she was finished and the lights went out, she was to walk off the stage, and no matter how thunderous the ovation, she was never to return for a bow. "My instruction was to walk off, period," Josephson later said. "People had to remember "Strange Fruit," get their insides burned with it."[77]

Though other singers, notably Nina Simone, have recorded "Strange Fruit," it remains Holiday's song, a testament to Josephson's determination to bring its cry for justice to his audiences and to the world. David Margolick reports that when Holiday first started singing "Strange Fruit," her mother asked, "Why are you sticking your neck out?" "Because it might make things better," Billie replied. "But you'll be dead." "Yeah, but I'll feel it. I'll know it in my grave."[78]

Testimony from Café Society audiences, anyone who ever head Holliay sing "Strange Fruit," and anyone who has ever sung it herself (in recent years it has been performed and recorded by a number of women's choruses) or even heard a recording, all attest to the power of the song and of her rendition. Yet, though it may have transformed and transfixed audiences, "Strange Fruit" could not save Holiday from bad health, a series of abusive relationships, and the drug and alcohol abuse that led to her death in 1959 at the age of 44. Toward the end of her life, she avoided singing "Strange Fruit." Drummer Lee Young, the brother of legendary saxophonist Lester Young, said that Holiday "didn't like to sing it because it hurt her so much. She would cry every time she would do it."[79]

Backlash and Resistance

As the 1940s began, the folk movement continued to promote proletarian solidarity. In 1941, Pete Seeger, who had dropped out of Harvard to pursue a folk singing career, was introduced to Lee Hays and Millard Lampell, singers who had rented an apartment together on the Lower East Side. The following February, Seeger, Hays and Lampell sang together at the national meeting of the American Youth Congress. They were soon joined by Woody Guthrie, whom Pete Seeger had met at a benefit for displaced workers, and the four named themselves the Almanac Singers. Other singers, both Black and White, joined them over the years.

The Almanac Singers were unique among the many left-wing folk groups of the '30s and '40s in their conscious effort to create a community in which daily life, songwriting, and performance were all part of the communal whole, "paralleling the principles of primitive communism familiar from time immemorial.... They believed that any creative effort was apt to be more socially meaningful and artistically satisfying if it was the product of a group experience rather than that of only one individual."[80] Out of this collaboration came some of the most enduring songs of the labor movement: "Talking Union," "Union Maid," "We Shall Not Be Moved," and their rendition of Florence Reece's "Which Side Are You On," recorded on their 1941 album *Talking Union*.

Like the workers' songs before them, the Almanacs' lyrics emphasized worker solidarity even as they continued to promote conventional ideas about women. "Union Maid," written by Woody Guthrie in response to a request for a union song from a female point of view, praises the union maid who "never was afraid / Of goons and ginks and company finks and deputy sheriffs who made the raid" and who "couldn't be fooled by a company stool, she'd always organize the guys." But the final verse, written later by Almanac members, advises girls "who want to be free" to "get you a man who's a union man and join the Ladies Auxiliary."[81] Feminists have updated this verse with several versions, including one by Nancy Katz, which first appeared in the 1973 edition of the IWW Little Red Songbook:

> A woman's struggle is hard,
> even with a union card;
> She's got to stand on her own two feet
> and not be a servant of a male elite.
> It's time to take a stand,
> keep working hand in hand,
> There is a job that's got to be done,
> and a fight that's got to be won.

Pete Seeger himself helped update this verse more than forty years after it first composition:

> You women who want to be free
> Just take a little tip from me
> Break out of that mold we've all been sold
> You got a fighting history
> The fight for women's rights
> With workers must unite
> Like Mother Jones, bestir them bones
> To the front of every fight.[82]

As one of the few integrated singing groups at the time, the Almanacs were also strongly influenced by Black gospel and spirituals. "Talking Union" was a reworking of a spiritual that began: "If you want to get to heaven, let me tell you what to do," and became "If you want higher wages let me tell you what to do/ You got to talk to the workers in the shop with you." Robert Darden documents the roots of many other labor and protest songs in the Black tradition: "Jesus is my Savior, I Shall Not be Moved" became "The Union is Behind Us, We Shall Not Be Moved," and "The Old Ship of Zion," was transformed into "Union Train" by a black cotton worker named Hattie Walls.[83]

However, by 1942, the Almanacs had begun to fragment: Pete Seeger, Millard Lampell and Peter Hawes went off to fight in World War II; other Almanac singers, including Beth Lomax Hawes, went to work for the War Department; and amid financial difficulties and philosophical differences, the cooperative was unable to continue. "We were orphans," recalled Pete Seeger many years later. "There was no [left-wing] organization that really made themselves responsible for us."[84] Perhaps the best assessment of the brief rise and fall of the Almanacs comes from Richard Reuss:

> Born in the cauldron of idealistic progressive ideology and social change prompted by extraordinary socio-political times—the heyday of the American communist movement, the rise of fascism, and the start of World War II—it's not surprising that the Almanac Singers' career was a brief roller coaster ride of creativity, friction, and unstable financial status.[85]

Yet, the end of the Almanacs was far from the end of left-wing folk music in America. In 1945, Pete Seeger returned from the War to form People's Songs, a New York organization that published a magazine of the same name, crusading for the unionism of the old Popular Front as well as the causes of the postwar era: civil rights and peace with Russia. *People's Songs* was the first of a series of magazines designed to encourage singing by all Americans, and though the organization lasted only until 1948, it had a number of successors, including *Sing Out*, founded by Pete Seeger and Irwin Silber in 1950 and still published today.

Like the labor activists who had found a political and cultural home in retreats like Nitgadaiget, mid-century activists brought their songs and their enthusiasm to left wing summer camps where, in the words of one movement veteran, campers learned to view singing as "a form of battle.... We sang everywhere: while cleaning up the bunk (you could do a whole 'Ballad for Americans'), walking from one activity to another, at meals, campfires and any formal gatherings."[86]

Among the forces leading to the demise of the Almanacs was the anti-communist backlash of the late 1940s and early 1950s, which targeted both men and women writers, artists, actors and musicians who had been associated with the Communist Party. Left wing Jewish camps like Nitgadaiget and Camp Kinderland were put on subversive lists.[87] Unions and labor choruses also felt the heavy hand of the witch-hunts. The membership of the New York *Freiheit Gesang Ferein*, which had numbered in the hundreds in the 1920s and 1930s, dwindled as singers worried about their safety and security. It was at this time that the chorus changed its name to the Jewish People's Philharmonic and its focus from communism to Yiddishism, emphasizing Yiddish language and culture rather than politics.[88] The Paterson *Freiheit Gesang Ferein*, too, managed to survive by shifting its focus from politics to Yiddish culture, although historian Robert Snyder says that "liberal and ex-Communist members of the chorus sustained a tradition of singing for peace and brotherhood that gave political meaning to their performances. Black spirituals, sung in support of the Civil Rights movement, also gave a progressive flavor to concerts."[89]

One labor chorus that did manage to survive was the ILGWU Chorus in Wyoming Valley, Pennsylvania, founded in 1947 by Min and Bill Matheson. In addition to fostering union solidarity through group singing, the chorus performed shows and annual reviews that raised money for mainstream organizations like the Knights of Columbus, the Salvation Army, and the Boy Scouts. Embedding themselves in the community, the Wyoming Valley chorus was able to win over their audiences with songs about labor history and the lives of working people. Kenneth Wolensky also hypothesizes that "simplicity of style, along with clever wording, may have contributed most to the success of the show and the chorus's work as a whole."[90]

The ideals that motivated the people's choruses found their way into the Civil Rights movement, the folk movement, and eventually into the women's music movement of the mid- and late- twentieth century. And although the virulence of the anti-Communist denunciations of the 1950s has mostly faded into history, echoes of the old Red Menace could be heard in late twentieth century attacks on the LGBT community, as AIDS and pedophilia replaced the demon of communist infiltration in the diatribes of right wing extremists like David Noebel, who denounced both the "communist subversion of music" and the dangers of AIDS and secular education.[91] Although mainstream critics reject Noebel's extremism, even as prominent a chronicler of folk and protest music as Serge Denisoff follows the line of those who view the Popular Front folk musicians of the '30s as tools of the Communist party.[92] In response, Ronald D. Cohen provides this assessment of left wing '30s politics:

> Woody, Pete Seeger ... and their friends were homegrown radicals, proud of their heritage and trying to make the country benefit everyone. While they perhaps saw the Soviet Union as somewhat of a model for the good society, even the source of world revolution, they had no real interest in any allegiance to a foreign power.... "I speak for the union people that see a union world," [Woody] wrote.... "I speak for the human beings of this human race."[93]

"Freedom in the Air": Music and the Civil Rights Movement

In 1962, Pete Seeger's conviction for contempt of Congress was overturned on a technicality and Seeger was free to begin the next phase of his activist singing career. A few months later, he accepted an invitation to sing at a church in Albany, Georgia, where a long campaign for civil rights had ended with Dr. Martin Luther King in jail and cross burnings on southern lawns. Seeger's initial idea was to present "a crash course in the history of the protest song," but the congregation failed to respond, wanting to sing "If I Had a Hammer" and "Hold On" with their own words and melodies. Realizing that the freedom song movement was "a different sort of folk music than one encounters among the pampered, groping, earnestly searching young people one meets in the Greenwich Villages of the North," Seeger advised SNCC—the Student Nonviolent Coordinating Committee, then mobilizing for the protests in Albany—to establish its own singing group. Shortly afterwards, Cordell Reagon, his wife Bernice Johnson Reagon, Jim Forman, and Rutha Mae Harris formed the Freedom Singers and began traveling around the South, raising awareness and recruiting organizers.[94]

The Freedom Singers were a testament to the Rev. C.T. Vivian's assertion: "I would think that a movement without music would crumble. Music picks up people's spirits. Any time you can get something that lifts your spirits and also speaks to the reality of your life, even the reality of oppression, and at the same time is talking about how you can really overcome, that's terribly important stuff."[95]

Numerous accounts testify to the power of singing to inspire, connect and fortify Black and White activists as they marched, rallied and endured beatings, jailing and the threat of death. "The people were cold with fear," activist Vernon Jordan later recalled, "until music did what prayers and speeches cold not do." *New York Times* folk music critic Robert Shelton called the new movement "probably the greatest mass topical songwriting rage in this country since the days of the labor movement in the Nineteen Thirties."[96]

James Farmer, national director of the Congress of Racial Equality (CORE) and a participant in the 1961 Freedom Rides, remembered a night in Mississippi's Hinds County Jail when a voice called from the cell block below to the freedom riders, "Sing your freedom song." Farmer went on, "We sang old folk songs and gospel songs to which new words had been written, telling of the Freedom Ride and its purpose." The female freedom riders in another wing of the jail joined in, "and for the first time in history, the Hinds County jail rocked with unrestrained singing of songs about Freedom and Brotherhood."[97] Bernice Johnson Reagon, who would later found the *a cappella* group Sweet Honey in the Rock, and who would become a bridge between the Black Civil Rights movement and the women's music and women's choral movements of the late twentieth century, noted the power of group singing to help resolve differences that could not be solved by talking alone: "After the song, the differences among us would not be as great."[98]

In August, 1962, one of the luminaries of the Civil Rights movement, Fannie Lou Hamer, was on a bus headed for Ruleville, Mississippi, when the local police stopped the bus and a group of men in trucks drove by shouting racist threats. Fannie Lou and her fellow riders were headed home from Indianola, where they had tried unsuccessfully to register to vote. Nearly fifty years later, Charles McLauren, a civil rights leader who was on that bus, described what happened next:

> All while that bus is sitting there, trucks are driving by with men, white men in them and guns, and they are saying things like "Niggers, you gonna get killed. Niggers, there ain't gonna be no nigger vote." And they're hanging out of the windows and just gesturing toward us. So then, as we're sitting there and all are worried, a church song just kind of eases out of somebody. And somebody on the bus says, "That's Fannie Lou." You know, when she starts to sing, now they're looking to her for inspiration. They're looking to her now to just calm them, make them feel good…. I mean, just kind of eased out. You know and then it come out and then it rises softly, sweetly. She was deep. I think that was the beauty about her—was that she made you feel what she felt. I'll never forget.[99]

SNCC organizer Bob Moses called Fannie Lou Hamer "the lady who sings the hymns." In 1963, her voter registration efforts landed her in jail in Winona, Mississippi, where she was beaten so badly that she could hardly move. Once she and the others with her were finally put in their cells, they began to sing. "When you're in a brick cell, locked up there, well sometimes words just begin to come to you and you begin to sing," she said. "Singing brings out the soul."[100]

As they rewrote the words of older songs to fit the needs of the Civil Rights movement, singers often turned to gospel hymns. Bernice Johnson Reagon, who was raised in the Baptist Church where her father was a pastor, wrote that "the power of congregational singing has made tracks in my soul—I am who I am because I was raised in the shadows between the lines of my people living their lives out in a song."[101]

Reagon felt that her early musical experiences were directly connected to her Civil Rights activism. Many years later she wrote, "The relationship between singing and that struggle was crucial for me. The training for being a singing fighter had begun with learning about the role of music in African-American culture and the role of the artist in the leadership of the community."[102]

Africadian Voices and Musical Transformations

Gospel music and the singer-activists it inspired were not limited to the United States. Delvina Bernard grew up in the Black communities of Lake Loon and Cherrybrook, eight miles from Halifax, Nova Scotia. "To grow up there ... was to be surrounded by black elders, parents, children, workers, teachers, and churchgoers [and] the song and singing of the Cherrybrook (African) United Baptist Church," writes historian and former Canadian poet laureate George Elliot Clarke, who coined the term "Africadian" to describe the descendants of African-American slaves who settled on the east coast of Nova Scotia.[103] In 1981, Delvina Bernard founded Four the Moment, a gospel-based quartet inspired by Sweet Honey in the Rock. They made their debut at an anti-Ku Klux Klan rally in Halifax singing "Joan Little," Bernice Johnson Reagon's tribute to a Black woman who was tried and acquitted for killing the jailer who had sexually assaulted her. Though their personnel changed over the years, Four the Moment always included three Black singers and one White singer. They released three albums— *We're Still Standing*, *Four the Moment Live*, and *In My Soul*. In a 2017 interview, Bernard recalled the group's spiritual and musical debt to Sweet Honey in the Rock, their collaboration with George Elliott Clarke, and their commitment to racial and economic justice. She concluded: "Through our music, we were able to shape the definition of what it means to be an African Nova Scotian."[104]

Robert Darden, Michael Castellini, and others remind us that Black spirituals and gospel were "charged with meanings that escaped whites but resonated with blacks.... The disguised protest of black gospel music was merely part of a much larger world of covert resistance at work in the black community."[105]

In 1961, Reagon joined a SNCC demonstration in support of two SNCC representatives who had been arrested for trying to buy tickets at a White waiting room window in Albany, Georgia. After a show of solidarity, marchers assembled at Union Baptist Church, where Charlie Jones, one of the leaders of the protest, asked Bernice to sing.

> I began to sing "Over my head I see...." Usually in the opening line I always sang "trouble in the air"; however, since Albany had just had its first march that wasn't a homecoming or thanksgiving parade I did not see any "trouble." I saw "freedom," so I switched the words as I sang and everyone followed, raising up the song.

> > Over my head I see Freedom in the air
> > Over my head I see Freedom in the air
> > Over my head I see Freedom in the air
> > There must be a God somewhere.

> It was the first time my living had changed a song even as it came out of my body. Freedom![106]

The most famous transformation of a gospel song was the reworking of Charles Tindley's gospel hymn "I'll Overcome Someday." In 1945, striking Negro Food and Tobacco Union members adopted it for their picket line, and later they brought it to the Highlander Folk School. Still later, Zilphia Horton taught it to Pete Seeger, and in 1969, Seeger met Guy Carawan and encouraged him to visit the Highlander Folk School, where

Carawan learned "We Shall Overcome." Then, in 1960, at the founding convention of the Student Nonviolent Coordinating Committee in Raleigh, North Carolina, Carawan was asked to lead a song and picked "We Shall Overcome." Before long, the song had become the anthem of the Civil Rights Movement.[107]

"One cannot describe the vitality and emotion this one song evokes across the Southland," said Martin Luther King's chief of staff, Wyatt Tee Walker.

> I have heard it sung in great mass meetings with a thousand voices singing as one; I've heard a half-dozen sing it softly behind the bars of the Hinds County prison in Mississippi; I've heard old women singing it on the way to work in Albany, Georgia; I've heard the students singing it as they were being dragged away to jail. It generates power that is indescribable.[108]

"Rip" Patton, one of the original Freedom Riders who challenged Southern Jim Crow laws on integrated buses, later recalled, "Music brought us together—we can't all talk at the same time, but we can all sing at the same time. It gives you that spiritual feeling. It was like our glue."[109]

Civil rights activist Sally Belfrage described the singing of "We Shall Overcome" at the end of every meeting: "The only song that has no clapping, because the hands are holding all the other hands. A suspension from color, hate, recrimination, guilt, suffering—a kind of lesson in miniature of what it's all about. The song begins slowly and somehow without anticipation of these things: just a song, the last one before we separate.... A sort of joy begins to grow in every face: 'We are not afraid'—and just for that second, no one is afraid, because they are free."[110]

Sally Belfrage was one of many young white women who abandoned conventional expectations to join the movement. Her memoir, along with those of Debra Schultz and Sara Evans, documents the complicated relationships and conflicts among Black and White men and women in the Civil Rights movement.[111] According to Evans, young white women in the movement were motivated by the religious ethos of the movement, their own sense of cultural alienation, and a search for new role models. "As they exercised their ingenuity to find ways of relating to the movement and of communicating to other whites the demonic nature of racial barriers," she writes, "they also struggled to elaborate an understanding of community in which they could exist as equal persons, freed from both the passivity and the guilt of their internalized image as white southern women."[112]

Evans and her sister memoirists also describe the ways that men dominated these organizations, even as they struggled for racial equality. Women like Fannie Lou Hamer and Bernice Johnson Reagon played significant roles in the struggle, but when they sang for equality, they were singing for racial equality and not for women's empowerment. Not until 1973 would Reagon form Sweet Honey in the Rock as "a group of Black *women* singers"[113]; not until 1978 would the Combahee River Collective sponsor Varied Voices of Black Women, the first touring program of woman-identified Black performers. And not until the '70s would the young feminist and lesbian veterans of the Civil Rights and anti-war movements defy male domination of those movements and begin to speak—and to sing—in their own voices.

3

Singing for Our Lives:
The Women's Music Movement

The memoirs of Sara Evans, Sally Belfrage, and others document the coalitions—often shaky and difficult—built by White and Black women during the Civil Rights Era. Contributors to Gail Murray's edited collection, *Throwing Off the Cloak of White Privilege: White Southern Women Activists in the Civil Rights Era*, describe other such collaborations, such as The Fellowship of the Concerned and a handful of other interracial organizations that formed in the 1930s and '40s and continued working toward racial integration in the years that followed.[1]

Nevertheless, by the 1970s the coalitions that had drawn women from different ethnic communities and social classes were beginning to fragment into what has come to be known as identity politics. In her 2004 study, *Separate Roads to Feminism*, Benita Roth describes second wave activism as a profusion of feminisms (emphasizing the plural) emerging out of women's varied histories and cultures. She emphasizes the role of social and structural inequality in the construction of these various feminisms.[2] Gloria T. Hull, Patricia Bell Scott, and Barbara Smith, in their groundbreaking work, *All the Women Are White, All the Blacks are Men, But Some of Us Are Brave*, propose a number of reasons for the erasure of women of color from the mainstream women's movement: "the increasing involvement of single, middle-class white women (who often had the most time to devote to political work), the divisive campaigns of the white-male media, and the movement's serious inability to deal with racism."[3]

"The Lavender Menace"

By the 1970s Betty Friedan's *The Feminine Mystique* had become the bible for many in the second wave of the women's movement and had helped inspire the founding of the National Organization for Women. Friedan's book led White feminists to advocate for reproductive rights and sexual equality in the workplace, in schools, and in the public sphere; yet as bell hooks points out, Friedan's discussion of "the problem that has no name" ignored the question of "who would be called in to take care of the children and maintain the home if more women like herself were freed from their house labor and given equal access with White men to the professions."[4] Most accounts of the 1966 founding of the National Organization for Women highlight the role played by Friedan and other White feminists and virtually ignore NOW co-founder Pauli Murray, a Black lesbian civil rights activist who had been arrested for refusing to move to the back of the bus in Petersburg, Virginia fifteen years before Rosa Parks did the same, and had organized restaurant sit-ins in Washington, DC twenty years before the Greensboro sit-ins.[5]

Racism was not the only form of bigotry within mainstream feminism. In 1969, Ivy Bottini, an out lesbian who was then president of the New York Chapter of the National Organization for Women, had held a public forum titled "Is Lesbianism a Feminist Issue?" Fearing that the presence of out lesbians in the women's movement would provide ammunition for opponents who already equated feminism with man-hating and lesbianism, Friedan led a move to expel all lesbians, including Bottini, from NOW's New York Chapter, warning of a "lavender menace."

But lesbians in the New York NOW Chapter who had begun coming out to one another were growing impatient with the closet. In 1970, Bottini and her sister activists interrupted the Congress to Unite Women with a memorable demonstration. Karla Jay, one of those who participated in the action, recalled:

About three hundred women filed into the school auditorium. Just as the first speaker came to the microphone, Jesse Falstein, a GLF (Gay Liberation Front) member, and Michela [Griffo] switched off the lights and pulled the plug on the mic.... When Michela and Jesse flipped the lights back on, both aisles were lined with seventeen lesbians wearing their Lavender Menace T-shirts and holding the placards we had made. Some invited the audience to join them. I stood up and yelled, "Yes, yes, sisters! I'm tired of being in the closet because of the women's movement." Much to the horror of the audience, I unbuttoned the long-sleeved red blouse I was wearing and ripped it off. Underneath, I was wearing a Lavender Menace T-shirt. There were hoots of laughter as I joined the others in the aisles.

Then Rita [Mae Brown] yelled to members of the audience, "Who wants to join us?"

"I do, I do," several replied. Then Rita also pulled off her Lavender Menace T-shirt. Again, there were gasps, but underneath she had on another one. More laughter. The audience was on our side.[6]

The protesters read a paper titled "The Woman Identified Woman," the first major lesbian feminist manifesto; they eventually renamed themselves the Radicalesbians and went on to advocate lesbian visibility and separatism.[7] (In 1977, at the National Women's Conference in Houston, Friedan received a huge ovation for seconding the resolution to protect lesbian rights—a move more tactical than pro-lesbian—and in her 2001 memoir she wrote that she was "more relaxed about the whole issue now.")[8]

Academic feminists were waging culture wars of their own. In 1970, after a year of rallies, petitions and unofficial classes, the first women's studies program was established at San Diego State University, followed a year later by a women's studies program at SUNY-Buffalo. Like their sister initiatives in the mainstream women's movement, early women's studies courses dealt mainly with the lives and concerns of White women. Black women responded with their own initiatives: the decade that followed saw the founding of Kitchen Table: Women of Color Press, as well as the publication of numerous works by Black feminists. In 1978, Black feminists came together in the Combahee River Collective to set forth an agenda for Black feminism. The members of the Collective expressed their commitment to "working on those struggles in which race, sex, and class are simultaneously factors in oppression," anticipating by more than a decade Kimberlé Crenshaw's now-classic essay on intersectionality.[9]

Nevertheless, identity remained a dominant force in feminist politics for most of the 1970s, and was nowhere more evident than in the world of lesbian feminism. Like the Lavender Menace, lesbians around the country were defying the closet and coming together to affirm their identity. And as the decade wore on, women found that although identity politics could be a source of strength, it could also become a wedge dividing feminists from one another. This was particularly true in the lesbian/feminist community that gave birth to women's music of the 1970s and '80s.

I Know You Know:
The Birth of Women's/Womyn's/Wimmin's Music

Although the folk and protest singers of the 1950s and 1960s had challenged racial and economic oppression, their songs reflected conventional ideas about women, while the folk movement itself continued to be dominated by men. Dorian Lynksey's 2011 history of protest songs, *33 Revolutions per Minute*, devotes only three of its thirty-three chapters to women (Billie Holiday, Nina Simone and the feminist punk rock movement Riot Grrrl), even as Lynskey himself acknowledges that "the burgeoning women's movement [of the 1970s] was ill-served by protest music."[10]

Woody Guthrie, the Almanac Singers and their followers had sung about dispossessed hobos, farmers and workers. Bob Dylan, Tom Paxton, Phil Ochs, and even Joan Baez and Judy Collins sang to expose injustice and promote peace.

In a 2004 interview, Ronnie Gilbert, a founding member of the Weavers, recalled her frustration at being "the girl in the band.... I hated that every time we got a review, they would talk about me as the chick. They would always talk about what I wore. They never talked about what the men wore."[11]

Like Gilbert, Alix Dobkin began her professional life as a singer in the mainstream folk revival movement of the '60s. After a girlhood in the Communist movement of which her parents were a part, Dobkin arrived in New York carrying her guitar and was soon involved in the folk movement centered in Greenwich Village. Dobkin became a regular at the Gaslight, a folk club where just about everyone who was anyone in the '60s folk/protest movement performed. She shared warm memories of the movement's "cooperative, supportive values," but recalled that "no one, including me, ever questioned the conventional wisdom of the time that said 'two chick singers back-to-back is bad programming.' I heard and spoke that exact phrase many times myself to justify whole evenings of nothing but Jack Elliot/ Bob Dylan-wannabes-with-guitar." [12]

Meanwhile, feminists in the anti-war and social protest movements were beginning to sing a different tune. On a cold and sunny day in March 1970, the late Naomi Weisstein was lying on the couch in her Chicago apartment when she had a revolutionary idea.

> I was lying on the sofa listening to the radio—a rare bit of free time in those early hectic days of the women's movement.... First, Mick Jagger crowed that his once feisty girlfriend was now "under my thumb." Then Janis Joplin moaned with thrilled resignation that love was like "a ball and chain." Then The Band, a self-consciously left-wing group, sang: "Jemima surrender/I'm gonna give it to you."
>
> I somersaulted off the sofa, leapt up into the air, and came down howling at the radio: "Every fourteen-year-old girl in this city listens to rock! Rock is the insurgent culture of the era! How criminal to make the subjugation

and suffering of women so sexy? We'll...we'll organize our own rock band!"[13]

Weisstein was growing dissatisfied with the Chicago Women's Liberation Union, the umbrella organization that had been founded by Heather Tobis and the women who walked out of the 1965 SDS meeting in Champaign. Despite the CWLU's commitment to feminist issues of reproductive choice and workplace equity, Weisstein wrote that the organization "often placed its version of socialism ahead of feminism." As an example, she recalled a returnee from one of the Venceremos Brigades who had gone to Cuba to harvest sugar and had described

> how she preferred to cut cane with the Cuban men because the Cuban women were so "politically undeveloped." When I queried her preference, another CLWU'er whipped out her little red book and started quoting Mao Tse-tung. Some women at the meeting sighed with relief to see the problem so easily resolved. Watching this scenario unfold, I thought I was hallucinating. Where was the feminism?[14]

Weisstein was convinced that a change of consciousness, along with structural change, was essential to overthrowing oppression.

> "What about rock?" I said to myself, boiling over with my new idea. "Rock, with its drive, power, and energy, its insistent erotic rhythms, its big bright major triads, its take-no-prisoners chord progressions, was surely the kind of transforming medium that could help us to change our consciousness."[15]

Fired with the idea of radical rock, Weisstein and six friends formed the Chicago Women's Liberation Rock Band and began playing in Chicago and touring through the Midwest and the East Coast. "To combat the fascism of the typical rock performance where the performers disdain audiences and the sound is turned up beyond human endurance," Weisstein later recalled, "we were interactive with our audiences, rapping with them and asking them which songs they liked while keeping the sounds at a reasonable roar. We were playful, theatrical, and comical, always attentive to performance."[16]

Band member Susan Abod described the band's first performance at Grant Park:

> We did the Kinks' "You Really Got Me" but with a whole new set of lyrics that started with "Man," instead of "Girl," and we pranced holding our "cocks" like Mick Jagger, or whatever rock star we found really annoying, and it would just look ridiculous. And the audience was totally into the guerrilla theater of it. They'd shriek and grab at our legs like groupies. It was so much fun, laughing at a culture that had kept us down.[17]

In 1972, the band released a record, *Mountain Moving Day*, together with the New Haven Women's Liberation Band—a record that "became an underground classic for many feminists," Weisstein wrote. "This is when that congeries of styles and songs called Women's Music began."[18]

The Chicago Women's Liberation Rock Band (CWLRB) broke up in 1973, torn by conflicts over strategy and identity that were roiling the radical women's movement as a whole. Nevertheless, watching a tape of the band's farewell concert many years later, Weisstein was deeply moved:

> In the grainy shadows of that last tape, the audience is ecstatic, because beyond the CWLRB's flaws, beyond the disintegration of the last performance, the band still conveys celebration and resistance. Its performance deliberately sets up a prefigurative politics of strong, defiant women, absolute democracy, the players and the audience together in a beloved community.[19]

A year before Naomi Weisstein and her friends formed the Chicago Women's Liberation Rock Band, two sisters on the west coast were heading for Los Angeles, determined to "either sign with a label or go back to school." June and Jean Millington had come to California from the Philippines with their parents in 1961 and had already begun singing in an all-girl quartet, The Svelts, and a band they called Wild Honey. After a disappointing period in LA, the sisters were about to return home when Richard Perry, a leading Warner Brothers producer, heard them sing at an open mic night and arranged to have them signed to Reprise Records, a Warner subsidiary. As they prepared to release their first album, the band members and the executives at Warner agreed that they needed a new name—"a woman's name, something short, memorable and at once feminine and bold." The band settled on the name FANNY; as June would later explain, "We really didn't think of [the name Fanny] as a butt, a sexual term. We felt it was like a woman's spirit watching over us."[20] But by 1974, the release date of their fifth and final album, "internal tensions, accumulated strains, and the ordinary occupational hazards of making it in a man's world predicated on sex, drugs and rock and roll" had taken their toll on the band and led to FANNY's demise.[21]

As a group that identified primarily with rock, FANNY's importance for feminist history lay not in their repertoire but in their very presence on the music scene. Prior to their arrival, no all-female band in any genre of modern music, playing their own instruments and writing their own material, had ever achieved commercial success. Though they did not challenge the political structure of the record industry or of the wider society, the energy and quality of their songwriting defied the assumption that rock belonged to the boys—the same assumption that was being challenged by their more politically inclined sisters in folk and protest music. Years later, Susan Abod told Queer Music historian JD Doyle that the Chicago Women's Liberation Band had drawn some of their inspiration from FANNY: "They were our heroes, because...they were musicians, and there was politics in their behavior of wanting to do rock & roll, and liking women and wanting to do it with women."[22]

Just as FANNY was ending their career as a band, a group of women in a feminist studies course on women and music at Goddard/Cambridge Graduate School for Social Change was coming together to form yet another kind of band, one that would present old-timey folk music along with compositions reflecting current events. The New Harmony Sisterhood Band played their first public concert in New Haven in 1970. A decade later, band member Pat Ouellete recalled: "The women were very excited. That first time we played, some women showed up with a huge sign that said, 'A STANDING OVULATION FOR OUR SISTERS.'" [23]

True to its origin in the world of feminist studies, the band's work reflected a commitment to theory along with music. "We took a lot of time reading theory, reading culture theory, women's studies," explained band member Marcia Deihl.

> We put together our own theoretical base for our existence so that when we got up there in our early days and it sounded like crap, we still wanted to stay together for reasons that a lot of people might not even have known when they heard us play. We had a pretty theoretical view worked out of why we were doing this and what we were doing and how it all fit with challenging the culture. [24]

The New Harmony Sisterhood Band became a fixture in the New England women's community, playing benefits for women's centers, union drives, striking workers, and early nuclear power protests. In 1976, the group recorded *...And Ain't I a Woman,* an album that included a version of Sojourner Truth's famous speech set to music by band member Lanayre Liggera; "Draglines," a protest against strip mining with words and music by band member Deborah Silverstein; and a mixture of topical and traditional songs. [25]

Like Naomi Weisstein, New Harmony Sisterhood Band members saw their work as deeply political; in an interview with a *Guardian* reporter, band member Kendall Hale explained: "On the left, people don't believe to a large extent that cultural work is political work, and they don't really see it as a priority.

Most of the party-building groups do not really appreciate the importance of how people relate to culture."[26]

New Harmony broke up in 1980 in what Hale later described as "a traumatic divorce.... Belonging to a pack of wild women who howled at the moon and everyone else gave me the voice I'd always wanted. Singing from our hearts, we told stories that few people had ever heard. But underground conflicts, combined with different personal agendas, forced us to split up.... It was the end, but I didn't want to let go."[27]

One feminist band that did survive into the twenty-first century was The Deadly Nightshade, a New England-based rock and country band started by Pamela Brandt, Anne Bowen, and Helen Hooke. Between its founding in 1972 and its initial breakup in 1977, the band went from Western Massachusetts to the national stage, releasing one of the first feminist albums on a major label ("The Deadly Nightshade," on RCA in 1975), and appearing in venues from "Sesame Street" to *Ms.* Magazine's second anniversary party. After that event, a *New York Times* music critic praised their "camaraderie and openness to their audiences" and acknowledged the importance of feminist politics in an appreciation of the band's talent, adding, "Like all anthems of this communal age, feminist songs owe part of their appeal to the very sense that the individual listener is being swept up in something larger than himself or herself, something comforting and protective and invincible."[28]

The Deadly Nightshade reunited in 2008 and continued performing until Pamela Brandt's death in 2015 made their future uncertain. Their website continues to carry the admonition "Please Check Your Coats, Guns, and Preconceptions at the Door."[29]

Even before the founding of the early feminist bands, before the attempt to pass the Equal Rights Act, and before the Stonewall uprising, Maxine Feldman, a lesbian singer-songwriter in Los Angeles, had performed "Angry Athis," the first modern lesbian song on record. The title was a play on words: Athis was a woman to whom Sappho had dedicated one of her love poems and when the syllables were separated out, the title became

"Angry at This." In a 2002 interview with JD Doyle, Feldman described the song's genesis:

> I hadn't been playing the guitar for a year because I'd been thrown off the Boston coffee house circuit back in '63 for being queer and bringing around the wrong crowd. And I had just left Boston and I had been living down in New York, too. And Mayor Lindsay had sent these cops into gay bars where they would imitate gay guys, and as soon as the guys went outside, they would bust them.... There were many things, being thrown out of college, always having to hide who you were, it got me so damn angry that one night, when I arrived in Los Angeles, California... I wrote "Angry Athis"....We were all getting very tired of being invisible and losing our jobs, losing our schools, losing our parents, you know, who didn't understand us, people trying to convert us.... To me being queer is like breathing.[30]

"Angry Athis" was released as a single in 1971 and appeared in Feldman's album, *Closet Sale,* in 1979. *Closet Sale* also featured "Amazon," a song Feldman first introduced at the National Women's Music Festival in 1976 and which became the Michigan Womyn's Music Festival's opening song every year until MichFest ended in 2015.

Though Maxine Feldman's anger echoed the feelings of many defiant lesbians in the early 1970s, militant lesbianism was not the only path into women's music. Holly Near's first album, *Hang in There*, released in 1973, came out of Near's work with Free the Army (FTA), an anti-Vietnam War road show, and included songs like "No More Genocide" and "G.I. Movement." Near had founded her own label, Redwood Records, to promote songs with a wide focus on social justice, a focus she never abandoned even after she came out publicly as a lesbian in 1976. On the other hand, Alix Dobkin, who had already begun to identify as a lesbian, joined with Kay Gardner and Patches Attom (Pat Moschetta) in 1973 to release *Lavender Jane Loves Women*, "the very first album by, for, and about Lesbians in the history of the world."[31] The album cost \$3300 for the first 1,000 copies, all of which sold out in three months with no distribution other than mail orders and a few lesbian-feminist bookstores.[32] In addition to a lesbian rewrite of the Almanacs' "Talking Union" ("If you want high consciousness, I'll tell you what to do,/ You got to talk to a woman, let her talk to you"), *Lavender Jane* featured "The Woman in Your Life," a song Dobkin later called her "signature tune," and which eventually became an anthem of the women's music movement.[33]

Meanwhile, Cris Williamson, who had already released three folk-oriented albums inspired by her admiration for Judy Collins, had begun writing and performing woman-identified songs, as had Meg Christian, who was radicalized after watching Ti Grace Atkinson and Robin Morgan walk off the set of the David Frost TV show in response to the host's disrespectful treatment.[34]

Like folk music before it, women's music celebrated struggles against all forms of oppression. But now for the first time, women who had been second-class citizens in the male dominated folk and social change movements, lesbians who had been closeted all their adult lives, young women angry and offended by media stereotypes, heard their lives expressed in song. Many years later, Ginny Berson recalled:

> Meg was performing in nightclubs in Washington. We started to notice in the women's bathrooms, women running into the bathrooms and crying and sobbing, and what was going on was that Meg's music and the fact that Meg was paying attention to women in the audience was so moving to them that it was releasing something in them.[35]

At the same time, the women's music movement reflected the tensions of the feminist movement as a whole, as identity politics fueled arguments between lesbians and straight women over woman-only spaces and homophobia in the mainstream women's movement. Women of color decried racism in the White women's movement and refused to exclude Black men from their activism. In addition, Black women often found that their connection to the music of the Black church that had nurtured them was at odds with the experiences of White lesbians, who had known religion as oppressive and homophobic. Radical groups like the Redstockings began to distance themselves from mainstream feminism, calling for lesbian visibility and lesbian separatism. Lesbians feeling marginalized both by mainstream society and by a women's movement that continued to privilege heterosexuality began creating safe spaces for themselves—softball leagues, lesbian bars, women's bookstores, and above all, concerts organized by and for lesbian performers and audiences.

Sweet Honey in the Rock:
"We Do Use Instruments: Our Voices"

The audiences who laughed, cheered, and cried at concerts by Cris Williamson, Holly Near, Meg Christian and other women singer-songwriters were overwhelmingly White and overwhelmingly lesbian or woman-identified. Meanwhile, Black women like Linda Tillery, Judith Casselberry and Jacque DuPree, and Mary Watkins were performing music derived from gospel, jazz, blues, and other African and African American influences. It would be several years before these two constituencies joined forces, but in 1971, Bernice Johnson Reagon assembled ten women singers from a workshop she was leading at the Washington, DC Repertory Company and began a process that would transform the world of women's music and American music at large.

Reagon had come to Washington, DC to pursue a graduate degree at Howard University and was serving as the vocal director for the DC Repertory Company. There, she taught the choral style she had learned as a child in her father's Baptist church in Albany, Georgia, where "there are no auditions, one has but to enter the congregation and find the courage to sing."[36] During her second year as vocal director, she and several other women began talking about forming a singing group, and one evening she gathered ten strong women singers from her workshop.

"The first song I taught this group was 'Sweet Honey in the Rock'.... It was a quartet song I had heard as a child and it was time for it to have its way in my life," Reagon recalled. "When the group that first night got the chorus right, I said, 'Hum, that's the name of the group. Sweet Honey in The Rock.'"[37]

Later that evening, Reagon called her father and asked him about the song and its meaning.

> He told me that it was based on a religious parable [that] described a land that was so rich that when you cracked the rocks, honey would flow from them. From the beginning, the phrase—with sweetness and strength in it—resonated in a deeply personal way with me. It was another two years before I understood that for me and for the group, this land where the rocks were filled with honey was beginning to take shape and sound under the shade of that song as the experience and legacy of African American women in the United States of America.[38]

Sweet Honey gave their first performance on November 23, 1973 at Howard University and released their first album in 1976. Drawing on the African American gospel and spiritual tradition, singing of oppression, liberation, and solidarity, Sweet Honey at first seemed "peripheral" to the women's movement that was happening all around them, so much of which was concerned with White middle-class women. But after she joined a group of Black women talking to each other about their own lives, Reagon began thinking about the women she had known as a child in Southwest Georgia, "adult females who carried their weight and any weight they had to carry to get through the world and not break... females who broke under the weight of oppression, sexism, and their responsibilities. Were they not women? I had left them out!"[39] About this time, she learned of Joan Little, a Black woman who had killed her jailer during a forced rape in a North Carolina prison, escaped from jail, and become the target of a dead-or-alive warrant issued for her capture. The result was "Joan Little," a song included on Sweet Honey's first album. Reagon later wrote:

> Opening myself up to Joan Little's struggle—as I let in women who fell, women who were abused by their husbands, women whom I saw every day—things immediately got softer for me and I could breathe with less clinched teeth. It might have saved my very life, this letting broken women into my world. It meant that Sweet Honey would not test women at the door as to what we were carrying. We assumed that if you were grown, black, and female, you were carrying a load.[40]

Another early song came from the words of civil rights icon Ella Baker, prompted by events following the murder of Andrew Goodman, Michael Schwerner, and James Cheney in 1964. During the search for the three murdered Civil Rights workers, officials found the bones of unknown murdered Black men who had never been searched for. At the same time, the Schwerners and Goodmans were denied permission to have their sons buried beside James Cheney because of a Mississippi law making it illegal for Whites and Blacks to be buried together. Ella Baker reacted with a speech that became "Ella's Song." Originally commissioned for Joanne Grant's 1981 film *Fundi*, about the life of Ella Baker, "Ella's Song" appeared on Sweet Honey's 1983 album, *We All...Everyone of Us.* The lyrics are taken almost verbatim from Ella Baker's speech:

> Until the killing of black men,
> black mothers' sons
> Is as important as the killing of white men,
> white mothers' sons,
> We who believe in freedom cannot rest.[41]

Before long, Sweet Honey in the Rock was drawing enthusiastic audiences that crossed lines of race, gender, and sexual orientation. For Black women, Sweet Honey concerts were a powerful reflection of themselves and their history. Poet and novelist Alice Walker wrote: "These songs said: We do not come from people who have had nothing. We come rather from people who've had everything—except money, except political power, except freedom. We understand, at last, listening to Sweet Honey, what our freedom songs are for. They show us the way home, which is the whole earth."[42]

Over the years the membership of Sweet Honey grew and changed as women left or joined the group, but the style remained the same. Bernice Johnson Reagon herself described it best:

> To sing a Sweet Honey concert, it is necessary to sing songs in the nineteenth century congregational style, as well as the performance styles required for arranged concert spirituals, quartet singing, early and classical gospel, jazz, West African traditional, rhythm and blues, and rap—all in the same evening. Capacity and virtuosity differ from singer to singer, but everyone is challenged to move with intelligence from one sound palette to another, changing the places where the sound is produced in the body.... So many people in our audiences ask, "Why don't you use instruments?" And I respond, "We do use instruments—our voices."[43]

In 1977, when Sweet Honey had been performing for just four years, Reagon received a call from Amy Horowitz, a White Jewish activist working with Holly Near. Horowitz had discovered an album titled *Give Your Hands to Struggle: The Evolution of a Freedom Fighter/Songs by Bernice Reagon*, and "stared in amazement at the picture of this woman who had not only written the songs on the album ... but had also spent the past fourteen years working as a community organizer and scholar."[44] Horowitz played the album for Holly Near, and they decided to invite Sweet Honey to sing on an album Holly was then producing, Meg Christian's *Face the Music*.

All three—Bernice, Holly, and Amy—remembered the collaboration between Sweet Honey in the Rock and the lesbian separatists in California as an experience that laid bare the hazards of identity politics and underscored the challenges of building coalitions. In Bernice Johnson Reagon's words:

> We went from Washington, DC, where we sang for black people, churches, schools, theaters, folk festivals, and political rallies, to the radical, separatist, white-women-dominated, lesbian cultural network in California. Amy Horowitz was our bridge.... Being a woman did not prepare us for being a voice within and beyond the women's cultural network. It was culturally a white, middle-class coalition....Coalition work is hard and often threatening, but necessary to force change within a society such as ours.[45]

Despite the challenges, Redwood and Sweet Honey agreed to collaborate on the group's second album, *B'lieve I'll Run On... See what The End's Gonna Be*, released in 1978. Again, the challenges of coalition building proved almost too difficult to surmount.

"Cross-cultural feminist work was courageous," Holly wrote in her autobiography. "The nature of the conflict was, on Redwood's part, white ignorance of black history, culture, and struggle, coupled with the frustration and anger felt by white working-class lesbians as they too struggled to survive in a hostile world."[46]

Amy Horowitz, too, expressed her distress in a journal entry written during the 1978 album tour: "On tour with Sweet Honey in California I witness racism. I can smell it. It's not a theoretical term and it's not just out there. It's in the women's movement loud and strong and it is in me despite good intentions, despite what I know about anti-Semitism."[47]

An activist who described herself as "living on the borderland," Horowitz once wrote, "My passport is stamped with internal landscapes that struggle to coexist. I refuse to establish a hierarchy of importance out of the plurality that is me."[48] Working with Redwood to produce Sweet Honey's second album, Horowitz collaborated with Reagon to write a statement about working in coalition, which appeared in the album booklet. But in the end, the stress of working together proved too great and Sweet Honey and Redwood parted ways. "I grieved for many years to come," Holly later wrote.[49]

Olivia: The Soundtrack for a Lesbian Generation

As women continued to struggle with the complexities of identity and activism, they were continuing to build a women's music movement that would eventually help foster the coalitions that were proving so challenging. In 1973, a group of lesbian feminists founded the first women's music label, Olivia Records, and went on to produce the albums that became "the soundtrack for a generation awakening to lesbian activism."[50]

Olivia was born when Judy Dlugacz, who had abandoned plans for law school in favor of radical activism, met Meg Christian and her lover Ginny Berson at a lesbian bar in Washington, DC. Discovering their common interest in politics, performance, and production, Meg and Ginny invited Dlugacz to join their collective, the Furies, a radical lesbian cooperative whose members shared a house in DC.

Christian was already performing within the radical women's community and had acquired a reputation as "the librarian of women's music" for her constant searching in record bins to find works by women. During one of these searches she discovered Cris Williamson's first album and begun incorporating Cris's songs into her own performances at area clubs and coffeehouses. When she discovered that Cris was coming to DC, Christian brought her coffeehouse audiences with her to the performance.

Thirty-five years later, Judy Delugacz recalled:

When [Cris] stepped out on the stage at GW [George Washington University, site of the concert], 400 women were in there cheering and clapping. Cris had no idea what was happening. As she sang her first song, another round of applause erupted and Cris was so caught off guard, she forgot the words to "Joanna." Out of the audience came Meg's voice, singing the words back to her. And that's how they met... [After the concert] Meg went backstage with arms full of tapes of women's music for Cris and invited Cris to be interviewed by Meg on a women's radio show the next day.... While talking on the air about the difficulties of being a woman in the recording industry... Cris blurted out, "Why don't you just start a women's record company!" And that's all it took.[51]

Meg brought the idea back to the Furies and five women formed the original Olivia collective, named after a 1949 lesbian coming-of-age novel by Dorothy Strachey Bussy. After a 45 rpm single release with Cris Williamson's "If it Weren't for the Music" on one side and Meg Christian's cover of Carole King/Gerry Goffin's "Lady" on the other, Olivia's first full length LP was Meg Christian's debut album, *I Know You Know*. The album included a cover of "Joanna," Cris Williamson's song that had first brought them together, as well as "Ode to a Gym Teacher," the first in a long line of songs with a particular strain of lesbian humor full of in-jokes and inversions of conventional narratives. The lesbian gym teacher was "a cliché that had made it out of lesbian subculture only through tragic narratives of exposure and scandal such as in the 1961 film featuring Audrey Hepburn and Shirley MacLaine, *The Children's Hour*.... The song reclaims that otherwise-doomed relationship... [and] functions as a nostalgic in-joke."[52]

Olivia's second album, Cris Williamson's *The Changer and the Changed*, assured the future of Olivia records, selling over a quarter of a million copies in the next twelve years to become one of the biggest selling independent records of all time. Songs like "Waterfall," "Sister," and "Song of the Soul," became familiar anthems at women's gatherings; as historian Bonnie Morris writes, "After that, there was no stopping Olivia Records. Decked out in brocade vests and clean flannel shirts, sporting pins that declared WE ARE EVERYWHERE, smiling women stood in line for performances by Olivia artists."[53]

Following the success of *The Changer and the Changed*, a wide array of performers recorded on Olivia, including many from the Black music community. In 1975, Linda Tillery and Mary Watkins joined Olivia, and together with blues singer Gwen Avery and poet Pat Parker, launched the Olivia-sponsored tour Varied Voices of Black Women. A year later, Judy Grahn, a White lesbian poet whose work reflected her working class roots, collaborated with Pat Parker on Olivia's first spoken word album, *Where Would I Be Without You*. Gradually, Olivia became an arena where Black and White women worked together, fostering collaborations through music that often eluded the lesbian community on other fronts. *Where Would I Be Without You* drew on preexisting connections among Black lesbian artists and between White and Black lesbians involved in cultural production: Linda Tillery had worked at A Woman's Place bookstore and was a member of Gente, a lesbian support group for women of color that also included Pat Parker and Judith Casselberry.[54]

Collaborations outside the collective proved more difficult, however. In 1976, Holly Near, Meg Christian, Margie Adam and Cris Williamson embarked on a seven-city California tour where "the issues that tore society apart day after day began to tear us apart too," Holly later recalled. "We were women in search of a new world. We asked hard questions of ourselves. How could we call this a tour of women's music if we were all white? What about Holly being straight? This wasn't a lesbian concert. Or was it?"[55] After Holly and Meg fell in love and began a relationship, the contrasts between the Redwood community and the Olivia community became increasingly apparent.

> Olivia had lesbian feminist priorities and believed in world peace [Holly wrote]. Redwood had world-peace priorities and believed in lesbian feminism. I wanted to feminize the peace movement and globalize the lesbian movement. Olivia wanted to build networks that would serve the lesbian community and bring lesbians to that newly created cultural base.... Olivia and Redwood

didn't like or trust each other much, but we were in the forefront of women's music together. It was, in this Dickensian tale of two record companies, the best of times, it was the worst of times.[56]

In 1977, the Olivia collective faced an even bigger crisis when Sandy Stone, a trans woman who had been hired as an Olivia engineer, was outed by Janice Raymond, a radical lesbian who attacked Stone by name in her book, *The Transsexual Empire: The Making of the She-Male*.[57] Stone and Olivia began to receive hate mail that included threats to the Collective and death threats to Stone. The most devastating attacks came from lesbian separatists who characterized Stone as an imposter who "has never had to suffer the discrimination, self–hatred or fear that a woman must endure and survive in her life" and "cannot possess the special courage, brilliance, sensitivity and compassion that derives from that experience."[58]

The Olivia collective responded with a fierce defense of Stone as "a person, not an issue," asserting that "the process of sex reassignment is a long, grueling and painful one, requiring years of hard work prior to surgery…. Because Sandy decided to give up completely and permanently her male identity and live as a woman and a lesbian, she is now faced with the same kind of oppression that other women and lesbians face. She must also cope with the ostracism that all of society imposes on a transsexual."[59]

Olivia's understanding of transgender identity as another form of oppression stands out as virtually unique in 1970s identity politics; not until the twenty-first century would trans activism gain widespread support in the LGBTQ community (see chapter 9). Meanwhile, during a tour, threats from a paramilitary group called the Gorgons forced Olivia to maintain unprecedented security at a Seattle concert; a debate between Olivia representatives and women opposed to trans presence in the lesbian community erupted into screaming; and anti-trans separatists (dubbed TERF's, or Trans-Exclusionary Radical Feminists by the trans-inclusive women's community) threatened to boycott Olivia. Unwilling to let her presence threaten the collective, Stone finally left for Santa Cruz, where she was welcomed by the lesbian community and eventually earned a Ph.D. and entered academia.

Goldenrod and Ladyslipper: Endangered Species

With the proliferation of women's music on Olivia, Redwood, and Margie Adam's Pleiades label, producers needed reliable outlets to sell their records. Two distributors, Ladyslipper and Goldenrod, arose to fill this need.

Goldenrod was the brainchild of Terry Grant, a young lesbian in Lansing, Michigan. One day in 1975 she was visiting a friend:

> I was over at her house and she'd ordered this record from *Ms.* Magazine, on Olivia records, called *I Know You Know*.... This music was—you know how you just can't sit down sometimes, or you're standing and you have to sit down. So we were just standing up and sitting down and standing up and sitting down, staring at the album jacket, trying to figure out who these women were.... When I heard Meg Christian was going to come to the city of Lansing as an intermission act for the Berkley Women's Music Collective in April of '75, I contacted Olivia and said did they want me to sell Meg Christian's music at this concert. And they wrote back and said "yes" right away. Because Olivia was all about using music as a social justice tool and—to change the world.[60]

After the concert, Grant was left with a stack of extra LP's and in keeping with the *ad hoc* culture of the '70s, the Olivia collective suggested that she keep the albums and become a distributor. "So that's how Goldenrod started. Basically I sold at the one concert and they asked me and I said yes, and I had not been out for very long. And suddenly I'm going into music stores with basically very little disguise, lesbian music being women's music, and asking them to buy it and put it in their bins. I would never, ever, ever have become a salesperson by my own choice, ever."[61]

Gradually, Grant expanded Goldenrod's operations into other Michigan cities, finding representatives through community contacts, women's bookstores, and some of her old Girl Scout friends. Eventually, she added other labels and expanded outside Michigan to make Goldenrod a national distributor of women's music. Although in recent years the rise of the internet and the demise of independent bookstores and record stores has led Goldenrod to scale down its operations, Grant remains proud of the role Goldenrod played in the early days of the women's movement. "We weren't just a couple dozen women in a bar. We were a community…. The music was integral and unifying and beautiful and validating, but there was also looking across the concert hall…. and seeing yourself as part of a community of beautiful women.[62]

One year after Terry Grant founded Goldenrod, Ladyslipper Music began as the "fantasy of a comprehensive catalog of records by women" in the mind of Laurie Fuchs, a lesbian who had just moved to Durham, North Carolina from South Georgia, where her isolation inspired her to search for a way to connect with the wider lesbian community.[63]

Ladyslipper began in 1976 as a four-page resource guide devoted to the musical accomplishments of women artists. It was produced in three days in order to have it ready for the 1977 Michigan Womyn's Music Festival. It grew into a fully-fledged wholesale distribution business, eventually issuing records on its own label. Like Goldenrod, Ladyslipper is now an online enterprise, with a catalogue that continues to feature women musicians and an aural history project archiving interviews with women musicians, including Holly Near, Mary Watkins, Judith Casselberry, and Ferron— "with many more to come."[64]

Although Ladyslipper and Goldenrod were competitors, Terry Grant sees their relationship as more of a partnership.

> Ladyslipper had a much bigger catalogue than most of
> us. And so they sold in our territory products that we
> didn't carry…. And so Laurie and I were collaborators

and competitors and close friends.... I really believe that one could do business ethically and in a feminist manner and Laurie believed that too.... That was part of the point of what we were doing in women's music and feminist politics.[65]

"This Train Still Runs"

Looking back on the first twenty years of women's music, *Hot Wire* and *Paid My Dues* editor Toni Armstrong, Jr. wrote that "in the 1970s the feminist and lesbian movements married each other, and their most beautiful and powerful daughter was named 'women's music and culture.'"[66] The creators of this music and culture overcame all kinds of resistance—not only from the critics who claimed that women-identified music was "little more than propaganda in the key of C," but from all those who were intent on silencing lesbian visibility altogether. "Lesbian events and products ran into incredible resistance," Armstrong recalled, "publications refusing to run gay-related ads, concert venues unwilling to rent to women-only events, papers unwilling to print reviews, radio shows refusing to play lesbian-specific lyrics, TV shows not allowing accurate portrayals with happy endings."[67]

In a speech at the twenty-fifth anniversary of the National Women's Music Festival, singer-songwriter Margie Adam movingly recalled these struggles and addressed their significance for the present:

When we began calling what we were doing Women's Music, we were creating a space for women that had never existed before. There had never been concerts produced entirely by women, with sound and lights run by women—where all the musicians were women and the music was written by women. We came together in this woman's space to be together—to feel the power and beauty and possibility in this woman-loving space....

The work is not done. Women still seek out Women's Spaces. We still love looking at each other, hearing ourselves in the music.[68]

In October, 1995, Janis Ian stood on the stage at London's Royal Albert Festival Hall. Thirty years before this moment, sixteen-year-old Janis's "Society's Child," with its story of an interracial romance condemned by parents and teachers, had provoked death threats, boycotts by radio stations, and, in at least one case, jeers and shouts of "Nigger Lover!" from the audience at a performance in Encino, California.[69] In the intervening years, Ian had pursued her songwriting career, escaped from an abusive marriage, and come out as a lesbian. Now she was singing "This Train Still Runs," a song she had recorded a few years earlier.

One year later, Holly Near and Ronnie Gilbert recorded "This Train Still Runs" as the title track on a live album celebrating Gilbert's seventieth birthday. By this time, Holly Near had joined her peace activism with lesbian/feminist activism; Ronnie Gilbert had come out as a lesbian and brought the legacy of the folk movement to a musical partnership with Holly; and Janis Ian had come as a lesbian and as a survivor of domestic abuse in her 1993 album, *Breaking Silence*, on which "This Train" was first featured.

"This Train Still Runs" is an anthem of survival and a fitting song for these three women—folk singers, civil rights advocates, lesbian activists, and coalition builders—and, by extension, for all the musicians, producers, and audiences who defied convention to build a movement that transformed women's culture and women's lives.

Nothing is forever young
I'm not done - this train still runs
This train still runs.[70]

Part II

"Now We Are a Movement"

4

From Women's Music to Women's Choruses

By 1980, women's music had become, in the words of Alix Dobkin, "the heart of this new world."[1] Olivia Records had moved to Los Angeles in the mid-1970s and produced Cris Williamson's *The Changer and the Changed*, one of the highest grossing independent records of all time; also in California, Margie Adam had founded Pleiades Records and Holly Near had established Redwood Records. Sweet Honey in the Rock was bringing African American women's experiences to the women's music movement, along with artists like Mary Watkins, Linda Tillery and the duo Judith Casselberry and Jacque DuPree.

Lesbians who had previously felt invisible in popular culture were singing along with Alix Dobkin's "The Woman in Your Life." They were buying copies of Meg Christian's *I Know You Know*. And they were listening to Holly Near's first explicitly woman-identified album, *You Can Know All I Am*, released the same year that Near announced to the 2,000 women at the first Michigan Womyn's Music Festival, "I have fallen in love with a woman." At that moment, in the words of the late Kay Gardner, "women's music [became] synonymous with lesbian music, mainly because lesbians [were] the driving force of the women's music movement."[2]

Meanwhile, feminists, both straight and gay, were challenging restrictive birth control and abortion laws, workplace inequality, and sexist images of women in the mass media, while scholars inspired by the Civil Rights, anti-war, and women's movements, and by postmodernist philosophers like Michel Foucault and Jacques Derrida, were deconstructing everything from the U.S. educational system to the traditional canons of literature and the arts. Among them were the new musicologists, whose insights would find expression in Susan McClary's groundbreaking *Feminine Endings*, which explored the ways gender and sexuality informed conventional ideas about music, and in Christopher Small's *Musicking: The Meanings of Performing and Listening*.[3] Although Small did not write specifically about women's music, his analysis is particularly relevant to the history of feminist choruses. Music, he wrote, "is not a thing at all, but an activity, something that people do," based on relationships among performers, audience, conductor and composer.[4] Small described the traditional western concert hall as an alienating environment that "allow[s] no communication with the outside world," where the members of the orchestra [or chorus] are expected to remain silent and reserve any expression of approval or disapproval for a specific moment at the end of the performance, while the director or conductor

> imposes his authority from outside the ensemble, backed by all the institutions of concert life.... The conductor is the incarnation of power in the modern sense and represents the image of what all of us dream at times of doing and of what many in our time have tried to do in the field of social and political action: to resolve conflicts once and for all through the exercise of unlimited power.[5]

Although folk music, anti-war music and women's music had already begun to break down some of these barriers, women's choruses, with their commitment to collaboration and lesbian visibility, would carry the process even further.

Politics and Music Together: Women Like Me

Like most big cities in the United States, New York City in the 1970s was home to a growing gay rights movement that emerged in the wake of the Stonewall uprising of June,

1969, when thousands of gay, lesbian and transgender people defied police harassment and took to the streets of Greenwich Village. Following the Lavender Menace uprising described in the previous chapter, Radicalesbians organized in New York. Despite their short-lived existence (they disbanded in 1971), lesbian culture flourished in consciousness raising groups and in manifestos and other publications. Notable among these was Jill Johnston's *Lesbian Nation: The Feminist Solution*, originally published as a series of essays in the *Village Voice* and then in book form in 1973. Johnston argued for lesbian separatism, not merely as a sexual alternative but as a political choice: "The lesbian is the woman who unites the personal and the political in the struggle to free ourselves from the oppressive institution [marriage]... by this definition lesbians are in the vanguard of the resistance."[6]

Bold actions like these inspired young women who were discovering feminist politics. Among them was Roberta Kosse, a classically trained composer drawn to feminism after five years at a traditional conservatory studying with "men who had 'made it'" in the musical world. "I learned to write perfectly respectable atonal music," she told *Paid My Dues* in 1978,

> but the music came from my head, not my guts.... My friends in the movement were putting their energies into political issues and action oriented projects, and while I strongly supported them, I wanted—needed— my time to write music. I felt guilty. Was I being a "bad" feminist? There was so much to be done for the world of women. Was I merely indulging in luxury?[7]

Kosse began writing songs about women—a project she later described as "in the closet, as it were"—and organizing Women Like Me, a chorus "which basically consisted of my friends and members of my consciousness-raising group." Her master's thesis, "Portraits of Women," was a work for women's chorus and orchestra based on poems by women; it drew reactions from her colleagues ranging "from confusion to anger to outright amusement.... I had clearly gone beyond the boundaries of 'good taste,'" she recalled. "What was politics doing in art?"[8]

Politics—even feminist politics—was making its way into the world of music, but Kosse did not feel at home in the folk/ pop style of most women's music of the 1970s. After a period of depression and confusion, during which she was unable to write anything, Kosse suddenly had "a flash"—the inspiration

> to write a large work for a big chorus of women with a women's orchestra. My fantasy was having the whole women's community in New York turn out for a spectacular, unique event. My second thought was, *What, am I crazy? How could I ever pull it off? Do I really dare?* I did dare.[9]

The result was *The Return of the Great Mother*, an oratorio with a text based on stories from women's mythology, which Kosse co-authored with her friend, Jenny Malmquist. Members of Women Like Me recruited additional singers and raised money for the work's first performances at the Washington Square Church in Greenwich Village on May 14 and 15, 1977. Kosse later recalled:

> The first night, for women only, was sold out. As I stepped up to the podium to conduct my oratorio, I had a moment of panic. (What, am I crazy? How can I do this?) But there, facing me were forty smiling faces of women who believed in me, trusted me, and stayed with me for four months of hard work. I knew I was safe. I think that was the most exciting night of my life.... We received a long standing ovation, and I felt at that moment that I really had begun the integration of my music and my politics.[10]

Women Like Me went on to perform the oratorio in other cities, and eventually incorporated as Ars Pro Femina, a non-profit production company.

From "Leaping Lesbians" to Choral Collaboration

Like New York, Los Angeles in the early 1970s abounded with political organizing. Lesbians and gay men initially collaborated within the Gay Liberation Front, which sponsored the first Gay Pride March and the Gay Community Services Center. However, conflicts over strategy and philosophy began to divide the two communities. Lesbians said they often felt as though they were being asked, in spirit if not in fact, to make the coffee and take the minutes. They felt alienated from gay men's preoccupation with (gay male) sexuality; the men interpreted this as an attack on their newfound liberation. According to Lillian Faderman, the final blow came when the men decided to form a coalition with the Black Panthers, placing women's concerns on the back burner and allying with a group whose public image women viewed as "quintessentially macho."[11] By the mid-1970s lesbians had broken away to form their own cultural institutions, including the Feminist Women's Health Center; the Woman's Building, housing a lesbian-feminist art movement; and a lively lesbian press. In 1971, the West Coast Lesbian Conference attracted women from all over the country. A follow-up conference in 1973 drew 2,000 women from twenty-six states and several foreign countries. Olivia Records, which had begun as a lesbian collective in Washington, DC, moved to Los Angeles soon afterward because in LA, according to founder Ginny Berson, lesbians were integral to "everything that was feminist."[12] In addition to concerts and recordings, Olivia artists like Cris Williamson lent their talents to LA's lesbian feminist theater productions and to fund raisers for the Women's Building.

Gay and lesbian visibility in Los Angeles, as elsewhere in the country, sparked a hostile reaction from right-wing politicians and conservative Christian groups. California became the epicenter of the national backlash in 1978, when Orange County State Senator John Briggs gathered enough petitions to put Question 6 on the state ballot. Inspired by Anita Bryant's 1977 "Save Our Children" campaign, which had repealed a Miami ordinance barring discrimination based on sexual orientation, the Briggs Initiative, as it became known, sought to ban gays and lesbians from working in California's public schools and would have mandated the firing of any school employee, gay or straight, who engaged in "advocating, soliciting, imposing, encouraging or promoting of private or public homosexual activity directed at, or likely to come to the attention of school children and/or other employees."[13]

Though it was rejected by California voters after a vigorous campaign by an opposition including Hollywood celebrities, Governor Ronald Reagan, and President Jimmy Carter, the Briggs Initiative was only the most notorious legal attack on gay and lesbian teachers—attacks in places ranging from Oklahoma to Arkansas to Washington State, which played on the fears of parents with depictions of gay people as pedophiles eager to "recruit" innocent children into their "unnatural" lifestyle.

In 1978, the year of the Briggs Initiative, Sue Fink was working as a Los Angeles junior high school music teacher by day and lesbian singer-songwriter by night. She had already written and performed "Leaping Lesbians," a hilarious take on homophobia that appeared on Olivia's 1977 response to the Anita Bryant campaign, *Lesbian Concentrate.* (The album cover featured an image of a frozen orange juice can—an allusion to Bryant's role as a spokeswoman for Florida orange juice—with the words "Lesbian Concentrate: a Lesbianthology, 100% Undiluted.") As Sue became more widely known in the LA women's music community, her life "was starting to overlap," as she later put it, and a few students were beginning to recognize her at concerts. Eventually a parent of one of her students discovered that she was a lesbian and tried to have her fired. Finding it increasingly difficult to work as a lesbian teacher, Sue decided to quit her school job.

A year earlier, Sue had worked with a collective to organize the Los Angeles Women's Community Chorus. Directing the chorus combined her commitment to teaching with her desire to reach out into the community. "I was a choral conductor. That's what I did for my living. But I was always into community involvement stuff. I wanted to see everybody 'doing it,'" she told *Hot Wire* magazine in 1991.[14]

Like Roberta Kosse, Fink and her chorus saw their mission as both artistic and political. They developed a set of goals that reflected the goals of the lesbian feminist movement around them, resolving "to engender in ourselves and in the community a consciousness of all kinds of woman-oriented music—music by women, for women, about women—[and] to provide in our chorus a nurturing supportive space for women of all lifestyles, of all economic and ethnic backgrounds of all sexual preferences."[15]

The Los Angeles Women's Chorus would provide a forum for women composers, conductors, arrangers and musicians; a library of feminist choral music; and "a place where women [could] gain experience in many different musical roles, instead of a solidified hierarchy of defined and unchanging roles." Finally, Fink and her sister organizers envisioned "a relaxed setting where music making and singing is a positive experience, where no one feels intimidated. Excellence in musicianship and quality of music will be encouraged without sacrificing fun, spontaneity, support, and consciousness raising."[16]

The Peninsula Women's Chorus and the Vocal Orchestra

In 1975, Patricia Hennings, a 25-year-old third-generation Californian and recent Stanford alumna, was named director of a women's chorus in Palo Alto that would become one of the longest-lived choruses in the women's chorus movement. Midpenninsula chorus had been founded by Marjorie Rawlins in 1966 under the auspices of the American Association of University Women. Under Hennings's leadership, the chorus changed its name to the Peninsula Women's Chorus and went on to establish a reputation as one of the country's premier women's choruses, performing classical and contemporary works in the U.S. and abroad.

The PWC was also instrumental in reclaiming the history of one of the twentieth century's most remarkable women's choruses. In the fall of 1982, Helen Colijn, a survivor of a World

War II women's internment camp on the island of Sumatra, brought a handwritten manuscript to a PWC rehearsal. It contained music that two of the prisoners, Margaret Dryburgh and Norah Chambers, had written down as part of the repertoire for a chorus they called the Women's Vocal Orchestra. To help the women of the camp memorize the music, Dryburgh and Chambers had created an entire repertoire of classical selections using only syllables; the one exception was "The Captives' Hymn," which Dryburgh wrote and which soon became a camp favorite.

Under Patricia Hennings's leadership, the PWC began learning the music that the women of the camp had sung to bolster their spirits and support one another.

"Learning the vocal orchestra music at first was unbelievably difficult for the chorus of 1982," PWC member Mary Ager recalled. "It seemed impossible. How could we sing so long without words?" But by the time they actually presented the work, the chorus had come to see singing it as a unique mission. "We felt the importance of honoring those women who in 1943 had to sit down to sing because they were starving and sick, whose daily lives included coping with tropical diseases, malnutrition, living in filth and among rats, cockroaches, and bedbugs with no medications and very little food or water.... Gradually the PWC was transformed musically through the demands of performing this difficult music."[17]

In 1983, the chorus presented "Song of Survival" at St. Bede's Church in Menlo, Park, California, with members of the original women's vocal orchestra, including Helen Colijn, as their guests. The story was later made into a movie, *Paradise Road*, starring Glenn Close and Frances McDormand, and was retold in a musical by Eleanor Harder and Ray Harder. "Song of Survival" continues to be performed by choruses around the world, including the Sydney Women's Vocal Orchestra, an Australian choir that formed in 2002 specifically to learn this piece.[18]

Anna Crusis: "It Means Upbeat"

When Sue Fink and her collaborators founded the Los Angeles Women's Community Chorus, "it seemed an overwhelming task as we didn't know of other choirs which could serve as models." But in 1978, she found a kindred spirit at the other end of the country and another chorus—Cathy Roma's Anna Crusis Women's Choir in Philadelphia. "Cathy and I had never heard of each other, and I had no idea there was another women's chorus, but we were even doing some of the same music... Cathy and I started corresponding.... and we've become fast friends."[19]

Catherine Roma, founding director of Anna Crusis, is often referred to as the mother of the women's chorus movement. Raised in Philadelphia in a conservative Catholic family, Roma discovered Quakerism at Germantown Friends School and eventually became a Convinced Friend. In the late 1960s and early 1970s, she earned degrees in music and choral conducting at the University of Wisconsin-Madison and became active in socialist-feminist politics.

When Cathy Roma arrived at the University of Wisconsin in the fall of 1966, she found a campus community that had become a national center of resistance to the Viet Nam War. Students and professors were organizing teach-ins on the war; students marched, burned draft cards, and confronted army recruiters, and in October,1967, held a large protest against napalm manufacturer Dow Chemical Company, then recruiting on campus. Following the 1970 killing of four students by National Guardsmen during an anti-war protest at Kent State University in Ohio, UW students joined the national student strike that closed the university for five days.

Meanwhile, lesbians and gay men in Madison were organizing as well. During the fall of 1969, several men gathered at the St. Francis House (the Episcopal student center on University Avenue) to form what would become the first gay liberation organization in Wisconsin: the Madison Alliance for Homosexual Equality (MAHE). MAHE eventually evolved into the more politically active Gay Liberation Front, launching Wisconsin's first gay center, first gay hotline, first class on homosexuality, first local gay and lesbian speaker panels, and first gay conference. Drawing on the imagery of the anti-war movement, Madison began calling itself "the third coast" of the gay rights movement. As in other cities, lesbians formed their own communities and their own organizations.[20]

Cathy Roma had come to Madison to major in music, but she was soon caught up in the campus radicalism around her. "Within my first year already I knew there were too many things I wanted to take," she recalled many years later. "History was a big one. I took some philosophy.... I took some wonderful experimental educational kinds of courses and stuff like that — but history is where the political people went." The 1967 protest against the Dow Chemical Company (manufacturer of napalm) proved a turning point in her activism:

> I smelled all the tear gas and I saw people with bandanas covering their face and everything, and everybody obviously was being pushed back.... My friends were there, and I knew that some of them were billy-clubbed and gassed and all of that.... It was a really, really, really important time in my education. I was in the music school and doing my diligent practicing and everything, managing to find time, but that's what was going on outside of my studies, you know, my political work, or my understanding that I needed to be putting myself—I needed to stand, literally, with, backing up what I felt. I needed to put my body on the line.[21]

At the same time, Roma recalled, she was beginning to acknowledge her sexual identity.

> So we're talking about my political stuff going on in '67 and '68 but also that was about the time when I was beginning to realize that I wanted to act more on my feelings for women.... The lesbians that were visible ...

were using language and words that were still too scary for me. They were so out and they were so sure that they were lesbians, you know, and they were doing political stuff around that—I wasn't there yet. It wasn't really till 1970, late 1969, that I fell in love with the woman who I was with for five years, and so then I really sort of came out and understood things much differently.[22]

By the early '70s Roma had begun to feel comfortable as a lesbian. She and some political compatriots had organized a Free School for junior high and high school students in Madison. And she was flourishing musically, encountering a "wild and weird" world of music—"the whole twelve-tone school and experimental music and Eric Satie, people who I hadn't been exposed to in high school." But like Roberta Kosse, Roma recalled that "it wasn't until later that I began to put all of these things together. So they were sort of happening separately. My classical music and my love for piano and everything [that] was happening."[23]

After Roma had finished her bachelor's degree, she enrolled in a master's program in piano performance, a course of study that was starting to feel more and more confining. She had initiated a choir of faculty and students at the Free School and was working with a boy choir in Madison when a conducting workshop convinced her that she needed to be "creating with people." Feeling that she needed "more experience and more teachers," she signed up for a workshop with Margaret Hillis, conductor of the Chicago Symphony Orchestra Chorus, and reconnected in Chicago with her old friend, women's studies professor Ann Gordon. Before long the conversation turned to choral music and conducting, and Roma expressed her desire to organize an event celebrating the upcoming American Bicentennial. "'OK, Ann, it's 1974—1976 is the bicentennial,'" she remembered saying to her friend. "'I want to tell the story of America through song, and how can I do it with the boy choir? You know, am I going to dress some of the boys up as girls?' And so Ann looks at me straight in the face and she says, "Why don't you start a women's choir?"'"

In retrospect, Roma was struck by her own limited perspective at the time.

> Even [with] my budding feminism and my lesbianism and my interest in women and my interest in music and everything, I couldn't make the connection, or I didn't make it immediately, because this is my experience. All of the women's choirs at the University of Wisconsin and other places that I know—and as a student conductor, I was in on the auditioning by the professors, and it was cruel in a way, because the very select women would be with the men, right, for the mixed choir, and then you had hundreds of women who really wanted to sing, and what did you do with them? You put them in the women's choir or glee club, whatever you want to call it, and they had a male conductor. And the position of the male conductor was always a plum, right? And then you had all of these women. So they were the leftovers, you know, and the repertoire was not very interesting.[24]

Roma's conversation with Ann Gordon set her on the path that would ultimately integrate her personal, political and musical lives. She returned to Madison to found a women's chorus of fifteen altos and fifteen sopranos, which she named Anna Crusis, inspired by the Greek term *Anacrusis*—"It means upbeat. It's that beat that moves into the downbeat. In music history, strong beats are masculine. Weak beats are feminine. So, it's turning that around."[25]

In 1976, Anna Crusis performed the work Roma and Gordon had written together at the Berkshire Conference on the History of Women in Bryn Mawr, Pennsylvania. The Berks, as it is known, was a fitting venue for Roma and Gordon to showcase their work. Founded in 1930 by women historians who felt themselves excluded from male academia, it had become a forum for the emerging discipline of women's history in the 1970s and continues to hold triennial meetings attended by thousands of feminist scholars and researchers.

Roma described "American Women: A Choral History" as "an unfolding of what women's lives were like and what women's struggles were like in the past," featuring "this great piece where we dressed up, wore little pieces of clothing that would indicate we were the male or the female for a discussion about getting the vote, the boys and the girls talking to each other. It was called Winning the Vote. There was humor, there was history—it was such creativity and collaboration with history and music and mime."[26]

Soon after the performance at the Berks, Roma moved to Philadelphia to teach at Abington Friends School. There she founded a new women's chorus, which she also named Anna Crusis. By this time, Roma had discovered the world of women's music. "[I was] wearing out the LPs on the record player of 'Lavender Jane' [Alix Dobkin's first album, *Lavender Jane Loves Women*], and some of those early LPs," she recalled.

> What fascinated me was that this music was about subjects that obviously hadn't been sung about before, or that I wasn't aware had been sung about before ... What I realized was that I was actually putting together these very important things—my Quaker peace and justice sensibilities, my interest in women, my lesbian self, and my classical training.[27]

Lesbian and gay activists in Philadelphia had already split into two factions by the 1970s: the male-dominated Gay Liberation Front and the Radicalesbians, who embraced radical separatism from liberal feminism and from gay male politics. However, although Roma and Anna Crusis identified as a feminist chorus, Roma's vision of feminism was very different from the radical separatists.

"We were always lesbian and straight women," she recalled, "almost in equal numbers, maybe usually more lesbian, but a very strong presence of heterosexual women." Then, as now, Roma valued "that coming together, that cross section of straight and lesbian women, because it's just powerful. It's strong, and it makes for a more politically conscious organization. And I love it. And I never wanted to have a choir of just lesbian women."[28]

Roma left Philadelphia in 1983 to pursue a doctorate in musical arts at the University of Cincinnati, where she founded and directed MUSE Women's Choir until her retirement in 2013. During her long career as a leader in the women's choral movement, she has remained true to the principles that motivated her back in 1975:

> When I started Anna, there was an importance to me to speak to all kinds of issues, because I come out of the antiwar, labor, peace and justice movements, and civil rights movement.... The fomenting of all of those movements coming together in the '60s, including the gay and lesbian liberation, I think that a cross section and a mix of women experienced in those different ways and areas made for a pretty amazing consciousness.[29]

Calliope: "Beautiful Voice"

Like Madison in the 1960s, Minnesota was home to active anti-war and gay rights movements, with much of the activity centered around university campuses. And just as in Madison, one of the earliest left-wing projects was a "free school." On June 20, 1969, in the first published account of gay liberation in Minnesota, a headline in the University of Minnesota student newspaper, *The Minnesota Daily*, proclaimed: "Free U starts 'homosexual revolution.'" "The Homosexual Revolution," a course taught at the left-wing Coffee House Extemporé, marked a shift from the closeted culture of the 1950s to the out and proud 1970s. Gay pride marches in Minnesota began with the first Twin Cities Pride Parade in 1972; the Twin Cities Pride Festival and various gay newspapers followed soon afterwards.[30]

As in other cities, lesbians developed institutions of their own. The Lesbian Resource Center opened in 1972, announcing its arrival in the new Women's Survival Catalog: "Gay Women in the

Minneapolis/St. Paul area have opened a Lesbian Resource Center in Minneapolis to better serve the needs of lesbians. We have found that other organizations are either too male- or straight-oriented, leaving us with a sense of invisibility. We are now coming out completely, affirming we are here." The Center housed A Woman's Coffeehouse, which became a popular alternative to the lesbian bar scene, where lesbians could socialize and discuss the issues facing them, and the Amazon Cooperative Bookstore, the first lesbian/feminist bookstore in the U.S and probably "the oldest in the English speaking world."[31] (According to historian Jim Elledge, Amazon Bookstore was the model for Madwimmin Books in Alison Bechdel's comic strip "Dykes to Watch Out For.")[32]

When they were not joining in intense discussions at A Woman's Coffeehouse or browsing the merchandise at Amazon, lesbians were gathering informally to sing together. In 1976, a group of Minneapolis women who had sung in a pick-up chorus at the Michigan Womyn's Music Festival returned home inspired to start a chorus of their own. Sarah Henderson, who joined the group not long afterwards, recalled the spirit of those early days:

> We were all people who had sung in a chorus in high school or in church choirs or even in college, but now we were out of the academic setting, most of us had left our churches, and we didn't have an outlet for singing. So that as much as any socio-political reasons was why we turned to *that*, to singing. Because it calls to the heart. And the spirit, of course. And then if you can throw in some sociopolitical and justice movement stuff too, why not?[33]

After a few weeks of singing "with different people showing up," the women realized that they "actually did need a leader, somebody to show us our warm-ups and suggest how we sing things, teach us stuff." They hired Nancy Cox, a local musician, to direct them—"for next to no money, because ... for a while there it wasn't fashionable to be well off, the idea was to make it with as little as you possibly could, and unfortunately that meant some people didn't make much of a living."[34]

Under Nancy's direction, the group performed a two-part arrangement of Cat Stevens's "Morning Has Broken" at the first women's service hosted by a local church. "A woman who was hoping to become a minister but hadn't been able to break the barriers was there leading it and she said, 'I have waited so many years for this.' It was so sweet. And people who were there all wanted to be there. It was not like a church service where you get dragged by your parents or you're there by expectations or things," Sarah remembered.[35]

The church appearance drew more women to the group, who named themselves Calliope. "We chose the name Calliope because it was one of the nine traditional muses, and one of our members knew about these things. Apparently the word Calliope means beautiful voice." The chorus continued to meet at members' homes and then eventually was given space at a local church.

> Sometimes things got double-scheduled, so we'd show up for our rehearsal space and somebody else was already there. So this church, many churches have you walk in and there are two staircases going up and around into the sanctuary. I remember standing on those two staircases facing each other to sing, with the director at the bottom between. And that worked fine except for warm up exercises. You know, standing on a stair and bending down to stretch towards your toes and hang your head and let your body swing a little, that's tricky on the stairs. But then, you know, one week somebody said, "We can rehearse at such and such place," and so the next week we rehearsed at such and such place.[36]

Although Calliope did not exclude straight women, in the early days it was "overwhelmingly lesbian," according to Sarah. It was not until many years later that the chorus "actually got down to writing a mission statement and saying who we are," and by that time there was no effort to put "lesbian" in the chorus publicity.[35]

As part of their efforts to build community among chorus members, Calliope instituted a group journal. "Each week somebody would take it and write down whatever they wanted," explained Sarah, "usually it'd be a bit of what we'd done that week, and then something about themselves, maybe, something about what they would like to see the chorus be." The chorus set aside a half hour at the end of each rehearsal when the woman who had had the journal at home that week read her entry aloud. Echoing the consciousness-raising groups of the era, singers would often write about their own life experiences. "You can't tell your story to the group in the middle of singing, and yet the group became close, and you wanted to tell your story and you wanted to be known."[37]

Exchanges in chorus discussion anticipated challenges that would arise in feminist choruses in the years to come. Sarah recalled:

> Most of us had been raised in a Christian church and had been damaged one way or another. We were a youngish group that hadn't gotten over that yet. So there were a lot of little comments that were anti-church, anti-Christian. And we did get called out on that once, by a woman singing out in the chorus whose partner was a minister and said, "You know, I am in fact a born again Christian.... I don't think we can assume that I'm the only one, and ... we can't assume that everybody agrees on all the issues."

For the women of Calliope, "a definite attempt to listen" was as essential as the mechanics of choral singing.

> Because whatever a person said, they were taking a brave step in writing their thoughts and reading them out loud to a group that might or might not agree with them. And they might agree [wholeheartedly], in which case applause would be no problem, but if somebody calls the group out on an issue, then applause is appropriate for their bravery, even if you still don't agree with them.[38]

Today, Calliope survives as the second-oldest women's chorus in the country. Over the years, the chorus has expanded its focus to address political issues in the wider world, but Calliope's mission statement remains true to the original mission to "provide a comfortable place for the feminist and lesbian communities to gather, celebrate, and renew spirits."

Singing for Change

During the 1970s, women active in contemporary peace and justice struggles organized dozens of other choruses to bring their advocacy for lesbian rights, reproductive freedom, disability rights and racial and gender equality to the wider community through music. Like Anna Crusis and Calliope, several are still alive and well; they include Artemis Singers of Chicago (founded in 1980 as the first women's singing ensemble in the U.S. to explicitly label itself a lesbian feminist chorus); Broad Cove Chorale (Hingham, MA, 1975); Cantalina (Cambridge, MA, founded in 1968 as a chorus for mixed voices and became a women's chorale in 1980); Peninsula Women's Chorus (Palo Alto, CA, founded as a university chorus in 1966 and reorganized as an independent women's chorus in 1975); the Rochester (NY) Women's Community Chorus (1978); and Windsong (Cleveland, 1979).

Many singers were already active in the lesbian community and incorporated this commitment into their choral missions. In Champaign-Urbana, volunteers at a shelter called A Woman's Place became the nucleus of an early chorus whimsically named Miss Safman's Ladies' Choir. In Houston, HeartSong founder Tori Williams organized a chorus support group for a member who had been diagnosed with thyroid cancer; in 1996, she expanded her efforts to co-found AssistHers, a city-wide organization that continues to provide assistance to and advocacy for lesbian women with a debilitating or life challenging disease. Judy Fjell's Song Circles inspired similar groups in other communities, including Davis, California, where Michelle Brodsky recalled, singers brought their songs to women in domestic violence shelters and "you'd have to get secret instructions because the shelters are unmarked locations. Sometimes people would just sit and listen but sometimes they'd sing along."[39]

Some choruses, like Anna Crusis and Women Like Me, embodied the vision of a particular composer or conductor; others, like Calliope, grew out of the collaboration of a group of women singing informally in each other's living rooms. Many, like the Los Angeles Women's Community Chorus, emerged from the lesbian/feminist community and have continued to affirm a women-centered identity; others, like Anna Crusis and Catherine Roma's Cincinnati chorus, MUSE, began with a political focus that included peace and racial equality. Yet despite their diverse origins and diverse choral cultures, women's choruses shared a common commitment: to provide a safe space for all women, to share the transformative power of choral singing with each other and with their audiences, and to advocate for social justice in their communities and their world.

5

The Birth of a Network

"Now We Are a Movement!" Women's Music Festivals

In 1973, after a "cultural night" at a Seattle Women's History Month celebration, feminist activist and philosopher Kate Millett was heard to say: "Now we are a movement, because we have music!"[1]

Returning home, Millett invited lesbian-feminist songwriters and poets to perform at the Sacramento Festival of Women's Music, the first such event in the country. During the years that followed, regional women's music festivals sprang up everywhere. Some, like the Chillicothe, Ohio Lesbian Festival and the Midwest Wimmin's Festival at Lake of the Ozarks, Missouri, were "womyn-only" (or "wimmin only") spaces that welcomed straight, bi and lesbian women (and later, trans women) and were held in parks, campgrounds, or other outdoor venues where women camped in tents or stayed in cabins. Others, like the Boston Women's Music Festival, took place indoors and did not explicitly use the word "lesbian" in the title, though lesbian feminist culture dominated the event. Other festivals sprouted up in Long Island, New York; San Diego; and the Pocono Mountains of Pennsylvania. Many of these festivals are still annual events; others have ceased to exist. Two of the best known, the National Women's Music Festival and the Michigan Womyn's Music Festival, became the pre-eminent national gatherings.

NWMF: "Beautiful Music from Women Who Loved Each Other"

Champaign-Urbana, identified by *Mother Jones* magazine in the 1970's as one of the country's top ten cities for progressive politics, was fertile ground for radical organizing. At the University of Illinois, the anti-Vietnam War movement mobilized against the university's acceptance of government research grants and the presence of military recruiters on campus. The Black Student Association, founded in 1967, submitted a list of demands to the administration, including a Black Studies program, a Black Cultural Center, and the hiring of Black RA's in the residence halls. The university's Gay Liberation Front, one of the first in the country, formed in 1972 and maintained a high profile, including a resource center and coffeehouse. Students also joined with community activists to achieve passage of Champaign's 1977 Human Rights Ordinance, which included sexual orientation (then described as "sexual preference") in its list of protected categories. Champaign was also the scene of the initial organizing meeting for the first March on Washington for Lesbian and Gay Rights, which materialized after the assassination of Harvey Milk in 1978. (See Chapter 7.) For feminists, both on and off campus, Champaign was an exciting place to be.[2]

"The primary energy was lesbian," recalled Mary Lee Sargent, a veteran of Champaign in the 1970's. "We had what we called a support group for the [women's] shelter. And we had a Thursday night group that met afterwards and discussed things to do with the shelter, but they also were a real social group and went out to the gay bar drinking and dancing till all hours— 'cause we were in our late twenties or early thirties and having our kind of —adolescence—you know, late." Previously closeted lesbians were discovering, "you know, there are others like me" and experiencing "a sense of power that 'Oh, we're changing the world.' It was a heady time and a very hopeful time."[3]

Nancy Melin, who was part of the Champaign lesbian community in the '70's and later sang with the feminist chorus Amasong (described in the next chapter), recalled being "a young lesbian, just out, and here are all these lesbians out in public, and it's still an environment where people were beaten up or killed back then.... So it was really exciting to be free and be open and feel okay. Here's all these other women, it was joyous, it was exciting."[4]

In May 1974, Kristen Lems, a young Champaign folksinger, and her sister approached the organizers of a local folk festival and asked why they were not seeking women performers. "I went in there and said to them, 'How could you have a folk festival that is all male? This is inconceivable to us,'" Lems recalled. "And they said there just weren't any women good enough. My sister and I were so outraged. What do you mean no women good enough? We put an ad in the paper that said: 'No women good enough? Come and audition for our women's folk festival.'"

The women's folk festival that Lems and her sister organized on the same night as the men's festival drew an overflow crowd. "From what I hear, theirs was very woebegone," said Lems.[5] She and her sister went on to organize the first National Women's Music Festival at the University of Illinois, where 800 women from all over the United States gathered to see and hear women performers and to share their own music and their lives.

The October 1974 issue of *Paid My Dues* featured extended accounts of women's experiences at the Festival. A writer named Margaret Marigold described workshops and performances by women's music icons Kay Gardner and Meg Christian, as well as lesser known musicians. In addition to these scheduled performances, an open mic was available on the mall all day. Marigold wrote, "It was so wonderful to lie on the grass in the sun and air, listening to beautiful music from women who loved each other."[6] Mary Lee Sargent recalled that during the Festival, the University of Illinois quad "would just be filled with groups of women and playing games and Frisbee and going to workshops. It was that feeling of, 'Oh, my gosh, there are so many of us and we're so powerful and we're creating all of this beautiful art and music.'"[7]

Amid the euphoria, some events at the Festival revealed divisions in the lesbian/feminist movement that would haunt future festivals and trouble the movement as a whole.

Some women objected to the presence of "a very few men, as organizers, as part of the equipment crew, and as audience," while others felt "it wasn't a real big deal." Resentment over the monopoly of the stage by a few "stars" led to "the 'takeover' of the stage by just about everybody." True to feminist process, the "takeover" became "a chance for the organizers to take criticism and praise and for the women to discuss grievances, and make plans for next year. Up till then, the stage had been used only by professionals, and now everyone was sharing it, and for a while, everyone sang."[8]

Michigan and Beyond

Two years after the first NWMF, Lisa Vogel and her sister, Kristie, along with their friend Mary Kindig, drew up a plan for a festival of their own in central Michigan.

"People said, 'You're nuts, you know. We're in Mount Pleasant, Michigan. What we've done is thrown one or two good keggers,'" Vogel recalled. "We literally had a party at our house, stopped the music at the most exciting moment and passed the hat. We had no money."

When they approached the organizers of the NWMF, "We went with a hand drawn ditto master that we had snuck in the university and done, you know with the little purple ink, and all the other producers who at that point were taking themselves very seriously were going, 'Wait a minute, you're doing this big thing that we're all talking about, what's up with those ditto masters?'"[9]

The Champaign women decided to take a chance on Vogel's plan, and in 1976 the first Michigan Womyn's Music Festival was held in the central Michigan college town of Mount Pleasant. Two thousand women came for three days and nights of performances held on one main stage.[10] The following year, the Festival moved to rural western Michigan, where it was produced, staffed and run entirely by women until it came to an end in 2015.

Before long, women's music festivals became the places where "the heart and soul of the movement came most alive."[11] From the beginning, they were safe spaces where women, especially lesbians, could live and love freely and where women were at the center rather than on the margins. Organizers educated themselves about everything from audio engineering to concert promotion to management and production.

Woman Sound, founded by sound engineer Boden Sandstrom in 1975, provided sound for festivals as well as women's music concerts. In her 2003 doctoral dissertation about the Michigan Womyn's Music Festival, Sandstrom wrote:

> Women [brought] various skills and crafts including carpentry (so that the stages could be built), truck and forklift driving, lifting and climbing, kitchen management and cooking for both workers and festiegoers, sound engineering and lighting design, stage management and production, box office and parking management, child-care and healthcare workers, artists for creative sign making, professional security and firefighting and innumerous other skills. Skilled women who were marginalized in traditionally male-dominated occupations were valued on their own terms. For many women, the process of building and creating an environment according to their own vision would begin to gradually erode layers of internalized powerlessness.[12]

Sign language interpreters were an integral part of festival performances, giving deaf lesbians the opportunity to participate in the festival experience, where hearing the music was only one part of the immersion in lesbian culture. In 1992, organizers of the fourth East Coast Lesbian Festival organized a pre-festival American Sign Language Intensive for Lesbians, which *Hot Wire* editor Toni Armstrong, Jr. described as "lesbian summer camp with a twist: when the 'counselors' say *no talking*, they mean it!"[13]

For the women in the forefront of the festival movement, the gatherings were overwhelming. "What we discovered there was that we were all lesbians," recalled singer-songwriter Cassie Culver. "And I tell you, our sense of power just went over the top. I mean, we were so high on the fact that we all existed."[14] Barbara "Boo" Price, who co-produced the Michigan Womyn's Music Festival from its inception until 1994, believes that the early years "were the organic creation of festival culture. Feminists—mostly lesbians—would go to great lengths to get together in large groups, brought by the excuse of their new 'women's music' but driven by a desire to affirm an identity as independent women forging a revolution."[15] Price goes on:

> There was an ecstatic quality to those first years of gatherings, punctuated by acts of social defiance: letting menstrual blood flow freely, throwing off shirts or all clothing, taking on male-identified jobs such as trench digging, tent stake sledging, stage rigging, tractor driving. Most of festival culture in the early days was the result of doing it all ourselves. The principle [sic] activity was sitting in front of the stage and waiting for or watching the concerts.[16]

Singer/activist Holly Near described her first visit to the women-only San Diego Women's Music Festival in 1975:

> I found women walking around looking tan and healthy and relaxed. Small groups were singing or fiddling under a tree. One woman was stretched out on a rock like a snake drying its skin and another woman recited poems to her, dancing gracefully around the rock. I discovered lesbians could be hippies too! The stage was built in a natural amphitheater and women sat on the slope, leaning against rocks, trees, and each other to listen to the music that many had waited all their lives to hear.[17]

In her 2006 dissertation on the Michigan Womyn's Music Festival, Laurie J. Kendall expounded on the idea of festival as a yearly "home" for women who "live liminal lives fifty-one weeks out of the year. They are like a diasporic people who visit their native homeland once a year where they soak up their cultural traditions and reinvest in their familiar relationships before returning to their lives in the diaspora."[18]

Coalition Building and Turning the Century

Women's music festivals could not escape the homophobia of the outside world or the internal identity crises that divided the women's movement in the 1970s and 80's, as Festival producer and ethnomusicologist Boden Sandstrom observed:

> The early festival culture was no less vulnerable to the strains of an endemic racism than the dominant culture from which it chose to separate. Women who had the financial means to organize, attend, or perform at women's music festivals were primarily white. General festival norms—everything from musical aesthetics, to food preferences, to camping acumen—reflected white predilections and experiences that tended to be more accessible to white participants.[19]

The November, 1981 issue of *Off Our Backs* included an article titled "Festival: Trouble and Mediation at Yosemite," documenting conflicts between White organizers and women of color at the Second Annual West Coast Women's Music and Cultural Festival. Kitchen workers went on strike, accusing Festival organizers Robin Tyler and Torrie Osborn of exploitation; Latinas claimed that White organizers had scheduled events so as to diminish the visibility of Latin American Solidarity Day; Jewish women (and some non-Jewish allies) protested what they considered the targeting of Robin by some women of color.

By the end of the Festival, women of color, White women, and Jewish women had all drafted separate statements: women of color demanded provisions for women of limited means and more diversity in staff; White women criticized the silencing of women of color and evidence of classism at the festival; and Jewish women stood in solidarity with women of color, but also criticized anti-Semitism. Their statements, and the events of the Festival as a whole, testified to the truth of Bernice Johnson Reagon's admonition in her Festival workshop, "Coalition Politics and Turning the Century": "Today, wherever women gather, it is not necessarily nurturing, it is absolutely hard work. You don't go into coalition work because you like it, the only reason you consider trying to team up with somebody who could possibly kill you is because you figure it's the only way you can stay alive."

Speaking not just of music festivals but also of the women's movement as a whole, Reagon reminded her listeners: "We must find people who integrate all these struggles.... What really counts is not what you do this weekend; it's what you do with this knowledge when you go back home Monday morning. Apply it. And then, do it every day you get up, and find yourself alive!"[20]

Struggles over race and power troubled other festivals as well. In 1989, some women of color boycotted the National Women's Music Festival after the board of directors failed to add two women of color to its all White membership. A few years later, Donna Eder, Suzanne Staggenborg, and Lori Sudderth interviewed dozens of NWMF participants and found that although most White participants were unaware of the boycott, many women interviewed did comment that they were concerned about the lack of racial diversity at the festival. The composition of the board was later altered to include women of color, but there remained obstacles to making the festival open to diverse groups of women. Eder and her co-researchers speculated that

...the apparent lack of interest in discussions of racism and identity on the part of some festival participants may be due in part to the fact that, for many, the function of the festival was to affirm a positive *lesbian* identity; they did not see it as the place to highlight differences among lesbians.[21]

Around the same time, African American musicologist Eileen Hayes and her friend Cindy Spillane visited eight women's music festivals and interviewed Black women musicians and attendees. The women Hayes interviewed often found these festivals oppressive (for example, "when white members of the festival gospel chorus changed male pronouns to female ones") but they appreciated the opportunity for Black women performers to connect with one another.[22] Hayes also visited Sistahfest, an all-Black lesbian cultural musical and political retreat founded in 1991 by United Lesbians of African Heritage (ULOAH), where "just hanging out with my cabin mates was funnier and more enjoyable than watching BET's *Comedy Jam*. Our collective presence was proof that the jelly beans at the bottom of the jar were not only black, but they rocked in ways that were as arguably compelling as the Afroed black lesbian feminist revolutionary stereotype." [23]

Linda Tillery, one of the few Black performers on the women's music concert circuit, acknowledged the challenges of being "an African American woman who was raised in a primarily black neighborhood in the inner city of San Francisco," with a musical background "based in jazz, rhythm and blues, and some gospel, with a very heavy dose of the blues." Tillery recalled asking herself, "*What on earth am I going to do for these women? How do I present who I really am to this audience, which may or may not have had exposure to the kind of music that is important to me?*"

Yet in spite of her apprehensions, Tillery found Michigan a welcoming environment. "The producers of the Michigan Womyn's Music Festival made it possible for me to present some programs that were really kind of groundbreaking," Tillery later recalled. "I would get an idea, Boo Price would hear it, and we'd toss it around. She would say, 'Well, why don't you do it if you think you can pull it together?'" One project that emerged from this collaboration was A Tribute to Black Women and the Blues, which Tillery called "an artistic expression of respect and gratitude paid to some women who might have been otherwise ignored ...one of the most satisfying moments of my life.... I can say that I was one of the women who was instrumental in exposing women's audiences to African-American music. And that too is a very satisfying thing for me."[24]

Bernice Johnson Reagon's observations about the joys and challenges of coalition building were amply demonstrated in the history of Sisterfire, a multicultural urban women's music festival that Sweet Honey in the Rock co-founded with Amy Horowitz in 1978, shortly after the ill-fated collaboration between Sweet Honey and Redwood Records described in Chapter 3. Horowitz was working full time as a producer for Sweet Honey when they decided that "the time seemed right to produce a 'women's cultural day.'....As Sarna Marcus, Bernice Reagon, Susan Allee, and Evelyn Harris bounced ideas back and forth, the name Sisterfire was born."[25] Horowitz later described the plan as an idea "born out of bold hopes and a special mix of naiveté and chutzpah.... We hardly slept. We were propelled by a sense of purpose and the task loomed enormous for a small crew of staff and volunteers high on hope and low on budget."

Three years later, the first Sisterfire Festival took place in Takoma Park Field in Washington, DC. "This festival is a demonstration of commitment to social change and hope," declared the Sisterfire statement of purpose. "We are building bridges between the women's movement and other movements for progressive social change. We are playing with fire, and we want nothing less from this event than to set loose the creative, fierce and awesome energies in all of us."[26]

Sisterfire eventually grew to a two day, four stage program with overnight camping and a marketplace of craftswomen. A 1984 article in *Hot Wire* described the atmosphere at the third festival as "festive and easygoing, with blankets spread across the grassy hillside for seating, old friends greeting each other, and crowds checking out the booths displaying crafts, publications, and food."[27]Sisterfire coordinator Ivy Young told

Hot Wire, "Since DC is a diverse city, we get volunteers from a variety of places. They're lesbian and straight, black and white, really multiethnic and multi-cultural."[28]

During its lifetime, Sisterfire featured an incredibly diverse lineup of performers, from ninety-two-year-old Elizabeth Cotton playing "Freight Train" on her left-handed guitar, to Alicia Portnoy, an Argentinian political prisoner, to Black novelist and theorist Alice Walker. Palestinian poet Hala Jabbour and Israeli poet Shelly Elkayam shared a stage, as did Yolanda King and Atalla Shabazz (daughters of Martin Luther King and Malcolm X, respectively). Cris Williamson, Margie Adam, Meg Christian, Holly Near, and a familiar lineup of women's music luminaries all made appearances, while Bernice Johnson Reagon and Sweet Honey remained the guiding force for the thousands "who celebrated this new woman-child."[29]

In 1987, after a year's hiatus, Sisterfire moved to a larger venue, with an audience of 5,000. *Hot Wire* hailed the festival's "triumphant return" and noted many "positive changes," including a computerized technical system, a re-structured Board of Directors, and the reorganization of committees for volunteers, including the important addition of an anti-racism committee and an international programming committee. The childcare area was named The Hearth and moved to the center of the festival area with its own programming. A Deaf community stage featured performances by deaf and hearing women. Sisterfire coordinator Penny Rosenwasser and Assistant Coordinator Marian Urquilla told *Hot Wire* that the festival was "the best ever in terms of attendance, weather, variety of acts, and artistry."[30]

Nevertheless, amid the celebration and diversity, Sisterfire was feeling the strains of culture clashes and identity politics. "There were White women who thought there was not enough women's music (read White) and Black women who thought there were too many White women," Amy Horowitz later wrote.

> There were straight people who wondered why there were so many gay and lesbian people around, and there were political people who thought the festival

was not addressing substantive issues, and there were festivalgoers who thought the performers were too politically oriented. There were women of color who claimed we were a racist institution and White women who denied the existence of racism within their circle. As sometimes happens from the accumulation of culturally based hurt, the festival was a tempting ground on which to unleash unexpressed disappointment and expectation.[31]

Matters came to a head during the 1987 festival, when two White lesbians asked two Black men to leave their crafts area because it was women-only space. According to most accounts, one of the men struck one of the women, who reported the incident to festival organizers. Caught between accusations of racism and the demands of lesbian separatism, some organizers tried to frame the incident as an episode of mutual violence. Writers in the lesbian press were quick to denounce this interpretation. Writing in the journal *Lesbian Ethics*, Anna Lee condemned the argument that "hitting as violence = exclusion as violence." She went on to point out that although the White lesbian excluded Black and White males from viewing her sculpture, she did not exclude Black women. Lee concluded, "The organizers of Sisterfire ignored black women in their definition of racism and what counts as a racist act."[32] Years later, in an essay on feminist political theory, lesbian feminist Bette Tallen suggested that the conflicting demands of gender and race were far from resolved. Tallen wrote, "When some lesbians defended the actions of the two Black men because of the reality of racism in the U.S.A., they ended up justifying woman-hating." [33]

The incident took festival organizers by surprise, and an article in the *Washington Blade* the following summer described their attempts to avoid similar clashes during the 1988 Festival. Roadwork officials prepared a flyer, to be handed out to all attendees at the gate, explicitly stating the Festival policy that the entire Festival site was open to all regardless of gender, with the exception of the women-only camping areas nearby.[34]

The January, 1989 issue of *Hot Wire* featured a positive account of the 1988 festival, but noted the sharp drop in attendance, which the reporter attributed in part to repercussions of the previous year's conflicts. Roadworks spokeswoman Dottie Green reminded readers that Sisterfire had always included men, though it would always be concerned with presenting and celebrating "women's creative spirit." She went on to acknowledge the role of separatism in the development of women's culture, but added that the time had come for women to broaden their scope, asserting, "We have got to march together [straight and gay, men and women], every kind, all doing it together. It's a human issue—we all deserve rights."[35]

Despite these efforts, the 1988 Sisterfire festival was the last. Amy Horowitz later wrote that the cultural, racial, and sexual clashes of 1987

> proved too heavy a load for the delicate suspension of the Sisterfire experiment. A national boycott, fueled by some of the women's music press, kept attendance down the following year and we stumbled, we did not survive the resultant withdrawal of support. I like to think that Sisterfire is sleeping in hibernation, gathering new strength and insights from the efforts of the first years. I like to think that she will wake up renewed again... soon.[36]

The Birth of a Network

Although Amy Horowitz's vision of a reawakened Sisterfire festival did not materialize, women's music festivals continued the hard work of coalition building. Conflicts over race, class, separatism, sexual radicalism, and later, transgender identity (discussed more fully in subsequent chapters) were not easily resolved, but organizers continued working together to create festival environments committed to feminism, consensus building and lesbian empowerment —environments that were ideal for the birth of a women's chorus network. Like Sue Fink and Cathy Roma, Kristen Lems, Lisa Vogel and their regional counterparts promoted music that expressed the struggle for peace and justice and the reality of women's lives. And in the pre-internet 1970's and 1980's, music festivals were enclaves where chorus members and directors from far-flung places could meet one another for the first time.

Many years later, Roma recalled those times:

> Imagine the year is 1972: there are no cell phones, no internet, no voicemail or answering machines. Yet, a network of women across the nation hooked up via sheer will. Women wanting to sing their lives, women writing lyrics expressing the emotion and experience of their everyday lives, women performing for one another, producing concerts (doing all skilled and technical jobs including lights and sound), recording, learning to play instruments usually considered unfeminine (traps, trumpet, bass, electric guitar, saxophone, etc) all coalesced around this thing called Women's Music.[37]

Roma also recalled how at Michigan and Champaign-Urbana she discovered "wonderfully creative, powerful songs and songwriters. One of the tracks that you could do at Michigan would be singing with the women's choir. They were fertile ground there, those activities, those festivals."[38]

If Cathy Roma was the mother of the women's chorus movement, Linda Ray (Echo) and Linda Small could be considered the midwives of the network that became its home. Echo was a member of The Kansas City Women's Chorus, and Linda Small, of the St. Louis Women's Chorus—two of the early midwestern choruses that had already begun exchanging songs—when they met up at the Michigan Womyn's Music Festival in 1980. Earlier that summer, singers in a workshop at the National Women's Music Festival had drawn up a list of names and addresses that they hoped would become the genesis of a women's chorus network, and Mardy Keener, a member of Miss Safman's Ladies' Choir in Champaign-Urbana, had sent out a mailing with a list of fifteen choruses. Keener addressed her letter to "Sister Singers" and added, "I obviously like that appellation—how about calling our network The Sister Singers Network?"[39]

Two months later, choral singers at the Michigan Womyn's Music Festival held a meeting where they drew up plans for a combined concert and a music sharing initiative, and joined in "a memorable rendition of *Aure Volante* sung in Italian and English simultaneously."[40] Following the meeting, singers who had attended the National Women's Music Festival circulated the list they had compiled and invited Michigan attendees to add their names. "Someone said, 'Well, we started this thing at National and here is the list,'" Echo recalled many years later. "Linda and I looked at each other and said, 'This never's gonna get off the ground unless someone takes this list and does something with it.' We had no way to duplicate it there because that was a rural setting, so we drug it home."[41]

That Fall, Echo and Linda sent out an expanded chorus list, a plan for sharing music, and a proposal for a Sister Singers choral performance at the 1981 NWMF. "We said, 'We need a logo or something or they won't think it's real'—as if it were," Echo recalled. "So, some people in our choir came up with a logo, put it on letterhead, made a bunch of copies, typed up a letter, typed up a thing and said, 'Send it out.'"[42] The new logo featured an image of a treble clef combined with the bottom cross of the traditional "woman" sign, superimposed on a curved staff line meant to suggest a rainbow.[43]

Enclosed with the letter was a directory based on the summer's lists and including contact information for fifteen women's choruses; the majority were from the Midwest, though California and Washington, DC were also represented. Sister Singers would eventually expand to other regions of the country and to both coasts, but the Network retains a strong midwestern presence to this day.

The midwestern genesis of Sister Singers, as well as of the National Women's Music Festival and the Michigan Womyn's Music Festival, contradicts the popular conception of the

Midwest as a barren cultural landscape. As Karen Lee Osborne and William J. Spurlin write in the introduction to their 1996 anthology, *Reclaiming the Heartland: Lesbian and Gay Voices from the Midwest*, "Looking at the Midwest through the lens of lesbian-feminist cultural practices [including women's music festivals] helps to ... dismantle the stereotype of the Midwest as a place for social conformity."[44] Festival historian Bonnie Morris points out that the Midwest "has often broken social codes to offer women opportunities." As examples she cites the World War II-era All American Girls' Baseball League that drew huge crowds to stadiums in small town Wisconsin, Michigan, Illinois and Indiana, and the tradition of "strong, capable farm women and wartime industrial workers, black and white."[45] Similarly, Martin F. Manalansan IV, Chantal Nadeau, Richard T. Rodríguez, and Siobhan B. Somerville remind readers that the importance of major cities like Chicago belies the image of the Midwest as exclusively rural and, by implication, unsophisticated.[46] In fact, one of the earliest women's choruses still singing, Artemis Singers of Chicago, proudly states on its website that Artemis was "one of the first women's singing ensembles in the U.S. to explicitly label herself a lesbian feminist chorus," and has been deeply involved with the women's/lesbian culture of Chicago since its founding in 1980.[47] In Cleveland, home to Windsong Feminist Chorus since 1979, *What She Wants: Cleveland's Monthly Feminist and Lesbian Newspaper* began publishing in 1973; in addition, the Gay and Lesbian Community Service Center of Greater Cleveland, which opened its offices in 1977, supported a wide variety of programs in the 1980s and 1990s, including a telephone hotline program, a calendar of events of interest to the gay/lesbian community, and outreach programs designed to combat homophobia in the larger community.[48]

Musicking in Kansas City

Initial plans for a Sister Singers concert at the 1981 NWMF were cut short when the University of Illinois evicted the NWMF from the campus. In a letter to the Network, Linda and Echo shared the bad news: "We have recently received frustrating news from Champaign. It seems someone in university hierarchies has decided the national Women's Music Festival is bad PR or some such idiocy. So if you can help that situation or know anyone who can please contact Music Festival Personnel and get on it quick!"[49] According to Nancy Melin, the move to banish the NWMF came from University President Stan Ikenberry, who was distressed by the open display of lesbian identity—in particular the sight of topless women playing Frisbee on the quad: "Rumor had it he didn't want these lesbians running around with no shirts on."[50] (The Festival incorporated as a not-for-profit organization called Women In the Arts/National Women's Music Festival Inc. and moved to the Indiana University campus in Bloomington, Indiana. It has since relocated in other midwestern universities and now takes place at various midwestern hotels.)

Linda and Echo's letter went on to announce that despite this setback, the Network planned to appear at the Midwest Wimmin's Festival in the Missouri Ozarks. That summer, four choirs—Women of the Heartland: Singing Our Lives; Artemis Singers; the Saint Louis Women's Choir; and the Kansas City Women's Chorus—performed at the Festival, which also featured a sixty-voice Network mass chorus. In addition, chorus members held a Network meeting where they discussed plans for future events along with "a responsible way in which we as a network can show our respect for the efforts of our own women arrangers and composers." Linda Small subsequently compiled a document titled "HOW TO SHARE MUSIC WITHOUT GETTING ARRESTED OR BEING POLITICALLY INCORRECT In 6 less-than-simple steps," which included a summary of copyright laws likely to affect women's choirs, along with guidelines for "Common Sense Courtesy," such as, "It is disrespectful of women musicians to perform their music (whether copyrighted or not) without giving [composers, writers and arrangers] credit on the stage and/or in the program."[51]

For the next three years, the Kansas City Women's Chorus and the St. Louis Women's Chorus organized annual performances at the Midwest Wimmin's Festival. By 1983, participation had grown to six choruses with seventy singers, and the Network was ready for a wider audience. In a planning document sent to all member choruses, the Saint Louis Coordinating Committee exuberantly declared that the time had come for "a Festival all our own" and added, "We thought we might call it the First Annual Women's Choral Festival." A national festival, the letter went on, would enable chorus members to meet their counterparts from all over the country, "to combine our voices in a massed choral concert and hear individual choruses sing," and "have time for fun playing Frisbee, exchanging back rubs, browsing in the Kansas City Women's Bookstore, etc." The letter called on member choruses to "SAVE THE DATES NOVEMBER 2, 3 AND 4, 1984 and set your sights on Kansas City, Missouri!" Choruses were also urged to consider the expenses associated with the festival (facilities rental, mailing costs for information, publicity) and adjust their budgets accordingly. Finally, the letter appealed for "Committees! This festival will only be successful if responsibility is shared by all. 'Now is the time for all good women' to add their talents to this enterprise."[52]

Like Chicago, Minneapolis, and Madison (described in the previous chapter), Kansas City was already home to a thriving gay and lesbian community when the Kansas City Women's Chorus began singing there in 1979. As early as 1966, the first planning meeting of ECHO, the Eastern Conference of Homophile Organizations, had been held in Kansas City (selected because "it was mutually inconvenient to everyone").[53] Two years later, Barbara Grier took over as editor of *The Ladder*, the first nationally distributed lesbian publication in the United States, and continued to edit the magazine from her home in Kansas City until it ceased publication four years later. Kansas City also boasted a twice-monthly free newspaper, the *Gay News-Telegraph*, which carried news of the gay and lesbian community and was distributed throughout Missouri, southern Illinois, and central Indiana, and continued publishing until 2000. In 1992, the paper, by then known as the *Kansas City News-Telegraph*, featured a retrospective titled "Excavating Our

Pride." It included the history of the city's many lesbian and gay advocacy organizations, as well as the Heart of America Sunday Softball League, a large number of social clubs, and New Earth Books, a lesbian-feminist bookstore. An article on "Women in Kansas City's Heritage" documented a lesbian separatist culture reminiscent of those in other American cities. As an example, the author recalls the Rail Room, a bar across from Union Station, which catered to railroad workers during the day but underwent "a magic transformation ... after a certain time of day. It was taken over by women and there was a halfway point in the room, unspoken and unmarked, past which no men ventured." Another article, headlined "The Churches: Not Always the Enemy," recounted that in addition to the local Metropolitan Community Church (a national denomination with a primary ministry to LGBT people), some of Kansas City's mainstream churches, including the Methodists, were among the community's "staunchest allies."[54]

The first National Women's Chorus Concert took place in 1984 at Kansas City's Trinity United Methodist Church and featured 130 voices from seven choruses based in Kansas, Missouri, Wisconsin, Illinois and Minnesota. Each chorus performed three or four selections, which included women's music favorites by Cathy Winter, Cris Williamson and Ysaye Barnwell; songs from the pop music repertoire (Cyndi Lauper's "Time After Time" and "The Rose"); a few classical pieces; and several folk songs. The Mass Chorus sang six songs, including "On Children," from Kahlil Gibran's *The Prophet* in a musical setting by Sweet Honey in the Rock singer Ysaye Barnwell, which, along with many of the other numbers on the 1984 concert program, remains a staple of programs across the Network.[55]

In the years to come, Sister Singers would grow to a network of three dozen choruses, with quadrennial festivals drawing hundreds of singers from all over the U.S. and featuring a wide range of songs, including commissioned works by women composers. Administration of the Network would require more formal organization, with a coordinating committee (referred to at various times in Network history as the Matrix, the Helm, and the Steering Committee), meeting annually. Network concerts no longer take place outdoors ("You'd get there and there's this big board and if you want to do a workshop, you just signed up, said, 'We're gonna do this workshop at this time under that tree'"), but the university settings where most Festivals now take place foster the same informal personal interaction in dorms and community housing. And, true to the initial emphasis on ethical values along with legal ones described in Linda Small's original guidelines, concert organizers continue to pay attention to feminist principles of respect, inclusion, and the primary worth of women's lives. Sign language interpretation and accessibility are taken for granted, as are scholarships and community housing opportunities for singers on limited incomes.

In traditional choral and symphonic performances, as Christopher Small points out, "most, if not all, of the audience will be strangers to us."[56] Audiences at community chorus performances may be neighbors or friends; those at folk music concerts may share political and social values and may even be invited to sing along; members of a church choir sing to their sister and brother congregants, who presumably share the same religious faith. But all of these musicking experiences (to use Small's term) retain the separation between singers and audience—the singers perform and the audience listens. At Sister Singers Festival concerts, the performers are the audience—or rather, choruses alternate roles, as each member chorus takes the stage to perform for the others, and then returns to see and hear the next chorus on the program. The culminating mass chorus is always a two-part affair, with half the choruses in attendance singing to the other half, and then reversing roles. In their blurring of the boundaries between performers and audience, Sister Singers Festivals evoke girlhood experiences at summer camp and the all-girl environment of the Girl Scouts, where, as Echo recalled, campers "sang before meals, after meals, even in the swimming pool. I mean, you always sang. It was just a part of life."[57]

*First Sister Singers
mailing list,
September 30, 1980*

*First National
Women's Chorus Concert,
1984*

First Annual
National Women's
Chorus
Concert

Participating choruses include:

130 voices from:

K.C., Mo.
St. Louis, Mo.
Chicago, Ill.
Manhattan, Ks.
Wichita, Ks.
Madison, Wi.
Minneapolis, Mn.

8:00 p.m.
Saturday, November 3, 1984
Trinity United Methodist Church
Armour & Kenwood   K.C., Mo.

Sixth Sister Singers Festival, Houston, 1991

Womasong, Asheville, North Carolina, undated photo

Common Woman Chorus,
Durham, NC,
undated poster

San Diego Women's Chorus,
1993

Program books,
2010

Artemis singers perform,
Chicago, 2010

Above: Catherine Roma conducts,
Chicago, 2010

Right: Composer Joan Szymko,
Chicago, 2010

142

Left: MUSE Chorus performs, Chicago, 2010

Below: A lighter moment with Womansong, Chicago, 2010

Below:Festival in Chicago, 2010

Above: Getting ready for the after-concert party, Chicago, 2010

Voices Rising
2011

SSN 30th anniversary Festival,
Champaign-Urbana, 2014

Amasong, 2012

Juneau Pride Chorus,
2016

The New Mexico Women's Chorus,
celebrating
"Changing the world one song at a time..."
presents:

We Shall Be Free!
Songs of Peace and Social Justice

New Mexico Women's Chorus,
2016

Saturday, January 16th, 2016 7 p.m.
First Unitarian Church, Albuquerque

Sunday, January 17th, 2016 4 p.m.
The Center for Spiritual Living, Santa Fe

"This project is made possible in part by New Mexico Arts,
a division of the Department of Cultural Affairs, and the
National Endowment for the Arts"

San Diego Women's Chorus, 2017

Rainbow Women's Chorus, San Jose, 2017

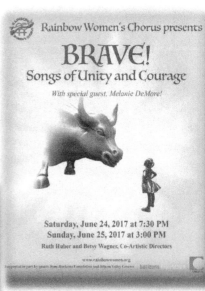

MUSE Women's Choir, 35th Anniversary concert, Cincinnati, 2018

Women in Harmony
2018

Women in Harmony poster
2018

6

Growing a Movement: Feminist Choruses and Feminist Leadership

Whether they are young girls singing in ancient Greek rituals, nuns in the convent at Rupertsberg, or modern-day college and university students, women's choruses must answer the same questions facing every group of people who sing together. How shall our chorus be organized? Who will lead us as we sing? What will constitute our repertoire and who will choose it? And what will be our relationship with our audiences and with one another? Traditionally, choral singers have had little to say about these matters, as religious tradition, ritual, or ruling authorities dictated the answers. More recently, some choirs have had more power over their choral lives. But for the choruses born out of the lesbian/feminist movement of the 1970s, choral organization meant more than just hiring a director or appointing a board. The motto stenciled on the T-shirts created for Womonsong of Madison spoke for many women's choruses: "Have meeting, will process."[1]

In the years following the first National Women's Choral Festival, feminist choruses appeared across the country. Some were the inspiration of a conductor, while others were created by women who were already singing together or were inspired by a particular event or political moment. But no matter how they began, one of the first questions they needed to answer was who would direct them. For choruses led by founding directors, the answer was obvious; in other cases, chorus members had to find a director who members felt was a good fit.

Choosing to direct a women's chorus was a unique commitment. Debbie Nordeen, who succeeded Linda Metzner as director of Womansong in Asheville, came to choral conducting after surviving cancer and experiencing "a major epiphany." Nordeen feels that "Womansong is my path for practicing what

I believe…. It's one thing to believe in something. It's one thing to say you're a Christian or Muslim or whatever your path is, but can you put it into practice without the words of it?" She describes conducting a women's choir as a deeply spiritual experience:

> Your voices are your souls. Your soul is expressed through the body, through the sound, through the breath, the heartbeat, and there you are all singing together. It's joy. It's beauty. And it brings peace, it brings harmony. The true, deep harmony. Not just the notes. The harmony of soul to soul doing something that unifies rather than divides.[2]

Patricia Hennings, who conducted the Peninsula Women's Chorus until her death in 2002, expressed similar sentiments when she wrote:

> As conductors, we must become the embodiment of the sound. There should be no gesture without meaning and no sound without purpose. Thus, we can expect that transformation of sound into spirit in rehearsal and performance, with beginning and advanced singers. The music will become the fabric of your choral community.[3]

Women chorus directors embraced the collective decision making that is an integral part of feminist process. Jackie Coren, former director of Philadelphia's Anna Crusis, says that "the challenge as a director is how to put a vision out and have people come along with that vision, but also to include them in the vision making. And I find sometimes my particular vision or my inclination may not speak to some of the women, and so as a director I just find that challenging in a good way, because I certainly couldn't steer that ship on my own."[4]

The directors who helped create women's choruses shared a relationship with their singers beyond pitch, rhythm and harmony: women's voices were not just producers of sounds, but expressions of women's authentic power to direct their own lives. Some directors came to choral conducting with academic backgrounds; some were nationally recognized composers or experienced conductors of other choruses looking for a musical home in the lesbian/feminist community.

Debbie Wachspress was pursuing graduate studies at SUNY/Geneseo and teaching music full time in the Rochester City School District when she assembled some friends to start the Rochester Women's Community Chorus in 1985. During the chorus's earlier incarnation as the Rochester Womyn's Community Chorus,

> Lesbian Separatism was the norm and a fun night out was doing guerilla theater at movie theaters and being arrested for committing acts of civil disobedience. Whoever led the group was not considered to be "in charge" nor was she a "conductor." That was deemed way too patriarchal. Everything was decided by consensus including how long to hold a particular note.

Wachspress decided that the "new" RWCC would be "more traditional. There would be a conductor and the music that was selected would be composed by both women and men. Lyrics would be scrutinized and, 'when necessary,' altered to fit our feminist politics."[5]

For Linda Metzner, founding director of Womansong in Asheville, North Carolina, directing a women's chorus was closely tied to her peace and justice commitment. Not long after starting the chorus in 1987, Metzner was vacationing in the Catskills when she had what she later described as a "thrilling spiritual inspiration" for a Womansong initiative: the New Start Fund, which would raise money for women in transition. "I especially wanted spiritually to encourage the idea that everyone has the right to a new start, wherever they are in their lives," she recalled. "I wonder if being at my family farm, full of memories of immigrants who came to America out of starvation to start life anew, helped me to envision the idea of the unending 'New Start.'"[6] Linda returned to the next Womansong rehearsal with a New Start proposal and the project has continued ever since.

Joanne Connolly was inspired to start Voices from the Heart in Portsmouth, New Hampshire, after attending a workshop with Ysaye Barnwell of Sweet Honey in the Rock. Connolly found it "amazing to do away with written music, and work together with other women to learn parts and create such soulful sounds. I wanted to recreate that experience in Portsmouth, NH."[7]

Bev Grant founded the Brooklyn Women's Chorus after years in the international folk and social justice movements, with a non-audition policy and a repertoire including many of her own songs. Though the group has maintained a multicultural repertoire and allied itself with many progressive international struggles, Grant's approach to diversity within the chorus membership differs from the course taken by Catherine Roma as director of MUSE, Cincinnati Women's Choir (see pp. 164-65).

> My feeling about this has changed over the years. From feeling like, "Oh my God! We have to recruit women of color! We have to! Or we're not legitimate!"—I moved away from that. I understand how intimidating it's gotta be for women of color to walk into the room and see 35 White women there, and me as the director, you know? They don't know me. They don't know my background, they don't know anything about me....So I don't feel like I have to legitimize *us* by trying to recruit.... I think what we're doing is legitimate.[8]

Kristina Boerger was feeling "tired [and] burned out" when she decided to move "from political activism to music activism." In 1990, she posted a flyer in downtown Champaign-Urbana that read "Creative Womyn, Take Note," inviting interested women to help form a new chorus. "I spelled womyn with a 'y,' which is a clue that lesbians should look at it.... I showed up and waited to see who else would walk through the door. I was afraid nobody would show—of course I was."'

Despite Boerger's apprehensions, a roomful of women showed up, ranging in age from twelve to fifty and varying widely in singing experience. Boerger named the chorus "Amasong: Champaign Urbana's Premier Lesbian/Feminist

Chorus," explaining, "There's lesbian-feminism with a hyphen, which refers to women who are lesbian and feminist. But if you put a diagonal slash between, then it means either/or.... It doesn't mean you have to be both to get in the choir. It means you've got to be one or the other."[9]

Not all choruses included the word "lesbian" in their title, but from the beginning, women's choruses were a safe place for lesbians, closeted or out. For many, singing in a feminist chorus was an important step on the road to becoming fully visible. A singer in the Phoenix Women's Chorus (formerly Arizona Women in Tune) recalled, "I was just coming out. I was raising my kids by myself and I had been divorced for years and I had no idea how to find lesbians anywhere ... except in bars." Just before a concert, she noticed the organist from her church sitting in the audience.

> I had not come out to her and I was sitting there and we were going to get up and sing ... I thought, "Oh, my gosh, I have to run up to her. I have to come out to them before I'm on that stage." So I went running up to her and I said, "Okay, Rose, I'm here because I'm coming—I'm out. You know, I'm lesbian or something." And she went, "Oh, that's wonderful," and gave me a big hug.[10]

Founding directors of the 1980s established Sister Singers as a network committed to social action. Cynthia Lawrence-Wallace had co-founded the San Diego LGBT Center and was a well-known anti-racism educator when she established the San Diego Women's Chorus in 1987. Catherine Roma moved from Philadelphia to Cincinnati in 1983 and soon afterwards founded MUSE, a women's chorus that has become a Sister Singers model of multiracial activism. Denver Women's Chorus founding director Carol White was inspired by a partnership with PFLAG (Parents, Families and Friends of Lesbians and Gays). In a 2014 keynote speech at the DWC's thirtieth anniversary celebration, White recalled the beginnings of the chorus. In 1967, while serving as Minister of Music in a Houston Methodist church, she was essentially fired for being gay and found myself out on the street with two worthless master's degrees, no job, no profession, no church, no money, no friends, no community, and nowhere to turn. And I sat there on that street corner forty-seven years ago, with my head in my hands, contemplating suicide and at the same time wanting desperately to do something about it.

After settling in Denver, White worked as a court reporter for thirty years. Then in 1980, she met a group of people starting a Denver chapter of PFLAG and everything changed.

I joined with them and served on the board of PFLAG here in Denver and [in 1984] the national convention of PFLAG was coming to Denver. I thought, "Wouldn't it be wonderful if we could recruit seventy women and put them together with the seventy men of the newly formed Denver Gay Men's Chorus and have a 140 voice PFLAG festival chorus to sing for that national convention?" So, I approached the PFLAG board, and they said "yes" and we were off and running.... Conducting had been my talent and my life and my reason for being before I was fired from the church for being gay. And now I was conducting again; only this time it was my own people, and we were actually singing in a choir.[11]

Living Room Singers

Not all early women's choruses were founded by directors. Some grew out of gatherings of "living room singers"—women who met to sing together for their own enjoyment and then discovered that they wanted to take their singing to the next level. A group of women who sang "in someone's living room" after a Ronnie Gilbert/Holly Near concert decided to become a chorus; after much discussion, they chose the name Columbus Women's Chorus ("it seemed like all the good names had been taken") and agreed in true feminist fashion that they "didn't want to exclude people, like the patriarchy, the general society has excluded people.... Even though we were all lesbian ... any woman who was comfortable with that, fine with us."[12] The Charlottesville Women's Choir began when a group of women responding to an ad in the local newspaper gathered at a non-profit coffee shop called The Prism. "There was an old piano there, and when I showed up there were three or four women sitting around a piano singing in harmony," recalled Estelle Philips.[13]

Windsong of Cleveland, Ohio began as the Cleveland Women's Choir, a small group that put on variety shows for a mostly-lesbian audience. Chorus member Ellen Catlin attended one of those early performances and joined the group, which sang all through the 1980s. "It was the heyday of the lesbian feminist community in Cleveland. It was a really fun time. It was vibrant. Cleveland just reflected everything that was going on all across the country with the development of women's music, the Michigan Womyn's Music Festival, you know, all that." Eventually the group decided to organize more formally. "We met in somebody's living room," recalled Ellen, "and we said, 'Okay, what are we going to call ourselves?' And somebody said, 'Windsong.' So, we said, 'Okay, that'll work.'"[14]

Other women's choruses were inspired by a particular event, a performance by another chorus, or just a desire to sing together. The Portland, Oregon, Lesbian Choir was born in 1986 when one woman posted a sign at a women's gathering stating "Lesbian Sing." The Southern Arizona Women's Chorus began in 1981 as a project for a University of Arizona graduate student; after his graduation, instead of disbanding, the group hired a director and continued singing. The DC Area Feminist Chorus (now Fortissima), started in 1978 when a group of women who had attended a Holly Near concert said, "We need to do this." Artemis Singers, the first women's singing ensemble in the U.S. to explicitly label themselves a lesbian feminist chorus, sang their first public performance at the second annual Chicago Gay/ Lesbian Community Band and Windy City Gay Chorus concert in 1980. In addition to their role as a founding chorus of Sister

Singers, Artemis was the only lesbian chorus to perform at the landmark 1982 gathering of gay and lesbian choruses in New York City, the founding event for GALA, the Gay and Lesbian Association of Choruses (discussed in the next chapter).

More Than Just a Job

Directors with academic credentials were often seeking a more collaborative environment than the university culture where they had been trained. Meredith Bowen, who directed Sistrum in Lansing, Michigan, after the departure of chorus founder Rachel Alexander, admits that she was "frustrated" at times because her choir was not interested in the music she had studied in graduate school. "I haven't been able to explore things like large works in the classical canon," she explains. "Like we can't explore Bach. We can't explore Mozart or Haydn. We don't do any of the large works; that's what I'm trained in." But for Bowen, the rewards of directing Sistrum far outweighed the challenges. "Women's choruses are special. I think it's because women like to work together. It's collaborative, the give and take that women have.... We create positive energy together."[15]

Joan Szymko, one of several director/composers in the women's chorus network, called her work with Aurora Chorus in Portland, Oregon her "education ... on progressive issues."

> I took these things to heart and I started arranging music because we sang about these issues and there was music that was going around the network but I didn't always like the arrangements or there was a specific song that someone came to music community with and said, "can we do this?" ....Even my becoming involved more with composing music was also out of necessity, out of a need to supply repertoire for this chorus.[16]

From the beginning it was clear to these directors that working with a women's chorus was more than just a job—

more, even, than just a career. Cindy Bizzell, who became director of the Common Woman Chorus in Durham, North Carolina, after singing with the chorus for several seasons, described "going through a lot of things in my own life where I was thinking about who I was and what kind of identity I had taken on and whether or not that was really me." For Cindy, as for many others, "the chorus was a great place to just feel like I didn't have to be anything that I wasn't."[17] Catherine Beller-McKenna, who had previously sung with Anna Crusis in Philadelphia, became director of Women in Harmony in Portland, Maine not long after finishing her doctorate in choral music. "I just really, really knew that this was for me," she said. "I love women's choral music. I love women's voices. I love the idea that the social justice is part of it."[18]

As part of their vision of feminist empowerment, women's choruses wanted to make their own decisions about who would direct them. The criteria for these decisions were often at odds with traditional ideas about choral directing. When the DC Area Feminist Chorus held interviews for director, they asked each applicant for her view of the conductor's role. One woman responded: "A conductor *conducts.*" Chorus member Marcia Knott recalled: "That attitude scared us. We weren't ready for that." The chorus eventually hired Deborah Weiner, a former music major who was "willing to take on the challenge of directing a chorus that was determined to make its own musical decisions."[19]

Miriam Davidson, who replaced Jackie Coren as Artistic Director of Anna Crusis, initially hesitated before assuming the role of director. Davidson had been an arranger, musician and singer, but did not see herself as a choral director. With the encouragement of her partner and the women of Anna Crusis, Davidson auditioned for the director post. "I think that was the transformative moment for me when I realized that everything that I had done kind of led me to this point," she recalled. "It was magic." Davidson described herself as "the shepherd of this incredible family of women who come together to share more than just making music together. It's a spiritual experience. It's a musically spiritual experience."[20]

While most women's choruses have chosen to work with a director, a few are self-directed. The Charlottesville Women's Choir was led by founding director Gaye Fifer for many years. After she left, the chorus established a leadership pattern with two or more people coordinating the choir and additional chorus members sharing the conducting. Estelle Phillips, who joined not long after the chorus's founding in 1984, had no musical training beyond piano lessons, but began conducting when she was offered the opportunity to direct a few pieces. "For me, conducting is very much an inner, unthinking process," she explained.

> That's the core of it that I do well and people were responding to, and then layered into that is a conscious studying of the music and practicing it in front of a mirror. But the basic ability to do it is innate—it's not a conscious process. It's just that I feel the music and it moves me and I'm able to express that in my face and my body movements such that the choir then responds to it.[21]

After working with a number of directors, Fortissima: DC's Feminist Singers (formerly the DC Feminist Chorus) also chose to be self-directed. Members of the chorus were "committed to activism and advocacy through music" and "recognized that improving as musicians and acting as trustees of the chorus are necessary to reach these goals. We are both voices raised in song and voices carrying our mission forward."[22]

Similarly, after singing with several conductors, Artemis Singers of Chicago decided to become self-directed with different choral members taking responsibility for different songs. In a statement posted on the Sister Singers web site, longtime Artemis member Midge Stocker wrote:

> Since Artemis Singers operates in an organic non-music hierarchical way, it has multiple artistic directors for any given concert and any member of the group can become an artistic director. All of the song selections are done by a consensus of the singers, and every singer has the opportunity to participate in the selection process

for every concert.... A magical thing happens when you
stand in front of a group of women. The respect I feel for
my sister singers when I'm directing them is enormous,
and some of the things I get to see/hear in them moves
me beyond words.[23]

Governance: Beyond "Seat of the Pants"

Whether they chose to work with a director or to share
directing responsibilities among themselves, choruses struggled
to sustain themselves as functioning organizations without
sacrificing feminist principles. "We don't want people telling
us what to do," Marte Parham recalled Houston's HeartSong
members saying. "We don't want to have a set of bylaws that
makes us do something we don't wanna do and if we're gonna
agree on something, here's the magic word, 'consensus.'"

Womansong of Asheville's governance was "seat of the pants,
kind of," according to director Debbie Nordeen. Eventually
the chorus developed a Wise Woman Council because "some
women have had horrible [associations with] the connotation of
the word 'board.'" Nordeen remembered "sitting in someone's
living room once in our Wise Woman Council.... She said, 'You
know, I looked at the bank account and in two months we're
gonna be broke.' And we go, 'Really, I had no idea we were gonna
be broke in two months.' So that's when we started to like get a
little more like 'Oh, well, we better be a little more organized.'"[24]

Choruses eventually realized that they needed some kind of
governance structure to manage finances, deal with publicity,
attend to the mechanics of rehearsing and performing, and
maintain a music library. Some choruses established 501(c)(3)
(non-profit) status, but others resisted becoming a legal entity.
Most choruses eventually needed to charge membership dues to
pay for rehearsal space rental and music, but many maintained
a sliding scale in keeping with a commitment to inclusiveness.
Cynthia Frank called the Mendocino Women's Choir "a 'no singer
left behind' group. If someone can't pay the dues, that's fine, we
want them to sing with us!"[25]

Unlike traditional choruses, feminist choirs also downplayed the audition process, making it as non-threatening as possible. Those that required auditions emphasized that they only required singers to match pitch; many, like Windsong Chorus of Cleveland, dispensed with auditions altogether, stating that "Membership is open to any woman who wants to find her voice and use it to speak a message through song." Fortissima: DC's Feminist Singers issued the following invitation to potential members: "No auditions, just a chance to come and meet us and see if the chorus your mother warned you about is the right place for you after all." Fortissima singer Carol Wheeler explained, "We have had people who, this is the first thing they've done and [would] be absolutely terrified to audition, stay and really enjoy themselves and relax into singing."[26]

Non-auditioned choruses connected their inclusiveness to the feminist ideal of eschewing competition in favor of collaboration. "The Aurora community of women is very much a feminist organization because it is an empowering place for women to be," said director Joan Szymko. "It's a place where they can just really be who they are…. You have to be able to hold your part and sing in tune, but there's no competitive audition in terms of how well you have to sing, you don't have to read music…. It's kind of like you can come at this from any place."[27] The Juneau Pride Chorus of Juneau, Alaska, organized as a project of Juneau PFLAG, described their audition process as follows: "We are basically not an auditioned chorus, but we do have an audition and it consists of three questions: are you supportive of gay, lesbian and bisexual issues, are you able to hold your part when the women next to you are singing a different part, and the third is, are you willing to serve on a volunteer committee because we're run by volunteers."[28]

As in every other aspect of choral organization, choruses initially approached music selection as a matter for consensus. Mary Robertson said that her choir, Soromundi of Eugene, Oregon, "started as a lesbian choir. Just a safe way to sing together" and selected their music together:

We retreat as a group in June, and listen together to fifty to eighty songs that have been submitted in advance by choir members. We consider and discuss the lyrics, the genres, the musicality, our abilities, the balance, our history, issues and politics for the coming year, or theme, and our past repertoire. From this we select a pool of about twenty songs to draw from for the next year.[29]

Similarly, Fortissima established a music committee in which "everybody who wants to, comes and brings songs. Then the song leaders will meet and divvy up the songs among themselves—who can lead what—and then we work out the rehearsal schedule as best we can."[30]

Many choruses began to add retreats to their choral schedule. A retreat offered the chance for more in-depth practice than a weekly rehearsal, as well as a chance for chorus members to strengthen their connections with one another. "It's not just more rehearsals," said Carol Wheeler of Fortissima. "The important part of that is we are cooking meals together and eating together and getting to know, especially, the new people."[31] Women in Harmony of Portland, Maine, began holding annual retreats at Camp Bishopswood, an Episcopal summer camp on the shores of Lake Megunticook in rural Maine. The three-day weekend included team building games, soprano and alto sectionals, and a Saturday night "Talent/No Talent Show" called "Femme Fire."[32]

As recently as 2008, a survey for Chorus America by Kelsey Menahan found that although many mainstream choruses had begun to provide accommodations for singers with disabilities, some still maintained rules or rehearsal spaces that effectively barred singers with crutches, wheelchairs, or other adaptations.[33] Long before the 1990 Americans With Disabilities Act became law, women's music festivals and women's chorus concerts were committed to making their rehearsal and concert spaces accessible to all singers and audience members. One chorus looking for a new rehearsal space had "a long list" of requirements:

> We needed to find a new space that was inexpensive and fully accessible and had parking and public transportation. We were quite demanding.... We were unable to find something that met all of our requirements. But some of them are non-negotiable.... We turned down a space that would have had a lot of other pros and we just couldn't do it because there was no way to use the bathroom.[34]

While mainstream choruses seldom provide sign language interpreters for their concerts, women's choral concerts and choral festivals have always been more than just singers on a stage. They have routinely included interpreters and actively welcomed members of the Deaf community. "Deaf people are a part of our society often excluded from information as well as participation by an insensitive or unknowing majority," declared two interpreters a 1985 *Hot Wire* article. "The women's music network has been developing and perfecting the use of concert interpreters for years, out of a genuine commitment to including all women who want to be a part of the evolving women's culture."[35] Sign language interpreter Kim Shaw, who identifies as hard of hearing, explained, "Seeing a performance that has an interpreter ... makes the music come alive to a degree that it does not when I'm only encountering it with my ears alone. When they have the visual element there and I really know what they're singing about, that's very powerful."[36]

Welcoming Women of Color

Though lesbian/feminist music festivals and choruses were in the forefront of deconstructing disability, building racial diversity proved more challenging. Like the mainstream women's movement and the women's music movement from which they sprang, early women's choruses were overwhelmingly White. Building choral partnerships across lines of race and ethnicity proved far more complicated—and painful—than many women anticipated. Nevertheless, identity conflicts and struggles over racism did not tear the Network apart, as happened in so many other lesbian/feminist groups in the '70s and '80s. One reason was that the Network continued to nurture partnerships with singers like Ysaye Barnwell and Bernice Johnson Reagon, coalition builders who mentored Sister Singers with honesty and love. In 1990, a meeting with Reagon inspired director Catherine Roma to begin a relationship that would help make MUSE the most racially diverse chorus in the Network and would inspire Network choruses for years to come.

The two first met in 1979 while Roma was still directing Anna Crusis in Philadelphia. "I went down to Washington, DC, and went to Dr. Bernice Johnson Reagon's house to talk about her coming up to Philadelphia to work with Anna Crusis to learn some of her music," Roma recalled. "She gave me tapes to take up from that visit to give to the choir to try and learn, because it's all from the oral tradition, and not much of it had been written down."[37]

Following this visit, Reagon came to Philadelphia to work with Anna Crusis.

> Bernice kept saying to me, "What repertoire are you singing? What kinds of repertoire are you choosing to program? And if you're an all-white choir and I come to your concert and I can hear myself even though I can't see myself but I can hear, something is happening. Then, that means something to me."[38]

When Roma moved to Cincinnati and founded MUSE, she continued her work with Reagon. In 1985 Reagon published *Compositions One*, her first book of original compositions, and soon afterward she offered to work with MUSE "to see ... if the notes on the page are really able to lift off the page."

> She came and did a workshop [Roma recalled], and worked some of the pieces that we had worked and changed them a little bit here and there.... She walked right up to people—she's short and strong and powerful ... and said, "Sing this," and she'd make a sound, and

they'd make a sound, and she'd say, "Hoooo," and she'd say, "Sing it back to me"... It was like unlocking gates of sound in people's bodies. And it was amazing.[39]

Reagon encouraged Roma to go beyond repertoire and address the racial and ethnic makeup of the chorus itself. By 1990 Roma was ready to put her commitment into action. MUSE had decided to keep its membership at forty-eight. "We didn't want to go above forty-eight because we wanted to be a community. We want to know each other and be involved in each other's lives. So, we started talking about, 'Well, how do we change ourselves? How do we attract more women of color? How do we reach out? How do we make that change?'" Since the number of singers was down to thirty-nine at that time, some members suggested that the chorus reserve seven slots for women of color. "Some people were very uncomfortable, saying, 'That's a quota system, you know, you can't do that.' And we talked about it, how do we change unless we make space? So, we figured out how we were going to reach out to different communities, different organizations."[40]

The decision to allot specific slots to women of color continued to generate controversy. "There were some people who didn't want us to do that," recalled Angie Denov, who has sung with the chorus since its founding. "I thought [it] made the most sense. You know, we would never have filled them if we got to the end of auditions and just said, 'Well, we didn't have seven people of color so we've got to fill them with someone.'"[41]

MUSE also targeted its audition announcements, sending notices to the *Cincinnati Herald*, the local African American newspaper. Soon afterward, the *Herald* published an article about MUSE and Roma joined the Martin Luther King coalition along with Gilda Turner, an African American union organizer who was one of the few women of color in the chorus at the time.

"Gilda was more connected," Roma recalled. "She was a Cincinnati person and was a member of the Union Baptist Church. She would go to black churches with her connections— she'd go to choirs, say we were going to put together a choir to sing the following year at the Martin Luther King program."[42]

Helping MUSE become more diverse did not end with merely bringing in more African American members; it meant insuring that the new members would feel at home in this mostly-White chorus.

"Cathy was a good caretaker," Angie Denov explained. "There's sort of a place where you go over the edge and now you've got enough African Americans to make them feel like they can stay. But you have to do caretaking to keep them in, especially in the beginning when you don't have very many people." Asked what she meant by caretaking, Angie went on to explain:

> Well, you know, if the policy per se says that you can't miss three rehearsals, or you can't be late, and someone in choir is having trouble in their lives, Cathy might let an African American woman who is like scraping by to make a living miss rehearsals or be late to rehearsal as long as they can do the singing when we needed them— and she wouldn't let you do that. It pissed some people off.... It's not exactly perfectly right if you were strictly going by the rules but that's what I mean by caretaking.[43]

Attracting more African American singers broadened MUSE's singing style as well as its membership. Roma speculated that the presence of African American voices encouraged chorus members "who loved to sing in their lower range. You know, nobody talks about the mature woman's voice. Voice teachers are worried that people are going to hurt their voices and stuff like that. But the experience of African American women is to use the full range of their voice and to just let it go."[44]

As part of her outreach into the African American community, Roma arranged a joint project with Pastor Todd O'Neal, director of the Ohio Unity Choir and a leading light in Cincinnati gospel music. Forty-eight MUSE members traveled on a rented bus to Marysville and Franklin Pre-release, the two women's prisons in the state of Ohio.

There was a lot of Jesus music. And I think if you know the history of the women's choral movement, there has been a decision on the part of a lot of the choristers, the singers, not to do sacred music necessarily, not to sing about Jesus and god and king and lord. There was just some visceral connection for some of the white women, the lesbians, that they were cast out of their church, that they couldn't go to church, couldn't feel comfortable there as lesbians, and that they were sinners, you know, the whole thing — so this strong, just, feeling.[45]

At this point the African American women began talking about their experiences.

What they tried to explain to the white women was that this music comes from a different place—it doesn't come from the same place as the church-going people who felt so uncomfortable and cast out—that for Back people, the church was the only place they could express themselves, the place that people could release, where they could be emotional, where they could let go, where they could shout, you know, where they could be free.[46]

The MUSE group reacted so intensely that Roma feared the choir "was going to explode, and that all the beginning work that we had done around race and around bringing people together and collaborations" would be undone. The following day, a snowstorm kept most people home, and chorus members were "calling each other, talking, talking, talking. Trying to share, trying to get through it." Ultimately, a group of eighteen singers decided to read James T. Cone's book, *The Spirituals and the Blues*, an exploration of these musical forms as cultural expressions of Black people. Eight chorus members calling themselves White Women Against Racism began meeting regularly and read another book, Judith Katz's *White Awareness*. Finally, the chorus invited two scholar activists from the University of Pennsylvania, Ellie DiLapi and

Gloria Gay, to conduct an anti-racism workshop, which proved so powerful that the chorus decided to invite them back in subsequent years.[47]

At about this time, African American chorus member Lois Shegog came to the podium during a MUSE rehearsal to conduct a piece. "It was obvious that she got a totally different sound from the choir," said Roma. "Different conductors get different sounds, because they conduct from a different place." Lois soon became MUSE's assistant conductor, and she and Cathy continued to work together to expand MUSE's reach and range.[48]

As part of the struggle to "move from being a choir that talks about diversity to becoming a diverse choir," MUSE joined the New Spirituals program in 1994, working with singers and composers to premier new works expressing traditional African American themes in a contemporary context. The initial collaboration launched a long-running collaboration with New Spirituals co-founder Linda Tillery, as well as workshops with a diverse array of guest artists, including Ethel Raim, ethnomusicologist and specialist in Balkan singing; jazz vocalist Rhiannon, a member of Bobby McFerrin's Voicestra; classical composer Kay Gardner; and Holly Near, as well as Sweet Honey in the Rock singers Bernice Johnson Reagon and Ysaye Maria Barnwell. The choir eventually documented these partnerships in a stirring video, "I Feel Like Going On: The legacy of the MUSE New Spirituals Project." As Roma points out in the introduction, Cincinnati was an appropriate place for the New Spirituals Project, for it was the Fisk Jubilee Singers' first stop on their 1871 inaugural U.S. tour.[49]

Growing the Network

Following the first National Women's Chorus Concert in 1984, organizers met to evaluate the success of the Festival and to look ahead to future Sister Singers events. In addition to organizational discussions, the Kansas City hosts read and tallied the evaluations that had come from concert attendees.

Singers had enjoyed the opportunity to exchange ideas with members of other choruses and to engage in spontaneous group singing. One woman wrote that she found the concert's location in a church to be "stifling," but most had positive responses to the festival as a whole. When asked what they liked best, one singer replied, "That it happened."[50]

Twelve choruses attended the second Festival, hosted by Madison's Womonsong in 1985. The Network continued the practice of community housing and welcomed children (including boys), for whom childcare was provided. The Festival took place over a fall weekend, with choral performances on Saturday and workshops on Sunday that included "goddess chants," "songs and sounds of birth," and "Collectivity: Process with a smile." Network founders Linda Small and Echo led a workshop called "Refocusing the Network: What does your chorus want and/ or need the Sister Singers Network to be?" suggesting that the Network was starting to think of itself as a permanent entity that would retain the collective spirit of its founding. This spirit continued at the 1986 Festival, hosted by Artemis Singers of Chicago, where Cathy Roma led a conducting workshop and Linda Small and Echo again led "Refocusing the Network." Another workshop reflected changing attitudes toward identity politics, asking participants to consider the question, "Lesbian-Feminist Choir: Is it an endangered species?"[51]

Following this Festival, planning committee member Ann Morris told *Hot Wire* writer Celia Guse, "The main exciting thing about the festival as an annual event ... is that it's perpetually a grassroots festival. It moves from city to city and has different planners each time. It's becoming an institution because it happens every year, but it's always fresh because there are new women planning it."[52]

In 1987 the Festival moved to the Hennepin Avenue United Methodist Church in Minneapolis. "We Make the Music" featured nine choruses singing individual sets and a Mass Choir with a program that reflected the growing range of the women's chorus movement. Songs included Kay Gardner's "When We Made the Music (The World Stopped to Listen)," a lyrical tribute to women's music that had been commissioned by Anna Crusis in 1977; "Shto Mie Milo," a popular Macedonian song sung in the "chest voice" Slavic music-style; "If You Love Me," a deceptively simple assertion of female independence by left-wing songwriting veteran Malvina Reynolds; and "Hasta La Victoria Siempre," a song celebrating indigenous Latin American women's resistance by Argentine singer-songwriter Suni Paz. The program book featured a statement of solidarity with the National March on Washington for Gay and Lesbian Rights (held the same weekend as the Festival and discussed more fully in Chapter 8) and a statement of support for the Las Madres of Minnesota Quilt Project, whose quilt honoring the women of Central America hung in the church lobby during the Festival. The program book also featured a restaurant and shopping guide to nearby Minneapolis and a listing of local points of interest, along with ads from local gay and gay-friendly businesses. Sister Singers Network was reaching out to the wider world, singing songs in diverse languages from diverse cultures, and beginning to partner with the gay community as well as other progressive groups.[53]

By this time, Sister Singers had grown to a Network of thirty-five choruses and twenty composer-arrangers. Administration now required more formal organization, and choruses were beginning to advocate for progressive causes beyond the lesbian community. In the summer of 1988, Linda Small and Echo invited member choruses to send representatives to an Autumn Evaluation—"a policy setting gathering of the Sister Singers Network and the National Women's Choral Festival" —to discuss possible membership in the newly founded GALA Choruses; relations between Sister Singers Network and the National Women's Choral Festival (which were still separate entities at this point); the benefits and drawbacks of becoming a 501(c)(3) (tax exempt) organization; and other questions related to organization and governance. That fall, women from ten choruses attended a reorganization meeting that voted to allow Sister Singers to continue as "an independent network of women's choral singers" with the National Choral Festival as one of its functions. Meeting representatives also decided to continue publishing a directory of choirs, to publish a newsletter, and to hold the next choral Festival in Kansas City in October, 1989. Much discussion took place about the kind of governance structure the Network would implement. "We don't need to reinvent this current group over and over," representatives declared in the Proceedings sent to the membership. "Some seem to want more universality in [the] group; others favor a smaller group that takes action, then consults with all the choruses." Participants came up with diagrams of three different governance models, which they titled "Hierarchy," "Matrix," and "Anarchy." In the end, they opted for "Matrix," which was represented by a circle linked to other surrounding circles. The central circle was to be the "hub—a switchboard type of function [that] takes incoming mail and sends it to the proper circle." The surrounding circles represented "people doing different tasks," including one circle with chorus representatives. Decisions were to be made by "people in little circles," including chorus representatives, who would meet periodically to make Network decisions by consensus.[54]

The 1989 Festival reflected the growth and greater complexity of the Network following the reorganization. Two hundred and fifty women from sixteen different choirs met at the Folly Theatre, a newly renovated Kansas City landmark. Pam Whiting, a local radio and TV personality, served as mistress of ceremonies, and a women's post-concert dance was held at the Americana Hotel. An article in the *Kansas City View* featured the Festival and quoted Lois Reborne, a KCWC founding member. "We're very excited about the festival being at the Folly. It's fun to have that legitimate space and all that room to move," she said, recalling the 1984 festival, also in Kansas City, when the choruses sang in a cramped church.[55]

"The Magic Music Makes," hosted by Houston's HeartSong, in 1991, was the first Sister Singers Festival held outside the Midwest and the first to feature a three-day format. For this Festival, which included fourteen choruses from ten states, organizers hired a professional producer and included both a public performance and a private concert for registrants only. An article in the *Houston Chronicle* about HeartSong described the chorus, quoted the director and several singers, and promoted the upcoming concert—all without ever mentioning the lesbian culture that was an integral part of the chorus's identity. Feminist choruses were making their way into the mainstream media—but invisibility still prevailed.[56]

In 1993, MUSE hosted the Sister Singers Seventh National Women's Choral Festival, with workshops by many of the New Spirituals collaborators, and a mass chorus with 300 participants from twenty choirs, including choruses from Vancouver and Ottawa and the Pre-Madonnas, a trio from London's feminist choir. Workshops at this Festival included "Looking at Our Racism," a panel on diversity, and meetings for the women of color, Jewish women, and lesbian teachers, along with the usual sessions on maintaining vocal health, choral directing, singing in harmony, and consensus building. Melanie DeMore, a founding member of Linda Tillery's Cultural Heritage Choir, who served as MC for the final performance, told participants, "The power to make music and to sing is a grand and miraculous one. It changes things. It changes the way the air looks. It changes the road."[57]

Inclusion and Diversity: New Challenges

The 1993 Festival showed that the Network was beginning to address issues of racism and inclusion. However, subsequent issues of the Network newsletter, *Across the Lines*, suggested that there was still a long way to go. In an article published shortly after the Festival, Ysaye Barnwell, who had presented a workshop, asked, "Why is the Network So White?" and answered her own question: "Most Women of Color would find little that was familiar, welcoming, appealing, empowering, or satisfying about being part of this network. Individual Women of Color would find little sense of self or affirmation of themselves as Women of Color and might not identify with being feminist or lesbian." She pointed out that Women of Color choirs and ensembles "are most often found in church-related contexts and sometimes have male accompanists or directors"—

arrangements that were problematic for many White lesbians. Barnwell ended her letter asking, "Are we to teach each other? and if so, how shall we teach each other? To what end?"[58]

In the same newsletter, Rochester Women's Community Chorus founding director Debbie Wachspress wondered:

> How did it happen that such passionate and talented women from throughout North America sang songs of gay pride, injustices, and struggle, but neglected to include our beautiful, strong sisters of color? We saw Ysaye Barnwell, Melanie DeMore, Linda Thomas Jones, Jacqueline Rago (all Women of Color). We made wonderful music with them. Why is it that we do not allow all of our sisters to join our individual chorus families? Why aren't our sisters of Color choosing to join our choral families?[59]

In response to these concerns, the Spring, 1994 newsletter announced the formation of a Women of Color caucus, a Jewish Women's support group, a disability caucus and an ASL interpreters caucus. A year later, however, the newsletter acknowledged, "The caucuses that were started at last year's planning meeting have not developed as hoped."[60] In February, 1996, participants at a Network planning meeting voted to continue supporting caucuses and urged chorus members to "nurture diversity in your life and nurture diversity in your chorus. Think of one thing that you could help change to make your chorus an open friendly place for a woman who is not of the dominant culture and then do it."[61] As subsequent history would show, making choruses more inclusive proved far more complicated—and painful—than many women anticipated. The coming decades would find Network members facing new challenges and building new coalitions while continuing to pursue the vision embodied in Linda Small's original guidelines—a vision of respect, inclusion, and the primary worth of women's lives that made singing together a force for transforming singers, audiences, and the wider world.

Part III

"A World Where All Voices Are Free"

7

From Separatism to Solidarity

While Sister Singers was growing from a mailing list to a network with a steering committee and a series of national festivals, gay men were organizing their own choruses, beginning in 1978 with the San Francisco Gay Men's Chorus, the first American choral group to include the word "gay" in its name. Earlier that year, the Briggs Initiative, seeking to ban gays and lesbians from working in California's public schools, had made California the epicenter of a national anti-gay backlash (see Chapter 4).

Among those in the forefront of the opposition was newly elected San Francisco Supervisor Harvey Milk, the first openly gay elected official in the U.S., whose election as an openly gay activist galvanized lesbians and gay men around the country.[1] One of those whom Milk inspired was Jon Sims, a high school band teacher who had come to San Francisco from Smith Center, Kansas. After hearing Milk deliver his famous "Give 'em hope" speech, urging lesbians and gays to come out of the closet, Sims formed the Gay Freedom Day Marching Band and Twirling Corps (now the San Francisco Lesbian/Gay Freedom Band), the first openly-gay musical group in United States history. That same year, Sims founded the San Francisco Gay Men's Chorus and on Oct. 30, 1978, the chorus held its first rehearsal.

Less than a month later, on November 27, Harvey Milk and Mayor George Moscone were assassinated by Supervisor Dan White. More than thirty years afterwards, Robert Rufo, one of the original members of the San Francisco Gay Men's Chorus, recalled the events of that day:

175

We'd only had about three rehearsals and ... my partner and I had heard that there was going to be a candlelight march, so we decided to go to that. And 3,000 people showed up for that march. We marched down Market Street in the Castro to the Civic Center. And when we got there, there were a lot of people there—a lot of anger, a lot of sadness, a lot of—what do we do now? I mean, you know, we had worked so hard to get Harvey Milk elected, and it was all taken away from us.

I had trouble finding the chorus, but I found them, and they passed out some sheets of music, [Mendelssohn's] "Thou Lord, Our Refuge," and we very quickly sang this song, and my thought was, the only way I could get through this was, thinking, "You gotta help these people with their sorrow. Maybe we can sing this song and give them some solace." So that's what we did, and it was over very quickly and many of us just slowly walked back to the Castro. We were so distraught and upset that evening, it's like, Harvey's gone, he's not gonna be replaced. I think in our own way we all became Harvey Milks. We wanted to continue his message. The chorus has always given a lot of hope to a lot of people. Within three years we were doing a national tour—nine cities in two weeks. Giving a lot of hope to people in all those cities.[2]

During the next five years, gay men's choruses sprang up in cities from Los Angeles to Boston. The New York City Gay Men's Chorus was only one year old in 1980 when they were invited to sing at a memorial service for two men killed in a drive-by shooting in front of two Greenwich Village gay bars. One year later, they became the first openly gay musical organization to perform at Carnegie Hall. By 1983, gay men's choruses had formed in Chicago; Dallas; Denver; Seattle; Portland, OR; Houston; Madison, WI; and other cities across the country. The Stonewall Chorale, based in New York City, became the first lesbian and gay chorus in the country in 1979, when women were invited to join the Gotham Male Chorus.

Coming Together: The Birth of GALA

In 1982, twelve choruses met in Chicago to plan a choral festival to be held in conjunction with the first Gay Games, a brainchild of former Olympic athlete Dr. Tom Waddell. Waddell conceived the Games as a means "to discover more about the process of our sexual liberation and apply it meaningfully to other forms of liberation"—a mission in perfect harmony with the goals of the growing gay chorus movement. That summer fourteen choruses performed at the West Coast Choral Festival, held in conjunction with the Games, and soon afterwards they founded GALA, the Gay and Lesbian Association of Choruses.[3]

The following year, the New York City Gay Men's Chorus organized COAST (Come Out and Sing Together), a choral festival featuring eleven gay men's choruses along with Artemis Singers, Chicago's lesbian chorus. In a generally positive review, *New York Times* music critic Edward Rothstein called the culminating concert at Avery Fisher Hall "an event that was at once political, ethnic, sexual and cultural" and wrote that "the very idea of a homosexual chorus is partly political, with singers being brought together ... partly as a demonstrative statement of open identification.... Even before the music began, the sight of 750 singers on stage caused the audience to stand and cheer."[4] As the first public concert by openly gay choruses, COAST was a landmark event. It was also the first time gay and lesbian choruses shared the stage.

GALA would eventually grow to include a significant number of women's choruses as well as mixed LGBT choruses, trans choruses and youth choruses, but it would be several years before lesbians and gay men came together in a unified movement. Meanwhile, many women's choruses were still preoccupied with questions of identity. When she founded Resonance in Boulder, Colorado, Sue Coffee wanted lesbian identity to be

> ... a non-issue—but it has to be an articulated non-issue instead of an invisible non-issue. There's a big difference. I give "the lesbian speech" every year, which we all agree is funny but helpfully straightforward: "This is a women's chorus, and there are a lot of lesbians in the chorus..."

That's the nutshell, and then there's a bit of elaboration ...which informs the culture, the humor, the messages, and the kinds of outreach we do.... Singers need to be fine with that or this wouldn't be the right chorus for them. I read once that choruses can be models for the kind of society we want to live in, and honestly, as the founding director, I need this chorus to be a community where I— and everyone—can feel authentic.... I also talk about the roots of the chorus in the GLBTQ choral movement and the women's music community, and tell the singers that we didn't invent ourselves. We wouldn't exist as this community-rich, intentional, relevant chorus without the inspiration of the GALA and Sister Singers networks and the singer-songwriters and festivals of the women's music movement. I think that's very important for the singers to understand, and it honors the lesbian roots while allowing us to define ourselves together in this moment, and to evolve organically.[5]

Betsy Parsons, who sang with Portland, Maine's Women in Harmony long enough to experience the chorus's evolution from lesbian-identified to woman-identified, agreed on the importance of recognizing the chorus's lesbian roots:

My contention is that until we as a chorus claim the lesbian part of our history, which we were never able to claim because of safety reasons at the time, until we're self-loving enough and proud enough to claim the lesbian part of our history and the contributions of lesbians to this wonderful group and make that a permanent part of the historical records and a part of what everybody knows about us, then we haven't in my view done an important developmental task that we need to do as a group.[6]

Identity: Lesbian and Feminist, Men and Women

The increasing presence of women's choruses in GALA presented an additional question: to join or not to join? Naomi Weinert, a longtime member of the Columbus Women's Chorus, explained why her chorus had decided to limit their wider choral affiliation to Sister Singers.

> The chorus provides a place to be musical but to perform music that has meaning, that has a purpose. And many of the Sister Singers choruses are also members of GALA. We've had a discussion many times, should we also belong to GALA. And that goes back to our founding again. We describe ourselves, we think of ourselves as a feminist chorus. We do not think of ourselves as a lesbian chorus.[7]

For Cathy Roma and MUSE, lesbian identity did not become a major issue until 1993, when Citizens for Community Values put forth a ballot referendum to remove gays and lesbians from the Cincinnati Human Rights Ordinance. "So, it went to a public vote," Roma recalled, "and the public vote said, by 68 percent, take that little clause out of the human rights ordinance. In fact, let's go further and let's say that it's legal to discriminate in housing and in employment if you're gay or lesbian in Cincinnati."[8]

The passage of Article 12 propelled Cincinnati's lesbian and gay community into the limelight and suddenly brought the issue of lesbian identity to the forefront of MUSE.

> That was the beginning of building more solidarity around that diversity because people saw—"Oh my God, this is real? This is really happening?" ....Husbands were dealing with people who said, "Your wife sings in that group — is she a lesbian?" ....Straight women totally became more aware of what it was like to be a lesbian person, and then the husbands who were married to the straight women in the choir, they had a whole education.[9]

Article 12 remained in force until 2006, when the City Council repealed it and added protection for transgender people. But despite the general move from separatism to inclusion, lesbian identity politics could still threaten the harmony of a women's chorus. In the late 1990s, one chorus experienced an identity crisis that threatened to destroy it entirely. The chorus had its origins in a lesbian discussion group that organized and hired a director in the early 1990s, after meeting in a member's living room for several years. Although the chorus did not use the word "lesbian" in its name, one of the singers who joined a few years later described it as "the women's chorus with a wink."

By the mid-90s, the chorus was seeking to expand its membership and some singers suggested more outreach to straight women. A lesbian who was then chairing the board recalled meetings in which "there were some very blatant discussions about how we really didn't want straight women in our chorus ... and [the director] was really pushing that agenda.... I was surprised," she added. "I was disappointed, and I didn't feel comfortable the way we were treating people in the chorus. I felt like as a group of women, we had that opportunity to treat everyone the same."

One of the other board members was a straight woman who was feeling increasingly marginalized. For weeks, she endured criticisms from the director that included accusations of "politicking" outside rehearsal and attacks on her singing (despite the fact that she was a trained singer who had been chosen for several solos). Finally, one night she walked out in the middle of a rehearsal. "For the very first time in my life I couldn't sing," she recalled. "Music had nothing for me because I put my faith in all of this and I was stripped entirely.... So I dropped right off of the chorus. And I took the rest of that semester off."

Finding herself faced with a chorus whose loyalties were now sharply divided, the director resigned and left to start another chorus. Nearly half of the chorus went with her; the singers who remained wondered how they could continue. One of the women who stayed recalled a meeting where the remaining members tried to decide whether they would remain a chorus. "[Would] we still sing? Would we just become a women's group that does, like, community service for women's concerns? It felt to me as if the weight was shifting toward no longer singing.... So I went to the center of the circle to say, 'We sing. That's who we are. That's what we're here for. That's personally what I'm on the planet for'.... Somehow that notion became like the defining new starting point."

Eventually, the chorus reconstituted itself with a new director and a new accompanist. Some of the members who had left decided to return, including the straight woman who had been the director's prime target. "Our very first concert," she recalled, "we walked into the church and the first song we sang was 'How Can I Keep From Singing'—and it was almost as if we were taking it over again.... We took it back, we took the church back, we took the chorus back, and with that, we were back."

Few women's choruses endured the extreme fragmentation described in this story. However, even as they built alliances between lesbian and straight singers, women's choruses remained fairly separate from their gay male counterparts. Sue Coffee, who directed the Denver Gay Men's Chorus before founding Resonance Women's Chorus, noted a number of cultural differences between the two, but went on to explain:

> I enjoyed the cultural anthropology of moving between the choruses. It was something I never imagined I'd experience. I loved conducting the men and I learned a ton from them. The men were easier in ways, which kept surprising me, until I got the feel of it. They were happier to be told what to do: "Just tell us what to wear," while performance clothing is often an eye-rollingly huge topic of discussion in a women's chorus. And on the other hand, the women will generally go deeper with me, eager to chew together on texts and concert themes. When I started with the gay men's chorus, I was struck by how much they laughed. Maybe other women laugh that much, but I don't think I did. That really changed me in life and in music. I realized that laughter is a crucial element of a good chorus rehearsal. But I also found that it was a double-edged sword, that humor sometimes short-circuited a moment of vulnerability.

Her experience directing the men's chorus gave Sue particular insight into the complex nuances of gender and race.

> I got an insider experience that was incredibly interesting—this is what it feels like to be a male in this society. I saw white gay men having a weirdly entangled experience, in which they were aware of ways they were oppressed because they were gay, but they were blind to ways they had privilege as men, and of course especially as white men. Women are more readily inclined to identify in coalition with others.

> I loved the differing energies between the men's and women's choruses, the way I could feel that in my hands as a conductor, so nuanced and beautiful, even more so because of the variety of sexual and gender orientations in the mix of these groups. I learned that "'gender energy" was an aesthetic element. There are different programming opportunities with each kind of chorus, and I loved moving between them. There are topics that people are perhaps used to hearing about from women, so the aesthetic arrest of some messages in a choral context is sometimes greater when it comes from a men's chorus.[10]

Tim Seelig, who has directed both men's and women's choruses—as founding director of the Turtle Creek Chorale, co-founder of the Women's Chorus of Dallas, and most recently, Artistic Director of the San Francisco Gay Men's Chorus—agreed about the many differences between the culture of women's and men's choruses, especially in the early days. Seelig noted that while women's choruses were often focused on issues of specific concern to women, such as violence against women and reproductive rights, gay men's choruses were "most often about being gay and singing."[11]

"We Were Kind of In It Together"

All of that changed in 1981 when the *New York Times* reported that doctors had diagnosed forty-one cases of "a rare and often rapidly fatal form of cancer among homosexual men" in the New York and San Francisco Bay areas.[12] During the next ten years, over 150,000 Americans, more than half of them gay men, would die of AIDS—more than twice as many people as died in the Viet Nam War.[13]

The early years of the epidemic were devastating to gay men's choruses. Tim Seelig, who was then directing the Turtle Creek Chorale, recalled the 1980s as a time when "we were singing for memorial services constantly, both of members and of people who were not members that just wanted some gay people to sing at a memorial service.... I can tell you that even with the Turtle Creek Chorale, with 250 members, there were many times when it got so bad I thought we're not going to have a choir left."[14] The Portland, Oregon, Gay Men's Choir, which grew to 150 members by 2015, lost 140 members over the years, many of whom kept singing as their health declined.[15]

The San Francisco Gay Men's Chorus (SFGMC) began a list called "The Fifth Section," which included the name of every chorus member who had died of AIDS and is still published in every SFGMC program; by 2012, the Fifth Section consisted of more than 300 SFGMC members. Gary Miller, one of the founders of the New York City Gay Men's Chorus, recalled that during the height of the epidemic, "From where I was standing, as conductor, half of the bass section was decimated. There was a weekend I'll never forget. We did three memorial services in two days. Two Saturday, one Sunday."[16]

The AIDS epidemic changed the culture of the gay male community and of gay men's choruses, from pure celebration to survival and support. In the face of government inaction and societal homophobia, gay men turned to one another and gay choruses became the only place for members to talk openly about the disease. Concert programs began to include AIDS requiems and chorus members "serenaded friends through their last breaths."[17]

Meanwhile, lesbian separatists, including those in women's choruses, watched as the medical establishment and the government turned their backs on the suffering of gay men and recognized a common enemy in the societal homophobia that stigmatized their gay brothers afflicted with the disease. In 2015, the on-line publication *Gay Star News* posted the results of a Reddit survey inviting survivors of the AIDS crisis to share their memories of the 1980s and early '90s. One contributor wrote:

> Lesbians who came to the aid of gay men at that time would be acknowledged as every bit as heroic as soldiers on the front lines of any war. When the AIDS crisis struck, it would be many of these same women who would go straight from their jobs during the day to acting as caregivers at night. They provided aid, comfort, and medical care to men withering away in hospices, men who'd already lost their lovers and friends to the disease and spent their last months in agony. They'd been abandoned by their own families, and were it not for lesbians—many if not most of them volunteers— they would have suffered alone.[18]

Among the lesbian choruses responding to the epidemic was HeartSong in Houston, Texas, the chorus that had hosted the 1991 Sister Singers festival. Houston, with a population of nearly two million, had recorded more than 3,000 AIDS cases by 1990, ranking it fourth among the nation's cities.[19] Five years earlier, in 1985, Mayor Louis Welch was running for re-election against progressive Kathy Whitmire. Welch was about to deliver a TV campaign speech describing the points of his plan to fight the epidemic when, unaware that the cameras were rolling, he remarked, "One of them is to shoot the queers." An estimated 146,000 people heard his comment, but the interview continued as if nothing had happened and Welch's campaign raised almost $70,000 in one day, although Whitmire ended up winning the election.[20]

It was against this background that the women of HeartSong turned their attention to the men dying of AIDS in Houston's hospitals and hospices. HeartSong had begun as an informal group of friends who regularly sang at an AIDS hospice and at the AIDS wing of a local hospital, and several founders were nurses who witnessed the physical and emotional ravages of the disease first hand.

"I was an ICU nurse when all this started," one singer recalled. "I remember our first patient that came and was in isolation; nobody wanted to go touch him... [One night] he was having a really hard time, and he was crying, his parents were fundamentalists. So, I crawled in bed with him—and just held him. I sang to him. I sang lullabies to him in fact. The music. It just broke the spell of the awfulness and the grief." Another chorus member who lived through those days said, "I think that the fact that HeartSong started at the same time that the AIDS epidemic was really heavy in this city, that that in some way had a community feeling. It was the lesbians that took care of the gay men that were dying then. Because there was such strife and hatefulness against the gay community then, as well as, you know, we were kind of in it together."[21]

Many other women's choruses confronted the epidemic. Artemis joined the Windy City Gay Chorus, the Chicago Gay Men's Chorus, the Chicago Gay and Lesbian Chorus, and the Chicago Children's Choir in "A Show of Concern: America Responds," a 1987 AIDS benefit billed as "one of the most star-studded live programs in the city's history." In Minnesota, Paul Petrella, a member of the Twin Cities Gay Men's Chorus, founded One Voice Mixed Chorus, bringing lesbians and gay men together in the face of the epidemic. "There was a time at least in the Twin Cities where the men and women's community were very, very separate," recalled Jane Ramseyer Miller, One Voice's current Artistic Director. "But as men and women came together working with and caring for people with AIDS and HIV, it really brought this community together. Paul Petrella decided that he wanted to create a chorus of men and women and a place where gay men and lesbians could gather and be community and family for each other, and that's where it began in 1988."[22] Other women's choruses began singing at AIDS hospices, partnering with AIDS support organizations, and performing at yearly observances of World AIDS day, held every December 1 since 1988.

Morality Politics and LGBT Resistance

Even before the AIDS crisis became national news, the movement for LGBT rights, which had begun with the Stonewall uprising ten years earlier, was facing serious challenges. Ronald Reagan's election to the presidency in 1980 and re-election in 1984 signaled a sharp turn to the right for American politics. Among those supporting the Reagan agenda were the expanding networks of the New Right, which mobilized technology and mass telecommunications to spread the message that homosexuality was a crime against God and that women belonged in the home and religion in the schools. This resurgence of *Kinder, Kirche, Küche* was led by Pat Robertson, whose Christian Broadcasting Network became the CBN Cable Network in 1981; Jim and Tammy Faye Baker, founders of the PTL (Praise the Lord) network (and later jailed for embezzlement); and Jerry Falwell, founder of the Moral Majority, who mobilized a national campaign against gay rights and the Equal Rights Amendment. In 1986, the Supreme Court ruled in *Bowers v. Hardwick* that private same-sex acts were not protected by law, agreeing with Georgia's attorney general Michael Bowers that "the very act of homosexual sodomy ... epitomizes moral delinquency."[23]

In 1988, Oregon voters approved Measure 8, an initiative sponsored by the Oregon Citizens Alliance. It repealed an existing executive order that had banned discrimination based on sexual orientation in the executive branch of state government and prohibited any job protection for gay people in state government. Four years later, the OCA sponsored ballot Measure 9, a broad initiative that would have eliminated all future and existing gay rights legislation, prohibited government promotion of homosexuality, and equated homosexuality with sadomasochism and pedophilia. Ballot measure 9 failed at the ballot box, 56-44%, but that same year, Colorado voters approved Amendment 2, denying any legal protection to gay, lesbian or bisexual people and repealing anti-discrimination laws that had already been enacted in Denver, Boulder and Aspen. Amendment 2 would not be overturned until 1996, when the U.S. Supreme Court ruled it unconstitutional in *Romer v. Evans.*[24]

The AIDS crisis gave anti-gay activists a platform for what Kenneth J. Meier and Donald P. Haider-Markel have called morality politics—the framing of ballot questions and other political initiatives in moral terms.[25] Opponents of gay rights had already begun to describe their actions as a moral crusade. "The thing that pushed me to be involved is, our culture was degenerating morally," said OCA founder Lon Mabon. "There's a lot of people who are deeply concerned about us as a society accepting homosexuality as a good and normal thing."[26]

As public awareness of the epidemic grew, anti-gay activists seized on public fears by portraying AIDS as the "gay plague" and conflating homosexuality and AIDS in new campaigns against gay civil rights. In California, four AIDS-related ballot initiatives appeared on the ballot in the 1980s, three of which were sponsored by long-time anti-gay activists. Proposition 64, sponsored by Lyndon LaRouche in 1986, would have made people with HIV/AIDS subject to quarantine by public health directors. It was successfully opposed by a coalition of gay rights, medical, and civil rights organizations, along with high profile politicians from both parties. Proposition 69, sponsored by LaRouche followers, appeared on the June 1988 ballot and would have made it possible for public health directors to quarantine persons with HIV/AIDS. This initiative too was defeated, by a strong 68-32 percent margin. The third initiative, Proposition 96, now called the Communicable Diseases Test Act, was the only one to pass and remains on the books to this day: it permits the testing of persons arrested for sex crimes and persons who may have exposed emergency workers to HIV. Proposition 96 probably succeeded because the civil rights community was devoting its full attention to defeating Proposition 102, which would have required physicians to report the names of persons testing positive for HIV/AIDS to government officials and would have enabled insurance companies and employers to deny insurance eligibility or employment based on HIV status. Proposition 102 was defeated in every California county; even Surgeon General Everett Koop spoke out against it.[27]

The combined backlash against gay and lesbian rights and AIDS galvanized the lesbian and gay community and made the 1980s and 1990s a time of renewed activism. Two events in particular spurred a massive 1987 March on Washington with the slogan, "For love and for life, we're not going back!" The first was the previous year's *Bowers* decision criminalizing consensual same sex relationships; the second was the Reagan administration's continuing silence in the face of the mounting AIDS crisis. Reagan's communications director, Pat Buchanan, called AIDS "nature's revenge on gay men" and Jerry Falwell said the disease was "not just God's punishment for homosexuals, it is God's punishment for the society that tolerates homosexuals."[28]

Half a million people joined the March on October 11, 1987, a date which eventually became National Coming Out Day. Among the other outcomes was the founding of ACT Up, the AIDS Coalition to Unleash Power, under the leadership of Larry Kramer.[29]

Although lesbians participated in the 1987 March, lesbian identity was generally subsumed under the heading of "gay." Neither the media nor the official March program paid much attention to lesbian oppression or to recent lesbian activism. Neither mentioned such important events as Audre Lorde's 1983 speech representing Third World lesbians and gay men at the twentieth anniversary celebration of Martin Luther King's March on Washington, nor the re-naming of the National Gay Task Force as the National Gay and Lesbian Task Force.[30] Historian Jean Balestery suggests that "this seemingly ideological erasure of lesbians in the 1987 March must be put in perspective with regard to the devastating, catastrophic AIDS crisis."[31]

Yet, as the survivor testimonies quoted above and the stories of HeartSong, Artemis, and other women's choruses clearly show, lesbians were in the forefront of the response to AIDS, both as activists and as caretakers. And as the AIDS crisis intensified during the 1980s and 1990s, GALA became an increasingly important place for lesbian and gay choral collaboration. In

1985 the GALA Board established a special fund to help women's chorus leaders attend its Leadership Conference in Washington, DC. Two years later, the Denver Women's Chorus became the first women's chorus to perform at a GALA Choruses Festival, singing alongside sixteen men's choruses. By 1995, women's choruses had become a regular fixture at GALA, and Sunny Hall, Artistic Director of Crescendo Women's Chorus, announced in the Sister Singers newsletter that the festival steering committee had added an additional concert slot to the festival schedule, "Women Celebrating Women Festival V," to "allow the women of GALA, SSN, and Tampa Bay [site of the Festival and home of Crescendo] to experience the expanding diversity that is women's choral music."[32]

The 1988 Sister Singers Autumn Evaluation (discussed in the preceding chapter) had included extensive discussions of what role, if any, Sister Singers choruses should play in GALA. Participants were invited to consider how the Sister Singers Network and GALA were similar and/or different; whether Sister Singers should become "a separate organization under GALA as an umbrella agency"; or whether the Network should continue to function as an entirely separate organization, with women's choruses choosing whether or not to join GALA. The Proceedings of the meeting, which ran to ten single-spaced typewritten pages, began with a section titled "Policy/Procedure Decisions" and stated choral representatives' feelings in no uncertain terms:

> Sister Singers Network shall continue as in independent network of women's choral groups. The National Women's Choral Festival shall continue and shall be a function of Sister Singers Network.
>
> Discussion: DO WE NEED A SEPARATE WOMEN'S NETWORK? (as opposed to a mixed network or being a sub-network of another network)
>
> CONSENSUS: Y E S ! ![33]

Although Sister Singers would remain independent, a growing number of women's choruses joined GALA during the 1990s. For many women's choruses, singing under joint auspices reflected the growing shift from separatism to solidarity; at the same time, the encounter between gay men's choruses and women's choruses often prompted a recognition of the differences between the two chorus cultures. Longtime members of the Denver Women's Chorus remembered their first encounter with GALA at a time when "the communities were completely separate and isolated. They didn't support each other, they didn't do each other's stuff.... We were separate and fine with that." But like many other choruses, DWC members remembered the AIDS crisis as the catalyst that brought the two choral communities together. "It was incredible to be part of GALA and watch this whole thing move through the choruses. Because what I saw was I think the men were—the men's choruses were pretty competitive, you know.... And then this hit. It was almost a growing up factor. To grow up, let the competition go. Because we [didn't] have energy to put against at this point. We [had] to pull together."[34]

In 1991, the New York City Gay Men's Chorus invited the Denver Women's Chorus to join them in a Pride concert at New York's Alice Tully Hall at Lincoln Center. Women who sang in that concert had warm memories of their reception by the men's chorus.

> The men opened their hearts up.... When we got there we found out that they'd had a meeting to talk over how do you talk to lesbians. How do you not offend women? Isn't it sweet? It was sweet! But it indicates to me we were very separatist. It was men, it was women, and there was really radical separation there. And when we went to New York there was a really coming together. We were made to feel very welcome. We were treated royally.[35]

An account in the NYCGMC twenty-fifth Anniversary Journal stated, "In the words of Holly Near, the two ensembles declared themselves 'brothers and sisters working together to make things right,'" and added that the DWC's performance of "The Ones Who Aren't Here," was "movingly offered to recall the community's losses."[36] This poignant song, dedicated to "all the lovers and friends kept from gathering," was originally written by John Calvi as a tribute to lesbians and gay men imprisoned by the closet and was performed by Meg Christian and Cris Williamson at their celebrated Carnegie Hall concert in 1982.[37] Its evolution into a lament for those lost to AIDS and frequently sung at AIDS memorials, suggests the journey that the two communities themselves had taken by the late 1980s.

Coalitions and Controversy

As more women's choruses joined GALA, the choral bonds between the lesbian and gay communities continued to strengthen. In 1990, Robbie Reasoner, a member of Calliope, described her chorus's experience at the 1989 GALA Festival in Seattle. "Calliope was privileged to hear women from Denver, Cincinnati, San Francisco, San Diego, Tacoma, Seattle, Portland [Oregon], and Los Angeles," she wrote. "We'd never had the opportunity to hear most of these choruses. GALA gave us a place to see and be seen by people from all over the United States and Canada." Reasoner went on to ask, "Was it worth it? Yes, Yes, and YES! ....The experience of being in one place with 2,500 other singers was too incredible for words.... The community feelings among the women and men at GALA sank into my heart and are still there today."[38]

A member of the Denver Women's Chorus recalled a similar sense of community at the 1992 GALA Festival in Denver, when "the Amendment 2 stuff was going down, and it was really horrible. And I saw the Denver choruses really pulled together. The men's chorus, the women's chorus specifically. I watched them and their performances and how they interacted with each other, and how they came together.... And I remember thinking to myself, 'That's the start of something new!'"[39]

These comments suggest that despite their differences, lesbian/
feminists and gay men were realizing that what connected them was
stronger than what separated them. Yet conflicts still arose, reminders
that differences between the two choral groups could still be divisive.
In 1992, the quincentenary of Columbus's arrival in North America,
members of Calliope participated in the same GALA Festival where
the Denver Women's Chorus experienced such a strong sense of
unity. Amid the usual veneration of Columbus, Sarah Henderson, a
founding member of Calliope, attended a concert by the Columbus
Gay Men's Chorus with the rest of her chorus.

> Being from Columbus, they sang a cute little ditty about
> the people arriving on the New World shores and it was
> gonna be real cute and very campy and stuff and Carol,
> our Native American member, heard the introduction to
> the song and walked out, and the rest of us sat there and
> listened to it, and I remember a line (*high pitched voice*),
> "The Indians look menacing!!" ....The song ended and
> the huge audience was erupting in great applause ... and
> there we were, in this one little section, taking up three
> rows right at the front, not applauding. Sitting very still
> with our hands in our laps not applauding.[40]

The Calliope singers held a meeting to decide what to do next.
Three members drafted a statement that one of the singers read
when Calliope took the stage to perform their set. "Basically [it]
said ...we've seen other examples, we ask everybody to join us
in the struggle to overcome the isms. And we didn't mention the
chorus by name, but people knew who it was, a lot of people
knew who it was."[41]

The Calliope statement drew an immediate reaction from
the audience:

> We did another song and then out of the big dark
> audience out there somebody yelled between songs,
> "Calliope your music's beautiful, but your politics suck!"
> and somebody else said, "Shut up," and somebody else
> said "But he's right"— and so there was some stuff going

on in the audience.... The previous GALA we'd gone to had been in Seattle in '89, and we'd been sorta darlings there. So, to come and sing our darling songs and then make this political statement, and the gay men's chorus movement was much more into being campy and social and not political, and certainly not political beyond gay rights. Not connecting with all the other issues that need to be dealt with.[42]

The next morning, a Calliope representative attended the GALA chorus representatives meeting. "It was packed to the gills," Sarah remembered, "and the topic of 'what Calliope did' came up and there were people who thought we should be kicked out of GALA. Well the nerve of us, criticizing another chorus. And I think some people would have liked to literally kick us. They were just furious." But not all the representatives at the meeting were hostile. "Eventually some people were saying, 'These issues need to be addressed,' and finally one guy from the Columbus Gay Men's Chorus said, 'Yeah, these issues need to be addressed, and while it's embarrassing to be singled out, you need a specific example, and if that happens to be my chorus, well, let it be, but let the discussions begin.'" Most important to Calliope was the sense of solidarity that arose within the women's chorus community. Women from other choruses offered to accompany the Calliope representative to the GALA meeting; members of the Portland Lesbian Chorus accompanied Calliope to the next performance hall after their reading of the statement; and Calliope members themselves "encouraged each other to wear our Calliope t-shirts and not try and be anonymous or anything. Wear that shirt, be open to the discussion, be brave, and we were, and it was fine."[43]

The controversy over Calliope's public statement did not end with the Festival, however. "What happened after that, sort of amazing. We got mail. We got piles of mail. Hate mail. Piles of hate mail. Some of it very disturbed ... and a lot of it from members of the Columbus Men's Chorus.... I think the haters actually went ahead and put pen to paper. And I think the people who were supporters did not realize how utterly necessary it was for them to let us know that, too."[44]

Yet despite the immediate resistance from some choral singers, the Columbus incident ultimately helped GALA move forward. Sandy, another Calliope singer, felt that "the event caused a lot of GALA people to start thinking in terms of, 'Hey, gays are not the only oppressed people in the world, and it will not do for us to be singing about [how] the Indians looked threatening.'"[45]

As subsequent chapters will show, the years that followed would see GALA's mission expand beyond gay issues to include racial, ethnic, religious, and gender awareness, just as the gay and lesbian community as a whole began forming alliances with other oppressed communities. Even as gay and lesbian chorus cultures remained distinct from each other, the rise of mixed choruses and the increasing presence of women in GALA made the LGBTQ chorus world as a whole a more unified community.

Alliances between men's and women's choruses were also fostered by the rise of umbrella arts organizations in which men's and women's choruses maintained their separate identities but supported one another and often performed together. The Rocky Mountain Arts Association was incorporated in the spring of 1982 to support the Denver Women's Chorus, the Denver Gay Men's Chorus, and, later, the Mosaic Youth Program—choruses that joined together to "provide educational, cultural and social enrichment for our audiences and ourselves.... We identify as an organization of gay, lesbian, bisexual and transgender (GLBT) people and supporters that is actively making a positive contribution to the entire community."[46] Flying House Productions, the umbrella organization for the Seattle Men's Chorus and the Seattle Women's Chorus, proudly bills itself as "the largest community chorus organization in North America, and stands out as the largest LGBT-identified men's and women's choruses in the world." Its president told ethnographer Wendy Moy, "The strength ... is the fact that we have this diverse and wonderfully complex and incredibly mission-focused organization that allows us to have both the men's chorus and the women's chorus.... under a single entity. To me it's like having a family where you have brothers and sisters."[47] Aria, the Windy City Women's Small Ensemble, debuted in Chicago in 1996 alongside the Windy City Gay Chorus, under the auspices of Windy City Performing Arts. Other joint choral ventures included the Central Pennsylvania Womyn's Chorus, formed in 1993 with the help of the Harrisburg Gay Men's Chorus; the Renaissance City Women's Choir, formed in Pittsburgh in 1996 in partnership with the men's chorus that had been established ten years earlier; and the Rainbow Women's Chorus of San Jose, California, initially a project of the Silicon Valley Gay Men's Chorus. In upstate New York, the Rochester Women's Community Chorus began when the director of the Rochester Gay Men's Chorus offered to help Debbie Wachspress organize a women's chorus, while in Houston, Texas, Bayou City Performing Arts grew out of the Montrose Singers, formed in 1979 by Andy Mills, and renamed the Gay Men's Chorus of Houston in 1992.

Women's Chorus, Male Director

The growing collaboration between men and women in the lesbian and gay chorus movement led some women's choruses to embrace the idea of a male director. One of the first was James Knapp. He was directing the Gay Men's Chorus of Houston at a state-wide choral festival in Dallas when "someone from the Dallas Women's Chorus screamed out in front of 350 singers ... 'Houston where are your women?'" Years later, Knapp recalled, "I was humbled to a place of movement—that haunted me. And I came back to Houston determined to do something about it."[48] Knapp recruited some of the women from HeartSong, which had disbanded by that time, to form the Bayou City Women's Chorus as a partner chorus of the Gay Men's Chorus of Houston under the aegis of Bayou City Performing Arts (BCPA), an organization that billed itself as "the best face of diversity in Houston," seeking "to provide opportunities for a wide range of Houstonians, fulfilling its mission of excellence in music, coupled with unity and pride."[49]

Founding members of the Bayou City Women's Chorus remembered James Knapp as someone who cared very deeply about the women. "This was not just—oh, you know, politically we have to have a women's choir, so let's try to get a few folks here. It was not about that at all. He cared about the women," one singer recalled.[50] Others remembered James's "guidance and his spirituality.... He always said, 'We are a family. You may be on a different path in life, but we are a family.'"[51]

Like many men who found their way to LGBT choral directing, Knapp had been fired from his job as church musician after the senior pastor learned he was gay. Though he was now directing two secular choruses, he continued to believe that "it's impossible to separate your faith from your work if you're a person of faith, which I am.... Those evenings in Houston at the Gay Men's Chorus or the Bayou City Women's Chorus—it was a community and there was spirit in that community. It wasn't Christian spirit, it wasn't Buddhist spirit, it wasn't Jewish spirit; it was human spirit coming together in a community." He also acknowledged the challenges of working with an organization that housed two choruses. "You've got to remember that in an umbrella kind of situation there can be resentment—of the women against the men, the men against the women, that whole big deal. From day one the men were the nurturers.... The men were very supportive of the women and wanted to see them succeed, and were going to do whatever it took."[52]

Although the men wanted to maintain "Gay Men's Chorus of Houston" as their name, the women of the new chorus felt differently.

"It was *never* a question about whether this was going to be a lesbian or a straight women's choir. It was going to be a women's choir.... Somebody was asking about what we were going to call it and I said, 'We will not call it the gay women's chorus,'" recalled Marte Parham. "And that was 100% agreement.... It will be BCWC (Bayou City Women's Chorus). And that was it. We never looked back."[53]

Another much-loved director, Dennis Coleman, retired in 2016 after 35 years directing the Seattle Men's Chorus and the Seattle Women's Chorus. Coleman had been leading the men's chorus for over two decades when a group of women who had sung in several short-lived Seattle-area women's choruses asked him to create a new women's chorus. Like James Knapp, Dennis Coleman heard their appeal as a call he could not refuse.

"There were a lot of feminist and lesbian women who had no specific chorus to communicate through song about issues," he explained. "They asked us to put together an organization similar to the men's chorus. We carefully considered the budget and implications and decided in the end it was our responsibility. It was our mission and we couldn't say no, even though it was going to be risky. We had to do it."[54]

Philip Swan, who has directed women's choirs at Lawrence University and elsewhere, found that both male and female colleagues initially questioned his choice to conduct women's choruses:

> My male counterparts believe this type of conducting is acceptable, but not exactly worthy of one's real time and effort.... Initially, my female colleagues have often unknowingly made me feel as though I am not a club member, but rather an outsider, due to my Y chromosome. Perhaps they think, "He may achieve adequate results with a women's choir, but how can there be a serious commitment to this genre? He must be biding his time, waiting to move to a mixed choir."

Feeling that he had been "relegated to what seems a liminal state of existence," Swan responded by seeking feedback from students and colleagues. The themes that emerged from these conversations echo the themes that have defined feminist choruses from the beginning: "fundamental sound, programming, belief in the individual and development of the whole person, and team building."[55]

Although women's choruses had generally positive responses to male directors, some occasionally encountered the same kinds of cultural dissonance that challenged choruses in GALA. Speaking of her chorus's male director, one singer admitted that she had "an issue with some of the things he says at rehearsals, that are very anti-feminist.... On our questionnaires last year, I wrote very clearly, 'I love him as a conductor, I think he's great, and I have a good time [singing] with him. But I do not want him speaking for the choir. This is a women's chorus, and that's very important to me.'"[56] Some women in choruses with male directors admitted that they would have preferred a woman:

> I still feel like there's a part of having a woman conductor that is a better fit.... I think we just inherently have a different kind of way of accessing and getting emotion from those people that we're conducting.... And I just feel like there's a common language there that sometimes gets a little bit missed. Not because anybody's a bad person– just because they're in this particular combination of chemistry and hormones."[57]

On the other hand, singers appreciated a male director who they felt respected them and made an effort to understand them as women: "He used to be much more uptight and much more rigid. And he's really like—grown, and he's mellowed out quite a bit. He's let a lot of us just kind of go 'Well okay, we're just gonna do our thing.'"[58]

In any case, by the 1990s the gay and lesbian choral communities had established alliances that would carry them into the twenty-first century. And as the millennium approached, the bonds that had begun to unite the lesbian and gay choruses of GALA helped heal women's choruses as well. Some of the singers who had seen their chorus split apart and nearly disappear over the conflict between lesbians and straight women (described earlier in this chapter), were still singing when their chorus reunited for a joint concert with the chorus that had broken away. "It was definitely the healing and rebalancing experience you would hope it would be," said one longtime singer. "We made beautiful music together and it was good for all of us."

8

New Century, New Directions

As the millennium approached, and as antiretroviral therapies brought a sharp decline in the number of AIDS deaths, lesbian and gay activists turned their efforts to wider social and legal issues. Two Supreme Court cases overturned previous discriminatory legislation: *Romer v. Evans*, in 1996, nullified Colorado's anti-gay Amendment 2; and in 2003, *Lawrence v. Texas* reversed the *Bowers* decision, which had criminalized consensual same sex relationships in Georgia (and by extension, everywhere else). Civil union partnerships were legalized in a handful of states in the early 2000s, anticipating the campaign for marriage equality that culminated in 2015 in *Obergefell v. Hodges* (discussed in Chapter 9). Within the LGBTQ community, Queer Nation and the Lesbian Avengers mobilized younger activists who challenged the terms "gay" and "lesbian" as politically conservative, while the movement for transgender rights, which would reach wide social and legal visibility in the twenty-first century (also discussed in Chapter 9), began to mobilize with the publication of Leslie Feinberg's *Transgender Liberation: A Movement Whose Time Has Come* in 1992.[1]

During these years, GLSEN (the Gay Lesbian and Straight Education Network), founded in 1990 by Kevin Jennings and a small group of teachers, grew to a national organization with a significant profile, producing regular school climate reports and advocating widely for LGBT students and teachers. PFLAG (Parents, Families and Friends of Lesbians and Gays), which had been advocating for lesbian and gay family members since 1972, also assumed a national focus, working on legal and social fronts for the rights and welfare of the entire LGBTQ community.

As the growing visibility of gay activists and gay issues both reflected and helped bring about the increasing acceptance of the LGBTQ community as whole, women's choruses began to reach out to broader constituencies, both gay and straight, even as they continued to advocate for those affected by HIV/AIDS. Starting in the late 1990s, women could be heard singing at folk festivals and arts festivals, at celebrations of Martin Luther King Day, and at fundraisers for organizations from inclusive summer camps to local theatre companies, as well as at Gay Pride marches and festivals, which had themselves become more open public celebrations of gay identity. In the early days, singing in a lesbian-identified chorus had itself been a courageous form of social action, but by the turn of the millennium choruses were able to expand their vision of social justice. As one member of the Phoenix Women's Chorus (formerly AZWIT, Arizona Women in Tune) explained, "Originally we saw the act of being out lesbians as the activist act, and now since we feel that we have gained a space where we can belong, we see our social justice element as being to work to increase diversity and compassion and acceptance of all different sorts of people."[2] Mary Lee Sargent, a long-time member of Amasong, expressed the spirit of this wider focus when she said, "I think that what Amasong being in the mainstream has meant is that we all feel safer."[3]

Embracing New Partnerships

Embracing diversity often meant partnering with other community groups and like-minded social organizations. Common Woman Chorus of Durham, North Carolina, highlighted a local food bank and an animal shelter in their Justice and Peace Concert. Afterwards an acquaintance told chorus member Janie MacNeela that what she remembered most about the concert was not only "a great evening of music," but the way the chorus "brought the whole justice and peace idea to life" by giving people the opportunity to donate to those local agencies.[4] Peggy Larson of Earthtones (St. Paul, Minnesota) reported that some of their most gratifying concerts were benefits for Mugalilwa School, "one of a few schools where women can get an education in Tanzania."[5] The Charlottesville (Virginia) Women's Choir decided to donate partial proceeds of their annual spring concert to community-based organizations, which included a local elementary school choir, an urban agricultural collective, the local Girl Scouts, and The Haven, an advocacy group working to end homelessness.[6]

Choruses also devoted entire concerts to a particular issue or organization. Voices Rising, of Jamaica Plain, Massachusetts, performed a program called "Take Up the Song," which featured "protest songs of every different kind," including, but not limited to, songs about gays and lesbians.[7] The Columbus Women's Chorus highlighted women's World War II history with "Notes of Courage," a concert that chorus member Naomi Weinert called "the heart and soul of the chorus." Chorus members paid musical tribute to the women featured in *Paradise Road*, the 1997 film (discussed in Chapter 4) based on the diaries, reminisences, and testimonies of women imprisoned in a Japanese prisoner of war camp who organized a vocal orchestra. Another part of the concert featured interviews with deaf women who had worked in the rubber factories in Akron during the War. "A whole Deaf community came to Akron to work in the rubber factories. And actually, the daughter of one of these women was one of our regular sign language interpreters. And so, she ... interviewed her mother."[8]

In 2009, the Orange County (California) Women's Chorus presented a concert titled "You Can't Sing That! Banned Books Set to Music," featuring an excerpt from "Anne Frank: A Living Voice," a musical setting of quotations from Anne Frank's diary; "Miss Celie's Blues," from the movie *The Color Purple*; choral settings of several songs from Lewis Carroll's *Alice in Wonderland*; and "Still I Rise," Rosephanye Powell's gospel-style anthem inspired by Maya Angelou's poem of the same name. Artistic Director Eliza Rubenstein acknowledged that "banned books may sound like an odd or scary theme for a concert, but these are some of the loveliest and most intelligent texts we've ever sung.... These works remind us that censorship usually succeeds only in blinding us to the colors and possibilities of language and life." The concert was presented in partnership with an independent bookshop in Laguna Beach and included a special display of banned books at the reception following the performance.[9]

As part of their outreach, women's choruses also began scheduling smaller, more informal performances for groups outside the concert hall. Cincinnati's MUSE Women's Choir performed "runouts"—smaller concerts "for less or more or no money," at which the audiences were often "folks who probably would never come to our concerts."[10] The Women's Chorus of Dallas embraced "outreach performances" as way of building audience support, as well as collaborating with groups such as AIDS service organizations, women's cancer prevention organizations, domestic violence prevention organizations, and MADD (Mothers Against Drunk Driving).[11] Many other choruses sang for like-minded groups or for members of their own chorus facing life crises. "We call it drive-by singing," Portland, Oregon's Aurora Chorus Director Joan Szymko explained. "There are times in the life of our community where women need healing, and so we will get groups together and go.... We just sing—some music that's very dear to everybody's heart."[12]

In 1996, Judy Fjell, the Montana based singer-songwriter whose Song Circles were described in Chapter 3, organized an *ad hoc* chorus of women to celebrate a Los Angeles showing of Judy Chicago's epic installation, The Dinner Party. "I'd written a song for Judy Chicago and the Dinner Party," Fjell recalled. "Eighty-some of us gathered in LA to sing for that exhibit.... That was my first experience with a pickup chorus, meaning that we had never rehearsed together before we met at the LAX Hilton in one of their conference rooms, and it was very exciting because a lot of these women weren't in a chorus.... Judy Chicago came to hear us at one point."[13]

Years later, members of Houston's HeartSong remembered singing at the inauguration of Texas Governor Ann Richards in 1991. One member recalled, "I just remember thinking, 'I cannot believe that we are going to the inauguration of Ann Richards.' I could not believe it. It was cold, and it was gloriously blue, and we sang like mad women, and it was the most amazing thing.... It was, you know, the shortest little blip of a minute that we sang our little heart, and then we were on and off the stage. But for us, it was just like the biggest deal."[14]

Rethinking Repertoire: "No Whining, No Flowers"

Mainstream women choral directors, too, were re-examining the repertoire they had taken for granted. Although many Sister Singers chorus directors came from the mainstream choral world, the lesbian/feminist identity espoused by women's choruses in the 1980s and early 1990s left the two communities fairly separate. But as women's choruses broadened their scope and music educators encountered the feminist theory and practice that was transforming the academic world, the paths of these two choral communities began to converge. Women choral directors started to challenge the unspoken rules that relegated their choruses to "singing sweet, pretty music, with very little substance."[15] Canadian choral director Hilary Apfelstadt noted that the majority of women's contemporary choral music had traditionally been "what I call 'butterflies and rainbows' music.... In my experience, women seek more substance than this, substance that can be found only in high quality music."[16] At Cornell University, Scott Tucker established a commissioning project for the Cornell University Chorus, informally titled "No Whining, No Flowers." Composers were invited to choose texts that would "explore topics that differ from the traditional women's repertoire themes of 'Oh woe, my man has left me,' and 'La la, look at the all the pretty flowers'— hence the title of the project."[17]

Music educators, too, began casting a critical eye at the mainstream texts intended for high school and college singers. In 2013, Lauren Estes examined thirteen monographs recommended by the American Choral Directors Association (ACDA) and found that these texts documented the ecclesiastical exclusion of female singing voices in church, but neglected to include the all-female choirs of the same eras. Similarly, the monographs failed to mention other historical examples (discussed in Chapter 2), such as the Venetian *Ospedali*, the German *Frauenchor*, and twentieth-century school and club-based women's choirs, thereby "preserving the hierarchy and thus the second-class status of women's choirs."[18]

Composer and choral music scholar Naomi Stephan conducted a similar survey after noting the predominance of men's choirs at several choral festivals, including the 1993 GALA Festival in Tampa, Florida. Stephan examined choral journals and conducted surveys among members of the IAWM (International Alliance for Women in Music) and the ACDA. The majority of her respondents believed that instrumentalists performed with a higher level of musicianship than choral musicians. They showed less interest in composing choral music than in instrumental, and deemed women's choral music less well written, less challenging and less complex than music for mixed choruses. She concluded, "The choral world has an undeniable bias in favor of men's and boy's choirs and SATB [Soprano, Alto, Tenor, Bass, i.e., mixed choruses]."[19]

Another music educator, Julia Eklund Koza, studied choral methods texts published between 1982 and 1992 and found that most were "constructed as how-to-do-it manuals," with "a static, finished model of teaching; a single, seamless image of the ideal choral experience" that left no room for debate or disagreement. Koza cited the gendered repertoire that other choral directors had observed: "slow ballads; lullabies; love songs; songs about nature; and soft, 'sweet,' diatonic pieces"—music that reflected "a traditional, White, middle-class definition of femininity. By contrast, pieces about adventure, travel, and drinking—lively, fast, loud, action music—often have been selected for boys."[20]

With a new awareness of these inequities, women's choral directors challenged the organizations that promoted them. In response to women's advocacy, the ACDA added a committee on women's choir repertoire and broadened its guidelines for overall repertoire selection to include cultural diversity.[21] And in 2004, MUSE director Catherine Roma brought the history and insights of the women's chorus movement to the ACDA with an article in *Choral Journal*. Writing as a choral director with roots in both academia and the lesbian/feminist women's music movement, Roma traced the history of women's choruses back to Sophie Drinker's mid-century research and connected the current proliferation of women's choral communities to the second wave of the women's movement in the 1970s. Declaring that "women's choruses no longer occupy the bottom of the choral hierarchy," she went on to highlight some of the contemporary women composers who were already familiar to singers in feminist choruses, including Ysaye Maria Barnwell, Gwyneth Walker, and Joan Szymko.[22]

"You say 'Y'all come' and then y'all don't come."

Even as they moved beyond the lesbian community to establish ties with the communities around them, most women's choruses (with the exception of MUSE, discussed in Chapter 6), remained overwhelmingly White. Almost every Festival featured at least one workshop on "how to diversify your chorus membership," often led by MUSE singers and directors, but as Cathy Roma discovered in the early 1990s, bringing racial diversity to a White chorus could be a challenging enterprise.

In 2005, The Common Woman Chorus of Durham, North Carolina, invited "Vanessa," the African American pastor of a primarily lesbian, African American congregation, to a chorus board meeting, an encounter described by CWC member Jennifer Womack in her 2009 master's thesis. "She sat as the lone point of color in a swathe of beige," Womack wrote. "Nine of us encircled the small living room possessing faces that might have closely matched that old crayon called 'Flesh' in the 1960's Crayola box, set apart only by heads of brown, gray, blonde and dye. The tenth, Vanessa, punctuated the room with her mahogany skin and tailored chartreuse shirt against the neutrals of the carpet and furniture."[23]

"You say 'Y'all come' and then y'all don't come," Vanessa told the group, and went on to describe the way well-meaning Whites tried to bridge racial barriers by inviting "Others" into their midst without "moving out of their own comfort zone into the physical, emotional, and spiritual spaces inhabited by people of color." She described the discomfort felt by her partner, who had been looking forward to making music with other lesbians: "She didn't feel welcomed."[24]

Vanessa went on to praise the chorus's desire for change, but added that the leaders of the CWC and her congregation needed to do much more groundwork before bringing their members together. "She [spoke] of being very intentional about confronting the '-isms' (racism, ageism, sexism, etc.), but acknowledge[d] that no matter how much leaders within a group desire to do this, the community as a whole needs to embrace the intent in order to achieve change."

Describing the atmosphere after Vanessa had left the meeting, Womack wrote:

> There was a solemnity, almost a palpable sense of earnestness among the CWC Board members to further analyze our own community and its perpetual lack of diversity. When we say "Y'all come" do we mean it, or is it simply a massaging of our own need to feel we have been open to Others? And are we willing to "Y'all come" in return? Vanessa's presence confronted us with these questions; her exit allowed us to ponder them within the incredible beige-ness of being.[25]

After the meeting Jennifer shared her account with the rest of the chorus, most of whom agreed they needed to broaden their outreach along the lines Vanessa had suggested. But five years later, an interview with seven Common Woman Chorus members revealed that racial diversity was a goal more easily envisioned than realized. Several singers believed that partnering with African American singers would mean expanding their choral repertoire to include "gospel or Christian music which many of our members are not keen on."

> It's partly a question of, do we need to modify what we sing in order to incorporate other people of other cultures? Part of the question came down to what is our identity

as a chorus and do we need to change our identity?—which would require a lot of work to try and go out and engage women with other groups or from other places or whatever. And do we sing the kind of music that would interest those people to participate with us? And, so part of the question to me was do we need to do that, you know? Is our identity as it is fine? We wish we had a more diverse membership, but it seems like it would require us changing who we are to accomplish that, and I don't know that we need to do that.[26]

CWC Director Cindy Bizzell's response echoed Bernice Johnson Reagon's advice to Catherine Roma in the early 1980s. Bizzell suggested the possibility of taking several spirituals that were already in the chorus repertoire and

do[ing] a clinic with them where we all learn the same music and they help us stylize it or they help us in that way. You have to create repertoire and sing pieces that when people of different ethnic groups might hear it or they might look and say, "Oh, I see somebody who looks like me," or "That sounds like music I sang growing up," or "I've heard that before." We have a couple people who from time to time feel to me like they want to take up the torch but it hasn't happened.[27]

Women from other choruses acknowledged that they too wanted to make their choruses more racially diverse but had not succeeded in doing so. Several pointed out that the lack of choral diversity mirrored the situation in the world outside. "I worked in a place where there's 21,000 employees," said a singer from the Bayou City Women's Chorus. "And lots and lots and lots of male and female African Americans, an incredibly diverse place. And what I've observed ... is that people segregate. They don't mix. And they're not encouraged to mix."[28]

The Huntsville (Alabama) Feminist Chorus noted that their audiences were often more diverse than their chorus membership. "Huntsville is a lot like other parts of the South and Alabama in that we do have quite racially organized communities and you can see it in the education system here and the public schools," said one chorus member. "But I will say that I feel like the audience of the chorus is more diverse than the chorus itself."

Sometimes even in a racially segregated community, a White chorus can reach out to a Black audience member. Another Huntsville singer recalled a concert with a social justice theme with at least one African American man in the audience.

> We were being a little bit apologetic for being so monocultural. We had sung a song ["Ella's Song," by Sweet Honey in the Rock] that said, "'Until the killing of black men, black mothers' sons, is as important as the killing of white men, white mothers' sons"—and he said it was so powerful to see a group of white people singing in racial solidarity and alliance and for him it was even like wow, he was crying and he said he had never experienced that before and it sort of shows me like a different possibility.[29]

Issues of race continued to challenge choruses in the North as well as in the South. Voices Rising, in Boston, Massachusetts, has tried to broaden its racial profile, but like most choruses in the women's network, it has remained mostly-White. "I know that some women of color, for instance, have not really felt welcome there or the music didn't really speak to them, so that's why they left," said chorus member Rebecca Gorlin.[30] Her chorus mate, Julie Regner, agreed, "It is something that we're constantly looking at and trying to figure out how to do—both in our music choice and where we advertise. And, unfortunately, for whoever it is … someone's gonna have to be the first to break in…. I think probably there may be some women who were turned off by the fact that we're not a diverse group right now so may be reluctant to join us and kind of be the one."[31] Columbus (Ohio) Women's Chorus member Naomi Weinert admitted, "Although the board talks about these things, I'm not sure they ever get communicated to the chorus…. We have not found Cathy Roma's secret … or we have not managed to tap into … community resources."[32]

Singing "Sisters"

Argerie Vasilakes, a longtime member of Cleveland's Windsong Chorus, described a conflict in which race and repertoire collided amid cultural confusion. The clash arose over a song the chorus had programmed for its spring concert, Gwyneth Walker's setting of Lucille Clifton's poem, "Sisters."

> It was the third time we've sung it but it was the first time that there arose a controversy about it. This song is about two sisters, it's a very playful song, two sisters who are growing up together and we encounter them at the beginning of the song as young girls who are shooing away mice and stepping on roaches and greasing their legs…. It's evocative of a time and a spirit…. What happened was that after an alto sectional some altos said, sort of whispering at a rehearsal to sopranos who were not there, "Something happened in our sectional the other day and we think that this song is racist and it's a not emblematic of the kind of philosophy that we have in our chorus and we shouldn't be singing it and if we do sing it then some of us are gonna protest and sit out the singing of it."[33]

Argerie noted that the protest was not lodged by the one Black woman in the alto section, but by White singers. She believed that the solution was to continue the dialogue among chorus members, "to have a conversation like this. Why do we think we'll be hurt if we do?"[34]

Clifton's poem figured in another choral debate, when the Grand Rapids Women's Chorus programmed the song for a 2002 concert. Chorus member Janice Scalza actually wrote to ask Lucille Clifton for her thoughts about a White women's chorus singing "Sisters." In her letter, Scalza wrote:

This past October, I attended a retreat with the chorus at which we discussed, for lack of a better word, our "guilt" about being mostly white women singing this song. The discussion involved whether we are "qualified" to present this song and also whether African American audience members would be insulted by our performing it. Would we offend them by singing about roaches and rats and talking in the language of young black girls who are sisters? ... Though we have all had the experience of being young and being sisters, we clearly have not had the experience of "being black or letting our hair go back." We love this song and we love the energy involved in singing it.... We absolutely love that we are singing it here in Grand Rapids Michigan. Yet, we struggle with the above questions in presenting it.... I would be most honored if you would consider giving us your insight on this.[35]

Clifton replied with an unqualified endorsement:

Thank you for your kind words. I have been asked this sort of thing and I'm not sure that my answer is adequate. What I do know is that the experience of being poor and feeling lonely is not a racial one; nor is it recent. People who believe that only black girls know the experiences in the poem tend to not realize that there are poor and young and learning to love oneself white and brown and red and yellow girls too. If I have traditionally been expected to understand myself perhaps through Your frames of reference, then so can you in Mine! Celebrate!!! Lucille Clifton.[36]

Adventures in Programming

As the debate over "Sisters" suggests, women's choruses faced new challenges as they moved their choral repertoire. By the late 1990s, women's choruses were performing songs from other cultures and in languages other than English as they expanded beyond their original lesbian/feminist focus. The seven choruses at the first national Sister Singers Festival in 1984 had performed songs by women's music notables (Cris Williamson's "Lullaby" was a particular favorite) along with rounds, chants, and some humorous takes, with a lesbian twist, on popular songs. The mass chorus included Ysyae Barnwell's "On Children," a musical setting of the text from Kahlil's Gibran's *The Prophet*, which would become a staple of women's music concerts and festivals.

Programs from the 1991 Festival in Houston and the 1993 Festival in Cincinnati showed that Network programming was becoming more adventurous. Choruses were still presenting gay-themed numbers, such as "To Be Strong," Laura Berkson's moving tribute to those affected by HIV, and "Simply Love," Holly Near's defiant defense of same sex love with its challenge to homophobia: "Perhaps you know there's something you should fear/ If my love makes me strong and makes you disappear/ It's simply love—my love for a woman." And the 1993 program also included Fred Small's "Everything Possible," perhaps the most-performed number by all LGBT choruses—a gentle lullaby that teaches a child, "You can be anybody that you want to be/You can love whomever you will/You can travel any country where your heart leads/And know I will love you still."[37]

One of the most remarkable stories in the women's chorus movement is the journey of a song that began as a protest against apartheid and became an anthem for LGBT choruses and their audiences. In 1984, South African singer-songwriter Labi Siffre was asked by the Aylesbury Multicultural Centre to chair a meeting of Black and White youth, with the goal of reducing hostilities between the two groups. Shortly after that, Siffre witnessed a scene on television in which a truck full of White South African police were shooting indiscriminately at Black protesters. Years later, he described what happened next:

I wanted to write a song about ... what had happened locally and what I had seen on this film about apartheid in South Africa. Then one day about two o'clock in the morning I went into the music room and I sat down at the keyboard and I opened my mouth and sang "The higher you build your barrier/ The stronger I become." My intention had been to write a song for Black youth and about apartheid. And I started to cry and I realized that I was writing in fact about my life as a gay child and adolescent and man being assailed by this constant attack on the validity of my existence by cowardly hypocritical people. You get to a point of "enough is enough." I'm not going to allow these people to hurt me anymore.

Siffre recalled reading an essay by a French art critic who had written "that if you write well about the particular, you write well about the general and generalities. And I realized that I had written a song that in fact did what I had intended. It did say something about apartheid. It did say something about Black youth. It also said something about being a Jew. It also said something about being disabled. But it was informed by my life as a gay child, adolescent, and adult."[38]

Before long, "Something Inside So Strong" was adopted by the gay rights movement in America, as well as overseas. It became even more widely known when the Flirtations ("the world's most famous, openly-gay, all-male, politically active, multicultural, a cappella singing doo-wop group") began singing it and recorded it in 1990 on their eponymously titled first album, *The Flirtations*. Years later, in an interview with Queer Music Heritage's DJ Doyle, Flirtations founder Jon Arterton recalled:

When I had a boyfriend in New York, very early on in our relationship he said, "You know, I know this song that would be great for you guys".... And he played me the original version of Labi Siffre singing that song, and I was just blown away....So we arranged it and we just started doing it. It's an amazing, just an amazing song.[39]

In 1999, Brooklyn Women's Chorus director Bev Grant discovered the song at a rally in Manhattan. "This guy came up with a cassette, he says 'You have to hear this!'....So I listened to it, and I arranged it for chorus." Not long afterwards, Grant was leading a Friday night concert for the People's Music Network."Pete Seeger was our star, and I taught everybody the song as the finale, and Pete fell in love with the song. And he got in touch with Labi Siffre in England and invited him over, and I was at this event somewhere in Westchester County where we sang it with Labi Siffre."[40]

"Something Inside So Strong" has since been performed and recorded by dozens of gay and lesbian choruses around the world. In 2017, Holler4, an activist women's choir in London, was invited to the main stage to lead the singing at the Women's March on London. One of their singers later tweeted, "Call me sentimental, but singing 'Something Inside So Strong' with 100,000 at #WomenMarchLondon [was] one of the most beautiful moments of my life."[41]

By the 1990s, choruses were also singing in languages other than English. The 1993 Cincinnati program included "Beau Soir," by French composer Claude Debussy; "Las Madres Cansadas," a Spanish translation by Joan Baez of her song "Weary Mothers"; and "Nigra Sum," Pablo Casals' setting of a text from the Song of Songs, which would frequently appear on future programs.[42]

Performing songs from other cultures and in other languages posed new challenges. "We try to get somebody to coach us on a language when we can get a native speaker," said Carol Wheeler of Fortissima. "We did a Welsh tune and we've got somebody that's a native Welsh speaker in their church that helped us with that. And I remember once in the earlier years of the chorus we did a Vietnamese song and somebody had a friend who had been in the Peace Corps and who called her answering machine and sang it into her answering machine so we could get the pronunciation."[43]

Pronunciation was not the only concern as choruses developed a multicultural repertoire. As choral director and scholar James Daugherty points out in an essay posted by GALA Choruses, "Enscoring such music ignores the fact that for much of world music the 'music' is not necessarily limited to pitches and rhythms and musical form. It also entails text, movement or dance, and social context—not as 'add-ons' but as part of the very meaning of music making. It is difficult, if not impossible, to communicate this multi-dimensional framework within the confines of a typical choral octavo."[44]

In an interview with MUSE's Catherine Roma, GALA Artistic Director Jane Ramseyer Miller noted that while "traditional choral festivals or events [may include] international music and it may be kind of technically beautiful ... there's no connection to the passion and the language and the culture that these people are singing about."[45] Evoking the ethos of the early labor and folk music movement, Roma agreed that choruses singing music from other cultures needed to "engage with the people from whom the struggle came."[46]

Similarly, in her 2006 dissertation on American Slavic choirs, Erica Quin-Easter drew on her own experiences with the Yale Women's Slavic Chorus to warn of "the promises— and the pitfalls—of musical multiculturalism," particularly the "appropriation and representation of other people's cultures [that] too often winds up reproducing unequal relations of power."[47]

For the mostly White members of the SABTQ [Soprano, Alto, Bass, Tenor, Queer] Women's Chorus of Honolulu, singing was inseparable from a strong awareness of colonial history. "I don't know how you cannot be aware of the fact that you are historically part of the aggressive culture that came here—and I think about it a lot," said Rose Adams. "A sense of loving it here and knowing that in a sense I don't belong here." As their chorus grew, singers strove to respect the native culture around them. "We have sung several songs in Hawaiian, which is great, to learn the language and try to honor it," explained Antonia Alvarez.

> And in the naming process, in one of those first meetings, we talked a lot about whether or not we should use a Hawaiian name, or whether we should root ourselves in Hawaii or in Honolulu.... Because as it ended up, the majority of our members were transplants. Hawaiian is our host culture. And so, honoring that in some of the songs that we sing, honoring it in the way that we sing

those songs, making sure, checking with *kumu*, with elders, with *kupuna*, about how we sing words, or is this song appropriate for us to say or not say?[48]

The story of MUSE's outreach to the African American community (described in Chapter 6) is another example of the challenges in choral encounters with cultures close to home. MUSE member Angie Denov recalled that when MUSE launched the New Spirituals Project (described in chapter 6), "we had very long discussions about singing this music.... There were some women in the choir who had trouble singing about God.... And there were a couple of members of MUSE who wouldn't sing the New Spirituals concert. They stayed in MUSE but they wouldn't do that concert.... It would break her heart any time Cathy would lose somebody over something like that," Denov added, "but we just kept telling her, that's the way it is ... and we have to keep doing what we need to do."[49]

Religious language had always been problematic in feminist choruses—for lesbians still feeling the pain of rejection by mainstream churches; for Jewish women feeling marginalized by the mainstream normalization of Christianity; for women who embraced the pagan or Wiccan concept of the goddess; and for atheists or women with no religious affiliation at all. Issues around religious language and observances became especially conspicuous during the winter holiday season, when mainstream choruses across the country were presenting holiday-themed programs full of Christmas music, sometimes with the obligatory song about Hanukkah (or in later years, Kwanzaa) tucked in like a strange visitor amid the tinsel and greenery. In general, gay men's choruses followed this practice; even GALA, with its stated commitment to diversity, staged a "Holiday Hullabaloo Blockbuster" at its 2016 Festival, billed as "a fun, festive, and fabulous look at some of the best Christmas, Kwanzaa, Hanukkah, and Winter Solstice songs performed by fifteen of your favorite GALA Choruses." This concert included twelve Christmas songs, one solstice song, one song about winter, and one Hanukkah song—Tom Lehrer's "Chanukah in Santa Monica," a lighthearted number evoking Tin Pan Alley and the Borscht Belt.[50]

Women's choruses found creative alternatives to these choral clichés. Some began presenting solstice concerts that celebrated the season without privileging any religion. Aurora Chorus director Joan Szymko described a holiday concert that she called "our traditional nontraditional event.... It's music that everybody can celebrate and relate to. It's about winter as a time of pulling in and introspection, a time of being together as a community and a family, about celebrating darkness into light.... It's truly about celebrating one human family at this time of year where so many come together to celebrate."[51]

In 2000, the Peninsula Women's Chorus commissioned "Psalm 121," a work that composer Libby Larsen called "a mountaintop in song." Chorus Director Patricia Hennings had told Larsen that she wanted to combine the biblical text ("I lift my eyes up to the hills/ From whence cometh my help?") with the writings of John Muir and "a place in the mountains where I've been going to since I was a little girl."[52] The final version remains true to the spiritual vision of the Biblical text while transforming it into a magnificent hymn to nature. Larsen wrote, "I wanted to create an unmistakable musical metaphor that suggested all the meanings of the word 'mountain': God, the challenge of accepting life in the face of death, the decision to confront great spiritual challenges, or simply accepting life as a mortal opportunity to love."[53]

Amasong Director Kristina Boerger led her chorus through a similar musical transformation when a friend gave her a tape with a song by Bobby McFerrin that she thought the chorus might sing. "And I thought, 'No, we probably can't,'" Boerger recalled. "But she gave me the tape and it was his setting of the words to the Twenty-Third Psalm. And he sings the first line: 'The Lord is my shepherd, I have all I need/ She makes me lie down'—and then it goes on like that. Well, of course you hear 'she' and your ears perk up immediately. *She*?"

Boerger loved the song and so did her chorus. "The music itself just shimmers," she said. "It's very simple. Everybody loved it. It's not something that you would catch certain other lesbian choruses ever singing because it comes from a patriarchal religious tradition."[54]

Bobby McFerrin himself explained how he came to write a version of the Twenty-Third Psalm with God as a woman.

> Psalm 23 is dedicated to my mother. She was the driving force in my religious and spiritual education, and I have so many memories of her singing in church. But I wrote it because I'd been reading the Bible one morning, and I was thinking about God's unconditional love, about how we crave it but have so much trouble believing we can trust it, and how we can't fully understand it. And then I left my reading and spent time with my wife and our children. Watching her with them, the way she loved them, I realized one of the ways we're shown a glimpse of how God loves us is through our mothers. They cherish our spirits, they demand that we become our best selves, and they take care of us.[55]

"Composing While Female"

In 1973, *High Fidelity Magazine* published a pair of opinion pieces responding to the question, "Why Haven't Women Become Great Composers?" Grace Rubin-Rabson, a widely published psychologist, professional pianist, and former college music instructor, attributed men composers' greater success to fundamental differences between males and females

> ... deriving from the sexual function.... With or without liberation, men will remain actively penetrating, women receptive, accounting for their readiness to accept and interpret. That this tendency is innate and not culturally conditioned appears in the laboratory study of baby monkeys reared together from birth without other social influences.... High-level human creativity is investigative, innovative, agonistic; receptivity and passivity will not conjure it into being.[56]

Rubin-Rabson's Freudianism may seem quaint to post-second-wave-feminist readers, but as late as 2011, Fiona Maddocks, the author of a well-reviewed book about Hildegard of Bingen, offered a similar response to the same question:

> Still we cannot escape the unanswered, unfashionable and, certainly, uncomfortable question: for all the many good, even excellent women composers, why has there not yet been a great one? Where is the possessed, wild-eyed, crackpot female answer to Beethoven, who battled on through deafness, loneliness, financial worry and disease to create timeless masterpieces? The answer, and I run for cover even raising the matter, may lie in biology or even psychopathology. If one should arrive, what a cry of joy and relief will be heard.[57]

On the other hand, musicologist Judith Rosen presented an argument that dates back as far as Virginia Woolf's classic *A Room of One's Own* and has generally dominated contemporary feminist thinking: women's failure to produce great fiction, music, or any other artistic creation is due not to their innate nature, but to the social, economic and psychological constraints of patriarchal society; removing these constraints will allow women to flourish freely alongside male writers, composers, and artists. This is also the argument put forth by composer Dale Trumbore:

> I think about being a female composer when I go to a new music concert with only white guys on the program, or when I see a list of competition winners and every single one of them is a white dude. We're conditioned not to notice this all-maleness, this whiteness. We come out of a long tradition where the best composers are, exclusively, white men. Rather than viewing each concert program as the astonishing lack of diversity it represents, we accept it as the norm.[58]

By the turn of the millennium, however, women composers were going beyond questions of access and representation to reconsider the composing process itself. Elizabeth Alexander, for example, described her composing process in relational terms:

> When I write for women's choirs, I find that I am powerfully influenced by a wide variety of extra-musical notions I have about women. If that last statement does not sound objective, it is because it is not! Those extra-musical notions are personal, and formed through the forty-eight years I have been on earth. They have been influenced by every woman I have known: my mother and grandmothers, my sister; my eleventh-grade history teacher; college friend; music colleagues, the neighbor across the street—the list goes on and on! So, when I imagine playful women, fierce women, earnest women, and joyful women, a host of impressions rises up in my mind different from what I imagine playful teenagers, fierce men, earnest children and joyful families to be.[59]

Like Alexander, choral conductor Shelbie Wahl responded to the question, "Do women compose differently than men?" by reframing the question itself:

> The point is not to discern categories of "masculine" and "feminine" music. Rather, the premise is that women may view a given situation through a different lens than their male counterparts—a lens that is colored and filtered by the cultural gender preconceptions in which all have evolved. Following this idea, it is not improbable to suggest that the creations of women composers may be different from the creations of men composers, simply because of the diverse life experiences of each.[60]

Women composers' collaborative approach made them ideal partners for choruses seeking to grow their choral repertoire while remaining true to their original mission of celebrating women. Joan Szymko was among several whose composing grew out of her work directing a women's chorus. "Early on, I was struck by the preponderance of 'fluff' repertoire found in the octavo market, beginning with the text/source material," Szymko said, adding that any text she set to music must be "artful [and] highly crafted."

> Where I come from as a choral musician and as a composer even, is I am expressing, you know, my own yearning for good. Well, what does that mean? I think that there is a desire to be in communion with. Okay, communion with what, who? It's not really that important—the object. It's that yearning to really truly be connected. And this is true connectivity. This is not the Internet or Facebook, or you know.... This is full embodied and sound energy and everything and it is transformative and transporting.[61]

Jan C. Snow had done some composing before she began singing with Windsong, Cleveland's Feminist Chorus. At the request of Windsong's Artistic Director, the late Karen Weaver, Snow began writing for Windsong and eventually became the chorus's resident composer. She too described her creative process in collaborative terms, recalling the genesis of one of her songs in a conversation with a singer-songwriter friend: "We were talking about our process and our writing.... He was saying, 'Oh everything I'm writing is crap and I'm not writing anything good.'"

Snow reminded her friend of a quote from writer/activist Anne Lamott: "It's what Anne Lamott called shitty first drafts. You write badly and then you have someplace to go. I said, 'One song leads to another.' And he said, 'You're right!' And that phrase, one song leads to another, then expanded: 'One song is never enough to carry you through.'"[62]

Snow's conversation with her friend became a Windsong favorite:

One song leads to another
it's first one, then the other
for one song is never enough
to carry you through.[63]

Snow has continued to compose for Windsong while still singing with the chorus, explaining, "I don't separate the two. They're together."[64]

Composer Elizabeth Alexander used Latin-jazz rhythms, clave accompaniment, finger snapping, and impromptu talking in her setting of a Zimbabwean proverb, "If you can walk you can dance, if you can talk you can sing," a women's chorus favorite that became her most performed work. Its message echoes Christopher Small's observation of traditional African societies, where the world "is not divided into the few 'talented' who play and sing and the many 'untalented' to whom they perform"; instead, "in the communal work of musicking ...everyone is able to and does take an active performing part."[65] Daniel J. Levitin tells a similar story about a shy friend who pursued his doctoral fieldwork in Lesotho, a small nation situated entirely within South Africa.

> Studying and interacting with local villagers, Jim patiently earned their trust until one day he was asked to join in one of their songs. So, typically, when asked to sing with these Sotho villagers, Jim said in a soft voice, "I don't sing."....The villagers just stared at Jim and said, "What do you mean you don't sing? You talk!" Jim told me later, "It was as odd to them as if I told them that I couldn't walk or dance, even though I have both my legs."[66]

A less well known but equally engaging composition by Elizabeth Alexander was "They Have Freckles Everywhere," a seven-part set of "character pieces" commissioned by Portland, Maine's Women in Harmony, which grew out of a collaboration between WIH and the Many Rivers Program of Portland's Hall Elementary School, where one of the chorus members happened to be a second grade teacher. During a visual arts residency at the Maine College of Art called "The Best Part of Me," Hall students were invited to identify a body part as the focal point for an accompanying photograph and poem. Setting the poems to music, Alexander wrote, "I became poignantly aware of how unabashedly children celebrate their bodies— while their adult counterparts have become habitually cautious about how we sit, walk, gesture, eat, speak, look.... I wrote a piece which orchestrates an uncommon occurrence: adults having fun with their bodies—in public!"[67] "Being Who You Are" dismantled stereotypes about both women and children, taking the children's poetry seriously enough to turn it into texts for adult singers and allowing the women to challenge ideas about body image through the words of their young collaborators.

In 1999, the Peninsula Women's Chorus participated in a similar collaboration when Patricia Hennings invited California Poets in the Schools, the largest writers-in-the-schools program in the country, to join with children, composers, and the chorus. CPITS poet-teachers began working with students in five San Francisco Bay area schools where PWC singers were already teaching. Eventually the children's poems were sent to three composers, Brian Holmes of San Jose, Ron Jeffers of Corvallis, Oregon, and Joan Szymko of Portland, Oregon, who turned them into a series of choral pieces that the chorus performed in a 2000 concert titled "A Young Poet Sings." Like the teachers and singers who participated in the Maine project with Elizabeth Alexander, California organizers insisted that the young poets' work be taken seriously. "We specifically said to the composers, 'Please don't write children's music. Write for an advanced women's chorus,'" Patricia Hennings later recalled.[68]

"Clangor, Clamor, Clapperclaw: Let Women Speak"

In 1994, composer Carol Matthews was approached by Sue Coffee, who wanted a new composition for the women's *a capella* group she was forming, Sound Circle. Matthews had previously composed a work for the Denver Women's Chorus, a large-scale collection of pieces built around the theme of lesbians in history, called "Masque of the Serpent," which the DWC had performed at the 1992 GALA Festival in Denver. Coffee's new group would be much smaller, only about twenty singers, and Matthews liked the idea, saying, "I want to write something that's really different." Sue said, "I wanted her to scare us, to give us something that would be so challenging that we'd know from then on that we could do anything."[69]

"Clangor, Clamor, Clapperclaw," the piece that Matthews eventually composed for Sound Circle, was one of the most challenging pieces any chorus had attempted. "It involved a lot of body percussion and clapping," Matthews explained. "And there was no text. It was just vocals." By the summer of 1996, the chorus had learned the piece and decided to perform it at the GALA festival in Tampa. When Matthews joined the chorus in rehearsals, she saw that Sue "had done a marvelous job of just taking the piece apart and teaching them a little bit at a time.... They knew bits and pieces of it really well but they had never been able to do it all the way through without stopping at that point." Composer and director discussed the piece, and Matthews told Sue that the piece "was about women's voices. That when the men control the instruments—the holy instruments and the drums—and when they control the language, the words, then what is left for women to sing? So, there are no words. And there are no instruments and no drums except our bodies. And this is the bell of alarm. This is the bell of a kind of freedom and a kind of call to let us speak. Let women speak." Then Matthews talked to the chorus. "I said to them, 'The way I conceive the piece is as if you were on the edge of a cliff with your toes over the edge, and you're leaning forward because it's so important to be seen, to be heard, that they hear you—what you have to say'.... I said, 'Don't be afraid of rushing. Just stay together and do it as hard as you can.' And they were terrified. I was so scared!"[70]

The piece premiered in the big concert hall at the Tampa Festival. Matthews recalled:

> I was sitting down in front, and they came out and Sue told the audience, "This is the women's cry, this is what

we want. We want the bell to say *Warning*, we want the bell to say *Freedom*, we want the bell so say, *Listen. Ascolte! Be aware!* That we are here. And we have voices." And then she went back and she started very soft, but very fast, and it goes [snapping her fingers] just like that. And they got through it, they just nailed it…. And then when she did the final cut-off, the hall was dead silent, and then it started—there was a wave that came from the back of the hall of people screaming and clapping and crying and carrying on. All the way up to the top of the stage. And it rocked Sound Circle—it literally rocked them back on their feet. That wave of sound just carried them back. And Sue almost forgot to acknowledge me, at the last minute she did. I was just jumping up and down![71]

"Sing for the Cure"

Two of the most celebrated commissions in the women's choral world premiered in the same year—2000—and have been performed around the world ever since. "Sing for the Cure" was commissioned by the Susan J. Komen foundation and created by Tim Seelig, then director of the Dallas Women's Chorus; "Where I Live" was the work of composer Diane Benjamin and was commissioned by the Denver Women's Chorus. Both works address the same topic—the breast cancer epidemic in the United States—with poems based on personal testimonies from victims, survivors, relatives, and caregivers. Each features moving musical accompaniment. Singers and their audiences never fail to find themselves deeply affected by these two works; yet, despite the similarities in their message, the stories behind their creation suggest different choral paradigms.

"Sing for the Cure" had its genesis when Nancy Brinker, founder of the Susan J. Komen Breast Cancer Foundation, approached Tim Seelig about composing a work that would highlight the work of the Komen Foundation in addressing the breast cancer epidemic. Brinker was inspired by "When We No

Longer Touch," a song cycle Seelig had written for the Turtle Creek Chorale highlighting the human dimensions of AIDS/HIV. Brinker wanted "an official kind of work—a musical work—for the Komen Foundation on the story of breast cancer—the story of breast cancer survivors, or families—something like you did around AIDS." Seelig was then conducting the Turtle Creek Chorale and its sister chorus, the Women's Chorus of Dallas, which had just lost its first member to breast cancer and included several survivors among its members.

> And, so it was a very poignant time for all of us, [Seelig recalled], and Nancy Brinker, in asking me to do this, wanted a big orchestral work with chorus, et cetera, and the only caveat was, they weren't going to give us any money to commission it...because the Komen Foundation gives all of its money just to education and research.... So, I stupidly said, "Well, sure, Nancy, I'll do that, why not." ...the Komen Foundation decided on "Sing for the Cure" and trademarked it early on, much like "Race for the Cure," so that it would always be the official work of the Komen Foundation.[72]

Seelig contacted Pam Martin, a Texas woman who had endured "a brush with death" through a brain aneurysm, to serve as lyricist for the project, and the Komen Foundation set up three days of interviews with breast cancer survivors and friends and family members of those who had not survived. "She interviewed them, she took notes, she taped their interviews. And then she went home and began to write, the most incredible lyrics imaginable. It took her quite some time, because it was just so heart wrenching that it took her a while to even get over the first three days. Pam did this all on spec, 'cause she knew we didn't have any money."[73]

Martin produced ten poems with narrations, and Seelig found composers to set them to music. The choruses booked the Dallas Symphony Center and the Dallas Symphony Orchestra and hired Maya Angelou to serve as narrator. Then he went about raising money to pay his lyricist, composers, and narrator, as well as the fee for the hall and orchestra. Seelig's account reveals his own determination as well as the ubiquitousness of the epidemic.

> As we began to raise money, we found a company that had headquarters in North Carolina [and] California, and an office in Dallas. And as fate would have it, they were having a meeting in Dallas.... They were on a break, they were having a conference, and so they ran me in and said, OK, tell your story.... I had nothing to show them, I had no music, but I did have some lyrics.... and I told them the story of the commissioning. And the president said, "Boy, I don't know, how much do you need to get started?" And I said, "Well, I could get started with $70,000." And he walked up to me and said, "You know, son, I don't think I've ever met anybody on more groundless ground than you are currently standing. But we want to support the women in our company who have had breast cancer. And so, we'll give you the money." So, within 20 minutes I had the first $70,000. It was absolutely amazing.[74]

"Sing for the Cure" premiered on June 11, 2000, and has been performed all over the world.Since it is a work for both men's and women's voices, the women's choruses who have sung it have joined with men's choruses, often from their own city: CHARIS women's chorus and the Gateway Men's Chorus of St. Louis; the Gay Men's Chorus of Houston and the Bayou City Women's Chorus; and the Richmond (VA) Women's Chorus singing with the Richmond Men's Chorus. Performances tend to be gala events; in 2009 Vox Femina Los Angeles and Voices of Hope Men's Chorus united for a performance with television star Florence Henderson—who had become a spokesperson for cancer awareness after losing her husband to the disease— as narrator.

The individual songs include many voices and many moods: The Community's Voice asks, "Who will speak for them?/ Who will make the choice?/ Give their pain a voice/ Share in their journey/ plead for their need?" The Partner's Voice is heard in "The Promise Lives On," sung by the entire chorus, and the voices of the survivors themselves range from mournful to defiant and even humorous. One of the most poignant songs is "Who Will Curl My Daughter's Hair," in which a mother prays for "one more year" to "give one more hug/ dry one more tear / mark one more inch upon the way / live to see them standing tall." In 2010, Kathy Latour, a breast cancer survivor and co-founder of the magazine CURE, recalled her role in the genesis of this song;

> During the writing of Sing for the Cure, the lyricist interviewed a number of women to understand what we face when confronted with breast cancer.... She wanted to get the perspective of a mother fearing she will not be able to raise her child. When the lyricist called me, I had just returned from a speaking engagement where I talked about our worst fear when we are diagnosed, and how it is the vision we see when we hear the words you have cancer. A number of people came up to me after the talk to tell me what they saw.... Then a petite woman walked up and said simply, "He doesn't know how to curl their hair." I relayed this story to the lyricist and then forgot about it. I wasn't able to attend the premiere, so I was thrilled when I got a call a few years later from director Dr. Tim Seelig, who asked if I would come talk to him about narrating a piece for another performance of Sing .... When I read the section he wanted me to narrate, I realized that the lyricist had incorporated my story into the narration and song that followed it.[75]

"Where I Live"

Like "Sing for the Cure," Diane Benjamin's "Where I Live" drew its inspiration from the stories of those affected by the breast cancer epidemic. But though they shared a common theme, they arose from different choral cultures.

"Where I Live" was commissioned by the Denver Women's Chorus in 1999, when Benjamin was serving as accompanist for Calliope Women's Chorus of Minneapolis. Frustrated by the standard SSA repertoire ("the published stuff for SSA is like written for girls' glee club, the ranges are stupid, they're all written for high school girls!"), Benjamin began arranging and composing for Calliope.[76] Meanwhile, the Denver Women's Chorus was discussing a commission for a work to present at the GALA Festival scheduled for San Jose the following year. When Artistic Director Marla Wasson proposed the breast cancer epidemic as the commission theme, the chorus immediately endorsed the idea. "Once we started bringing it up in the chorus, it just burst out," recalled DWC member Connie North. "Everybody knew somebody. We'd already had people in the chorus who'd had breast cancer ... [I]t was such a universal experience, even if you hadn't had it yourself.... It was beginning to be so obvious that it was such a widespread thing."[77] The chorus commissioned Benjamin to write a piece for them, raising the money from local donations. "The thing is, they really wanted something about breast cancer, but they didn't have any idea what," Benjamin recalled. "So I had really free rein about what I was able to do ... We were very fortunate in the Twin Cities at this time, we had a group called Women's Cancer Alliance.... It was really focused on breast cancer as a social issue, an environmental issue, and really trying to counteract the narrative of you know, let's just all examine our breasts and wear pink."[78]

Benjamin had a friend and sister chorus member who had been diagnosed with breast cancer shortly before she started writing the piece.

I started talking to her and also to her mother, which was really interesting, about the experiences of survivors, and I determined two things. First of all, I felt like every word of the piece should be by a survivor, except the first movement, which I wrote the lyrics for.... Every other word in that piece is written by a survivor, and that was really really, really, really important to me, and I think that that ties to sort of the way that women's choruses were formed, it was really to be about our voices, our experiences, so that was really important. And then the second thing was to really take that social justice position.[79]

In 2009, ten years after the piece was first commissioned, Benjamin's home chorus, Calliope, performed the piece in her hometown, Minneapolis. By this time, the piece had been performed forty times by women's choruses across the country. Shortly before the performance, *Minneapolis Star Tribune* reporter Kim Ode visited Calliope to speak with members of the chorus and to watch a rehearsal with Benjamin herself coaching the singers.

"The first several rehearsals were touch-and-go, the singers dissolving in tears at a particular phrase or unbidden memory," Ode reported. "In the midst of the fourth movement, 'Help Me,' Mary Lilja broke down, blindsided by how the lyrics mirrored a friend with breast cancer who always wished that people could meet her on her terms, then asked forgiveness for being so difficult."[80]

Other singers expressed similar emotions. "I'm just barely able to get my body through this even now," acknowledged Sarah McMahill, another Calliope member. Founding member Sarah Henderson, who had sung the piece with other groups, observed: "It's not always the women in the scarves who are crying. They're not the ones who get hit in the face with it."[81]

Both "Sing for the Cure" and "Where I Live" present the words of actual survivors and their friends and family members. Both are deeply affecting to the performers who sing these words and the audiences who hear them. But the compositional processes and the actual texts of the two works reflect markedly different cultural, social, and political approaches.

"Sing for the Cure" was trademarked by the Komen foundation as soon as it was commissioned, and has remained part of the Komen enterprise. Gayle L. Sulik, in her 2012 book,

Pink Ribbon Blues: How Breast Cancer Culture Undermines Women's Health, is one of many critics of "pinkwashing," a term coined by the San Francisco activist group Breast Cancer Action to describe "companies that raise funds for breast cancer while diverting attention from the company's potential hazards, such as producing chemicals or toxins that have been linked to the disease."[82] The Komen Foundation itself has pursued several questionable promotions, including pink-ribbon themed plastic water bottles (despite the fact that studies have linked BPA, a common ingredient in plastic water bottles, to malignant tumors); pink Kentucky Fried Chicken "buckets for the cure" (despite the known links between obesity and breast cancer); a Komen-trademarked perfume called "Promise Me," which was found to contain several potentially cancer-causing ingredients; and 1000 pink drill bits produced by Baker Hughes, a Houston oil company, for use in hydraulic fracturing ("fracking"), a process using over 700 chemicals, many of which are endocrine disrupters and have been found to increase the risk of cancer.[83]

The pink ribbon concept itself was inspired by the AIDS red ribbon campaign, which was inspired in turn by the yellow ribbons that had been displayed in solidarity with the hostages taken in Iran in 1979 and the American troops fighting in the Gulf War of the 1990s. In 1990, members of Visual AIDS, a group of artists advocating for people with HIV/AIDS, were inspired by the yellow ribbons to create the Ribbon Project, choosing the color red for its "connection to blood and the idea of passion— not only anger, but love."[84]

Unlike the Komen Foundation, the Visual AIDS Artists' Caucus sought to avoid any commercialization of the red ribbon symbol. The Visual AIDS website states, "The ribbon has never been copyrighted in the United States, to allow it to be worn and used widely as a symbol in the fight against AIDS." The statement goes on to declare the artists' intention "not to list any individual as the 'creator' of the Red Ribbon Project," but to keep the copyright image free "so that no individual or organization would profit from the use of the red ribbon," and to keep the Red Ribbon "as a consciousness raising symbol, not as a commercial or trademark tool."[85]

Among those who have performed both "Sing for the Cure" and "Where I Live" are the long-time members of the Denver Women's Chorus, the chorus that originally commissioned "Where I Live." "I've sung in both," said one chorus member, "and 'Sing For The Cure' is a wonderful piece too but ... it has a different feel—partly I suppose because 'Where I Live' was ours, you know, and 'Sing For The Cure' wasn't ours.... It's very moving, it's very wonderful—but it feels a little more commercial to me." Other chorus members noted the difference between singing a piece with a men's chorus and singing "Where I Live," which was written for women's chorus. "I miss[ed] that factor," said one singer. "I really enjoyed the parts of 'Sing for The Cure' where it's just us. I think that—that the women's viewpoint on that is very different from the men."[86]

Women's choruses continue to perform "Where I Live," with proceeds generally going to local breast cancer support and awareness groups. Choruses find the experience of singing it unlike any other performance. In her ethnographic study of the Common Woman Chorus, Jennifer Womack described "Where I Live" as a "coming-of-age milestone for the group.... In every interview I have conducted with both past and present members, the Breast Cancer Concert is mentioned.... Twenty-one years into their existence, it was the season in which the chorus reached adulthood."[87]

In an effort to involve the audience and raise awareness, many choruses follow Benjamin's recommendation for question-and-answer periods after a performance. Like "Sing for the Cure," "Where I Live" transforms the words of sufferers and survivors alike into moving musical poetry. But while "Sing for the Cure" and the Komen Foundation emphasize the search for "the cure," "Where I Live" goes beyond empathy and hope to prevention, pointing to the environmental factors that have contributed to the epidemic. Interspersed with the final movement, "My Body," is a spoken segment naming chemicals associated with cancer.

"I was really fortunate to find this book called *1,001 Household Chemicals*, and I just thought, Oh we just need to name these toxins, we do a lot of naming," Benjamin recalled. "I thought, Well, you know, we need to call out what's killing us. I got paid

$2,000 from the Denver women's chorus. It seemed like a whole lot of money but I wasn't answerable to somebody's corporate board of directors."[88]

Keeping the Network Alive

While individual choruses were widening their social action networks and expanding their repertoire, the Network itself continued to serve as a unifying force. In February, 1996, representatives from six choruses gathered in Cincinnati at a Network meeting hosted by MUSE and featured in the May 1996, issue of *Across the Lines*. In addition, the newsletter carried a front-page invitation from the Portland Lesbian Choir, which had volunteered to host the next Sister Singers Festival in 1998. "We are excited about bringing a festival to our town," the choir declared, extolling the opportunities a West Coast festival would offer: "We are excited about sharing the diversity of this area's women's choirs (three in Portland alone). And we are excited about the chance to show all of you the beauty of the Pacific Northwest.... Oregon is a beautiful place and Portland is a friendly city with a large and active lesbian community."[89] The article also reflected the Network's increasing concerns about the surrounding political world, acknowledging that there might be some apprehension about Oregon's recent anti-gay initiatives (see chapter 7), but assuring readers that "the Portland area has consistently rejected these initiatives," and that "public officials, churches and civic organizations" had come forth to help defeat the three statewide ballot measures.[90] The stage was set for Sister Singers' first west coast Festival. Shortly after the meeting, however, financial and other difficulties forced the Portland Lesbian Choir to cancel.

The years that followed were a difficult time for the Network. Though individual choruses continued to grow and thrive, SSN was not able to sponsor another Festival for several years, and the newsletter, too, lapsed. Finally, in 1999, women attending the National Women's Music Festival and the GALA leadership conference began discussing Sister Singers and realizing how much the Network had meant to them over the past twenty years. Artemis Singers of Chicago, one of the Network's founding choruses, stepped forward to host a planning meeting with the aim of reviving the Network. "We invited people to come and we got a roomful," recalled Artemis singer Midge Stocker. "We were prepared to step in because we think this is really, really important for the women's choral network, for the women's community."[91]

Among the roomful of women at the 1999 meeting were Janice Scalza and Sheryl Mase, representing the two-year-old Grand Rapids Women's Chorus. "Sheryl and I had just gotten together as girlfriends," Janice recalled. "And then when we got to the meeting, Sheryl and I, you know, started to have a lot of energy for each other, but also for the rest of the group that was there.... And our relationship was forming, our relationship with our chorus was forming, and then we stepped into this wonderful group of women that we realized were us, but all around the country."[92]

Buoyed by the spirit at the meeting, Janice and Sheryl volunteered to host the next Festival in Grand Rapids, with the understanding that Michigan's other women's chorus, Sistrum of Lansing, would help out. "I think everyone in the room was nervous," Janice recalled, "except for Sheryl and me, because we had all this confidence and faith that we could do this. Well, then what ended up happening is, you know, as you can imagine, women in the room were very excited, as were we, but we ended up having to call home."

Sheryl added, "My feeling was we can do this. And how fun will this be and how amazing and there's women across the country that want to attend a festival and crave to get together and share their commonalities and their passion for music and, you know, social justice issues and everything else. I just thought, 'We can do this.'"[93]

The chorus immediately began planning for the 2001 Festival, which would be called "Under Northern Lights"—a title "which basically came from a ferry ride that Lori [GRWC Director Lori

Tennenhouse] and I took on the Badger Ferry going across Lake Michigan." The Festival planners also decided on a theme for themselves, inspired by the fish in the Grand River. "We titled ourselves, 'The Salmon Singers'.... We threw a big party for the planners very early on with a very strong punch." "A fish tank full of punch," Sheryl added. "Fish tank with bobbers. With little ice cube fishes. I can't stress to you enough the value of making things fun for the planning committee."[94]

To help fund the Festival, planners reached out to local sponsors, even securing grants from corporations and a welcome proclamation from the mayor.

> We determinedly made it an international festival by inviting Canadian choruses. We just went in and embellished and made it seem like the best thing that was ever gonna happen to the city, and it was international and we were gonna be providing all of this revenue when all of these people descended on Grand Rapids. Part of it was bluster and part of it was, you know, actual real, heartfelt excitement.... When the festival was over, Sheryl and I were recognized with hometown hero awards.[95]

"Under Northern Lights," held during Memorial Day weekend, 2001, included performances by twenty-two women's choruses, two mass choruses, and guest performances by women's music legends Margie Adam, Sue Fink, Rhiannon, and Kay Gardner. Looking back on the Festival ten years later, Janice and Sheryl agreed that along with revitalizing the Network, "Under Northern Lights" was a catalyst for their chorus. "Why do you want to do this? It's such a hard thing to convey," said Sheryl. "Because you love the music, you feel strongly about the social issues. And there's an intangible—there's that networking with women all over the place that are likeminded. That, to me, is just so important."

"It's given back in incredible ways over the years," Janice agreed, "not only for our own chorus and Sistrum.... We've been able to help rejuvenate the Network.... We paid the people we needed to pay and then we turned over, I think, $18,000 or $19,000 to the Network to say, 'Here, go have another festival now.'" Sheryl added, "It's that whole idea of creating more body of music. So, we've started commissioning. We didn't have anything but going forward from there, our chorus, it just kind of hits you over the head—we need to contribute to the body of women's music."[96]

In 2006, the San Diego Women's Chorus fulfilled Janice's invitation to "go, have another festival now," and Sheryl's suggestion to enrich the repertoire by commissioning music by women composers. "Western Sol," the ninth Sister Singers Festival and the first to take place on the West Coast, also marked the Network's twenty-fifth anniversary with the Network's first commissioned work, "Ode to Women," Argentinian-American composer Josefina Beneditti's setting of a poem by Pat Mora. The text is a tribute to women and to music, and the song has been performed several times since at individual choral concerts and GALA Festivals:

> Listen to the place where life grows
> the inner seedbed of music
> that curls and branches....
> Listen, for when the *mujeres* gather
> O when women gather
> to hold hands together
> their hums rise and ripple, sway
> like candles, a symphony of light.[97]

Eleven choruses attended the San Diego Festival. Organizer Teri Siciliani acknowledged that one of the issues arising in the planning was the fact that the San Diego Women's Chorus, the host chorus, was led by a male director. "And for us it was, you know, 'Yeah, well, we want to maybe host a festival but we've got a male director. How's that gonna play out?'"

Members of the Sister Singers Co-Coordinating Committee and organizers of past festivals were immediately supportive. "They were very clear that it was really what we decided to have—to be our festival about—what our rules were. There were not set rules of what you have to do to produce a Sister Singers festival—it can have the flavor to reflect and should have the flavor to reflect who you guys are as a chorus and to invite others to join in that."[98]

Teri's observations were an apt description of the Sister Singers Network as choruses prepared to move into the twenty-first century. "You know, as the women's movement has evolved, so, I think, have the Festivals. There's a lot of difference about how we feel about things than we did thirty years ago.... I think it's important not to be static because if you are static in any way in your life, then it just dies eventually."[99]

As women's choruses moved beyond the millennium, Sister Singers was very much alive. The first decades of the twenty-first century would bring new struggles and new challenges for the LGBTQ movement and for the women's choruses who continued to sing for social justice.

9

Into the Future

During the first decades of the twenty-first century, the LGBT community advanced toward equality at a pace few could have predicted. In 2003, the Supreme Court repealed *Bowers v. Hardwick*, ending the criminalization of consensual same-sex sexual activity. In 2011, the repeal of "Don't Ask, Don't Tell" allowed LGBT people to serve openly in the military. And most notably, the campaign for marriage equality, which had engaged activists at the state level for decades, finally culminated in *Obergefell v. Hodges* on June 26, 2015, when the Supreme Court declared marriage equality the law of the land.

The marriage campaign had begun at the state level in the early 1990s, when a handful of states began passing laws that pre-emptively prohibited same sex marriages. By the turn of the century, the LGBT community and their allies had mobilized, and in 2004, Massachusetts became the first state to legalize same-sex marriage. Advocates continued to pursue a state-by-state strategy until 2013, when the Supreme Court issued two decisions that gave strong impetus to the marriage equality movement. Ruling on *U.S. v. Windsor*, the Court held that Edith Windsor, who had legally married Thea Spyer in Canada in 2007, was entitled to Spyer's estate after the latter's death. The decision effectively overturned DOMA, the 1996 Defense of Marriage Act, which had held that the terms "spouse" and "marriage" applied only to opposite-sex unions. On the same day, the Court also overturned Proposition 8, a 2008 California ballot initiative that had added a provision defining marriage as a union between one man and one woman to the state constitution.

In the years leading up to and immediately following the *Windsor* decision, women's choruses were at the forefront of statewide campaigns for marriage equality—campaigns that could be harrowing as well as inspiring. In November, 2013, debate over marriage equality in the Hawaii State Legislature turned into an all-day session that drew "raucous crowds," according to the *Honolulu Civil Beat*, and forced the House and Senate Sergeants-at-Arms to order opposing demonstrators into separate areas divided by barricades.[1]

November 6, 2013, was rehearsal night for the Women's Chorus of Honolulu, whose rehearsal space at St. Clement's Church happened to be a short way from the Legislature. Two years later, founding member Antonia Alvarez recalled, "Hundreds and hundreds of protesters were brought out by the busload to the Capitol, chanting, shouting... You could hear the chanting in our rehearsal space, and the week of the vote was just awful, almost unbearable." Alvarez found the experience especially traumatic because of the work she was doing during the day.

> I was doing trainings on LGBT safety and equality during the day, and people [were] coming up to me and saying how their families are being torn apart by this vote. The Leg' was hearing all of this testimony, it would go into three, four in the morning. Our teenagers were staying up at night, telling their story and then having pediatricians come in telling how it's totally correct and fine, and then the grandparents of that child would go in an hour later and say ... they're gonna die—it was just incredibly painful. It was really important to have the women's chorus coming in and singing some of the songs that we had that helped us heal— "Circle Round for Freedom, Circle Round for Peace"—just coming together and singing.[2]

As statewide marriage campaigns proliferated, women's choruses continued to march, rally, and sing. In 2005, the

Common Woman Chorus of Durham, North Carolina, presented "Love and Marriage," a celebration of marriage equality. Local religious leaders from the North Carolina Religious Coalition for Marriage Equality read a Declaration of Faith that they had recently presented to the North Carolina General Assembly, and the pastor of the local Metropolitan Community Church performed a same-sex commitment ceremony. According to the chorus website, "The concert was followed by a raucous wedding reception complete with wedding cake and champagne. By popular demand, the chorus presented a reprise performance of this event in 2006."[3]

Voices Rising of Boston partnered with Another Octave: Connecticut Women's Chorus in 2009 to produce "Love is Here to Stay," a marriage equality concert at the Unitarian Society of New Haven. The same year, the two choruses joined for "Five!" a concert celebrating five years of marriage equality in Massachusetts, and co-produced "The Joy of We" at Eliot Church in Newton, featuring Mark Koval's "We the People: A Musical Exploration of Marriage Equality in America."[4]

2009 also saw the defeat of a Maine campaign to uphold a same-sex marriage law that had been passed by the legislature and sent to referendum by gay rights opponents. During the campaign, Portland Maine's Women in Harmony sang at several rallies, including one at First Parish Unitarian Church where members of the Maine Gay Men's Chorus joined them in a performance of "Two Weddings," a plea for marriage equality by a WIH member writing about the meaning of marriage for her heterosexual son and her lesbian daughter.[5] (Marriage equality did finally come to Maine three years later, when voters approved a new Question One, this time framed as an endorsement of same-sex marriage, and marriage equality became state law.)

In 2012, the Seattle Men's Chorus and the Seattle Women's Chorus joined in a five-city tour to present "Voices United for Marriage," a concert in support of Washington State's Ballot Referendum 74. After the measure's success, the men's chorus featured a double marriage ceremony during their December holiday concert. Retired judge Anne Levinson, a former Seattle deputy mayor and longtime advocate for LGBT equality, officiated at the on-stage marriage of two couples, one from each chorus. The Seattle Women's Chorus joined the men to sing "One Hand, One Heart," from *West Side Story*.[6]

In 2012, Calliope Women's Chorus of Minnesota performed at the Marriage Equality Open House sponsored by the Macalester-Plymouth Marriage Equality Committee and Minnesotans United for All. The event was part of a campaign featured in *How Love Won: The Fight for Marriage Equality*, a documentary chronicling the successful campaign to defeat an anti-gay amendment to the state constitution. The defeat of the amendment made Minnesota the first US state to reject a constitutional ban on same-sex marriage; during the campaigns that followed in other states, *How Love Won* was shown at film festivals around the country and overseas.[7]

By 2015, thirty-seven states had legalized same-sex marriage by legislative action, court decision, or, in three states, by popular vote on a ballot initiative. In view of these developments, and in the wake of the *Windsor* and Prop. 8 rulings, activists decided that the time was right to move to the national stage. *Obergefell v. Hodges* was named for Jim Obergefell, who had sued the state of Ohio to allow the death certificate for his late spouse to read "married"; the case included five other couples from four states—Michigan, Ohio, Kentucky, and Tennessee—some of whom were biological or adoptive parents.

In its 5-4 decision, the Court ruled that the fundamental right to marry was guaranteed to same-sex couples by both the Due Process Clause and the Equal Protection Clause of the Fourteenth Amendment to the Constitution.[8] Writing for the majority, Justice Anthony Kennedy asserted, "It would misunderstand these men and women to say they disrespect the idea of marriage.... They ask for equal dignity in the eyes of the law. The Constitution grants them that right."[9]

Although some in the LGBT community viewed marriage as a reactionary institution privileging monogamous state-sanctioned unions over the many kind of families that LGBT people had created, the widespread public reaction to the *Obergefell* decision was joyful celebration. Supporters uploaded rainbow flags to their social media pages, couples began planning their weddings, and Mary Bonauto, the Maine attorney who had argued the case before the Supreme Court, called the decision "a day for equality, for liberty and justice under law."[10] That night, the crowd gathered on Pennsylvania Avenue saw the White House lit up in rainbow colors as President Obama, who had expressed his support for same-sex marriage three years earlier, tweeted a rainbow-colored avatar with the message, "If you liked our avatar, you'll love the view from Pennsylvania Avenue tonight," and the hashtag "#LoveWins."[11]

Yet even as marriage equality became the law of the land and queer people made their way into the mainstream media, hate crimes and anti-gay initiatives were on the rise. Mark Potok, a senior fellow at the Southern Poverty Law Center, spoke for many when he suggested that as the majority of society became more tolerant of L.G.B.T. people, opponents tended to become more radical.[12] Trinity University Associate Professor Amy Stone agreed, asserting that anti-gay activists "tend to use these moments to frighten the general public, relying on fears about trans women in bathrooms or locker rooms. Usually these moments tap into pre-existing panics about gender or sexuality, not necessarily spawning new ones."[13]

What Matters

Heaven help me for I am lost
what a price my love did cost
but here I am standing strong and I am free
(From "What Matters," ©1999 Randi Driscoll
Swim Swam Swum Songs/BMI)

The most notorious hate crime of the late 1990s was the murder of Matthew Shepard in 1998. Aaron McKinney and Russell Henderson met Shepard at a bar in Laramie, Wyoming, offered him a ride home, and drove to a remote rural area where they robbed, pistol-whipped, and tortured him. His death six days later inspired demonstrations and protests around the world that ultimately culminated in the passage of the Matthew Shepard and James Byrd, Jr. Hate Crimes Prevention Act, signed by President Obama in 2009. The Act expanded the federal hate crimes law to include crimes motived by a victim's actual or perceived gender, sexual orientation, gender identity, or disability. (James Byrd was an African American man who was tied to a truck by two white supremacists, dragged behind it, and decapitated in Jasper, Texas, in 1998.)

The growth of social media and the Internet meant that news affecting the LGBT community, and political news in general, traveled almost instantaneously. And just as quickly, the community responded with rallies, vigils, political activism—and music. One of the most powerful musical responses was "What Matters," written soon after the murder of Matthew Shepard. In words expressing the spirit of the entire LGBT chorus movement, Randi Driscoll described the genesis of the song:

> When I first heard the tragic story of Matthew Shepard's death I was saddened and outraged. I wanted to kick in my television set, scream and cry. Instead, I went to my piano to find solace in my music. What transpired was the song, "What Matters."....I have spent years touring to promote the single and raise awareness by performing the song at clubs, benefit concerts, vigils and Pride festivals. This work and this song are the most important things I have ever done in my life. I am continuously inspired by the angels around us that do so much to see that this type of hatred and ignorance is stopped.[14]

Kevin Robison's choral arrangement of "What Matters" became a mainstay of the LGBT chorus repertoire. Within a decade, "What Matters" had been performed by over fifty choruses internationally, including the Gay Men's Chorus of Los Angeles at the Disney Hall and the New York City Gay Men's Chorus at Carnegie Hall. In 2010, Voices Rising Artistic Director

Leora Zimmer led a mass chorus performance of "What Matters" at the tenth National Sister Singers Choral Festival in Chicago.[15]

Despite the national horror at the murder of Matthew Shepard and the passage of the Hate Crimes Prevention Act, the Southern Poverty Law Center reported 15,351 LGBT hate crime offences during the years from 1995-2008.[16] Between 2000 and 2015, data from the FBI and from local and national print and on-line newspapers documented anti-gay violence in at least thirty states. The victims included a fifteen-year-old junior high school student shot by a classmate in Oxnard, California, because he was perceived as gay; a woman stabbed to death at a bus stop in Newark, New Jersey by a man whom she had told she was a lesbian while rejecting his advances; a three-year-old boy in Tampa, Florida, who died of brain injuries sustained when his father repeatedly threw him against a wall because he was concerned that the child was gay; and dozens of transgender men and women who were shot, stabbed, beaten and strangled to death.[17]

The backlash against LGBT rights escalated legislatively as well. In 2012, Jack Phillips, a baker in Lakewood, Colorado, refused to provide a wedding cake for a gay couple, citing his religious beliefs against same sex marriage. The case went all the way to the Colorado Supreme Court, which refused to hear the case, leaving in place the Colorado Civil Rights Commission's decision ordering Phillips to make cakes for same-sex ceremonies or face legal action. Phillips abandoned baking altogether, but in 2016 his attorney filed a petition asking the Supreme Court to rule on the case. On June 4, 2018, the Court ruled in favor of Masterpiece Cakeshop on the grounds that some members of the Colorado Civil Rights Commission, which had originally heard the case, had made comments that the Court considered to reveal an anti-religion bias. Gay rights advocates, including the American Civil Liberties Union, which had represented the couple, emphasized that the ruling was a narrow one that did not challenge Colorado's non-discrimination laws and affirmed the rights of LGBT people in general.[18]

The Phillips case encouraged anti-gay activists in other states to pursue the "religious exemption" argument. In 2016 the Georgia legislature passed a so-called religious liberty bill, which would have prevented government penalties against anyone refusing to serve or hire a person if doing so would violate a "sincerely held religious belief." The bill was vetoed by Governor Nathan Deal after "a steady stream of corporate titans" threatened to pull investments from Georgia if it became law.[19]

And then, as the first anniversary of the Supreme Court marriage decision approached, and in the middle of one the bitterest presidential campaigns in recent years, Omar Mateen, a twenty-nine-year-old security guard, perpetrated an attack that was the deadliest single mass shooting and the deadliest incident of violence against LGBT people in United States history, and the deadliest terrorist attack on U.S. soil since the September 11 attacks of 2001. The attack killed forty-nine people and wounded fifty-three others inside Pulse, a gay nightclub in Orlando, Florida, and provoked a statement from the United Nations Security Council and vigils around the world. Gay choruses again responded, with special concerts, vigil performances, and a special tribute and performance by the Orlando Gay Chorus at the 2016 GALA Festival.[20]

As in the past, the backlash did not stop LGBT activists and their allies from continuing the battle for full equality. In addition, during the first decades of the twenty-first century, choruses joined with other communities and sang for struggles that faced the country at large. Several choruses produced programs around the theme of climate change, such as, "Sea Change," a 2015 concert by Resonance Women's Chorus of Boulder, described as "an exploration in sound and song of the emotional experience of living with climate change, and an attempt to simply be with the 'not knowing' that underlies all of our wonderings and fears about the Earth's future and our own."[21] Windsong Chorus of Cleveland partnered with the Cleveland International Film Festival for two showings of *Letters from Baghdad*, a documentary about Gertrude Bell, a British spy who helped draw the borders of Iraq and has been called "the female Lawrence of Arabia." And well before the subject of immigration gave rise to a national debate, several choruses offered concerts focusing on the experiences of those who chose or were forced to leave their homelands. "Land of Our Dreams," a 2007 concert by the Central Pennsylvania Womyn's Chorus, included songs from Africa, Central and South America, India, and Eastern Europe, interspersed with spoken reflections from members of PAIRWN, The Pennsylvania Immigrant and Refugee Women's Network.[22] In 2011, Portland, Maine's Women in Harmony presented "Moving On: Immigration in Song," a concert featuring a commissioned song cycle, "(F) light," with text by Tucson-based poets Wendy Burk and Eric Magrane and music by former Women in Harmony member Erica-Quin-Easter. In her program notes for "(F)light," Quin-Easter described the work as "a song cycle exploring ... themes of migration, culture, identity, and environment in the Canadian border regions of Maine and the Mexican border regions of Arizona."[23]

"When She Sings, Her Voice Carries Far"

"Moving On" included a guest performance by Pihcintu, a multinational girls' chorus based in Portland, a city which happens to be a refugee resettlement community with immigrants from all over the world. The Women in Harmony-Pihcintu partnership had begun a year earlier when Music Director Catherine Beller-McKenna approached Pihcintu founder-director Con Fullam, an award-winning singer, songwriter and producer whose musical journey had taken him from Sidney, Maine ("60 or so people, 600 or so cows"), to Nashville and back home to Maine. The grandson of an Irish immigrant, Fullam founded Pihcintu after hearing local teachers describe the challenges faced by Portland's refugee children; he envisioned the chorus as a way for these children to find healing and support and become part of a community. He chose the name "Pihcintu," which means "When she sings, her voice carries far" in the language of the Passamaquoddy, one of Maine's indigenous peoples. Although he had originally intended to include both boys and girls, Con found that cultural taboos made it impossible to attract and keep boys, and Pihcintu eventually became a girls' chorus.[24]

Amanda Allen, a member of the Women in Harmony community relations team, served as the liaison between the two choruses and soon began learning about the lives of the Pihcintu girls. "The oldest, [who are] sixteen and seventeen, have very vivid memories of being in Sudan and being afraid for their lives every day. And seeing people be killed, and losing their family members. Some of the girls are moved from home to home. I found out with a lot of the girls from going to pick them up that there would be ten to eleven people in this two-bedroom apartment."[25]

As part of her work with Pihcintu, Amanda was asked to chaperone a 2011 trip to Washington, DC, where the girls sang at "Bridges to a New Future," a convention sponsored by the U.S. Office of Refugee Resettlement. Delegates from around the world gave the girls a standing ovation, and the *Today* show featured a heartwarming segment with Con leading the girls in song.[26] Behind these public celebrations, Amanda's role as chaperone gave her a glimpse into the girls' private lives.

> Some of the girls were a handful, and Con was very careful not to put some of them together. But there were three girls that begged and begged to be together. When I looked at them, and they seemed very stressed, and earnestly sad, I relented and said, "OK, you can be together and I'll chaperone you." And so, we shared a room together, the three of them in this huge bed, these nine- to eleven-year-old girls would sleep cocooned, all three together, so close, and I realized that's how they always sleep. I didn't realize they were cousins. When I would pick them up I just assumed that they were friends at each other's house—what I would do growing up. But they all lived together.[27]

The collaboration between Pihcintu and Women in Harmony proved both challenging and rewarding. Amanda had worried that "it would be mayhem and no one would know what to do with that type of chaos. And that did happen," she admitted. "There were the girls that wanted to talk through the whole thing, and didn't want to pay attention and didn't want to learn from us, and there were members of the chorus that were very taken aback by that." But there were also successes. With some chorus members, "it just clicked, and there was great understanding and acceptance. We paired them with other members in the chorus and members of Women in Harmony would help and teach the songs to Pihcintu. Then they in turn would teach us songs. They really opened up to teaching us their songs."[28]

Amanda and her sister singers soon realized that their standard choral procedure was very different from the singing styles of the Pihcintu girls. "The challenge for Women in Harmony was to sing a song that we weren't reading the music, and that we could relax a little bit. Maybe move around. The energy of the girls was so different. I think that threw a curve, even for our director, who works with children, but I didn't know if she would realize that it would be quite so different."

Amanda had some afterthoughts about what might have strengthened the collaboration. "I think it was disruptive, disruptive to our chorus, and I think a lot of chorus members would say that's what they remember, even though the end result was very successful, it was a wonderful concert." With hindsight, she wishes that some of the Women in Harmony singers had met with Pihcintu in the girls' own "more informal and relaxed rehearsal space." On reflection, "It was a lot to invite them into our rehearsal, as structured as rehearsal is, and how much we try to accomplish in that two hours' time span."

Despite these difficulties, Amanda considered "Moving On" a success for both the audience and the chorus. "We're a little more loosened up," she said. "It really showed the audience that we were having fun, and that we enjoyed that, even though it might not have been in everyone's comfort zone.... We did a rap with them, which is so unlike our singing style, but ... to bring that to us and to be able to teach that to us, they're so proud of that."[29]

Traveling Abroad: More Than Just Singing

As they broadened their outreach, women's choruses were traveling—to Sister Singers and GALA Festivals, to collaborations with choruses in other cities, and in some cases, outside the United States. In 2009, MUSE received an invitation to an international summit sponsored by *Justica Global*, a non-governmental human rights organization headquartered in the Dominican Republic. Thirty MUSE members traveled to Santo Domingo for "*Arte y Revolución*," where they sang in several concerts and participated in a panel on the role of the arts in social justice organizing.

"Our first morning in the capital, we gave an impromptu concert on the steps of the National Archives One," recalled MUSE singer Katie Johnson. "The sunny hall was filled with archive technicians and national leaders gathered to commemorate the institution's oral history radio program. The audience gasped at Lois's voice [Lois Shegog, MUSE's African American Assistant Director] in 'I'm Gon' Stand,' and one woman even cried during the '*Duerme Negrito*,' remembering her mother singing that song to her as a child."

The visit offered many other informal singing opportunities. "We rehearsed with a local *a cappella* ensemble that arranges, performs, and spreads the word about Dominican music. They workshopped *El Pambiche* [and] suggested ways to improve the feel of syncopation. We ended up dancing with choir member[s] ... and Cathy worked on the possibility of commissioning an arrangement for MUSE from the director."[30]

MUSE members agreed that the trip was about more than just singing. "To see with our own two eyes the poverty, pollution, and trash filling the streets was not easy, and to see the mixture of people, the vivid colors, the crowds, Spanish words, and children dancing is what I see as the living spirit of this country," wrote Julie Lessard. "It's a reminder that there is still fighting to be done, and justice to be achieved.... I feel blessed to be a part of this choir which strives for so much of what the conference and the people from *Justicia Global* strive for in their own country every day."[31]

Other women's choruses traveled abroad to participate in international choral festivals. The Peninsula Women's Chorus won third prize in the women's concert division at the 2006 Béla Bartók Choir Competition in Debrecen, Hungary, and performed at the San Juan Coral International Choral Festival in San Juan, Argentina, in 2015. Other women's choruses have traveled to Normandy, France, for a World War II commemorative ceremony (Southern Arizona Women's Chorus); to Cuba (Voices from the Heart, New Hampshire); and to Italy (Women's Voices, New Hampshire).[32]

In 1999 Champaign's Amasong Chorus participated in a choral exchange with a mixed chorus in Pilsen, Czechoslovakia, which had been arranged through a Czech friend of an Amasong member. "It was a marvelous, marvelous experience," recalled Kathie Spegal. "The first time ... we sang in the carriage house [of a museum], which is beautiful. They'd set up chairs and it was just a little raised platform and we stood there and sang and we did a couple of Cajun songs, which they loved because of the rhythm, and 'Shenandoah,' and of course our 'Cradle Me,' which everybody likes to hear... They understood the rhythm and the harmony, 'cause they didn't always understand the words."

After a concert in Prague, the Czechs set up a reception in an adjoining room with food and wine. "The longer the night went and the more they drank, the more gregarious they got, and we all ended up on stage together and they taught us a Czech song. And so, we all sang it together." The following summer, Amasong hosted some of the Czech singers, who performed in Champaign. Did they know that Amasong was a lesbian-identified chorus? "I don't know what they knew," said Kathie. "I don't know what they understood and on what level but it wasn't an item of discussion. We just all loved music. So, it really didn't make any difference."[33]

"Music for a Purple Country"

Sue Coffee's two choruses, Resonance and Sound Circle, have organized collaborative concerts after every presidential election since George W. Bush's victory in 2004. "In 2004 we were sitting in Sound Circle rehearsal the week after the election and everybody was paralyzed by grief," Sue recalled, "and everyone we knew had been home watching TV and crying to themselves. People were isolating in their grief. Somebody said, 'Let's sing, let's do a concert.' We threw together a concert called 'No One is an Island: Music for a Purple Country.'" Sound Circle and Resonance were joined by the Denver Gay Men's Chorus, which Sue was also directing at the time. "We pulled from repertoire we knew, and it all spoke exactly to the moment," she added.[34]

By 2008 the choruses knew they wanted to present another election concert. "This time it was premeditated and ... I was trying to plan a program with enough flexibility to deal with either outcome," she explained. When the news of Barack Obama's election became official,

> ... everybody was dancing outside on the [Boulder] Pearl Street Mall. The concert was called "How Can I Stop From Singing!" We had Sound Circle, Resonance, and the small group of the Denver Gay Men's Chorus. The Low-Flying Knobs, a women's marimba group in town, opened the show with Zimbabwean marimba music.... And a number of other local artists and song leaders joined us. We opened the doors—it was a free concert—and people flooded in. We estimated 1,200 people in about a minute—a bit scary, honestly. They came in so fast—it was fantastic. We were plugged into the zeitgeist and got to feel all the energy of it.[35]

Obama's re-election in 2012 was the occasion for another election concert, "Sweet Land: Choices of Dignity," in which Boulder musicians and activists came together for a performance "inspired by the challenges of the presidential election, reflecting on our lives, our history, and our shared future."[36]

Trans Singers: "I Wanna See You Be Brave"

With the Supreme Court deciding in their favor, the White House on their side, and public opinion moving toward support for gay rights, activists began tackling what many viewed as the next frontier for their community: transgender advocacy. The very public transition of Olympic athlete Bruce Jenner to Caitlin Jenner, a self-proclaimed trans woman, helped normalize trans identity for thousands of Americans, as did the increasing number of trans characters on shows like "Transparent," featuring an aging father who begins living as a woman, and "Orange is the New Black," in which trans actress Laverne Cox played a trans woman prisoner. Among the heroes of the burgeoning movement for trans equality was Nicole Maines, a trans girl whose parents sued the Orono School District for denying Nicole access to the girls' bathrooms at her elementary and middle schools. In 2014, The Maine Supreme Court ruled in favor of the Maineses, stating that the district had violated the Maine Human Rights Act prohibiting discrimination based on sexual orientation. In 2015 the National Center for Transgender Equality reported growing acceptance of trans people by family members, coworkers, classmates, and friends, and President Obama became the first American president to utter the word "transgender" in a State of the Union address, condemning "the persecution of women, or religious minorities, or people who are lesbian, gay, bisexual or transgender."[37]

Advocates expressed optimism at the sudden appearance of trans people in the mass media. Hayden Mora, deputy chief of staff at the Human Rights Campaign and a transgender man, told CNN that that "the more people who know transgender people, the more they will understand, accept and support us." Similarly, trans activist and author Riki Wilchins declared, "We are at a social inflection point on transgender issues. Civil rights for minorities come in fits and starts. We're on an upswing now."[38]

Transgender students were the particular targets of so-called bathroom bills—laws and school policies that ordered trans students to use the bathroom corresponding to the gender on their birth certificate. The most notorious of these was North Carolina's HB-2, stating that individuals in government operated buildings (including public schools) may only use restrooms and changing facilities corresponding to the sex identified on their birth certificates. This law also overturned the city of Charlotte's non-discrimination policy, which had been in place since early 2016. Wrangling over these laws continued until March 2017, when, under pressure from the NCAA, which threatened to withhold championship events from the state through 2022, the House and Senate voted to repeal HB2 and replace it with House Bill 142, establishing the legislature as the sole authority to regulate access to bathrooms, showers, and changing facilities and instituting a moratorium on any new local ordinances on regulating public accommodations or private employment practices until December 1, 2020.[39]

Liberals and progressives regarded the uproar over bathrooms as a thinly disguised campaign against the trans community, pointing to the absence of any evidence that allowing trans students or adults to use the bathroom corresponding to their gender identity had endangered anybody else. In a 2015 national survey, seventeen school districts covering 600,000 students reported that they had experienced no problems after implementing transgender protections.[40] Similarly, as of 2017, neither the Transgender Law Center, the Human Rights Campaign nor the American Civil Liberties Union had found a single case of a transgender person harassing or threatening a cisgender person in a bathroom.

In a widely-shared twitter post, actor-turned activist George Takai drew a parallel between the Civil Rights movement and the current movement for LGBT rights, tweeting, "It's not about bathrooms... as it was never about water fountains."[41] Rev. William Barber II, president of the North Carolina NAACP, agreed. "This is not about bathrooms. It's about whether or not you can codify hate and discrimination into the laws of the state."[42]

The issue of trans identity had arisen in the lesbian community as far back as 1977, when threats by anti-trans women had forced Sandy Stone out of her job as an Olivia Records engineer, despite the Olivia collective's strong support. (See Chapter 3). In 1979 Janice Raymond's *The Transsexual Empire: The Making of the She-Male*, attacked Stone personally and condemned transsexuals for "rap[ing] women's bodies by reducing the real female form to an artifact, appropriating this body for themselves."[43]

The issue surfaced again in 1991 when Michigan Womyn's Music Festival organizers evicted Nancy Burkholder, a trans woman, informing her that the festival was open to "natural, women-born-women only."[44] This event coincided with the publication of Stone's transsexual manifesto "The Empire Strikes Back," in which she deconstructed medical and philosophical ideas about trans identity throughout history, ending with an appeal to transsexuals to "use the strength which brought us through the effort of restructuring identity, and which has also helped us to live in silence and denial, for a revisioning of our lives."[45]

Fueled by their anger at MichFest's treatment of Burkholder and by the transphobic rhetoric of Raymond and others, activists organized Camp Trans, an annual demonstration outside the MichFest gate. Though trans women were eventually admitted to the Festival, the conflict continued to simmer; as late as 2001, the Festival handout included a statement saying that although no womon's [sic] gender will be questioned on the land," organizers would continue "to run the Festival in a way that keeps faith with the womyn-born-womyn policy, which may mean denying admission to individuals who self-declare as male-to female transsexuals or female-to-male transsexuals now living as men (or asking them to leave if they enter)."[46] By 2015, the issue was still not resolved, and a coalition of LGBT rights groups had launched a petition calling for founder Lisa Vogel to meet with trans advocates. The meeting never took place; instead, on April 21, Vogel announced in a Facebook post that the 2015 Festival would be the last. Although Vogel's post did not mention the trans-inclusion controversy, many believed it played a significant role in the Festival's demise.

The trans controversy at Michigan touched on larger issues in the LGBT community stretching back to the lesbian separatism of the 1970s. Lesbians who continued to insist that only those born with XX chromosomes were real women—derisively labeled TERFs (Trans Exclusionary Radical Feminists) by trans advocates—espoused an essentialist concept of identity that had been largely discredited by the LGBT movement at large and by queer studies, which argued that gender itself was a fluid social construction rather than a fixed biological absolute.

Despite their deep connections to the women's festival movement, and to Michigan in particular, women's choruses had long since abandoned the exclusionary politics of lesbian separatism. Even choruses who had kept the term "lesbian" in their name, like the Portland (Oregon) Lesbian Choir and Artemis Singers (Chicago's Lesbian Feminist Chorus), featured mission statements emphasizing that all women were welcome regardless of sexual orientation. Of the 100+ American choruses listed on the Sister Singers website in 2017, most made no reference to trans identity, focusing instead on the need to match pitch, the importance of regular attendance at rehearsals, and the rewards of joining a community of women singers. Fifteen choruses mentioned gender identity or trans identity as part of their inclusive mission. The Common Woman Chorus of Durham, North Carolina, offered membership to "anyone who identifies as a woman, enjoys choral singing, and can commit to the chorus' regular rehearsal schedule." Fortissima: DC's Feminist Singers declared themselves "open to all sopranos and altos, regardless of gender." Anna Crusis described their choral community as "diverse in age, ethnicity, sexual orientation, gender expression, and culture," and added, "We create space for conversation and opinion and work together to create an environment in which all voices are heard." Several other chorus websites mentioned the trans community in their general mission statements; Voices Rising of Boston even included a link to the National Center for Trans Equality in their statement of principles.[47]

Although women's choruses were generally trans-friendly, it was not until an alto in Minnesota's One Voice Mixed Chorus approached Artistic Director Jane Ramseyer Miller to say that she was beginning her physical transition by taking testosterone, that LGBT choruses began paying specific attention to trans singers. "I was clueless about the process," Miller wrote in a 2016 post on the GALA blog, "but suggested that we check in every few months for a range check. Within the next year, to my amazement, Jan's voice moved seamlessly from alto through tenor and eventually settled at a solid bass 2. Aside from learning to read a new clef, he experienced relatively few vocal issues in the process."[48]

A year later, another One Voice singer transitioned, but this time the process was much more complicated and included vocal fatigue, hoarseness, and serious difficulty singing. Miller wrote that she was "fascinated by the experiences of these two singers, and I felt helpless to address their vocal issues. I began reading and talking to vocal experts, and finally found one who had worked with transitioning singers."[49]

As a result of these conversations, One Voice Mixed Chorus hosted the world's first Transgender Voices Festival in April 2004. The festival included vocal workshops for transitioning voices, workshops exploring identity and voice, and training for voice teachers and conductors. It culminated in the founding of TransVoices, a new Twin Cities chorus for transgender singers.

Miller's interactions with trans singers led her to write, "I began to understand that voice is incredibly important to transgender people. The pitch of someone's voice can determine whether or not they 'pass' as their identified gender. Because transgender voices do not always 'match' outward gender expression, trans people may be silenced from speaking or singing out of fear or embarrassment. The situation is particularly sensitive for those transitioning from male to female (M2F)."[50] Miller's observation suggests a parallel between the experiences of trans singers and those of women, especially lesbians, in feminist choruses. In both cases, "finding one's voice" has a double meaning: it refers to the physical act of singing and it also suggests defying the silencing that has oppressed women and trans people alike. The desire to express an authentic voice has inspired trans choruses, not only in big cities like Chicago, Boston, and Los Angeles, but in less likely places like Kansas City; Manchester, New Hampshire; and Atlanta. One of the earliest trans choruses to challenge multiple social stereotypes was the Transcendence Gospel Choir of

San Francisco, who were featured in *The Believers*, a 2006 documentary, and who recorded an album titled *Oh Happy Day* with the San Francisco Gay Men's Chorus. Kathleen McGuire, then Artistic Director of the SFGMC, was struck by the parallel between the SFGMC's origin in the wake of the Harvey Milk assassination (discussed in Chapter 7) and the Transcendence Gospel Choir's mission to come forward as "cultural warriors" in the twenty-first century. She organized a joint concert featuring the two choruses, and in 2004 they collaborated on *Oh Happy Day*, an album of gospel songs.[51]

The relationship between visibility and backlash that had characterized gay rights history since the 1970s was nowhere more evident than in the public portrayal of trans Americans. As discussed above, the growing presence of trans people in the media and in public life provoked right wing legislators and religious conservatives to concoct bathroom bills and other anti-trans initiatives. Gay rights groups and their allies rallied to support this newly visible constituency and, as in the past, the voices of choral singers were often able to go beyond marches and rallies in disarming their adversaries. In a burst of public visibility that would have been unthinkable a decade earlier, trans choruses began making their way into the mainstream media: The *LA Weekly* featured an article on the Trans Chorus of Los Angeles; the Butterfly Music Transgender Chorus of Boston was featured on the National Public Radio midday news program, "Here and Now," as well as on ABC News and in the *Boston Globe*; and NPR's "Weekend Edition Saturday" highlighted several trans choruses, including the Heartland Trans Chorus of Kansas City and the Trans Chorus of Los Angeles.[52] Within the mainstream choral world, a 2016 article on the Chorus America website included trans choruses in a discussion of "community engagement stories."[53]

The singing lives of women's choruses and trans choruses have not generally coincided outside quadrennial GALA festivals, where all the choruses under the LGBT umbrella meet in song. However, there have been several notable exceptions. In 2016, Resonance Women's Chorus of Boulder invited members of Phoenix, the Colorado Trans Community Choir and Arts Collective, to join them in their spring concert, "Each of Us." The concert featured Sara Bareilles's "Brave," originally written to support a friend coming out of the closet. The lyrics spoke to the entire LGBT community, but seemed especially apt for singers: "Say what you wanna say/ And let the words fall out / Honestly—I wanna see you be brave ..."[54]

An even more remarkable collaboration is the story of A.P. and Cyndi Hopper, whose life together has been intimately bound up with LGBT choruses. After attending Jane Ramseyer Miller's 2004 workshop, A.P., a trans woman, joined One Voice and became the chorus's bass section leader. A blatantly transphobic comment at a GALA workshop led A.P. and several others to speak with Miller. One Voice had already developed guidelines for working with trans singers; Miller "took our guidelines to the GALA board and said, 'These are our guidelines, I think we all need to be on this page.'" The One Voice guidelines that GALA eventually adopted focused on helping trans singers adjust to their post-transition voices, and fostering respect through the use of gender-neutral language and programming.[55]

While she was still singing with One Voice, A.P. was invited to become the accompanist and Assistant Director of Calliope, one of the longest-lived choruses in the Sister Singers network. "Working with Calliope is just amazing," she said. "The women of Calliope are just an amazing group of women. It's just been a wonderful experience."[56]

Like many trans people, A.P. was married before her transition, and like some other trans women, she remained married to her pre-transition spouse, Cyndi. But unlike most couples, A.P. and Cyndi's marriage is a musical partnership as well. Cyndi Hopper was an early member of Calliope and continued singing with the chorus as her husband transitioned and assumed the dual roles of Calliope's accompanist and Assistant Director. One Voice and Calliope have played a central role in A.P. and Cyndi's lives.

"One Voice was very instrumental in A.P.'s coming out," Cyndi recalled. "She's known since she was nine that she was different, as a little boy.... Since we've married it's been a real blossoming for A.P. because of the way the world was changing and because she got involved in that trans choir that mixed her in with One Voice.... We've been married now seventeen years [and] every year the female side became stronger and stronger and stronger."

In addition to coming to terms with A.P.'s transition, Cyndi experienced her own emotional transition within Calliope:

> A.P. just played for one concert and then everybody fell in love with her, and then it was "Do you think we can hire A.P.?" And then they said, "Well, this is Cyndi's group, we have to be sure Cyndi's okay with that." And I was like, "Well, what am I gonna do? What am I gonna say? I'm not gonna say no, you can't have the wonderful A.P. as your accompanist because I refuse to accept that." So, I just had to sort of step back and say, "Okay, that's fine for the greater good." I've been a very independent woman all my life and I kinda wanted to have my own little thing—but it's been great and the group really, really, really loves her and it hasn't detracted from my participation in the group either. So ... you just go with the flow and you know, it was kinda hard the first year ... but now I don't care anymore, she's such a part of the group now.[57]

While Cyndi and A.P.'s story may be unique, it embodies the values of love and shared commitment that have inspired women's choruses and the LGBT chorus movement from the beginning—values embodied in the GALA vision of "a world where all voices are free."

Queer Youth Take the Stage

As they turned their attention to trans identity and trans oppression, LGBT choruses also began to advocate for gay youth. Organizations like PFLAG and GLSEN (discussed in the previous chapter) had been working to combat anti-gay bullying in schools and communities for years, and had begun to focus on so-called conversion therapy—psychological and religious procedures intended to "cure" young people of homosexuality. As of 2017, six states and the District of Columbia, along with fifteen cities, had banned conversion therapy for minors, with bills pending in a handful of other states. Conversion therapy had been debunked by mainstream medical and psychological associations as ineffective and potentially harmful to gay youth, but anti-gay forces persisted. And as they did, the LGBT community and its singers persisted as well.

One of those in the forefront of the gay youth choral movement was Carol Siriani, who founded the first queer youth choir in North America in 2001. In the late 1990s, Carol Siriani was conducting the Vancouver Lesbian and Gay Choir (now known as Out in Harmony) in a performance of Harry Chapin's "Cat's in the Cradle," when someone placed an open pepper spray canister on the floor directly behind her. Years later, Siriani recalled "the smell of the inside of the ambulance while the kind attendants explained the physical, but not the emotional symptoms of both short-term and long-term exposure to pepper spray."

In addition to conducting the VLGC, Siriani was a newly hired teacher in the Coquitlam School District, (a suburb of Vancouver), where daily she watched "the bullying of students and teachers," much of it aimed at lesbian and gay students. The plight of these students, combined with the impact of the attack she had suffered, led her to form Gay Lesbian And Supportive Singing, or GLASS.

"I saw a way to make an impact by showing them how to become activists rather than victims," she recalled. "GLASS is the result of our dream after that incident.... They are so much more than our future, they are our now."[58]

Although GLASS went "on hiatus" when Siriani moved to Surrey (another Vancouver suburb), other gay youth choruses soon appeared. By 2017, the GALA membership list included ten youth choruses. Some, like GenOUT of Washington, DC, Mosaic Youth Chorus of Denver, and Omaggio LGBTQ Chorus of Phoenix, sing under the auspices of an adult gay chorus or an umbrella LGBT arts organization that includes men's and women's choruses. Others, like Diverse Harmony of Seattle and Bridging Voices of

Portland, Oregon, identify as Gay Straight Alliances, extending the GSA mission of support and safety from the classroom to the concert stage. Youth Pride Chorus of New York operates under the auspices of the non-profit Big Apple Performing Arts and the New York Lesbian, Gay, Bisexual & Transgender Community Center, while Dreams of Hope (Pittsburgh), and Perform Out (Kansas City) sing as freestanding youth choirs mentored by supportive adult directors and advisors.[59]

LGBT youth choruses arose in the shadow of long-standing myths about gay pedophilia. From Anita Bryant's 1977 "Save Our Children" campaign to the various ballot referenda targeting LGBT teachers, to twenty-first century attacks on Gay-Straight alliances in public schools, gay people working with youth have always been vulnerable to suspicions about "recruitment" and indoctrination. LGBT activists who recalled their own difficulties as gay adolescents defied these assumptions, but even the most committed were mindful of the need to protect themselves and the youth they served. As youth choruses proliferated, a set of guidelines for rehearsals and performances with minors appeared on the GALA web site. And while many mainstream organizations were posting similar guidelines (posts by Catholic dioceses were particularly noticeable in the wake of the child abuse scandals of the early twenty-first century), the guidelines that appeared on the GALA website suggested a special awareness of the jeopardy felt by gay adults working with youth. Viewed in the context of anti-gay stereotyping by the religious right, the prohibition on inappropriate touching and sexual intimacy took on added resonance, and a notice in the center of the post, highlighted in red, declared: "Important: meet with an attorney to insure that your youth and your organization are protected."[60]

Women in lesbian/feminist choruses were also careful to avoid any suspicion of "recruitment." A number of choruses included age limitations in their membership guidelines, although a very few accepted girls as young as ten or twelve or admitted girls who were accompanied by a singing adult. More often, women's choruses considered youth membership on an *ad hoc* basis. These discussions could become heated, as women wrestled with the tension between their own need for safety and their desire to support adolescent girls who might be searching for safe spaces. Several women's choruses resolved the conflict by mentoring youth choirs. Oregon's Soromundi and the Portland Lesbian Choir both invited members of Bridging Voices, Portland's GSA Youth Choir, to perform in their concerts. In Cincinnati, MUSE Artistic Director Rhonda Juliano co-founded the Diverse City Youth Chorus with the support of MUSE and the Cincinnati Men's Chorus.[61]

Whatever anxieties singers may have felt, the LGBT choral movement continued to mentor youth choruses and to feature them at GALA festivals. In 2010, GALA Executive Director Robin Godfrey called youth choruses "the largest growing segment of our chorus population."[62]

At the 2016 GALA Festival in Denver, eight youth choruses performed in a Blockbuster concert titled, "Youth Invasion from Gay to Z." The individual performances included some staples of the adult LGBT chorus repertoire—John Lennon's "Imagine" and a rousing rendition of "I Am What I Am," from *La Cage Aux Folles*. But the final number, which the eight youth choruses sang together on the GALA stage, combined the message of gay visibility and pride with a youthful energy unmatched even at a GALA Festival. The medley began with "Will I," a poignant lament from the musical *Rent* ("Will I lose my dignity? / Will someone care?/ Will I wake tomorrow/ From this nightmare?"), and ended with a rousing version of Walk the Moon's "Shut Up and Dance."

Nicholas Petricca, who wrote "Shut Up and Dance," once said that part of the inspiration for the song came from "picturing myself in high school ... being this incredibly uncomfortable, awkward adolescent dude."[63] On that last night of the 2016 GALA Festival, "Shut Up and Dance" was an anthem for LGBTQ youth and their enthusiastic adult audience:

> Oh, don't you dare look back
> Just keep your eyes on me
> I said you're holding back
> She said shut up and dance with me.[64]

Queer youth were still at risk in their schools and LGBTQ adults still faced discrimination and worse in the wider world, but the sight of two dozen gay adolescents celebrating their lives on the GALA stage reminded the lesbian and gay singers in the audience, if they needed reminding, of how far their own musical activism had taken them in the struggle for full equality.[65]

Taking Stock

By the second decade of the twenty-first century, Sister Singers was still breaking new ground. The 2010 Festival, hosted by Artemis Singers of Chicago, brought twenty-three performing member choruses and nearly 650 participants to Loyola University, where ensembles from Alaska to Florida and from California to Massachusetts performed for one another for four music-filled days, and then joined for two mass chorus performances on the last night of the Festival.

The mass chorus performances included familiar songs from the women's chorus repertoire—Elizabeth Alexander's "Where There is Light in the Soul," Joan Szymko's setting of "Arise My Love," and Kevin Robison's choral arrangement of "What Matters." The final number was brand new—"A Universal Dream," by California composer Jenni Brandon, commissioned especially for the Festival. Jenni and Artemis member Meta Hellman drew the text from the Preamble to the Constitution and the writings of Chicago reformer Jane Addams. The premiere happened to fall on July 4—an auspicious date for a musical tribute to Chicago's pioneer reformer and to the ideals embodied in the Constitution.

"A Universal Dream" begins with Jane Addams's ringing words: "What is it the radicals seek?/ Free speech and free thought/ Promises fulfilled/ Liberty guaranteed." Interspersed with the verses are the opening lines of the Preamble: "We the People/ Establish Justice/ We the People/ Insure tranquility." The piece ends with a soaring descant consisting of the word "Liberty" in seven languages, from "Liberdad" (Spanish) to "Inkululeko" (Zulu/South African).[66]

When the evening was over, singers wandered out to watch the fireworks and celebrate at the Piper Hall Mansion on the Loyola campus. But it wasn't long before the Network began planning for 2014—a year that would mark the thirtieth anniversary of the first Sister Singers Festival.

"Returning to Our Roots"—the theme of the 2014 Festival—took Sister Singers back to Champaign, where, in 1980, a group of choral singers at the National Women's Music Festival had signed a membership list for an organization they hoped would become a network. Hosted by Amasong, Champaign-Urbana's Premier Lesbian/Feminist Chorus, the 2014 Festival featured performances by seventeen choruses, a guest performance by the activist duo Emma's Revolution, and another new commission by Boulder composer Andrea Ramsey, "Lineage," with a text from a poem by African American poet Margaret Walker. But most of all, the 2014 Festival was a time for women's choruses to consider their journey—a journey closely tied not only to the LGBT rights movement, but to social justice movements all over the world. By 2014, the women's choral movement had moved from separatism to coalitions, and from the closet to the community.

Election 2016: "Singing Together Keeps Our Hearts Aloft"

The election of Donald Trump in 2016 left many in the progressive community in deep shock and grief, confronting a frightening reality few had anticipated. Once again, Sue Coffee and her two choruses organized a concert for the community, called "The Quiet Work of Centuries" and inspired by words of John F. Kennedy about the role of artists in society. It was described on the Resonance website as "an evening of singing and community, balm for the campaign-weary soul, a meditation on home, alienation, and 'other.'"[67] Sue recalled:

As I went to sleep on election night, knowing everyone in my community felt as sick as I did, I was perversely cheered all of a sudden when I realized the concert would be much better now. The repertoire was essentially the same, with a few additions, but the context created more need and therefore more impact, offering some food for thought about the role of art. Doing this series of concerts, responding to the ups and downs, conceptualizing for months in advance, thinking about what the audience needs, has been a great laboratory for me.[68]

Shortly after the 2016 election, a post that seemed to resonate with women's choruses all over the country began making the rounds on the Internet. The post originated with Aimee Van Ausdall, a Denver woman who had participated in the January 21 March for Women's Lives. Van Ausdall wrote:

This morning I have been pondering a nearly forgotten lesson I learned in high school music. Sometimes, in band or choir, music requires players or singers to hold a note longer than they actually can hold a note…. In those cases, we were taught to mindfully stagger when we took a breath so the sound appeared uninterrupted…. Let's remember MUSIC…. Together, we can sustain a very long, beautiful song for a very, very long time. You don't have to do it all, but you must add your voice to the song.[69]

On January 21, 2017, the day after the presidential inauguration, millions of women, men, and children from every continent on the planet participated in the Women's March—the largest single-day protest in U.S. History.[70] Women's choruses joined the marches in their home cities; some gave impromptu performances, but in other places the crowds were so big that singers were unable to find one another. Those who were unable to attend the march pored over Facebook posts and photo essays in newspapers and magazines.

One of those who experienced the march through newspaper photos was Ruth Huber, co-artistic director and composer-in-residence of the Rainbow Women's Chorus of San Jose. The result was a new composition inspired by those images. Huber's description of how she came to write "Signs" provides an apt finale to this history of women's choruses:

> The Women's March of January 21, 2017, was an historic, unprecedented outpouring of "nasty women and their friends" united in protest and burgeoning hope for the future. Sparked by a five-word Facebook post ("I think we should march"), thousands of activists, movement leaders, and ordinary people turned out in all fifty states and around the world. Because Rainbow Women's Chorus had our twenty-year anniversary concert that day, I was unable to attend local events, but a friend sent me a link to a photo essay from the *New York Times*. I spent about thirty minutes perusing images of impassioned women and men, some in pink hats, all carrying an array of cardboard signs. I wrote down the messages that leapt out at me, and their voices began to sing, resulting in SIGNS: Voices from the Women's March. There were a few favorites that I had to leave out. From a boat in Antarctica: "Penguins for Peace" and "Seals for Science." And finally, "A nation is not defeated till the hearts of women are on the ground." In these dark times, singing together keeps my heart aloft.[71]

Endnotes

Introduction

1. "The Chorus Impact Study: How Children, Adults, and Communities Benefit from Choruses," Chorus America website, 2009, accessed October 3, 2018, https://www.chorusamerica.org/publications/research-reports/chorus-impact-study.
2. Joe Robinson, "Is Your Work Ethic Keeping You from Living Your Life?", *Huffington Post Blog*, December 7, 2010, updated November 17, 2011, accessed July 12, 2018, http://www.huffingtonpost.com/joe-robinson/why-the-work-mind-leaves-_b_790703.html.
3. Karyn O'Connor, "The Anatomy of the Voice, *Singwise*, accessed July 11, 2018, http://www.singwise.com/cgi-bin/main.pl?section=articles&doc=AnatomyOfVoice.
4. Lynn O'Brien, interview with the author, July 26, 2015.
5. Björn Vickhoff et al., "Music Structure Determines Heart Rate Variability of Singers," *Frontiers in Psychology* 9 (July, 2013), accessed August 26, 2018, https://doi.org/10.3389/fpsyg.2013.00334.
6. Don Lee, "Choruses and Community Wellness," *ChorusAmerica*, April 2, 2013, accessed July 11, 2018, https://www.chorusamerica.org/singers/choruses-and-community-wellness.
7. The Military Wives, *Wherever You Are* (London, HarperCollins, 2013). The Military Wives were the subject of a BBC TV series, *The Choir: Military Wives;* a hit single; and an album, *Stronger Together.* They can be seen performing at https://www.youtube.com/watch?v=0hR6O7VxKaQ.
8. The YMCA Jerusalem Youth Chorus website, accessed August 26, 2018, http://ymca.jerusalemyouthchorus.org.
9. Young@Heart website accessed August 26, 2018, www.youngatheartchorus.com.
10. Encore: Our Story," Encore Creativity for Older Adults website, accessed August 26, 2018, http://www.encorecreativity.org/index.php/about-encore/68-our-story.
11. Wendy White, interview with the author, October 8, 2015.
12. Michael Todd Krueger, instructions to the Silvertones Senior Chorus.
13. Estelle Phillips, interview with the author, July 3, 2010.
14. Janice Kinney, "'Making Church': The Experience of Spirituality in Women's Choruses" (PhD. diss. University of Washington, 2010), 58, ProQuest 3445507.
15. Janice Scalza, interview with the author, July 3, 2011.

16. Don Lee, "The Evolution of GLBT Choruses," *ChorusAmerica*, June 20, 2013, accessed July 11, 2018, https://www.chorusamerica.org/singers/evolution-glbt-choruses.

17. "ANNA At-A-Glance," Anna Crusis website, accessed August 26, 2018, https://annacrusis.org/page/anna-glance.

Chapter 1

1. Victoria Doubleday, "The Frame Drum in the Middle East: Women, Musical Instruments and Power," *Ethnomusicology* 43, no.1 (Winter,1999): 107, accessed July 10, 2018, http://www.jstor.org/stable/852696.

2. Ibid., 108.

3. Layne Redmond, *When the Drummers Were Women: A Spiritual History of Rhythm* (New York: Three Rivers Press, 1997), 21.

4. Ibid., 47-48.

5. Marija Gimbutas and Miriam Robbins Dexter, *The Living Goddesses* (Berkeley and Los Angeles: University of California Press, 2001); Riane Eisler, *The Chalice and the Blade* (New York: Harper Collins, 1995); Merlin Stone, *When God Was a Woman* (New York: Houghton Mifflin, 1976).

6. Rita Gross, *A Garland of Feminist Reflections: Forty Years of Religious Exploration* (Berkeley and Los Angeles: University of California Press, 2009), 163.

7. Sarah Pomeroy, *Goddesses, Whores, Wives and Slaves: Women in Classical Antiquity* (New York: Schocken Books, 1975, 1995), x.

8. Sophie Drinker, *Music & Women: The Story of Women in their Relation to Music* (New York: Coward & McCann, 1948, The Feminist Press, 1995), 63. All citations refer to the Feminist Press edition.

9. Ibid., 281-82.

10. Ruth Solie, "Afterword," *Music & Women*, 355.

11. Exod. 15:20-21, *The Torah: New Jewish Version, The Torah: A Modern Commentary* (New York: Union of American Hebrew Congregations, 1981).

12. Carol Meyers, "Miriam, Music, and Miracles," in *Miriam, the Magdalen, and the Mother*, ed. Deirdre Good (Bloomington: University of Indiana Press, 2005), 32.

13. Frank M. Cross, Jr. and David Noel Freedman, "The Song of Miriam," *Journal of Near Eastern Studies* 14, No. 4 (October 1955): 239; Cross, "The Song of the Sea and Canaanite Myth," in *Canaanite Myth and Hebrew Epic: Essays in the Religion of the People of Israel* (Cambridge, Massachusetts: Harvard University Press, 1973, 1999). For feminist interpretations of Miriam, see Phyllis Trible, "Bringing Miriam Out of the Shadows," in *A Feminist Companion to Exodus-Deuteronomy*, ed. Athalya Brenner (Sheffield England: Academic Press, Ltd. 1994);

Rita Burns, "Has the Lord Indeed Spoken Only Through Moses? A Study of the Biblical Portrait of Miriam" (Ph.D. Diss., Marquette University, 1980), https://epublications.marquette.edu/dissertations/AAI8104800/; and Fokkelien van Dijk-Hemmes, "Traces of Women's Texts in the Hebrew Bible" in *On Gendering Texts: Female and Male Voices in the Hebrew Bible*, ed. Athalya Brenner and Fokkelien van Dijk-Hemmes (Leiden, The Netherlands: E.J. Brill, 1996).

14. Wilda C. Gafney, *Daughters of Miriam: Women Prophets in Ancient Israel* (Minneapolis: Fortress Press, 2008), 80.

15. Carol Meyers, "Miriam, Music, and Miracles," 36, 37. See also Peggy R. Sanday, "Female Status in the Public Domain," in *Woman, Culture, and Society*, ed. Michelle Zimbalist Rosaldo and Louise Lamphere (Stanford: Stanford University Press, 1973), 189-206.

16   Musa Dube, *Postcolonial Feminist Interpretations of the Bible* (St. Louis: Chalice Press, 2000), 74; Susan Ackerman, "Why Is Miriam Also among the Prophets? (And Is Zipporah among the Priests?)," *Journal of Biblical Literature* 121, No. 1 (Spring, 2002), 47-80, accessed July 9, 2018, http://www.jstor.org/stable/3268330.

17. George Hinge, "Cultic Persona and the Transmission of the Partheneions," in *Aspects of Greek Cult: Context, Ritual and Iconography*, ed. J. Jensen, et al. (Aarhus: Aarhus University Press 2009), 217.

18. Calame, *Choruses of Young Women in Ancient Greece*, trans. Derek Collins and Janice Orion, new and revised Edition (Lanham, Maryland: Rowman and Littlefield, 2001), 14, 261.

19. Eva Stehle, *Performance and Gender in Ancient Greece: Nondramatic Poetry in its Setting* (Princeton: Princeton University Press, 1979), 31-33. See also Diane J. Rayor, "Competition and Eroticism in Alcman's Parthenaion [1PMG]," American Philological Society Association Annual Meeting Abstracts (Decatur, Illinois, 1987), 80.

20. Eva Cantarella, "Gender, Sexuality, and Law," in *The Cambridge Companion to Ancient Greek Law*, ed. Michael Gagarin & David Cohen (Cambridge, UK: Cambridge University Press 2005), 252-53.

21. Josine Blok, "Virtual Voices: Toward a Choreography of Women's Speech in Classical Athens," in *Making Silence Speak: Women's Voices in Greek Literature and Society*, ed. André Lardinois and Laura McClure (Princeton: Princeton University Press, 2001), 106.

22. Mary deForest, "Female Choruses in Greek Tragedy, *Didaskalia*, IV, No. 1 (Spring 1997), accessed July 10, 2018, http://www.didaskalia.net/issues/vol4no1/deforest.html.

23. Pomeroy, *Goddesses, Whores, Wives and Slaves*, 71, 88.

24. Kay O'Pry, "Social and Political Roles of Women in Athens and Sparta," *Saber and Scroll* 1, Issue 2 (Summer 2012); edited and revised April 2015, 11, accessed August 18, 2018, https://pa02217736.schoolwires.net/site/handlers/filedownload.

ashx?moduleinstanceid=23317&dataid=29076&FileName=Social%20
and%20Political%20Roles%20of%20Women%20in%20Athens%20
and%20Sparta.pdf.

25. Evan Bowie, "Alcman's First Parthenion and the Song the Sirens
    Sang," in *Archaic and Classical Choral Song: Performance, Politics and
    Dissemination*, ed. Evan Bowie and Lycia Athanassaki (Berlin: Walter
    deGruyter, 2011), 38.

26. André Lardinois, "The parrhesia of young female choruses in Ancient
    Greece," in *Archaic and Classical Choral Song*, 170.

27. Calame, *Choruses of Young Women*, 257.

28. Lardinois, "The parrhesia of young female choruses," 172.

29. James William Smith, "Political Parthenoi: The Social and Political
    Significance of Female Performance in Archaic Greece" (Ph.D. diss.,
    University of Exeter, 2013), 250, 251, accessed July 12, 2018, http://
    hdl.handle.net/10871/10901.

30. Eva Cantarella, *Pandora's Daughters: The Role and Status of Women in
    Greek and Roman Antiquity*, trans. Maureen B. Fant (Baltimore: Johns
    Hopkins University Press, 1993), 21.

31. Barbara Newman, "Sybil of the Rhine," in *Voice of the Living Light:
    Hildegard of Bingen and Her World*," ed. Barbara Newman (Los
    Angeles: University of California Press, 1998), 1.

32. Fiona Maddocks, *Hildegard of Bingen: The Woman of Her Age* (New
    York: Doubleday Image Books, 2001, 2003), 54-55.

33. Margaret Berger, *On Natural Philosophy and Medicine: Selections from
    Cause et Cure* (Rochester, New York: D.S. Brewer 1999), 100.

34. Nathaniel M. Campbell, Beverly R. Lomer, and K. Christian McGuire,
    "The *Symphonia* and *Ordo Vertutum* of Hildegard von Bingen,"
    International Society of Hildegard von Bingen Studies, accessed July 9,
    2018, http://www.hildegard-society.org/p/music.html.

35. Margot Fassler, "Composer and Dramatist," in Newman, *Voice of the
    Living Light*, 154.

36. Christopher Page, *The Owl and the Nightingale: Instrumental Practice
    and Songs in France, 1100-1300* (Berkeley & Los Angeles: University of
    California Press 1989) 156.

37. Bruce Holsinger, *Music, Body, and Desire in Medieval Culture, Hildegard
    of Bingen to Chaucer* (Stanford: Stanford University Press, 2001), 2,
    107.

38. Michelle Edwards, "Women in Music to ca. 1450," in *Women and Music:
    A History*, 2nd ed., ed. Kaarin Pendle (Bloomington: Indiana University
    Press, 2001), 47.

39. A good sample can be heard at https://www.youtube.com/
    watch?v=TuzvAeyw0wk.

40. Hildegard of Bingen, *Scivias*, trans. Columbia Hart and Jane Bishop,
    with an introduction by Barbara Newman and preface by Caroline
    Walker Bynum (New York: Paulist Press, 1990), 59.

41. Marilyn Mumford, "A Feminist Prolegomenon for the Study of Hildegard of Bingen," in *Gender, Culture and The Arts: Women, the Arts, and Society,* ed. Ronald Dotterer and Susan Bowers (Selinsgrove, Pennsylvania: Susquehanna University Press,1993), 2.

42. Joseph L. Baird and Radd K. Ehrmann, introduction to *The Letters of Hildegard of Bingen, Vol, I,* trans. Joseph L. Baird and Radd K. Ehrmann (New York: Oxford University Press, 1994), 5.

43. Maddocks, *Hildegard of Bingen*, 91.

44. John Van Engen, "Abbess: 'Mother and Teacher,'" in *Voice of the Living Light*, 38.

45. Lorna Marie Collingridge, "Music as Evocative Power: The Intersection of Music with Images of the Divine in the Songs of Hildegard of Bingen" (Ph.D. diss., School of Theology, Griffith University, 2003), Chapter 8, Note 1, 249, accessed July 9, 2018, https://www120.secure. griffith.edu.au/rch/file/db79c53d-d57e-bb6f-6aed-f5604599c01f/1/ Collingridge_2004_01Thesis.pdf.

46. Mistress Tengswich to Hildegard, Letter 52, *The Letters of Hildegard von Bingen, Vol. 1,* trans. Baird and Ehrmann, 127.

47. Ibid., Letter 52r, 129.

48. Norman F. Cantor, *The Civilization of the Middle Ages* (New York: Harper Perennial, rev. ed., 1994), 356.

49. Bruce Holsinger, "The Flesh of the Voice: Embodiment and the Homoerotics of Devotion in the Music of Hildegard of Bingen (1098-1179," *Signs* 19, no. 1 (Autumn, 1993), 98, accessed July 10, 1018, http://www.jstor.org/stable/3174746.

50. Barbara Newman, *Sister of Wisdom: S. Hildegard's Theology of the Feminine* (Berkeley and Los Angeles: University of California Press, 1987), 14.

51. Hildegard of Bingen, Letter to the Bishop of Mainz, ca. 1178, "Epistola XLVII," *S. Hildegardis, abbatissae: Opera omnia*, vol. 197 of *Patrologiae curcus completus . . .Series prima* [Latin], ed. Jacques Paul Migne (Paris: Petit-Montrouge, 1855), trans. Barbara L. Grant, reprinted in *Women in Music: An Anthology of Source Readings from the Middle Ages to the Present*, ed. Carol Neuls-Bates, rev. ed. (Boston: Northeastern University Press, 1996), 19.

52. Ibid.

53. Laura Patterson, "The Late 20th Century Commercial Revival of Hildegard of Bingen" (master's thesis, Washington University in St. Louis, 2010), 3-4, accessed August 18, 2018, https://openscholarship. wustl.edu/cgi/viewcontent.cgi?article=1476&context=etd.

54. Matthew Fox, *Illuminations of Hildegard von Bingen* (Rochester, Vermont: Bear and Company, 2002), 43-44.

55. Joan Szymko, "*Viriditas*: The Breeze That Nurtures All Things Green," in *Take Up the Song: Building a Community of Heart and Soul and Voice*, ed. Patricia Hennings (Corvallis, OR: earthsongs, 2003), 24-25.

56. Laura W. Macy, "Women's History and Early Music," in *Companion to Medieval and Renaissance Music*, ed. Tess Knighton and David Fallows (Berkeley and Los Angeles: University of California Press, 1997), 96.

57. Micky White, "Vivaldi and the Pietà," accessed August 18, 2018, http://www.excellence-earlychildhood.ca/documents/Micky_White.pdf.

58. Richard Cross, "Vivaldi's Girls: Music Therapy in 18th Century Venice," accessed July 9, 2018, http://www.users.cloud9.net/~recross/why-not/Vivaldi.html.

59. Ibid.

60. Amanda Holloway, "The Red Priest Unfrocked," *The Times of London*, October 19, 2007, accessed July 10, 2018, reprinted at http://www.classicalmusicguide.com/viewtopic.php?t=19042.

61. William Packer, "Vivaldi and the Chorus of Unwanted Children," *Financial Times.com*, August 29, 2005, accessed July 11, 2018, http://www.toddtarantino.com/hum/vivaldiarticle.html.

62. Meredith Bowen, "Sacred Music from The Convents of Seventeenth-Century Italy: Restoration Practices For Contemporary Women's Choirs" (Ph.D. diss., Michigan State University, 2016), 22-23, accessed July 9, 2018, https://doi.org/10.25335/M5RX4Q.

63. Quoted in Bowen, 24.

64. Michael Talbot, "Tenors and Basses at the Venetian 'Ospedali,'" *Acta Musicologica* 66, no. 2 (July - December, 1994): 131, accessed August 29, 2018. 123-138. DOI: 10.2307/932767. https://www.jstor.org/stable/932767.

65. Patricia O'Toole, "A Missing Chapter from Choral Methods Books: How Choirs Neglect Girls," *The Choral Journal* 39, no.5 (December 1998), 22.

66. *Vivaldi's Women*, directed by Rupert Edwards (2006: BBC Wales), DVD. Courtesy of Richard Vendome, used by permission.

67. Ibid.

68. Ibid.

69. Ibid.

70. Vivaldi's Women Facebook Page, accessed July 12, 2018, https://www.facebook.com/Vivaldis-Women-191192901080329.

71. Sophie Drinker, *Brahms and His Women's Choruses* (Published and Copyright by Author under the auspices of MusuRGiA Publishers, Merion, Pennsylvania, 1952), 10, accessed August 18, 2018, https://archive.org/stream/brahmshiswomensc00drin/brahmshiswomensc00drin_djvu.txt.

72. Rachel Dickey, "The Women's Chorus Emergence and Evolution in 19th Century Germany" (Mus.D. diss., Indiana University, 2015), 10, accessed July 10, 2018, https://scholarworks.iu.edu/dspace/handle/2022/19875.

73.	Celia Applegate, "The Building of Community Through Choral Singing," in *Nineteenth Century Choral Singing*, ed. Donna M. DiGrazia (New York: Taylor and Francis, 2013), 13-14.

74.	Dickey, 13.

75.	Drinker, *Brahms and His Women's Choruses*, 3.

76.	Dickey, 14, 29, 34-35, 53.

77.	Drinker, *Brahms and His Women's Choruses*, 18.

78.	Franziska Meier, Diary Entry for April 1, 1859, quoted in Drinker, *Brahms*, 27.

79.	Meier, Diary Entry for April 15, 1859, quoted in Drinker, *Brahms*, 27.

80.	Ibid, 29.

81.	Ibid, 33.

82.	Brahms to Clara Schumann, Sept. 30, 1859, quoted in Drinker, *Brahms and His Women's Choruses*, 43.

83.	Jan Swafford, *Johannes Brahms: A Biography* (New York: Alfred A Knopf, 1997), 30.

84.	Ibid.

85.	Drinker, *Brahms and his Women's Choruses*, 56.

86.	Meier, Diary Entry, August 1, 1859, quoted in Drinker, 25.

87.	Meier, Diary Entry, August 15, 1859, quoted in Drinker, 28.

88.	Victoria Meredith, "The Pivotal Role of Brahms and Schubert in the Development of the Women's Choir," *The Choral Journal* 37, no. 7 (February 1997), 9, accessed July 11, 2018, http://www.jstor.org/stable/23551511.

89.	Drinker, *Brahms and His Women's Choruses,* 68.

90.	Ibid., 71-72.

91.	Friedchen Wagner, *Memoirs of Friedchen Wagner*, quoted in Drinker, *Brahms and His Women's Choruses*, 74.

92.	Brahms to Franziska Meier, quoted in Drinker, *Brahms*, 76.

93.	Anna Lenz to Sophie Drinker, July, 1935, quoted in Drinker, *Brahms*, 79.

Chapter 2

1.	Celia Applegate, "The Building of Community Through Choral Singing," in *Nineteenth Century Choral Singing*, ed. Donna M. DiGrazia (New York: Taylor and Francis, 2013), 3.

2.	Lucy Poate Stebbins and Richard Poate Stebbins, *Frank Damrosch: Let The People Sing* (Durham, NC: Duke University Press, 1945), 140.

3.	Stacy Horn, *Imperfect Harmony: Finding Happiness Singing with Others* (Chapel Hill: Algonquin Books, 2013), 95.

4.	Quoted in Horn, 98.

5.	Francie Wolff, *Give the Ballot to the Mothers: Songs of the Suffragists - A History in Song* (Springfield, MO: Delinger's, 1998).

6. Barbara Welter, "The Cult of True Womanhood: 1820-1860," *American Quarterly* 18, no.2, Part 1 (Summer, 1966): 151-174.

7. https://www.youtube.com/watch?v=J6pxXI_V4RM.

8. Sheryl Hurner, "Discursive Identity Formation of Suffrage Women: Reframing the 'Cult of True Womanhood' Through Song," *Western Journal of Communication* 70, no. 3 (July 2006): 239-40.

9. Quoted by Carolyn DeSwarte Gifford, "Temperance Songs and Hymns," in *Religions of the United States in Practice*, ed. Colleen McDannell, vol. 1 (Princeton: Princeton University Press, 2001), 159.

10. Quoted in Gifford, 164.

11. "Club Movement" in "DeColonizing Our History: A Restorative History Website," accessed July 9, 2018, http://decolonizingourhistory.com/club-movement.

12. Linda Whitesitt, "Women as 'Keepers of Culture': Music Clubs, Community Concert Series, and Symphony Orchestras," in *Cultivating Music in America: Women Patrons and Activists since 1860*, ed. Ralph P. Locke and Cyrilla Barr (Berkeley and Los Angeles: University of California Press 1997), 66.

13. Ibid.

14. Quoted in *Women in Music: An Anthology of Source Readings from the Middle Ages to the Present*, rev. ed., ed. Carol Neuls-Bates (Boston: Northeastern University Press, 1996), 189, 191.

15. Henry Edward Krehbiel, "Concert of the Rubenstein Club," *New York Tribune,* April 18, 1890, quoted in Horn, 42, 43.

16. Quoted in Horn, 45-46.

17. William Rogers Chapman papers, New York Public Library Archive, accessed July 9, 2018, https://timesmachine.nytimes.com/timesmachine/1911/12/15/104886190.html?pageNumber=13.

18. Horn, 94; Whitesitt, 66-67, 71.

19. "Rubenstein Club," *The Encyclopedia of Cleveland History*, accessed August 20, 2018, http://ech.case.edu/cgi/article.pl?id=RC3.

20. Monica J. Hubbard, "Women's Choirs: Anonymous No More!" in *Take Up the Song*, 116-119.

21. Evelyn Brooks Higginbotham, *Righteous Discontent: The Women's Movement in the Black Baptist Church, 1880-1920* (Cambridge, MA: Harvard University Press, 1993), 1.

22. Jenna Jackson, *Singing in my Soul: Black Gospel Music in a Secular Age* (Chapel Hill: University of North Carolina Press, 2004), 35.

23. Ibid., 38, 34.

24. Quoted in Jackson, 35.

25. Robert Darden, *People Get Ready: A New History of Black Gospel Music* (New York: Continuum International Publishing Company, 2004), 58-60.

26. Darden, 116; Tim Brooks, *Lost Sounds: Blacks and the Birth of the Recording Industry, 1890-1919* (Champaign: University Illinois Press, 2005), 193; "Our Music," Fisk Jubilee Singers website, accessed August 29, 2018, http://fiskjubileesingers.org/the-music/.
27. Darden, 119-120.
28. Ida Husted Harper, ed., *The History of Woman Suffrage*, vol. 5 (New York: Source Book Press, 1970), 56, quoted in Roslyn Leigh Brandes, "'Let Us Sing as We Go': The Role of Music in the United States Suffrage Movement" (master's thesis, University of Maryland, 2016), 62, accessed August 20, 2018, https://drum.lib.umd.edu/handle/1903/18403.
29. Quoted in Darden, 120.
30. Darden, 120.
31. Samuel A. Floyd, *The Power of Black Music: Interpreting Its History from Africa to the United States* (Oxford: Oxford University Press, 1996), 63.
32. Luvenia A. George, "Lucie (Lucy) Campbell Williams: Her Nurturing and Expansion of Gospel Music in the National Baptist Convention, U.S.A., Inc.," in *We'll Understand It Better By and By*, ed. Bernice Johnson Reagon (Washington DC: Smithsonian Institution Press, 1992), 113.
33. Pamela Palmer, "Lucie E. Campbell-Williams: A Legacy of Leadership through the Gospel," August 1, 2008, 2008 Rhodes Institute for Regional Studies, 15, accessed July 12, 2018, https://dlynx.rhodes.edu/jspui/bitstream/10267/23978/1/2008-Pamela_Palmer-Lucie_E_Campbell_Williams-Blankenship.pdf.
34. *Say Amen, Somebody*, directed by George T Nirenberg, (GTN Productions, 1982), DVD.
35. Darden, 171.
36. Studs Terkel, "Louis Armstrong, 1962," in *And They All Sang: Great Musicians Talk About Their Music* (London: Granta Books, 2007), 146.
37. Susan F. Martin, *A Nation of Immigrants* (New York: Cambridge University Press), 107-108).
38. History of Nord-Amerikanischer Sängerbund, accessed July 10, 2018, http://nasaengerbund.org/index.php?p=1_58_History-NASB; N. Lee Orr, "The United States," in *Nineteenth Century Choral Singing*, 487.
39. Richard Reuss with Joanne Reuss, *American Folk Music and Left-Wing Politics, 1927-1957* (Lanham, Maryland: Scarecrow Press, 2000), 41; Judith Tick, *Ruth Crawford Seeger: A Composer's Search for American Music* (New York: Oxford University Press, 1997, 2000), 194.
40. Emanuel S. Goldsmith, *Modern Yiddish Culture: The Story of the Yiddish Language Movement* (New York: Fordham University Press, 1976, expanded ed. 2000), 92.

41. Alice Kessler-Harris, "Labor Movement in the United States," *Jewish Women's Archive*, accessed July 11, 2018, https://jwa.org/encyclopedia/article/labor-movement-in-united-states.

42. Diane Lapis, "Nitgedaiget: A Vanished Utopia," *Dutchess County Historical Society 2015 Yearbook*, Volume 94, 131-145; Jacob Schaefer, *Mit Gesang Tzum Kampf* (New York, NY: International Workers Order, 1932).

43. Marion Jacobson, "With Song to the Struggle: An Ethnographic and Historical Study of the Yiddish Folk Chorus" (Ph.D. diss., New York University, 2004), 73, accessed July 11, 2018, ProQuest [2004.3114198].

44. Ellen Koskoff, "The Sound of a Woman's Voice: Gender in a New York Hassidic Community," in *Women and Music: A Cross-Cultural Perspective*, ed. Ellen Koskoff (Champaign: University of Illinois Press, 1989), 217-18.

45. Jacobson, 62.

46. Debbie Friedman, *A Journey of Spirit*, directed by Ann Coppel, (Ann Coppel Productions, 2003), DVD.

47. Jacobson, 89.

48. "Milestones," Jewish People's Philharmonic Chorus website, accessed July 11, 2018, http://www.thejppc.org/id16.html.

49. Robert Snyder, "The Paterson Jewish Folk Chorus: Politics, Ethnicity and Musical Culture, *American Jewish History* 74, no. 1 (September, 1964): 31, accessed July 12, 2018, http://www.jstor.org/stable/23882496.

50. Jacobson, 90.

51. Industrial Workers of the World, "Minutes of IWW's Founding Convention – Part 1," accessed July 11, 2018, https://iww.org/about/founding/part1.

52. The entire film *With Babies and Banners* is available on YouTube at https://www.youtube.com/watch?v=pa75V-tdBko and on the Internet Archive at https://archive.org/details/withbabiesandbannersstoryofthewomensemergencybrigade.

53. Sarah Eisenstein, *Bread and Roses: Working Women's Consciousness in the United States 1890 to the First World War* (London and New York: Routledge, 1983), 32.

54. Oppenheim's poem was not published until 1946, in the IWW newspaper *Industrial Solidarity*, and historians disagree on whether the words inspired or were inspired by the signs of the Lawrence strikers and/or by Schneiderman's speech (see Note 53, above).

55. *Pride*, directed by Matthew Warchus (Pathé/BBC Films, 2014), DVD, available for rental at https://www.youtube.com/watch?v=Jv4XKNUAzCM.

88888

56. Jennifer Meixelsperger, "The Struggle is Real: Propaganda and Workers Songbooks Published by the Workers Music League, 1934-35" (Ph.D. diss., University of Wisconsin, 2015), 13, accessed July 11, 2018, https://dc.uwm.edu/etd/820.

57. John Steinbeck, "Foreword," in *Hard Hitting Songs for Hard-Hit People*, ed. Alan Lomax, Woody Guthrie, and Pete Seeger (New York: Oak Publications, 1967), 8.

58. Mark Krasovic, "Ex-Slave Interviews in the Depression Cultural Context," in *Been Here So Long: Selections from the WPA American Slave Narratives*, accessed February 1, 2017, http://newdeal.feri.org/asn/hist02.htm,. (Site discontinued.)

59. Kenneth J. Bindas, *All of this Music Belongs to the Nation: The WPA's Federal Music Project and American Society* (Knoxville: University of Tennessee Press, 1995), 16-17.

60. Michael Fried, "W. Elmer Keeton and His WPA Chorus: Oakland's Musical Civil Rights Pioneers of the New Deal Era, *California History* 7, no. 3 (Fall 1996): 242-43, accessed July 10, 2018, https://www.jstor.org/stable/25177596?seq=1#page_scan_tab_contents.

61. Reuss, 103.

62. Eleanor Flexner, "History of American Women 'Living Newspaper' Drama," *Daily Worker*, March 5, 1951, 11, quoted in Kate Weigand, *Red Feminism: American Communism and the Making of Women's Liberation* (Baltimore: The Johns Hopkins University Press, 2001), 114.

63. Eleanor Flexner, writing as Betty Feldman, "Singing of Women, Important Achievement in People's Theatre," *Daily Worker*, April 5, 1951, 11, quoted in Weigand, 114.

64. James R. Barrett, "Rethinking the Popular Front," *Rethinking Marxism* 21, no. 4 (October 2009): 544.

65. John A. Lomax, *Our Singing Country* (New York: Macmillan 1941, Minneola, New York: Dover Publications reprint, 2000), ix, accessed July 11, 2018, http://www.traditionalmusic.co.uk/our-singing-country/our-singing-country%20-%200013.htm.

66. Ibid., xvi.

67. Judith Tick, *Ruth Crawford Seeger: A Composer's Search for American Music* (Oxford: Oxford University Press, 1997), 200.

68. Beth Lomax Hawes, *Sing it Pretty* (Champaign: University of Illinois Press, 2008), 22-23.

69. Quoted in Michael Denning, *The Cultural Front: The Laboring of American Culture in the Twentieth Century* (London and New York: Verso, 1996), 296.

70. Denning, 299-300.

71. Ibid., 138.

72. Quoted in Harry Goldman, "Pins and Needles: An Oral History" (Ph.D. diss., New York University 1977), 74.

73. Harold Rome, "Chain Store Daisy," in *Reading Lyrics*, ed. Robert Gottlieb and Robert Kimball (New York: Pantheon, 2000), 409.
74. Denning, 306.
75. "Cotton Club of Harlem," *Blackpast.Org: An Online Reference Guide to African American History*, accessed July 9, 2018, http://www.blackpast.org/aah/cotton-club-harlem-1923.
76. David Margolick, *Strange Fruit: Billie Holiday, Café Society, and an Early Cry for Civil Rights* (Philadelphia, Running Press, 2000), 40.
77. Ibid., 50.
78. Ibid., 47.
79. Quoted in Margolick, 126.
80. Reuss, 156-57.
81. Woody Guthrie "Union Maid," Woody Guthrie website, accessed August 20, 2018, http://www.woodyguthrie.org/Lyrics/Union_Maid.htm.
82. Nancy Katz, "Union Maid," in *Songs of the Workers To Fan the Flames of Discontent*, 34th ed. (Chicago, IL.: Industrial Workers of the World, 1973), 46; *Carry It On: A History in Song and Picture of the Working Men and Women of America*, ed. Pete Seeger and Bob Reiser (New York: Simon & Schuster, 1985), 153-54.
83. Pete Seeger, *Talking Union and other Union Songs*, The Almanac Singers, Washington DC: Folkways Records, 1955, liner notes; Robert Darden, *Nothing But Love in God's Water* (University Park: Pennsylvania State University Press, 2014), 75, 99.
84. Quoted in Reuss, 174.
85. Ibid., 173.
86. Ernie Lieberman, quoted in Robbie Lieberman, *"My Song is My Weapon": People's Songs, American Communism, and the Politics of Culture, 1930-1950* (Urbana, IL: University of Illinois Press, 1989), 61-62.
87. Lapis, 141.
88. Marion Jacobson, "From Communism to Yiddishism: The Reinvention of the Jewish People's Philharmonic," in *Chorus and Community*, ed. Karen Ahlquist (Champaign: University of Illinois Press, 2006), 205-206.
89. Robert Snyder, "The Paterson Jewish Folk Chorus: Politics, Ethnicity and Musical Culture, *American Jewish History* 74, no. 1 (September, 1964: 39, accessed July 12, 2018, http://www.jstor.org/stable/23882496.
90. Kenneth C. Wolensky, "'We're Singing for the Union': The ILGWU Chorus in Pennsylvania Coal Country, 1947-2000," in *Chorus and Community*, 229. Lesbian-feminist choruses would use this same strategy as they emerged from the closet to the community in the late 20th century (see Chapter 7).
91. Ronald D. Lankford, Jr., *Folk Music U.S.A.: The Changing Voice of Protest* (New York: Schirmer Trade Books, 2005), 129.

92. Serge Denisoff, "Urban Folk 'Movement' Research: Value Free?" *Western Folklore* 28, no. 3 (July, 1969): 187, accessed July 10, 2018, http://www.jstor.org/stable/1499264.

93. Ronald D. Cohen," Woody the Red?" in *Hard Travelin': The Life of Woody Guthrie*, ed. Robert Santelli and Emily Davidson (Hanover, NH: Wesleyan University Press/University of New England, 1999), 145-146.

94. Dorian Lynskey, *33 Revolutions Per Minute: A History of Protest Songs, from Billie Holiday to Green Day* (New York: Harper Collins, 2011), 47-48.

95. Quoted in Guy and Candy Carawan, eds, and comps., *Sing for Freedom: The Story of the Civil Rights Movement Through Its Song* (Montgomery, Alabama: New South, Inc., 2007), xxii.

96. Robert Shelton, "Songs a New Weapon Civil Rights Battle, *The New York Times,* August. 20, 1962, accessed July 12, 2018, http://www.nytimes.com/learning/teachers/archival/19620820songsweapon.pdf.

97. Sanford Wexler, *The Civil Rights Movement: An Eyewitness History* (New York: Facts on File, 1993), 134.

98. Bernice Johnson Reagon, "In Our Hands: Thoughts on Black Music," *Sing Out!* 24 (January/February 1976: 1–2, 5.

99. *The American Future: A History, Presented by Simon Schama*, (BBC Two, 2008), DVD.

100. Quoted in Charles Marsh, *God's Long Summer: Stories of Faith and Civil Rights* (Princeton: Princeton University Press, 2008), 17, 22.

101. Bernice Johnson Reagon, "Singing for my Life," in *We Who Believe in Freedom: Sweet Honey in the Rock...Still on the Journey*, ed. Bernice Johnson Reagon and Sweet Honey in the Rock (New York: Anchor Doubleday, 1993), 141.

102. Bernice Johnson Reagon, "Foreword," in *Reimaging America: The Arts of Social Change*, ed. Mark Obrien and Craig Little (Philadelphia: New Society Publishers, 1990), 3.

103. George Elliott Clarke, "Gospel as Protest: the African-Nova Scotia Spiritual and the lyrics of Delvina Bernard," in *Rebel Musics: Human Rights, Persistent Sounds, and the Politics of Music Making*, ed. Daniel Fischlin and Ajay Heble (Montreal and New York: Black Rose Books, 2003), 110-11.

104. Zamani Miller, "Legacy of Four the Moment: Interview with Delvina Bernard," October 27, 2017, Africentric TV, accessed July 11, 2018, https://www.youtube.com/watch?v=owFGw290R5I.

105. Michael Castellini, "Stand In, Stand Up and Sing Out!: Black Gospel Music and the Civil Rights Movement" (master's thesis, Georgia State University, 2013), 5-6, accessed July 9, 2018, http://scholarworks.gsu.edu/history_theses.

106. Reagon, "Singing for My Life," 154. For a rousing and joyous rendition of this song by a premier women's chorus, see Anna Crusis Women's Choir, https://www.youtube.com/watch?v=gOaEa4DHhis.

107. Deanna F. Weber, "The SNCC Freedom Singers: Ambassadors for Justice," in *We Shall Overcome: Essays on A Great American Song*, ed. Victor V. Bobetsky (Lanham, Maryland: Rowman and Littlefield, 2015), 31.

108. Quoted in Carawan and Carawan, 8.

109. Quoted in Trymaine Lee, "Singing with the Freedom Riders: The Music of the Movement," *Huffington Post*, May 30, 2011, accessed July 11, 2018, https://www.huffingtonpost.com/2011/05/30/gospel-and-the-freedom-ri_n_868299.html.

110. Sally Belfrage, *Freedom Summer* (New York: Viking Press, 1965; Charlottesville: University Press of University of Virginia, 1990, 1999), 245-246.

111. Debra Schultz, *Going South: Jewish Women in The Civil Rights Movement* (New York: New York University Press, 2001); Sara Evans, *Personal Politics: The Roots of Women's Liberation in the Civil Rights Movement and the New Left* (New York: Vintage, 1980).

112. Evans, 53-54.

113. Reagon, "Let Your Light Shine—Historical Notes," in *We Who Believe in Freedom*, 19, emphasis in original.

Chapter 3

1. Gail Murray, ed., *Throwing Off the Cloak of Privilege: White Southern Women in the Civil Rights Era* (Gainesville: University Press of Florida, 2004).

2. Benita Roth, *Separate Roads to Feminism: Black, Chicana, and White Feminist Movements in America's Second Wave* (Cambridge, UK: Cambridge University Press, 2004).

3. Gloria T. Hull and Barbara Smith, "Introduction: The Politics of Black Women's Studies," in *All the Women Are White, All the Blacks are Men, But Some of Us Are Brave*, ed. Gloria T. Hull, Patricia Bell Scott, and Barbara Smith (New York: The Feminist Press, 1982), xvi.

4. bell hooks, *From Margin to Center*, 3rd ed. (New York: Routledge, 2015), 1-2.

5. "Finding Pauli Murray," National Organization for Women website, accessed July 11, 2018, http://now.org/about/history/finding-pauli-murray.

6. Karla Jay, *Tales of the Lavender Menace* (New York: Basic Books, 2000), 143.

7. Miriam Schneir, ed., *Feminism in Our Time: The Essential Writings, World War II to the Present* (New York: Vintage Books, 1994), 160-61; Flora Davis, *Moving the Mountain: The Women's Movement in America Since 1960* (Champaign: University of Illinois Press, 1999), 266.

8.   Michelle Kort, "Portrait of the Feminist As an Old Woman: Betty Friedan Has Survived Fame, Bitter Feuds and Heart Surgery. Now, in a New Book, She Celebrates Life, Aging and Family," *Los Angeles Times Magazine*, October 10, 1993, accessed July 11, 2018, http://articles.latimes.com/1993-10-10/magazine/tm-44091_1_betty-friedan/7; Betty Friedan, *Life So Far* (New York: Touchstone, 2001), 249.

9.   The Combahee River Collective, "The Combahee River Collective Statement," copyright © 1978 by Zillah Eisenstein, accessed July 12, 2018, http://americanstudies.yale.edu/sites/default/files/files/Keyword%20Coalition_Readings.pdf; Kimberlé Crenshaw, "Mapping the Margins: Intersectionality, Identity Politics, and Violence against Women of Color," *Stanford Law Review* 43, no. 6 (July 1991): 1241-1299.

10. Lynskey, 176, note.

11. Ronnie Gilbert, interviewed by Kate Weigand, March 10, 2004, Voices of Feminism Oral History Project, Sophia Smith Collection, Smith College, Northampton, Massachusetts, accessed July 10, 2018, https://www.smith.edu/libraries/libs/ssc/vof/transcripts/Gilbert.pdf.

12. Alix Dobkin, *My Red Blood, A Memoir of Growing Up Communist, Coming into the Greenwich Village Folk Scene, and Coming Out in the Feminist Movement* (New York: Alyson Books, 2009), 170-71.

13. Naomi Weisstein, "Days of Celebration and Resistance: The Chicago Women's Liberation Rock Band, 1970-1973," in *The Feminist Memoir Project: Voices from Women's Liberation*, ed. Rachel Blau DePlessis and Ann Snitow (New Brunswick, New Jersey: Rutgers University Press, 2007), 350.

14. Ibid., 351.

15. Ibid., 353.

16. Ibid.

17. CWLU Herstory Website Editorial Committee, "The Chicago Women's Liberation Rock Band," accessed July 9, 2018, https://www.cwluherstory.org/cwlu-workgroups-articles/chicago-womens-liberation-rock-band.

18. Weisstein, 356-57.

19. Ibid, 361.

20. Quoted in "Fanny: Godmothers of Chick Rock: About Fanny," Fanny webstite, accessed July 10, 2018, http://www.fannyrocks.com/about-2/how-it-began/

21. Barbara O'Dair, *Trouble Girls: The Rolling Stone Book of Women in Rock* (New York: Random House, 1997), 418.

22. Susan Abod, interviewed by JD Doyle, Queer Music Heritage, accessed July 9, 2018, queermusicheritage.com/apr2012s.html. This and all subsequent Queer Music Heritage posts used courtesy of JD Doyle.

23. Pam Annas, Marcia Deihl, and Pam Ouellete, "The Politics of Music—Carrying It On: An Interview with the New Harmony Sisterhood Band," *Radical Teacher*, no. 13 (March, 1979): 15.

24. Ibid., 16.

25. New Harmony Sisterhood Band, *And Ain't I a Woman?* Liner Notes, accessed July 11, 2018, http://media.smithsonianfolkways.org/liner_notes/paredon/PAR01038.pdf.

26. Kendall Hale, *Radical Passions: A Memoir of Revolution and Healing* (iUniverse, 2008).

27. Ibid.

28. John Rockwell, "The Pop Life Deadly Nightshade Trio Speaks Well of Women," *The New York Times*, Sept. 13, 1974, accessed August 20, 2018, http://www.nytimes.com/1974/09/13/archives/deadly-nightshade-trio-speaks-well-of-women-the-pop-life.html.

29. The Deadly Nightshade website, accessed August 20, 2018, http://www.thedeadlynightshade.net/Home.html.

30. Maxine Feldman, interviewed by JD Doyle, April 2002, Queer Music Heritage, accessed July 10, 2018, http://queermusicheritage.com/apr2002s.html.

31. Alix Dobkin website, www.alixdobkin.com.

32. Cynthia Lont, "Women's Music: No Longer a Small Private Party," in *Rockin' the Boat: Mass Music and Mass Movements*, ed. Reebee Garofalo (Boston: South End Press, 1992), 244.

33. Alix Dobkin, interviewed by JD Doyle, Queer Music Heritage, May 2002, accessed July 10,2018, http://queermusicheritage.com/may2002s.html.

34. Linda Rapp, "Christian, Meg," *GLBTQ Encyclopedia*, accessed July 12, 2018, http://www.glbtqarchive.com/arts/christian_m_A.pdf.

35. Ginny Berson, interviewed in *Radical Harmonies,* directed by Dee Mosbacher (WomanVision, 2002), DVD.

36. Bernice Johnson Reagon, "Let Your Light Shine: Historical Notes," in *We Who Believe in Freedom*, 14.

37. Ibid., 16.

38. Ibid.

39. Ibid., 31.

40. Ibid.

41. Ibid., 21

42. Alice Walker, "Sweet Honey in the Rock—The Sound of Our Own Culture," in *We Who Believe in Freedom*, 9-10.

43. Reagon, "Let Your Light Shine, in *We Who Believe in Freedom*, 34.

44. Amy Horowitz, "Some Factors in the Equation" in *We Who Believe in Freedom*, 184.

45. Reagon, "Let Your Light Shine," 32-33.

46. Holly Near, *Fire in the Rain...Singer in the Storm: An Autobiography* (New York: William Morrow, 1990), 137.

47. Horowitz, 186.

48. Ibid.

49. Near, 139.

50. Bonnie Morris, "Olivia Records: The Production of a Movement," *Journal of Lesbian Studies* 19 (2015): 291, accessed July 11, 2018, DOI: 10.1080/10894160.2015.1026699.

51. Judy Dlugacz, "Judy's View: Olivia Back Then" (August 1, 2007), http://www.olivia.com/Connect/Voices/judy_s_view/archive/2007/08/01/Olivia-Back-Then.aspx. (Site discontinued. Used by permission.)

52. Sarah Doughter, "Sex and Laughter in Women's Music," *Current Musicology*, no. 90 (Fall 2010): 45, accessed July 10, 2018, https://academiccommons.columbia.edu/catalog/ac:178252.

53. Morris, 298.

54. Ibid., 291.

55. Near, 113.

56. Ibid., 119-120

57. Janice Raymond, *The Transsexual Empire: The Making of the She-Male* (Boston: Beacon Press, 1979).

58. "Open Letter to Olivia," reprinted in Matt Abernathy, "Transphobic Radical Hate Didn't Start with Brennan: The Sandy Stone-Olivia Records Controversy," *The Trans-Advocate*, n.d., accessed July 11, 2018, http://transadvocate.com/transphobic-radical-hate-didnt-start-with-brennan-the-sandy-stone-olivia-records-controversy_n_4112.htm.

59. Quoted in Abernathy.

60. Terry Grant, interview with the author, January 5, 2016.

61. Ibid.

62. Ibid.

63. Susanna J. Sturgis, "Ladyslipper: Meeting the Challenge of Feminist Business," *Hot Wire* 1, no. 2 (March, 1985): 36, accessed July 12, 2018. This and all other *Hot Wire* articles can be accessed at http://www.hotwirejournal.com/hwmag.html.

64. Ladyslipper music Women's Music Aural Herstory Interviews, accessed August 20, 2018, https://archive.org/search.php?query=Ladyslipper%20Music.

65. Grant, interview.

66. Toni Armstrong, Jr., "Playing to the Highest Common Denominator," in *The Woman-Centered Economy: Ideas, Reality, and the Space in Between*, ed. Loraine Edwalds and Midge Stocker (Chicago: Third Side Press, 1995), 229.

67. Ibid.

68. Margie Adam, Speech at 25th National Women's Music Festival, June 19, 1999, accessed July 9, 2018, http://www.margieadam.com/speeches-writings/25th-national-womens-music-festival-speech.

69. Janis Ian, "Prologue," in *Society's Child* (NY: Penguin Books, 2008), xii-xxii.

70. Janis Ian and Jess Leary, "This Train Still Runs," © Rude Girl Pub. (50%)/WB Music Corp., accessed August 21, 2018, https://www.janisian.com/lyrics/thistrainstillruns.php. Janis Ian's version is available at https://www.youtube.com/watch?v=oHf03Gnicxs.

Chapter 4

1. Dobkin, *My Red Blood,* 208.
2. Kay Gardner, interviewed in *Radical Harmonies.*
3. Susan McClary, *Feminine Endings: Music, Gender, & Sexuality,* 2nd. ed. (Minneapolis: University of Minnesota Press, 2002); Christopher Small, *Musicking: The Meanings of Performing and Listening* (Middletown, Conn.: Wesleyan University Press, 1998).
4. Small, 2.
5. Ibid., 81, 86.
6. Jill Johnston, *Lesbian Nation: The Feminist Solution* (New York: Simon and Schuster, 1973), 276-77.
7. Roberta Kosse, "Chronicle of a Feminist Composer," *Paid My Dues* 2, no. 3 (Spring 1978): 6. All issues of *Paid My Dues* are available online courtesy of JD Doyle at http://queermusicheritage.com/pmd1.html.
8. Ibid.
9. Ibid., 7.
10. Ibid.
11. Lillian Faderman and Stuart Timmons, *Gay LA: A History of Sexual Outlaws, Power Politics and Lipstick Lesbians* (New York: Basic Books, 2006), 181-182.
12. Ibid., 189.
13. Diane Ehrensaft and Ruth Milkman, "Sexuality and the State: The Defeat of the Briggs Initiative and Beyond, Interview with Amber Hollibaugh," *Socialist Review* 9, no. 3 (May-June 1979), reprinted in Amber Hollibaugh, *My Dangerous Desires: A Queer Girl Dreaming Her Way Home* (Durham and London: Duke University Press, 2000), 43-61.
14. Sue Fink, interviewed by Toni J. Armstrong Jr., *Hot Wire: The Journal of Women's Music and Culture* 7, no. 2 (May 1991): 3.
15. Sue Fink, "Los Angeles Women's Chorus," *Paid My Dues* 2, no. 3 (Spring 1978): 9.
16. Sue Fink, interviewed by Toni J. Armstrong Jr., 9.
17. Mary Ager, "The PWC and the Vocal Orchestra Music of *Song of Survival,*" in *Take Up the Song,* 54.
18. Sydney Women's Vocal Orchestra website, accessed September 1, 2018, https://swvo.wordpress.com/about.
19. Sue Fink, Interviewed by Toni J. Armstrong, Jr., 3.

20. Scott C. Seyforth and Nichole Barnes, "'In People's Faces for Lesbian and Gay Rights': Stories of Activism in Madison, Wisconsin, 1970 to 1990," *The Oral History Review* 43, no. 1 (Spring, 2016): 81–97, accessed August 21, 1018, https://elpa.education.wisc.edu/docs/WebDispenser/elpa-documents/in-people-s-faces-for-lesbian-and-gay-rights-stories-of-activism-in-madison-wisconsin-1970-to-1990.pdf?sfvrsn=0.

21. Catherine Roma Interviewed by Joyce Follet, June 19 and 20, 2005, Voices of Feminism Oral History Project, Sophia Smith Collection, Smith College, Northampton, Massachusetts, 19-20.

22. Ibid., 24.

23. Ibid., 22.

24. Ibid., 29-30.

25. Ibid., 35.

26. Ibid., 43.

27. Ibid., 38, 41.

28. Ibid., 45

29. Ibid., 46.

30. Dick Hewetson, *History of the Gay Movement in Minnesota and the Role of the Minnesota Civil Liberties Union* (Minneapolis: Friends of the Bill of Rights Foundation, 2013), accessed July 10, 2018, https://www.qlibrary.org/wordpress/wp-content/uploads/2014/04/MN_Gay_Movement_MCLU.pdf.

31. Joan Wallner, "Founding Mothers: Twenty-five years at Amazon," *Minnesota Women's Press*, January 25, 1995, 19, 27.

32. Judith Kegan Gardiner, "Bechdel's Dykes to Watch out For and Popular Culture," in *Queers in American Popular Culture, Volume I*, ed. Jim Elledge (Santa Barbara: Praeger, 2010), 93.

33. Sarah Henderson, interview with the author, July 25, 2015.

34. Ibid.

35. Ibid.

36. Ibid.

37. Ibid.

38. Ibid.

39. Michelle Brodsky, interview with the author, August 13, 2010.

Chapter 5

1. Joanna Cazden, "Lawrence, Kate, and Lilith," *Folkworks* 5, no. 2 (March-April 2005): 5.

2. University of Illinois at Urbana-Champaign Archives: Student Life and Culture, accessed August 22, 2018, http://archives.library.illinois.edu/slc/research-education/timeline/1970-1979.

3. Mary Lee Sargent, interview with the author, August 18, 2011.

4. Nancy Melin, interview with the author, July 21, 2013.

5. Kristen Lems, interviewed in *Radical Harmonies*.
6. Margaret Marigold, "National Women's Music Festival, *Paid My Dues* l, no. 3 (October 1974): 15.
7. Sargent, interview.
8. Marigold, 15-16.
9. Lisa Vogel, interviewed in *Radical Harmonies*.
10. Boden Sandstrom, "Performance, Ritual and Negotiation of Identity in the Michigan Womyn's Music Festival" (Ph.D. diss., University of Maryland, 2002), 109, accessed August 22, 2018, ProQuest [3080281].
11. Narrator, *Radical Harmonies*.
12. Sandstrom, 111.
13. Toni Armstrong, Jr., "Silent Pre-Fest," *Hot Wire* 9, no. 1 (January 1993): 36.
14. Sandstrom, 107.
15. Bonnie Morris, *Eden Built by Eves: The Culture of Women's Music Festivals* (Los Angeles: Alyson Books, 1999), 35-36.
16. Ibid., 24.
17. Near, 107.
18. Laurie J. Kendall, "From the Liminal to the Land: Building Amazon Culture at the Michigan Womyn's Music Festival" (Ph.D. diss., University of Maryland, 2006), 8, accessed August 22, 2018, ProQuest 3212615, https://drum.lib.umd.edu/bitstream/handle/1903/3499/umi-umd-3329.pdf?sequence=1&isAllowed=y.
19. Boden Sandstrom, "Women's Music, Passing the Legacy," in *Women's Culture: The Women's Renaissance of the Seventies*, ed. Gayle Kimball (London: Scarecrow Press, 1981), 111.
20. Loraine Hitchins and td, "festival: trouble & mediation at yosemite," *Off Our Backs* 11, no. 1 (November 1981): 12-13, 25, accessed July 10, 2018, https://www.jstor.org/stable/i25774082.
21. Donna Eder, Suzanne Staggenborg and Lori Sudderth, "National Women's Music Festival: Collective Identity and Diversity in a Lesbian-Feminist Community," *Journal of Contemporary Ethnography* 23, no. 4 (Jan. 1995): 500, 502.
22. Eileen Hayes, *Songs in Black and Lavender: Race, Sexual Politics, and Women's Music* (Chicago: University of Chicago Press, 2010), 55.
23. Ibid., 112-13.
24. "In their Own Voices: Self-Portraits of Festival Performers: Linda Tillery," in Morris, *Eden Built By Eves*, 107-108.
25. Horowitz, 191.
26. Ibid., 192-192.
27. Rena Yount, "Sisterfire," *Hotwire* 1, no. 1 (November 1984): 28.
28. Ibid.
29. Horowitz, 193.
30. Nancy Seeger, "Welcome Back Sisterfire 1987," *Hot Wire* 4, no. 1 (November, 1987): 38.

31. Horowitz, 193.

32. Anna Lee, "For the Love of Separatism," *Lesbian Ethics* 3, no. 2 (Fall, 1988), accessed July 11, 2018, http://www.feminist-reprise.org/docs/leelovesep.htm.

33. Bette S. Tallen, "How Inclusive Is Feminist Political Theory? Questions for Lesbians," in *Just Methods: An Interdisciplinary Feminist Reader*, ed. Alison M. Jaeger, updated ed. (New York: Routledge, 2016), 211.

34. "Sisterfire Music festival to ignite next weekend," *The Washington Blade*, June 24, 1988, 3, accessed July 12, 2018, http://digdc.dclibrary.org/cdm/ref/collection/p16808coll24/id/14766.

35. Nancy Seeger, "Sisterfire '88," *Hot Wire* 5, no. 1 (January, 1989): 31.

36. Horowitz, 193-94.

37. Muse Choir Website, http://www.musechoir.org/writings/artistic/252. (Link discontinued. Used by permission.)

38. Catherine Roma, interviewed by Joyce Follet, 50-51.

39. Mardy Keener, "Letter to Chorus Mailing List, June 9, 1980," Sister Singers Network Archive, 1981-2003, Sophia Smith Collection, Smith College, Northampton, Massachusetts.

40. Linda Small and Linda Ray, "Letter to Chorus Mailing List, October 28, 1980," Sister Singers Network Archive.

41. Linda Ray (Echo), interview with the author, July 5, 2010.

42. Ibid.

43. Linda Small and Linda Ray, "Letter to Chorus Mailing List, October 28, 1980," Sister Singers Network Archive.

44. Karen Lee Osborne and William J. Spurlin, eds., *Reclaiming the Heartland: Lesbian and Gay Voices from the Midwest* (Minneapolis: University of Minnesota Press, 1996), xvii.

45. Morris, *Eden Built by Eves,* 37.

46. Martin F. Manalansan IV et al., "Introduction: Queering the Middle: Race, Region and a Queer Midwest," in *Queering the Middle: Race, Region, and a Queer Midwest, A Special Issue* of *GLQ: A Journal of Lesbian and Gay Studies* 20, no.1-2, ed. Martin F. Manalansan et al., 2014): 3, accessed September 30, 2018, https://read.dukeupress.edu/glq/article/20/1-2/1/34879/Queering-the-MiddleRace-Region-and-a-Queer-Midwest.

47. "Our Herstory," *Artemis Singers* website, accessed July 9, 2018, https://artemissingers.org/herstory.

48. "What She Wants," *The Encyclopedia of Cleveland History*, accessed July 12, 2018, http://ech.case.edu/cgi/article.pl?id=WSW.

49. Linda Ray and Linda Small, "Letter to Sister Singers, January 2, 1981," Sister Singers Archive.

50. Nancy Melin, interview.

51. Linda Small, "How to Share Music Without Getting Arrested for being Politically Incorrect," Sister Singers Archive.

52. Saint Louis Coordinating Committee, "Letter to Sister Singers, June 12, 1984," Sister Singers Archive.

53. Scoop Phillips, "The Making of a Community," *Kansas City News-Telegraph*, "Excavating Our Pride" Feature Supplement, March 1992, accessed July 12, 2018, https://library2.umkc.edu/spec-col/glama/pdfs/history/article-phillips2.pdf.

54. Phillips, "The Churches: Not Always the Enemy," *Kansas City News-Telegraph*, "Excavating Our Pride," March, 1992, accessed July 12, 2018, https://library2.umkc.edu/spec-col/glama/pdfs/history/article-phillips1.pdf.

55. "Combined Chorus Concert," First National Women's Chorus Concert Program, Sister Singers Archive.

56. Christopher Small, 39.

57. Linda Ray (Echo), interview.

Chapter 6

1. Melba Jesudason and Sally Drew, "Feminist Music and WOMONSONG Choir of Madison, Wisconsin, *Studies in Popular Culture* 15, no. 1 (1992): 70, accessed July 11 2018, http://www.jstor.org/stable/23414480.

2. Debbie Nordeen, interview with the author, November 7, 2009.

3. Patricia Hennings, "The Heart of the Matter," in *Take Up the Song*, 15.

4. Jackie Coren, interview with the author, August 6, 2011.

5. Deborah Wachspress, e-mail message to the author, June 18, 2015.

6. Quoted in Marilyn Hubbard, "We Know Why We Sing," *WNC Woman*, Oct. 28, 2012, accessed July 10, 2018, http://www.wncwoman.com/2012/10/28/we-know-why-we-sing.

7. Voices from the Heart website, accessed July 12, 2018, http://www.voicesfromtheheart.org.

8. Bev Grant, interview with the author, November 3, 2014.

9. Kristina Boerger, *Amasong Chorus: Singing Out*, directed by Jay Rosenstein (New Day Films, 2003), DVD. Available for download on Vimeo, https://vimeo.com/86911054.

10. Phoenix Women's Chorus (formerly Arizona Women in Tune), group interview, March 8, 2011.

11. Carol White, Keynote Speech at the Denver Women's Chorus 30th anniversary dinner, Denver, May 17, 2014.

12. Naomi Weinert, interview with the author, July 2, 2010.

13. Estelle Phillips, interview with the author, July 3, 2010.

14. Ellen Catlin, interview with the author, July 3, 2010.

15. Meredith Bowen, interview with the author, May 9, 2010.

16. Joan Szymko, interview with the author, August 31, 2010.

17. Cindy Bizzell, interview with the author, December 17, 2010.

18. Catherine Beller-McKenna, interview with the author, October 5, 2009.

19. Susanna J. Sturgis, "The D.C. Area Feminist Chorus," *Hot Wire* 2, no. 1 (November 1985): 48.
20. Miriam Davidson, "Miriam Davidson—Interview," GALA Choruses Blog, March 21, 2104, accessed July 10, 2018, http://galachoruses. org/blog/miriam-davidson-interview.
21. Estelle Phillips, interview.
22. "Mission and Vision," Fortissima: DC's Feminist Singers website, accessed July 10, 2018, http://www.fortissima.org/mission_vision. shtml#.WQpTZ1Pyul.
23. Midge Stocker, "Self Directed Chorus," Sister Singers website, accessed July 12, 2018, http://www.sistersingers.net/Tools/ SelfDirectedChorus.shtml#.WQpUAFMrKlM.
24. Debbie Nordeen, interview.
25. Cynthia Frank, e-mail communication to the author, September 2, 2015.
26. Windsong website, accessed July 12, 2018, http://windsongcleveland. org; Fortissima website; Carol Wheeler, interview with the author, August 10, 2014.
27. Joan Szymko, interview.
28. Marsha Buck, interview with the author, April 11, 2011.
29. Mary Robertson, e-mail communication to the author, Aug. 5, 2014.
30. Carol Wheeler, interview.
31. Ibid.
32. Catherine Beller-McKenna, e-mail to Women in Harmony, September 12, 2011.
33. Kelsey Menahan, "With Access and Accommodation for All, *The Voice*, December 2008, accessed July 11. 2018, https://www.chorusamerica. org/management-governance/access-and-accommodation-all, reposted at http://www.performingartsconvention.org/file/ Vol32No2%2008-09%20Accessibility.pdf
34. Kim Shaw, interview with the author, July 1, 2010.
35. Jody Steiner and Laurie Rothfeld, "ASL Interpreting for Concerts: An Interpreter's Voice," *Hot Wire* 2, no. 1 (November 1985): 8.
36. Kim Shaw, interview.
37. Catherine Roma, interview with the author, April 7, 2010.
38. Ibid.
39. Catherine Roma interviewed by Joyce Follet, 71; Bernice Johnson Reagon, *Compositions One* (Washington, D.C.: Songtalk, 1986).
40. Catherine Roma, interviewed by Follet, 72.
41. Angie Denov, interview with the author, August 1, 2013.
42. Catherine Roma, Follet interview, 73.
43. Angie Denov, interview.
44. Catherine Roma, Follet interview, 74
45. Ibid., 80.
46. Ibid., 81.

47. James H. Cone, *The Spirituals and the Blues* (Maryknoll, New York: Orbis Books, 1991); Judith H, Katz, *White Awareness: Handbook for Anti-Racism Training* (Norman: University of Oklahoma Press, 1978); Catherine Roma, Follet interview, 81.

48. Catherine Roma, Follet interview, 61.

49. "I Feel Like Going On," The New Spirituals Project, accessed July 11, 2018, https://www.youtube.com/watch?v=A2jxPTWh_zs.

50. "First National Women's Chorus Evaluations," Sister Singers Archive.

51. "National Women's Choral Festival 2," 1985 Program Book, Sister Singers Archive.

52. Celia Guse, "The Third Annual Women's Choral Festival," *Hot Wire* 3, no. 2 (March 1987): 60.

53. "We Make the Music," 1987 Program Book, Sister Singers Archive.

54. Linda Ray (Echo), interview and Sister Singers Archive.

55. Steve Walker, "Women's chorus sets issues to music," *The KC View*, October 18-31, 1989, Sister Singers Archive.

56. Barbara Karkabi, "Songs from the heart: For 50 women, amateur choral group HeartSong is a refuge from Houston's hectic pace," *The Houston Chronicle*, April 14, 1991, "Heartsong Clippings and Miscellaneous," Queer Music History, accessed August 23, 2018, http://www.houstonlgbthistory.org/heartsong-clippings.html.

57. "A Feminist Fourth," Sister Singers Festival Program, Sister Singers Archive; Catherine Roma and Marilyn Ebertz, "The Seventh National Women's Choral Festival: A Feminist Fourth," *Hot Wire* 10, no 1 (January 1994): 57.

58. Ysaye Barnwell, "Reflections on the Festival," *Across the Lines: The Sister Singers Newsletter* (1993), Sister Singers Archive.

59. Debbie Wachspress, "A Reflection from Rochester," *Across the Lines* (1993), Sister Singers Archive.

60. *Across the Lines* (1995), Sister Singers Archive.

61. Angie Denov, "Thoughts on Diversity and SSN: The Diversity Caucuses," *Across the Lines*, May, 1996, Sister Singers Archive.

Chapter 7

1. Michael Ward and Mark Freeman, "Defending Gay Rights: The Campaign Against the Briggs Amendment in California," *Radical America* 13, no. 4 (July-Aug.1979): 11-26, accessed August 23, 2018, https://library.brown.edu/pdfs/1125404303746164.pdf.

2. Robert Rufo, "34 Years Later, Harvey Milk's Legacy Lives On," accessed July 12, 2018, https://www.youtube.com/watch?v=AT1TO075xwk.

3. John Quinn, "Local Businessman to Wrestle in Gay Games VI," *Between the Lines,* July 13, 2006, accessed August 23, 2018, https://pridesource.com/article/19498; https://galachoruses.org/about/history.

4. Edward Rothstein, "CONCERT: 'FIRST GAY CHORAL FESTIVAL," *The New York Times*, September. 9, 1983, accessed August 23, 2018, https://www.nytimes.com/1983/09/13/arts/concert-first-gay-choral-festival.html.

5. Sue Coffee, interview with the author, April 10, 2009.

6. Betsy Parsons, interview with the author, September 5, 2008.

7. Naomi Weinert, interview.

8. Catherine Roma, Follet interview, 77.

9. Ibid.

10. Sue Coffee, interview.

11. Tim Seelig, interviewed by JD Doyle, "Gay & Lesbian Choruses: The History & Music of the Gay & Lesbian Choral Movement, *Queer Music History*, November 2010, accessed July 12, 2018, http://queermusicheritage.com/nov2010.html.

12. Lawrence K. Altman, "Rare Cancer Seen in 41 Homosexuals," *The New York Times*, July 3, 1981, accessed July 9, 2018, http://www.nytimes.com/1981/07/03/us/rare-cancer-seen-in-41-homosexuals.html.

13. Liz Hamel et al., HIV/AIDS In The Lives Of Gay And Bisexual Men In The United States, The Henry K Kaiser Foundation, September 25, 2014, accessed July 10, 2018, http://kff.org/hivaids/report/hivaids-in-the-lives-of-gay-and-bisexual-men-in-the-united-states.

14. Seelig, interviewed by JD Doyle.

15. Kathy Aney, "Gay men's choir sang through adversity," *East Oregonian*, April 10, 2015, accessed July 9, 2018, http://www.eastoregonian.com/eo/local-news/20150410/gay-mens-choir-sang-through-adversity.

16. Joyce Wadler, "A Baton Is Passed, but the Chorus Sings On," *The New York Times*, June 25, 1998, accessed July 12, 2018, http://www.nytimes.com/1998/06/25/nyregion/public-lives-a-baton-is-passed-but-the-chorus-sings-on.html.

17. Meredith May, "Gay Men's Chorus Carries On," *SFGate*, June 4, 2006, accessed July 11, 2018, http://www.sfgate.com/health/article/Gay-Men-s-Chorus-carries-on-A-quarter-century-2533823.php.

18. Joe Morgan, "Survivors of 1980s AIDS Crisis Reveal What Happened to Them," *Gay Star News*, February 2, 2015, accessed July 11, 2018, http://www.gaystarnews.com/article/survivors-1980s-aids-crisis-reveal-what-happened-them020215.

19. Bruce Lambert, "In Texas, AIDS Struggle Is Also Matter of Money," *The New York Times*, January 5, 1990, accessed July 11, 2018, http://www.nytimes.com/1990/01/05/us/in-texas-aids-struggle-is-also-matter-of-money.html?pagewanted=all.

20.	Chrislove, "Remembering LGBT History: 'Shoot the Queers': Houston's 1985 Anti-Gay Referendum and Backlash," *The Daily Kos*, May 20, 2012, accessed July 9, 2018, https://www.dailykos.com/story/2012/05/20/1093065/-Remembering-LGBT-History-Shoot-the-Queers-Houston-s-1985-Anti-Gay-Referendum-and-Backlash.

21.	HeartSong Women's Chorus, group interview with the author, September 13, 2014.

22.	Jane Ramseyer Miller, "Jane Ramseyer Miller— Interview," GALA Choruses Blog, October 11, 2013, accessed July 11, 2018, http://galachoruses.org/blog/jane-ramseyer-miller-interview.

23.	*Bowers v. Hardwick*, accessed July 9, 2018, https://www.law.cornell.edu/supremecourt/text/478/186.

24.	George T. Nicola, "Oregon Anti-Gay Ballot Measures," *Gay and Lesbian Archives of the Northwest*, accessed July 11, 2018, https://www.glapn.org/6013OregonAntiGayMeasures.html; Amy L. Stone, *Gay Rights at the Ballot Box* (Minneapolis; University of Minnesota Press, 2012), 21; Stephen Zamansky, "Colorado's Amendment 2 and Homosexuals' Right to Equal Protection of the Law," *Boston College Law Review* 35, no. 1 (1993), accessed July 12, 2018, http://lawdigitalcommons.bc.edu/bclr/vol35/iss1/6; Doug Linder, *Exploring Constitutional Conflicts: The Gay Rights Controversy*, accessed July 11, 2018, http://law2.umkc.edu/faculty/projects/ftrials/conlaw/gayrights.htm.

25.	Kenneth J. Meier, *The Politics of Sin* (New York: Taylor & Francis, 1994, Routledge, 2015); Donald Haider-Markel, "AIDS and Gay Civil Rights: Politics and Policy at the Ballot Box," Research Gate, January 1999, accessed July 10, 2018, https://www.researchgate.net/publication/258821782_AIDS_and_Gay_Civil_Rights_Politics_and_Policy_at_the_Ballot_Box.

26.	Marc Ramirez, "Lon Mabon Sets 'Em Straight," *Seattle Times*, October 3, 1993, accessed July 12, 2018, http://community.seattletimes.nwsource.com/archive/?date=19931003&slug=1724056.

27.	Haider-Markel, 353, 354-55, 370.

28.	Will Kohler, "Today in Gay History—June 19, 1983: Founder of the Moral Majority Jerry Falwell: 'Aids is God's Punishment for Homosexuals,'" *Back2Stonewall*, accessed July 11, 2018, http://www.back2stonewall.com/2018/06/june-19-1983-founder-moral-majority-jerry-falwell-aids-gods-punishment-homosexuals.html.

29.	"The History of Coming Out, *Human Rights Campaign*, accessed July 12, 2018, http://www.hrc.org/resources/the-history-of-coming-out; Marc Stein, "Memories of the 1987 March on Washington," *OutHistory.org*, accessed July 12, 2018, http://outhistory.org/exhibits/show/march-on-washington/exhibit/by-marc-stein.

30. Jean E. Balestery, "The Role of Lesbians in the 1979 and 1987 Marches on Washington for Lesbian and Gay Rights," posted by Urvashi Vaid, *Lesbian Concentrate*, August 20, 2010, accessed July 9, 2018, http://urvashivaid.net/wp/?p=394.
31. Ibid.
32. *Across the Lines*, October, 1995, Sister Singers Archive.
33. "Planning/Invitational Letter"; "Minutes of 1988 Meeting," Sister Singers Archive; capitals and punctuation in original.
34. Denver Women's Chorus, group interview with the author, March 15, 2015.
35. Ibid.
36. New York City Gay Men's Chorus 25th Anniversary Journal, 57, accessed July 11, 2018, https://issuu.com/jimvivyan/docs/nycgmc25/61.
37. John Calvi website, accessed July 9, 2018, http://www.johncalvi.com.
38. *Across the Lines* 1, no. 1 (October 1990): 2-3, Sister Singers Archive.
39. Denver Women's Chorus, interview.
40. Sarah Henderson, interview with the author, July 25, 2015.
41. Ibid.
42. Ibid.
43. Ibid.
44. Ibid.
45. Quoted in Julia Balén, *A Queerly Joyful Noise: Choral Musicking for Social Justice* (New Brunswick, NJ: Rutgers University Press, 2017), 108.
46. "About," Rocky Mountain Arts Association website, accessed August 23, 2018, https://www.rmarts.org/about.
47. Wendy K. Moy, "Come Together: An Ethnography of the Seattle Men's Chorus Family" (Ph.D. diss., University of Washington, 2015), 43, accessed August 23, 2018, https://digital.lib.washington.edu/researchworks/bitstream/handle/1773/33215/Moy_washington_0250E_14101.pdf?sequence=1, ProQuest [3688950].
48. James Knapp, interview with the author, September 18, 2014.
49. "About BCPA," Bayou City Performing Arts website, accessed July 9, 2018, http://www.bcpahouston.org.
50. Lori Heidelberger, interview with the author, September 12, 2014.
51. Jamie Miller, interview with the author, September 12, 2014.
52. James Knapp interview.
53. Marte Parham, interview with the author, September 12, 2014.
54. Tom Keogh, "Leader, Advocate, Legend," Seattle Choruses Blog, June 6, 2016, accessed July 12, 2018, http://www.seattlechoruses.org/blog/leader-advocate-legend/#sthash.2iLmvDQ4.dpuf.
55. Philip A. Swan, "The Y Factor in an X Chromosome World," in *Conducting Women's Choirs: Strategies for Success*, ed. and comp. by Debra Spurgeon (Chicago: GIA Publications, 2012), 134.

56. Unnamed singer.
57. Ibid.
58. Stephanie J., choral singer.

Chapter 8

1. Leslie Feinberg, *Transgender Liberation: A Movement Whose Time Has Come* (New York: World View Forum, 1992).
2. Unnamed singer, Phoenix Women's Chorus, Group Interview, March 8, 2011.
3. Mary Lee Sargent, in *Amasong Chorus: Singing Out*.
4. Janie MacNeela, interview, with the author, December 17, 2010.
5. Peggy Larson, e-mail communication to the author, July 27, 2010.
6. "About Us," Charlottesville Women's Choir website, accessed July 9, 2018, http://www.cville-womens-choir.org/?page_id=28.
7. Julie Regner, interview with the author, July 1, 2010.
8. Naomi Weinert, interview.
9. "Orange County Women's Chorus Presents 'You Can't Sing That!'", press release, April 20, 2009. http://www.ocwomenschorus.org/sites/default/files/OCWC-PR-You-Can't-Sing-That.pdf. (Site discontinued.)
10. Angie Denov, interview.
11. Melinda Imthurn, e-mail post, ChorusWomen Yahoo Group, August 4, 2011.
12. Joan Szymko, interview.
13. Judy Fjell, interview with the author, June 9, 2010.
14. Marte Parham, interview.
15. Shelbie Wahl, "By Women, For Women: Choral Works for Women's Voices," in *Conducting Women's Choirs*, 145.
16. Hilary Apfelstadt, "Practices of Successful Women's Choir Conductors," *Choral Journal* 39, no. 5 (December 1998): 35, accessed July 9, 2018, https://acda.org/files/choral_journals/December_1998_Apfelstadt_H.pdf.
17. "No Whining, No Flowers," Cornell Chorus Commissioning Project, accessed July 11, 2018, http://cuchorus.com/commissioning-project.
18. Lauren Estes, "The Choral Hierarchy Examined: The Presence of Repertoire for Women's Choirs in Monographs on Choral Literature and Choral History" (master's thesis, Syracuse University, 2013), 40, accessed July 10, 2018, http://surface.syr.edu/cgi/viewcontent.cgi?article=1009&context=thesis.
19. Naomi Stephan, "Is it Just (,) You Girls? A Plea for Women's Choral Music," *Journal of the International Alliance for Women in Music* 11, no. 2 (2005): 2-3.

20. Julia E. Koza, "Getting a Word in Edgewise: A Feminist Critique of Choral Methods Texts," *The Quarterly* 5, no. 3 (Fall, 1994), Reprinted in *Visions of Research in Music Education* 16, no. 5 (Autumn, 2010): 72, accessed July 11, 2018, http://www-usr.rider.edu/~vrme/v16n1/volume5/visions/fall8.

21. American Choral Directors Association Women's Choir Repertoire & Standards Leadership, accessed July 9, 2018, https://acda.org/ACDA/Repertoire_and_Resources/Repertoire_specific/womens_choir_History.aspx.

22. Catherine Roma, "Women's Choral Literature: Finding Depth, *The Choral Journal* 44, no. 10 (May, 2004): 30, 34-35, accessed July 12, 2018, http://www.jstor.org/stable/23555441.

23. Jennifer Womack, "Singing for Our Lives" (master's thesis, The University of North Carolina at Chapel Hill, 2009), 20, accessed August 23, 2018, https://cdr.lib.unc.edu/record/uuid:3fada1d3-2dab-4c6b-9200-2edbe4e717b2, ProQuest [1467319].

24. Ibid., 22.

25. Ibid., 22-23.

26. Common Woman Chorus, group interview, December 17, 2010.

27. Cindy Bizell, interview with the author, December 17, 2010.

28. Unnamed singer, Bayou City Women's Chorus founders, group interview, September 12, 2014.

29. Erin Reid, interview with the author, August 27, 2015.

30. Rebecca Gorlin, interview with the author, July 1, 2010.

31. Julie Regner, interview.

32. Naomi Weinert, interview.

33. Argerie Vasilakes, interview with the author, July 26, 2015.

34. Ibid.

35. Janice Scalza to Lucille Clifton, reprinted in "Lucille Clifton Writes on Experiencing Her Poetry," Gwyneth Walker's website, accessed August 23, 2018, https://www.gwynethwalker.com/clifton.html.

36. Lucille Clifton to Janice Scalza, reprinted in Walker, "Lucille Clifton Writes on Experiencing Her Poetry."

37. © Holly Near, Simply Love," © 12000 Calico Tracks Music; Fred Small, "Everything Possible," © 1983 Pine Barrens Music.

38. "Something Inside So Strong," BBC Soul Music, Series 18, Episode 3, accessed July 9, 2018, http://www.bbc.co.uk/programmes/b040hx6j.

39. Jon Arterton interviewed by JD Doyle, Michael Callen Tribute, accessed August 23, 2018, http://www.queermusicheritage.com/may2013s.html.

40. Bev Grant, Interview with the author, November 3, 2014.

41. Sophie Hemery, Twitter Post, *Holler4*, accessed July 10, 2018, http://www.holler4.co.uk/womens-march-on-london.html.

42. All chorus programs from Sister Singers Archive.

43. Carol Wheeler, interview.

44. James Daugherty, "Ethnic/Multicultural Choral Music: Thinking Out of the Box," accessed July 10, 2018, http://galachoruses.org/documents/events/Daugherty-ETHNIC-MULTICULTURAL-CHORAL-MUSIC.pdf.

45. Catherine Roma interviewed by Jane Ramseyer Miller, Gala Choruses Blog, July 28, 2014, accessed August 24, 2018, https://galachoruses.org/blog/cathy-roma-and-jane-ramseyer-miller.

46. Ibid.

47. Erica Quin-Easter, "Singing in Another Voice: Exploring the Mystery of Multiculturalism with American Slavic Choirs" (master's essay, University of Southern Maine, 2006), 24.

48. Rose Adams and Antonia Alvarez, interview with the author, July 9, 2015.

49. Angie Denov, interview.

50. GALA Choruses 2016 Festival Schedule, accessed July 10, 2018, http://galachoruses.org/documents/events/festival2016/Festival-Schedule-Of-Events.pdf; complete program, 35, in possession of the author.

51. Szymko interview.

52. Libby Larson, "I Lift My Eyes to the Mountains—Psalm 121: In Memoriam Patty Hennings," in *Take Up the Song*, 19.

53. Ibid., 20.

54. *The Amasong Chorus: Singing Out.* https://vimeo.com/86911054, at 28 minutes.

55. Omega Institute, "Sing Your Prayers: an Interview with Bobby McFerrin," *HuffPost*, 6/11/2016, accessed July 11, 2018, https://www.huffingtonpost.com/omega-institute-for-holistic-studies/bobby-mcferrin_b_1582043.html.

56. Grace Rubin-Rabson, "Why Haven't Women Become Great Composers?" *High Fidelity* 23, no 2 (February, 1973): 49.

57. Fiona Maddocks, "Women Composers: Notes from the Musical Margins," *Guardian UK Observer*, March 13, 2011, accessed July 11, 2018, https://www.theguardian.com/music/2011/mar/13/london-oriana-choir-women-composers.

58. Dale Trumbore, "Composing While Female," Center for New Music, August 17, 2015, accessed July 12, 2018, http://centerfornewmusic.com/composing-while-female.

59. Elizabeth Alexander, interviewed in Nancy Menk, "Writing for Women's Voices: A Conversation with Composers," in *Conducting Women's Choirs*, 171.

60. Iris Levine and Shelbie Wahl, Women's Choirs: Model Repertoire Repertoire as Model," *The Choral Journal* 51, no. 11 (June-July, 2011): 56, accessed July 11, 2018, http://www.jstor.org/stable/23561627.

61. Joan Szymko in Menk, "Writing for Women's Voices," 173; interview with the author.

62. Jan C. Snow, interview with the author, July 25, 2015.

63. "Another Song", © Jan C. Snow. Used by permission.

64. Jan C. Snow, interview.

65. Small, *Musicking*, 208.

66. Daniel J. Levitin, *This is Your Brain on Music: The Science of a Human Obsession* (New York: Penguin, 2006), 6-7.

67. Elizabeth Alexander, Program Notes, "Being Who You Are," Women in Harmony Concert, May 19-20, 2007, in possession of the author.

68. Patricia Hennings with Marie des Jardines, "'A Young Poet Sings,'" in *Take Up the Song*, 82.

69. Sue Coffee, e-mail communication to the author, May 18, 2017.

70. Carol Matthews, interview with the author, May 20, 2016.

71. Ibid.; A video of this performance is available at https://www.youtube.com/watch?v=VNpeRVZeDd4.

72. Tim Seelig, interviewed by Kris Schindler, "An Interview with the Conductor of Sing for the Cure: Dr. Timothy Seelig," accessed July 12, 2018, https://www.youtube.com/watch?v=9B4tLzLruvQ.

73. Ibid.

74. Ibid.

75. Kathy Latour, "Sing for the Cure," *CURE*, May 6, 2010, accessed July 11, 2018, http://www.curetoday.com/articles/sing-for-the-cure.

76. Diane Benjamin, interview with the author, September 7, 2015.

77. Connie North, interview with the author, March 15, 2015.

78. Diane Benjamin, interview.

79. Ibid.

80. Kim Ode, "Calliope Sings of Women's Health," *Minneapolis StarTribune*, May 13, 2009, accessed August 24, 2018, https://www.highbeam.com/doc/1G1-199872467.html.

81. Ibid.

82. Gayle Sulik, *Pink Ribbon Blues: How Breast Cancer Culture Undermines Women's Health* (New York: Oxford University Press, 2011), 370.

83. Think Before You Pink, a Project of Breast Cancer Action, Accessed July 12, 2018, http://thinkbeforeyoupink.org.

84. "The Red Ribbon Project, "*Visual Aids*, accessed July 12, 2018, https://www.visualaids.org/projects/detail/the-red-ribbon-project.

85. Ibid.

86. Denver Women's Chorus, group interview.

87. Womack, 32.

88. Diane Benjamin, interview; Grace Ross Lewis, *1001 Chemicals in Everyday Products* (New York: John Wiley & Sons, 1999).

89. "Portland to Host 8th Festival," *Across the Lines,* May, 1996, 1,3, Sister Singers Archive.

90. Ibid.

91. Midge Stocker, interview with the author, May 29, 2011.

92. Janice Scalza and Sheryl Mase, interview with the author, July 23, 2011.

93. Ibid.

94. Ibid.

95. Ibid.

96. Ibid.

97. Pat Mora, "Ode to Women," In *Adobe Odes* (Tucson: University of Arizona Press 2006), 92-93.

98. Teri Siciliani, interview with the author, May 29, 2011.

99. Ibid.

Chapter 9

1. Nathan Eagle, "Same-Sex Marriage Debate Splits Hawaii State Capitol in Two—Literally," *Hawaii Civil Beat*, November 8, 2013, accessed July 10,2018, http://www.civilbeat.org/2013/11/20358-same-sex-marriage-debate-splits-hawaii-state-capitol-in-two-literally.

2. Antonia Alvarez, interview.

3. "About Us," Common Woman Chorus website, accessed July 9, 2018, http://www.commonwomanchorus.net/2007/aboutus.htm.

4. "Our Herstory," Voices Rising website, accessed July 12 2018, http://www.voicesrising.org/about-voices-rising/our-herstory.

5. Rita Kissen, "Two Weddings," 2009, accessed August 24, 2018, https://www.youtube.com/watch?v=ZrJk07-k6cY.

6. "Historical Timeline," Seattle Choruses website, accessed August 24, 2018, https://www.seattlechoruses.org/learn/history/; "Seattle Men's Chorus & Seattle Women's Chorus Celebrate Marriage Equality in Washington State," https://www.youtube.com/watch?v=YueVSEOSXe8.

7. "Performance: Marriage Equality Open House," Calliope Women's Chorus website, accessed July 9, 2018, https://calliopewomenschorus.org/2012/09/18/upcoming-performance-marriage-equality-open-house; *How Love Won: The Fight for Marriage Equality*, directed by Michael McIntee, 2016, accessed July 10, 2018, www.howlovewon.com.

8. *Obergefell v. Hodges,* 2, accessed July 11, 2018, https://www.supremecourt.gov/opinions/14pdf/14-556_3204.pdf.

9. Ibid., "Opinion of the Court," 28.

10. Scott Dolan, "Maine reacts to Supreme Court ruling affirming same-sex marriage in all states," *Portland Press Herald*, June 26, 2015, accessed July 10, 2018, http://www.pressherald.com/2015/06/26/maine-reacts-to-supreme-court-ruling-affirming-same-sex-marriage-in-all-states.

11. "Year on Twitter: #LoveWins in the United States," posted December 14, 2015, accessed July 12, 2018, https://twitter.com/i/moments/672083334550446080?lang=en.

12. Haeyoun Park and Iaryna Mykhyalyshyn, "L.G.B.T. People Are More Likely to Be Targets of Hate Crimes Than Any Other Minority Group," *The New York Times*, June 16, 2016, accessed, July 12, 2018, https://www.nytimes.com/interactive/2016/06/16/us/hate-crimes-against-lgbt.html?_r=0.

13. Quoted in Brandon Griggs, "America's transgender moment," *CNN*, June 1, 2015, accessed July 10, 2018, http://edition.cnn.com/2015/04/23/living/transgender-moment-jenner-feat/index.html.

14. Randi Driscoll, "Randi Driscoll/Kevin Robison/What Matters," *Choralicious*, the Yelton Rhodes Music Blog, accessed July 10, 2018, http://choralicious.com/YRMblog/?p=32.

15. "About Randi Driscoll," Randi Driscoll's website, accessed July 10, 2018, http://www.randidriscoll.com/bio?i=y; Sister Singers Network 10th National Choral Festival, Program, in possession of the author.

16. Southern Poverty Law Center, *SPLC Intelligence Report*, 2010 Winter Issue, (February 27, 2011), accessed July 12, 2018, https://www.splcenter.org/fighting-hate/intelligence-report/2011/anti-gay-hate-crimes-doing-math.

17. Cynthia Laird, "Breaking News: Vigil for Slain Oxnard Teen," *Bay Area Reporter*, February 5, 2008, accessed September 30, 2018, https://www.ebar.com/news///238760/breaking_news:_vigil_tues_for_slain_oxnard_teen; Ramin Setoodeh, "Young, Gay and Murdered in Junior High," *Newsweek*, July 18, 2008, accessed August 28, 2018, https://www.newsweek.com/young-gay-and-murdered-junior-high-92787; Ronald Smothers, "Newark Preaches Tolerance of Gays Year After Killing," *The New York Times*, May 12, 2004, accessed July 12, 2018, http://www.nytimes.com/2004/05/12/nyregion/newark-preaches-tolerance-of-gays-year-after-killing.html; "Florida Man convicted of murdering 3-year-old "gay" son, Advocate.com, July 19, 2005, accessed July 10, 2018, https://web.archive.org/web/20050722234735/http://www.advocate.com/news_detail_ektid18908.asp; Mark Leon Goldberg, "New Report: Every Third Day a Trans Person is Killed," *UN Dispatch*, July 21, 2009, accessed July 10, 2018, https://www.undispatch.com/new-report-every-third-day-a-trans-person-is-killed.

18. James Esseks, "In Masterpiece, the Bakery Wins the Battle But Loses the War," ACLU website, accessed September 4, 2018, https://www.aclu.org/blog/lgbt-rights/lgbt-nondiscrimination-protections/masterpiece-bakery-wins-battle-loses-war.

19. Greg Blustein, "BREAKING: Nathan Deal vetoes Georgia's 'religious liberty' bill," *Atlanta Journal-Constitution*, April 9, 2016, accessed July 9, 2018, https://politics.myajc.com/blog/politics/breaking-nathan-deal-vetoes-georgia-religious-liberty-bill/yVAFf868i7ilsrwT9zpH3L/.

20. "Orlando Gay Chorus Speech and Song for Pulse Victim's at GALA Denver 2016," accessed August 24, 2018, https://www.youtube.com/watch?v=U1urPSxm7Gc.
21. "Past Performances," Resonance Women's Chorus website, accessed August 24, 2018, http://www.resonancechorus.org/past-performances.html.
22. "Letters from Baghdad," Windsong, Cleveland's Feminist Chorus website, accessed August 24, 2018, http://windsongcleveland.org/new-events/2017/4/7/letters-from-baghdad-ciff; "Land of Our Dreams," Central Pennsylvania Womyn's Chorus website, accessed July 9, 2018, http://www.cpwchorus.org/programs/landofourdreams.pd.
23. Erica Quin-Easter, Program Notes, "Women in Harmony: Moving On: Immigration In Song," Portland Maine, May 14-14, 2011, in possession of the author.
24. "Bio," Con Fullam website, accessed August 24, 2018, http://www.confullam.com/bio.html; Erik Philbrook with Brianne Galli, "Pihcintu, A Unique Multicultural Chorus from Maine, Gives Children from War-torn Countries Hope and a Voice," ASCAP website, accessed July 12, 2018, https://www.ascap.com/playback/2012/02/radar-report/pihcintu.aspx.
25. Amanda Allen, interview with the author, August 7, 2013.
26. This segment is available at https://www.youtube.com/watch?v=szWy64ZANpM.
27. Amanda Allen interview.
28. Ibid.
29 Ibid.
30. Katie Johnson, "Earth, Water, Fire and Love Stories from the Dominican Republic, MUSE Choir Writings: Activism, March 29, 2009. http://www.musechoir.org/writings/activism/428. (Link discontinued. Used by permission.)
31. Julie Lessard, "Earth, Water, Fire and Love Stories."
32. "About the Peninsula Women's Chorus," Peninsula Women's Chorus website, accessed July 12, 2018, http://www.pwchorus.org/?q=about; "News," Southern Arizona Women's Chorus website, http://www.southernarizonawomenschorus.org/news.html; "Our Trips," Voices from the Heart website, accessed August 24 2018, https://www.voicesfromtheheart.org/our-trips/; "Tour," Women's Voices website, accessed August 24, 2018, http://womensvoiceschorus.org/news/tour/.
33. Kathie Spegal, interview with the author, July 21, 2013.
34. Sue Coffee, interview.
35. Ibid.
36. "Past Performances," Resonance Women's Chorus of Boulder website; John Aguilar, "One Action, One Boulder aims to tap past for future benefit," Boulder Daily Camera, January 14, 2012, accessed July 9, 2018, http://www.dailycamera.com/ci_19743288.

37.   S. E James et al., "The Report of the 2015 U.S. Transgender Survey" (Washington, DC: National Center for Transgender Equality, 2106), accessed July 11, 2018, http://www.transequality.org.); Barack Obama, "Remarks by the President in State of the Union Address, January 20, 2015," accessed July 11, 2018, https://obamawhitehouse.archives.gov/the-press-office/2015/01/20/remarks-president-state-union-address-january-20-2015.

38.   Griggs, "America's transgender moment."

39.   Greg Lacour, "How North Carolina Got Here (updated)," *Charlotte Magazine*, March 2017, accessed July 11, 2018, http://www.charlottemagazine.com/Charlotte-Magazine/April-2016/HB2-How-North-Carolina-Got-Here.

40.   Rachel Pereclay, "Seventeen School Districts Debunk Right-Wing Lies About Protections for Transgender Students," *Media Matters for America*, June 3, 2015, accessed July 12, 2018, https://mediamatters.org/research/2015/06/03/17-school-districts-debunk-right-wing-lies-abou/203867.

41.   George Takai, "It's Not About Bathrooms," Twitter post, February 23, 2017, accessed July 12, 2018, https://twitter.com/georgetakei/status/834907705349386240?lang=en.

42.   Katie Zezima, "'Not about bathrooms': Critics decry North Carolina law's lesser-known elements," *The Washington Post,* May 14, 2016, accessed July 12, 2018, https://www.washingtonpost.com/national/not-about-bathrooms-critics-decry-north-carolina-laws-lesser-known-elements/2016/05/14/387946ec-186b-11e6-924d-838753295f9a_story.html?utm_term=.84316dd69349

43.   Raymond, 104.

44.   Cristan Williams, "Michigan Womyn's Music Festival," accessed July 12, 2018, *The TransAdvocate*, April 9, 2013, http://transadvocate.com/michigan-womyns-music-festival_n_8943.htm.

45.   Sandy Stone, *The Empire Strikes Back: A Posttransexual Manifesto*, accessed July 12, 2018, https://sandystone.com/empire-strikes-back.pdf.

46.   Emi Koyama, "A Handbook on Discussing the Michigan Womyn's Music Festival for Trans Activists and Allies," accessed July 11, 2018, http://www.confluere.com/store/pdf-zn/mich-handbook.pdf.

47.   Join Us," Common Woman Chorus website; "We Want Bread, But We Want Roses too," Fortissima: DC's Feminist Singers website; "Audition for Anna," Anna Crusis Women's Choir website, http://annacrusis.org/page/audition-anna; "Our Vision," Voices Rising website.

48.   Jane Ramseyer Miller, "Creating Choirs That Welcome Trans Singers," GALA Choruses Blog, February 8, 2016, accessed July 11, 2018, http://galachoruses.org/blog/creating-choirs-that-welcome-trans-singers.

49.   Ibid.

50.   Ibid.

51. "Transcendence Gospel Choir," Transfaith website, accessed July 12, 2018, http://www.transfaithonline.org/explore/christian/traditions/black/transcendence_gospel_choir; Rona Marech, "Singing the gospel of Transcendence: Nation's first all-transgender gospel choir raises its voices to praise God and lift their own feelings of self-love and dignity," *San Francisco Chronicle*, April 18, 2004, accessed July 11, 2018, http://www.sfgate.com/bayarea/article/SAN-FRANCISCO-Singing-the-gospel-of-2791956.php.

52. Catherine Womack, "LA's First Trans Chorus is Drowning Out the Nasty Rhetoric," *LA Weekly*, May 5, 2016 accessed July 12, 2018, , http://www.laweekly.com/arts/las-first-trans-chorus-is-drowning-out-the-nasty-rhetoric-6899760; CJ Janovy, "Transgender Choruses Harness the (Changing) Power of Voices," heard on "Weekend Edition Saturday," May 21, 2016, accessed July 11, 2018, http://www.npr.org/sections/deceptivecadence/2016/05/21/478863157/transgender-choruses-harness-the-changing-power-of-voices; "Chorus Helps Trans Men and Women Find Their Voice," "Here & Now," accessed July 9, 2018, http://www.wbur.org/hereandnow/2015/06/30/butterfly-transgender-chorus; Avianne Tan, "Boston Chorus Empowers Transgender Singers by Helping Them Find Their Voices," *ABC News*, December 10, 2015; accessed July 12, 2018, http://abcnews.go.com/US/boston-chorus-empowers-transgender-singers-helping-find-voices/story?id=35699949.

53. Kelsey Menahan, "The Butterfly Music Transgender Chorus: A Safe Space for Transgender Singers," in "Beyond Outreach: Four Community Engagement Stories," Chorus America website,, May 3, 2016, accessed July 11, 2018, https://www.chorusamerica.org/education-training/beyond-outreach-four-community-engagement-stories.

54. Kelly Morris, "Sara Bareilles: 'Brave' Was inspired by Close Friend's Coming Out," *The Seattle Lesbian*, February 3, 2014, accessed July 1, 2018, http://theseattlelesbian.com/sara-bareilles-brave-was-inspired-by-close-friends-coming-out.

55. A.P. Hopper, interview with the author September 8, 2015.

56. Ibid.

57. Cyndi Hopper, interview with the author, July 26, 2015.

58. GLASS Youth Choir Facebook page, accessed July 10, 2018, https://www.facebook.com/Glass-Youth-Choir-262930367096569/info/?tab=page_info.

59. Gord Goble, "Surrey choir shines light on life's serious issues – but still has fun doing it," *Surrey NOW-Leader*, May 12, 2016, accessed July 10, 2018, http://www.bclocalnews.com/entertainment/379257691.html?mobile=true; "Meet Our Youth, GALA Choruses website, accessed July 10, 2018, http://galachoruses.org/resource-center/youth/meet-our-youth.

60. "Protecting Youth and Your Chorus," GALA Choruses Resource Center, http://galachoruses.org/resource-center/youth/protecting-youth-and-chorus.

61. "About Soromundi," Soromundi: Lesbian Chorus of Eugene website, accessed July 12, 20187, http://soromundi.wixsite.com/soromundi/about; Faye Militante, e-mail message to the author; Diverse City Youth Chorus Facebook Page, accessed July 10, 2018, https://www.facebook.com/pg/diversecityyouthchorus/about/?ref=page_internal.

62. Robin Godfrey, interviewed by JD Doyle, 'Gay & Lesbian Choruses: The History of the Gay & Lesbian Choral Movement: The Script, Part 1, "The History and The Music," *Queer Music Heritage*, November 2010, http://queermusicheritage.com/nov2010s.html.

63. Rob LeDonne, "Inside 'Shut Up and Dance,' WALK THE MOON's number one hit," *American Songwriter*, March 5, 2015, accessed July 11, 2018, https://americansongwriter.com/2015/03/inside-shut-up-and-dance-walk-the-moons-number-one-hit.

64. Nicholas Petricca, Kevin Ray, Sean Waugaman, Eli Maiman, Ryan Mcmahon, Ben Burger, "Shut Up and Dance," Warner/Chappell Music, Inc.

65. This memorable performance is available on YouTube at https://www.youtube.com/watch?v=Wgmq6rMuKEQ.

66. "A Universal Dream," Commissioned by Sister Singers Network and premiered on July 4, 2010, © 2009 Jenni Brandon, accessed July 9, 2018, https://www.youtube.com/watch?v=yoHyPBqLdTU.

67. "Past Performances," Resonance Women's Chorus of Boulder website.

68. Sue Coffee, interview.

69. Aimee Van Ausdall, Facebook post, January 31, 2017, used by permission.

70. Matt Broomfield, "Women's March against Donald Trump is the largest day of protests in U.S. History, say political scientists," *Independent*, January 23, 2017, accessed July 9, 2018, http://www.independent.co.uk/news/world/americas/womens-march-anti-donald-trump-womens-rights-largest-protest-demonstration-us-history-political-a7541081.html.

71. Ruth Huber, e-mail communication to the author, May 30, 2017.

Bibliography

"A Feminist Fourth: Sister Singers Festival Program." Sister Singers Archive 1981-2003, Sophia Smith Collection, Smith College, Northampton, Massachusetts.

A Journey of Spirit. Directed by Ann Coppel. Ann Coppel Productions, 2003. DVD. www.ajourneyofspirit.com.

"A Sense of Place, The Women's Philanthropy Institute at the Center on Philanthropy at Indiana University." March 2010. Accessed July 9, 2018. http://www.cfgnh.org/Portals/0/Uploads/Documents/Public/A-Sense-of-Place-FINAL.pdf.

Abod, Susan. Interview by JD Doyle. Queer Music Heritage. queermusicheritage.com/apr2012s.html. All Queer Music Heritage posts courtesy of JD Doyle.

"About." Rocky Mountain Arts Association website. Accessed August 23, 2018. https://www.rmarts.org/about.

"About Randi Driscoll," Randi Driscoll's website. Accessed July 10, 2018. http://www.randidriscoll.com/bio?i=y.

"About Soromundi." Soromundi: Lesbian Chorus of Eugene website. Accessed July 12, 2018.http://soromundi.wixsite.com/soromundi/about.

"About the Peninsula Women's Chorus." Peninsula Women's Chorus website. Accessed July 12, 2018. http://www.pwchorus.org/?q=about.

"About Us." Charlottesville Women's Choir Website. Accessed July 9, 2018. http://www.cville-womens-choir.org.

"About Us." Common Woman Chorus website. Accessed July 9, 2018. http://www.commonwomanchorus.net/2007/aboutus.htm

—." Women's Voices Chorus website. Accessed July 12, 2018. http://womensvoiceschorus.org/about.

Ackerman, Susan. "Why Is Miriam Also among the Prophets? (And Is Zipporah among the Priests?)." *Journal of Biblical Literature* 121, no. 1 (Spring, 2002): 47-80. Accessed July 9, 2018. http://www.jstor.org/stable/3268330.

Adam, Margie. 25th National Women's Music Festival Speech (1999). Accessed July 9, 2018. http://www.margieadam.com/speeches-writings/25th-national-womens-music-festival-speech.

Adams Rose. Interview with the author, July 9, 2015.

Ager, Mary. "The PWC and the Vocal Orchestra Music of *Song of Survival.*" In *Take Up the Song: Building a Community of Heart and Soul and Voice*, edited by Patricia Hennings and the Peninsula Women's Chorus, 53-64. Corvallis, Oregon: Earthsongs, 2003.

Aguilar, John. "One Action, One Boulder aims to tap past for future benefit." *Boulder Daily Camera*, January 14, 2012. Accessed July 9, 2018. http:// www.dailycamera.com/ci_19743288.

Alexander, Elizabeth. Program Notes, "Being Who You Are." Women in Harmony Concert, Portland, Maine, May 19-20, 2007. In possession of the author.

Allen, Amanda. Telephone interview with the author, August 7, 2013.

Altman, Lawrence K. "Rare Cancer Seen in 41 Homosexuals." *The New York Times*, July 3, 1981. Accessed July 9, 2018. http://www.nytimes. com/1981/07/03/us/rare-cancer-seen-in-41-homosexuals.html.

Alvarez, Antonia. Interview with the author, July 9, 2015.

Amasong Chorus: Singing Out. Directed Jay Rosenstein. New Day Films, 2003. DVD.

Aney, Kathy. "Gay men's choir sang through adversity." *East Oregonian*, April 10, 2015. Accessed July 9, 2018. http://www.eastoregonian.com/ eo/local-news/20150410/gay-mens-choir-sang-through-adversity.

Annas, Pam, Marcia Deihl, and Pam Ouellete. "The Politics of Music— Carrying It On: An Interview with the New Harmony Sisterhood Band." *Radical Teacher* 13 (March, 1979): 14-20. Accessed July 9, 2018. http://www.jstor.org/stable/20709201.

Apfelstadt, Hilary. "Practices of Successful Women's Choir Conductors." *Choral Journal* 39, no. 5 (December 1998): 35-41. Accessed July 9, 2018. https://acda.org/files/choral_journals/December_1998_ Apfelstadt_H.pdf.

Applegate Celia. "The Building of Community Through Choral Singing." In *Nineteenth Century Choral Singing*, edited by Donna M. DiGrazia, 3-20. New York: Taylor and Francis, 2013.

Armstrong, Toni Jr. "Playing to the Highest Common Denominator." In *The Woman-Centered Economy: Ideas, Reality, and the Space in Between*, edited by Loraine Edwalds and Midge Stocker, 219-230. Chicago: Third Side Press, 1995.

—. "Silent Pre-Fest." *Hot Wire* 9, no. 1 (January 1993): 36. All *Hot Wire* articles can be accessed at http://www.hotwirejournal.com/hwmag. html.

Arterton, Jon. Interviewed by JD Doyle. Michael Callen Tribute. Accessed August 23, 2018. http://www.queermusicheritage.com/may2013s.html

"Audition for Anna." Anna Crusis Women's Choir website. Accessed July 9, 2018. http://annacrusis.org/page/audition-anna.

Baird, Joseph L. and Radd K. Ehrmann. Introduction to *The Letters of Hildegard of Bingen, Vol. I*. Translated by Joseph L. Baird and Radd K. Ehrmann. New York: Oxford University Press, 1994.

Balén, Julia. *A Queerly Joyful Noise: Choral Musicking for Social Justice*. New Brunswick, NJ: Rutgers University Press, 2017.

Balestery, Jean E. "The Role of Lesbians in the 1979 and 1987 Marches on Washington for Lesbian and Gay Rights," posted by Urvashi Vaid. *Lesbian Concentrate*, August 20, 2010. Accessed July 9, 2018. http://urvashivaid.net/wp/?p=394.

Barnwell, Ysaye. "Reflections on the Festival." *Across the Lines: The Sister Singers Newsletter*, no. 9 (1993): 11. Sister Singers Archive 1981-2003, Sophia Smith Collection, Smith College, Northampton, Massachusetts..

Barrett, James R. "Rethinking the Popular Front." *Rethinking Marxism* 21, no. 4 (October 2009): 531-50.

Bayou City Performing Arts website. Accessed July 9, 2018. http://www.bcpahouston.org.

Bayou City Women's Chorus founders. Group interview with the author, September 12, 2014.

Belfrage, Sally. *Freedom Summer*. Charlottesville: University Press of University of Virginia, 1990, 1999. First published 1965 by Viking Press.

Beller-McKenna, Catherine. E-mail message to Women in Harmony, September 12, 2011.

—, Catherine. Interview with the author, October 5, 2009.

Benjamin Diane. Interview with the author, September 7, 2015.

Berger, Margaret. *On Natural Philosophy and Medicine: Selections from Cause et Cure*. Rochester, New York: D.S. Brewer, 1999.

Bindas, Kenneth J. *All of this Music Belongs to the Nation: The WPA's Federal Music Project and American Society*. Knoxville: University of Tennessee Press, 1995.

Bizell, Cindy. Interview with the author, December 17, 2010.

Blok Josine. "Virtual Voices: Toward a Choreography of Women's Speech in Classical Athens." In *Making Silence Speak: Women's Voices in Greek Literature and Society*, edited by André Lardinois and Laura McClure, 95-116. Princeton: Princeton University Press, 2001.

Blustein, Greg. "BREAKING: Nathan Deal vetoes Georgia's 'religious liberty' bill." *Atlanta Journal-Constitution*, April 9, 2016. Accessed July 9, 2018. https://politics.myajc.com/blog/politics/breaking-nathan-deal-vetoes-georgia-religious-liberty-bill/yVAFf868i7ilsrwT9zpH3L/.

Bowen, Meredith. Interview with the author, May 9, 2010.

—. "Sacred Music from The Convents of Seventeenth-Century Italy: Restoration Practices For Contemporary Women's Choirs." Ph.D. diss., Michigan State University, 2016. Accessed July 9, 2018. https://doi.org/10.25335/M5RX4Q.

Bowers v. Hardwick. Legal Information Institute, Cornell Law School. https://www.law.cornell.edu/supremecourt/text/478/186.

Bowie, Evan. "Alcman's First Parthenion and the Song the Sirens Sang." In *Archaic and Classical Choral Song: Performance, Politics and Dissemination*, edited by Evan Bowie and Lycia Athanassaki, 33-66. Berlin: Walter deGruyter, 2011.

Brandes, Roslyn Leigh. "'Let Us Sing as We Go': The Role of Music in the United States Suffrage Movement." Master's thesis, University of Maryland, 2016. Accessed July 9, 2018. https://drum.lib.umd.edu/handle/1903/18403.

Brandon, Jenni. "A Universal Dream." Commissioned by Sister Singers Network and premiered on July 4, 2010, © Jenni Brandon 2009. Performance available at https://www.youtube.com/watch?v=yoHyPBqLdTU.

Brodsky, Michelle. Interview with the author. August 13, 2010.

Brooks, Tim. *Lost Sounds: Blacks and the Birth of the Recording Industry, 1890-1919*. Champaign: University Illinois Press, 2005.

Broomfield, Matt. "Women's March against Donald Trump is the largest day of protests in U.S. History, say political scientists." *Independent*, January 23, 2017. Accessed July 9, 2018. http://www.independent.co.uk/news/world/americas/womens-march-anti-donald-trump-womens-rights-largest-protest-demonstration-us-history-political-a7541081.html.

Buck, Marsha. Interview with the author. April 11, 2011.

Burns, Rita. "Has the Lord Indeed Spoken Only Through Moses? A Study of the Biblical Portrait of Miriam." Ph.D. diss., Marquette University, 1980. Accessed July 9, 2018. https://epublications.marquette.edu/dissertations/AAI8104800/. ProQuest [8104800].

Calame, Claude. *Choruses of Young Women in Ancient Greece*. Translated by Derek Collins and Janice Orion. New and Revised Edition. Lanham, Maryland: Rowman and Littlefield, 2001.

Calvi, John. http://www.johncalvi.com.

Campbell, Nathaniel M., Beverly R. Lomer, and K. Christian McGuire. "The *Symphonia* and *Ordo Vertutum* of Hildegard von Bingen." *International Society of Hildegard von Bingen Studies*. Accessed July 9, 2018. http://www.hildegard-society.org/p/music.html.

Cantarella, Eva. "Gender, Sexuality, and Law." In *The Cambridge Companion to Ancient Greek Law*, edited by Michael Gagarin & David Cohen, 236-253. Cambridge University Press 2005.

—. *Pandora's Daughters: The Role and Status of Women in Greek and Roman Antiquity*. Translated by Maureen B. Fant. Baltimore: Johns Hopkins University Press.

Cantor, Norman F. *The Civilization of the Middle Ages*. Rev. ed. New York: Harper Perennial, 1994.

Catlin, Ellen. Interview with the author, July 3, 2010.

Carawan, Guy and Candie, eds. and comp. *Sing for Freedom: The Story of the Civil Rights Movement Through Its Songs*. Montgomery, Alabama: New South, Inc., 2007.

Castellini, Michael. "Stand In, Stand Up and Sing Out: Black Gospel Music and the Civil Rights Movement." Master's thesis, Georgia State University, 2013. Accessed July 9, 2018. http://scholarworks.gsu.edu/history_theses.

Cazden, Joanna. "Lawrence, Kate, and Lilith." *Folkworks*, no. 2 (March-April 2005): 5. Accessed July 9, 2018. https://folkworks.org/FWIssues/FWv05n02/FWv05n02.pdf.

Chapman, William Rogers. William Chapman Rogers Papers. New York Public Library. Accessed July 9, 2018. https://timesmachine.nytimes.com/timesmachine/1911/12/15/104886190.html?pageNumber=13.

"Chorus Helps Trans Men and Women Find Their Voice. "NPR Here & Now," broadcast June 30, 2015. Accessed July 9, 2018. http://www.wbur.org/hereandnow/2015/06/30/butterfly-transgender-chorus.

Chrislove. "Remembering LGBT History: 'Shoot the Queers': Houston's 1985 Anti-Gay Referendum and Backlash." *The Daily Kos*, May 20, 2012. Accessed July 9, 2018. https://www.dailykos.com/story/2012/05/20/1093065/-Remembering-LGBT-History-Shoot-the-Queers-Houston-s-1985-Anti-Gay-Referendum-and-Backlash.

Clarke, George Elliott. "Gospel as Protest: the African-Nova Scotia Spiritual and the lyrics of Delvina Bernard." In *Rebel Musics: Human Rights, Persistent Sounds, and the Politics of Music Making*, edited by Daniel Fischlin and Ajay Heble, 108-19. Montreal and New York: Black Rose Books, 2003.

Clifton, Lucille. Letter to Janice Scalza, reprinted in Gwyneth Walker, "Lucille Clifton Writes on Experiencing Her Poetry." Gwyneth Walker's website. Accessed July 9, 2018. http://www.gwynethwalker.com/clifton.html.

"Club Movement." DeColonizing Our History: A Restorative History Website. Accessed July 9, 2018. http://decolonizingourhistory.com/club-movement.

Coffee Sue. E-mail message to the author, May 18, 2017.

—. Interview with the author, April 10, 2009.

Cohen, Ronald D." Woody the Red?" in *Hard Travelin': The Life of Woody Guthrie*, edited by Robert Santelli and Emily Davidson, 138-152. Hanover, New Hampshire: Wesleyan University Press, 1999.

Collingridge, Lorna Marie. "Music as Evocative Power: The Intersection of Music with Images of the Divine in the Songs of Hildegard of Bingen." Ph.D. diss., School of Theology, Griffith University, 2003. Accessed July 9, 2018. https://www120.secure.griffith.edu.au/rch/file/db79c53d-d57e-bb6f-6aed-f5604599c01f/1/Collingridge_2004_01Thesis.pdf..

Cone, James H. *The Spirituals and the Blues*. Maryknoll, New York: Orbis Books, 1991.

Coren, Jackie. Interview with the author, August 6, 2011.

"Cotton Club of Harlem." *Blackpast.Org: An Online Reference Guide to African American History*. Accessed July 9, 2018. http://www.blackpast.org/aah/cotton-club-harlem-1923.

Crawford, Sidnie White. "Traditions about Miriam in the Qumran Scrolls." *Faculty Publications, Classics and Religious Studies Department, Paper 97.* University of Nebraska/ Lincoln, 2003. Accessed July 9, 2018. http://digitalcommons.unl.edu/classicsfacpub/97.

Crenshaw, Kimberlé. "Mapping the Margins: Intersectionality, Identity Politics, and Violence against Women of Color." *Stanford Law Review* 43, no. 6 (July, 1991): 1241-1299.

Cross, Frank M., Jr. "The Song of the Sea and Canaanite Myth." In *Canaanite Myth and Hebrew Epic: Essays in the Religion of the People of Israel*, 121-144. Cambridge, Massachusetts: Harvard University Press, 1973, 1999.

Cross, Frank M., Jr. and David Noel Freedman. "The Song of Miriam." *Journal of Near Eastern Studies* 14, no. 4 (Oct., 1955): 237-250.Accessed July 9, 2018. http://www.jstor.org/stable/543020.

Cross, Richard. "Vivaldi's Girls: Music Therapy in 18th Century Venice." Accessed July 9, 2018. http://www.users.cloud9.net/~recross/why-not/Vivaldi.html.

CWLU Herstory Website Editorial Committee. "The Chicago Women's Liberation Rock Band." Accessed July 9, 2018. https://www. cwluherstory.org/cwlu-workgroups-articles/chicago-womens-liberation-rock-band.

Darden, Robert. *Nothing But Love in God's Water.* Vol.1, *Black Sacred Music from the Civil War to the Civil Rights Movement.* University Park: Pennsylvania State University Press, 2014.

—. *People Get Ready: A New History of Black Gospel Music.* New York: Continuum International Publishing Company, 2004.

Daughterty, James." Ethnic/Multicultural Choral Music: Thinking Out of the Box." GALA Choruses website. Accessed July 10, 2018. http://galachoruses.org/documents/events/Daugherty-ETHNIC-MULTICULTURAL-CHORAL-MUSIC.pdf.

Davidson, Miriam. "Miriam Davidson—Interview." GALA Choruses Blog, March 21, 2104. Accessed July 10, 2018. http://galachoruses.org/blog/miriam-davidson-interview.

Davis, Flora. *Moving the Mountain: The Women's Movement in America Since 1960.* Champaign: University of Illinois Press, 1999.

deForest, Mary. "Female Choruses in Greek Tragedy. *Didaskalia* V, no, 1 (Spring 1997). Accessed July 10, 2018. http://www.didaskalia.net/issues/vol4no1/deforest.html.

Denisoff, Serge. "Urban Folk 'Movement' Research: Value Free?" *Western Folklore* 28, no. 3 (July, 1969): 183-197.Accessed July 10, 2018. http://www.jstor.org/stable/1499264.

Denning, Michael. *The Cultural Front: The Laboring of American Culture in the Twentieth Century.* London and New York: Verso, 1996.

Denov, Angie. "Thoughts on Diversity and SSN: The Diversity Caucuses." *Across the Lines: The Sister Singers Newsletter,* no. 7 (May, 1996). Sister Singers Archive 1981-2003, Sophia Smith Collection, Smith College, Northampton, Massachusetts.

—. Interview with the author, August 1, 2013.

Denver Women's Chorus. Group interview with the author, March 15, 2015.

Dickey, Rachel. "The Women's Chorus Emergence and Evolution in 19th Century Germany." Mus.D. diss., Indiana University, 2015. Accessed July 10, 2018. https://scholarworks.iu.edu/dspace/handle/2022/19875.

Diverse City Youth Chorus Facebook Page. Accessed July 10, 2018. https://www.facebook.com/pg/diversecityyouthchorus/about/?ref=page_internal.

Dlugacz, Judy. "Judy's View: Olivia Back Then." August 1, 2007. http://www.olivia.com/Connect/Voices/judy_s_view/archive/2007/08/01/Olivia-Back-Then.aspx. (Site discontinued. Used by permission.)

Dobkin, Alix. Interviewed by JD Doyle. Queer Music Heritage. http://queermusicheritage.com/may2002s.html.

—. *My Red Blood: A Memoir of Growing Up Communist, Coming into the Greenwich Village Folk Scene, and Coming Out in the Feminist Movement.* New York: Alyson Books, 2009.

Dolan, Scott. "Maine reacts to Supreme Court ruling affirming same-sex marriage in all states." *Portland Press Herald*, June 26, 2015. Accessed July 10, 2018. https://www.pressherald.com/2015/06/26/maine-reacts-to-supreme-court-ruling-affirming-same-sex-marriage-in-all-states/.

Doubleday, Victoria. "The Frame Drum in the Middle East: Women, Musical Instruments and Power." *Ethnomusicology* 43, no. 1 (Winter, 1999): 101-134. Accessed July 10, 2018. http://www.jstor.org/stable/852696.

Doughter, Sarah. "Sex and Laughter in Women's Music." *Current Musicology* 90 (Fall 2010): 35-56. Accessed July 10, 2018. https://academiccommons.columbia.edu/catalog/ac:178252.

Drinker Sophie. *Brahms and His Women's Choruses.* Published and Copyright by Author under the auspices of MusuRGiA Publishers, Merion, Pennsylvania, 1952. Full text available online at https://archive.org/stream/brahmshiswomensc00drin/brahmshiswomensc00drin_djvu.txt.

—. *Music & Women: The Story of Women in their Relation to Music.* New York: Coward & McCann, 1948. Reprinted with preface by Elizabeth Wood and afterword by Ruth Solie. NY: The Feminist Press, 1995.

Driscoll, Randi. "Randi Driscoll/Kevin Robison: what matters." Choralicious, the Yelton Rhodes Music Blog. http://choralicious.com/YRMblog/?p=32.

Dube, Musa. *Postcolonial Feminist Interpretations of the Bible.* St. Louis: Chalice Press, 2000.

Eagle, Nathan. "Same-Sex Marriage Debate Splits Hawaii State Capitol in Two—Literally." *Hawaii Civil Beat*, November 8, 2013. Accessed July 10, 2018. http://www.civilbeat.org/2013/11/20358-same-sex-marriage-debate-splits-hawaii-state-capitol-in-two-literally.

Eder, Donna, Suzanne Staggenborg, and Lori Sudderth. "National Women's Music Festival: Collective Identity and Diversity in a Lesbian-Feminist Community." *Journal of Contemporary Ethnography* 2, no. 4 (Jan. 1995): 485-515.

Edwards, Michelle J. "Women in Music to ca. 1450." In *Women and Music: A History,* 2nd ed., edited by Kaarin Pendle, 26-53. Bloomington: Indiana University Press, 2001.

Ehrensaft, Diane and Ruth Milkman. "Sexuality and the State: The Defeat of the Briggs Initiative and Beyond: Interview with Amber Hollibaugh." *Socialist Review* 9, no. 3 (May-June 1979): 55-72.

Eisenstein, Sarah. *Bread and Roses: Working Women's Consciousness in the United State 1890 to the First World War.* London and New York: Routledge, 1983.

Eisler, Riane. *The Chalice and the Blade.* New York: Harper Collins, 1995.

Esseks, James. "In Masterpiece, the Bakery Wins the Battle But Loses the War." ACLU website. Accessed September 4, 2018. https://www.aclu.org/blog/lgbt-rights/lgbt-nondiscrimination-protections/masterpiece-bakery-wins-battle-loses-war.

Estes, Lauren. "The Choral Hierarchy Examined: The Presence of Repertoire for Women's Choirs in Monographs on Choral Literature and Choral History." Master's thesis, Syracuse University, 2013. Accessed July 10, 2018. http://surface.syr.edu/cgi/viewcontent.cgi?article=1009&context=thesis.

Evans, Sara. *Personal Politics: The Roots of Women's Liberation in the Civil Rights Movement and the New Left.* New York: Vintage, 1980.

Faderman Lillian and Stuart Timmons. *Gay LA: A History of Sexual Outlaws, Power Politics and Lipstick Lesbians.* New York; Basic Books, 2006.

"Fanny: Godmothers of Chick Rock: About Fanny." Fanny website. Accessed July 10, 2018. http://www.fannyrocks.com/about-2/how-it-began.

Fassler, Margot. "Composer and Dramatist." In *Voice of the Living Light: Hildegard of Bingen and Her World,"* edited by Barbara Newman, 149-175. Los Angeles: University of California Press, 1998.

Feinberg, Leslie. *Transgender Liberation: A Movement Whose Time Has Come.* New York: World View Forum, 1992.

Feldman, Maxine. Interview by JD Doyle. Queer Music Heritage. http://queermusicheritage.com/apr2002s.html.

"Finding Pauli Murray." National Organization for Women website. Accessed July 11, 2018. http://now.org/about/history/finding-pauli-murray.

Fink, Sue. "Los Angeles Women's Chorus." *Paid My Dues* 2, no. 3 (Spring 1978): 9-11. All issues of *Paid My Dues* are available online courtesy of JD Doyle at http://queermusicheritage.com/pmd1.html.

—. "True Live Adventures in Women's Music." Interview with Toni J. Armstrong Jr. *Hot Wire: The Journal of Women's Music and Culture* 7, no. 2 (May 1991): 2-5.

"First National Women's Chorus Concert Program: Combined Chorus Concert." Sister Singers Network Archive, 1981-2003, Sophia Smith Collection, Smith College, Northampton, Massachusetts.

"First National Women's Chorus Evaluations." Sister Singers Archive 1981-2003, Sophia Smith Collection, Smith College, Northampton, Massachusetts

Fjell, Judy. Interview with the author, June 9, 2010.

"Florida Man convicted of murdering 3-year-old "gay" son. *Advocate. com*, July 19, 2005. Accessed July 10, 2018. https://web.archive.org/web/20050722234735/http://www.advocate.com/news_detail_ektid18908.asp.

Floyd, Samuel A. *The Power of Black Music: Interpreting Its History from Africa to the United States*. Oxford University Press, 1996.

Fox, Matthew. *Illuminations of Hildegard von Bingen*. Rochester, Vermont: Bear and Company, 2002.

Frank, Cynthia, e-mail message to the author, Sept. 2, 2015.

Fried, Michael. "W. Elmer Keeton and His WPA Chorus: Oakland's Musical Civil Rights Pioneers of the New Deal Era." *California History* 7, no. 3 (Fall 1996): 236-249. Accessed July 10, 2018. https://www.jstor.org/stable/25177596?seq=1#page_scan_tab_contents.

Friedan, Betty. *Life So Far*. New York: Touchstone, 2001.

Fullam, Con website. Accessed July 10, 2018. www.confullam.com.

Gafney, Wilda C. *Daughters of Miriam: Women Prophets in Ancient Israel*. Minneapolis: Fortress Press, 2008.

GALA Choruses 2016 Festival Schedule. http://galachoruses.org/documents/events/festival2016/Festival-Schedule-Of-Events.pdf.

Gardiner, Judith Kegan. "Bechdel's Dykes to Watch out For and Popular Culture." In *Queers in American Popular Culture,* Vol. 2, edited by Jim Elledge, 61-101. Santa Barbara: Praeger, 2010.

George, Luvenia A. "Lucie (Lucy) Campbell Williams: Her Nurturing and Expansion of Gospel Music in the National Baptist Convention, U.S.A., Inc." In *We'll Understand It Better By and By*, edited by Bernice Johnson Reagon, 109-19. Washington DC: Smithsonian Institution Press, 1992.

Gifford, Carolyn DeSwarte. "Temperance Songs and Hymns." In *Religions of the United States in Practice*, Vol. I, edited by Colleen McDannell, 158-170. Princeton: Princeton University Press, 2001.

Gilbert, Ronnie. Interview by Kate Weigand, March 10, 2004. Voices of Feminism Oral History Project, Sophia Smith Collection, Smith College, Northampton, Massachusetts. Accessed July 10, 2018. https://www.smith.edu/libraries/libs/ssc/vof/transcripts/Gilbert.pdf.

Gimbutas, Marija and Miriam Robbins Dexter. *The Living Goddesses*. Berkeley and Los Angeles: University of California Press, 2001.

GLASS Youth Choir Facebook page. Accessed July 10, 2018. https://www.facebook.com/Glass-Youth-Choir-262930367096569/info/?tab=page_info.

Goble, Gord. "Surrey choir shines light on life's serious issues—but still has fun doing it." *Surrey NOW-Leader*, May 12, 2016. Accessed July 10, 2018. http://www.bclocalnews.com/entertainment/379257691.html?mobile=true.

Godfrey, Robin. Interviewed by JD Doyle. Gay & Lesbian Choruses: The History of the Gay & Lesbian Choral Movement: The Script, Part 1, "The History and The Music." Queer Music Heritage, November 2010. http://queermusicheritage.com/nov2010s.html.

Goldberg, Mark Leon. "New Report: Every Third Day a Trans Person is Killed." *UN Dispatch*, July 21, 2009. Accessed July 10, 2018. https://www.undispatch.com/new-report-every-third-day-a-trans-person-is-killed.

Goldman, Harry. "Pins and Needles: An Oral History." Ph.D. diss., New York University 1977.

Goldsmith, Emanuel S. *Modern Yiddish Culture: The Story of the Yiddish Language Movement*. Expanded ed. New York: Fordham University Press, 2000. First published 1976.

Gorlin, Rebecca. Interview with the author, July 1, 2010.

Gottlieb, Robert and Robert Kimball, eds. *Reading Lyrics*. New York: Pantheon, 2000.

Grant, Bev. Interview with the author, November 3, 2014.

Grant, Terry. Interview with the author. January 5, 2016.

Griggs, Brandon. "America's transgender moment." *CNN*, June 1, 2015. Accessed July 10, 2018. http://edition.cnn.com/2015/04/23/living/transgender-moment-jenner-feat/index.html.

Gross, Rita. *A Garland of Feminist Reflections: Forty Years of Religious Exploration*. Berkeley and Los Angeles: University of California Press, 2009.

Guse, Celia. "The Third Annual Women's Choral Festival." *Hot Wire* 3, no. 2 (March 1987): 28-29, 60.

Guthrie Woody. "Union Maid." Woody Guthrie website. Accessed July 10, 2018. http://www.woodyguthrie.org/Lyrics/Union_Maid.htm.

Haider-Markel Donald. "AIDS and Gay Civil Rights: Politics and Policy at the Ballot Box." *Research Gate*, January 1999. Accessed July 10, 2018. https://www.researchgate.net/publication/258821782_AIDS_and_ Gay_Civil_Rights_Politics_and_Policy_at_the_Ballot_Box.

Hale, Kendall. *Radical Passions: A Memoir of Revolution and Healing.* iUniverse, 2008.

Hamel, Liz, Jamie Firth, Tina Hoff, Jennifer Kates, Sarah Levine, and Lindsey Dawson. *HIV/AIDS In The Lives Of Gay And Bisexual Men In The United States*. The Henry K Kaiser Foundation, Sep 25, 2014. Accessed July 10, 2018. http://kff.org/hivaids/report/hivaids-in-the-lives-of-gay-and-bisexual-men-in-the-united-states.

Hawes, Beth Lomax. *Sing it Pretty*. Champaign: University of Illinois Press, 2008.

Hayes, Eileen. *Songs in Black and Lavender: Race, Sexual Politics, and Women's Music*. Chicago: University of Chicago Press, 2010.

HeartSong Women's Chorus. Group interview with the author, September 13, 2014.

Heidelberger, Lori. Interview with the author, September 12, 2014.

Hemery, Sophie. Twitter Post. *Holler4*. Accessed July 10, 2018. http://www. holler4.co.uk/womens-march-on-london.html.

Henderson, Sarah. Interview with the author, July 25, 2015.

Hennings, Patricia with Marie des Jardines. "'A Young Poet Sings,'" in *Take Up the Song*, 82-86.

Hennings, Patricia. "The Heart of the Matter." In *Take Up the Song*, 15. Originally published in *The Choral Journal* 27, no. 6 (January 1987): 37-41. Accessed July 10, 2018. http://www.jstor.org/stable/23553518.

Hewetson, Dick. *History of the Gay Movement in Minnesota and the Role of the Minnesota Civil Liberties Union*. Minneapolis: Friends of the Bill of Rights Foundation, 2013. Accessed July 10, 2018. https://www. qlibrary.org/wordpress/wp-content/uploads/2014/04/MN_Gay_ Movement_MCLU.pdf.

Higginbotham, Evelyn Brooks. *Righteous Discontent: The Women's Movement in the Black Baptist Church, 1880-1920*. Cambridge: Harvard University Press, 1993.

Hildegard of Bingen. "Letter to the Bishop of Mainz." Translated by Barbara L. Grant. In *Women in Music: An Anthology of Source Readings from the Middle Ages to the Present*, rev. ed., edited by Carol Neuls-Bates, 18-20. Boston: Northeastern University Press, 1996.

—. *Scivias*. Translated by Columbia Hart and Jane Bishop, with an
introduction by Barbara Newman and preface by Caroline Walker
Bynum. New York: Paulist Press, 1990.

Hill, Joe. "The Rebel Girl." *The Little Red Songbook, 34ᵗʰ Edition*. Chicago:
Industrial Workers of the World, 1974.

Hinge George. "Cultic Persona and the Transmission of the Partheneions."
In *Aspects of Greek Cult: Context, Ritual and Iconography*, edited by J.
Jensen, G. Hinge, P. Schultz, and B. Wickkiser, 215-236. Aarhus: Aarhus
University Press 2009.

"Historical Timeline." Seattle Choruses website. Accessed August 24, 2018.
https://www.seattlechoruses.org/learn/history/.

"History of Nord-Amerikanischer Sängerbund." Nord-Amerikanischer
Sängerbund website. Accessed July 10, 2018. http://nasaengerbund.
org/index.php?p=1_58_History-NASB.

Hitchins, Loraine and td. "festival: trouble & mediation at yosemite." *Off Our
Backs* 11, no.10 (November 1981): 12-13, 25. Accessed July 10, 2018.
https://www.jstor.org/stable/i25774082.

Holloway Amanda. "The Red Priest Unfrocked." *The Times of
London*, October 19, 2007. Accessed July 10, 2018. http://www.
classicalmusicguide.com/viewtopic.php?t=19042.

Holsinger, Bruce. "The Flesh of the Voice: Embodiment and the Homoerotics
of Devotion in the Music of Hildegard of Bingen 1098-1179." *Signs* 19,
no. 1 (Autumn, 1993): 92-125. Accessed July 10, 2018. http://www.
jstor.org/stable/3174746.

—. *Music, Body, and Desire in Medieval Culture, Hildegard of Bingen to
Chaucer*. Stanford: Stanford University Press, 2001.

hooks, bell. *From Margin to Center*. New York: Routledge, 2015.

Hopper, A.P. Interview with the author, September 8, 2015.

Hopper, Cyndi. Interview with the author, July 26, 2015.

Horn, Stacey. *Imperfect Harmony: Finding Happiness Singing with Others*.
Chapel Hill: Algonquin Books, 2013.

Horowitz, Amy, "Some Factors in the Equation." In *We Who Believe in
Freedom: Sweet Honey in the Rock...Still on the Journey*, edited by
Bernice Johnson Reagon and Sweet Honey in the Rock, 179-200. New
York: Anchor Doubleday, 1993.

How Love Won: The Fight for Marriage Equality. Directed by Michael
McIntee. 2016. Accessed July 10, 2018. www.howlovewon.com.

Hubbard, Marilyn. "We Know Why We Sing." *WNC Woman*, Oct. 28, 2012.
Accessed July 10, 2018. http://www.wncwoman.com/2012/10/28/
we-know-why-we-sing.

Hubbard, Monica J. "Women's Choirs: Anonymous No More!" In *Take Up the Song*, 116-119.

Huber, Ruth. E-mail communication to the author, May 30, 2017.

Hull, Gloria T. and Barbara Smith. "Introduction: The Politics of Black Women's Studies." In *All the Women Are White, All the Blacks are Men, But Some of Us Are Brave*, edited by Gloria T. Hull, Patricia Bell Scott, and Barbara Smith, xvii-xxxvi. New York: The Feminist Press, 1982.

Huntsville Feminist Chorus. Group interview with the author, August 27, 2015.

Hurner, Sheryl. "Discursive Identity Formation of Suffrage Women: Reframing the 'Cult of True Womanhood' Through Song." *Western Journal of Communication* 70, no. 3 (July 2006): 234-60.

"I Feel Like Going On." The New Spirituals Project. Accessed July 10, 2018. https://www.youtube.com/watch?v=A2jxPTWh_zs.

Ian, Janis. "Prologue." In *Society's Child*, xiii-xxii. New York: Penguin Books, 2008.

Imthurn, Melinda. E-mail post. *ChorusWomen Yahoo Group*, August 4, 2011.

Industrial Workers of the World. Minutes of IWW's Founding Convention— Part 1. Accessed July 11, 2018. https://iww.org/about/founding/part1.

Jackson, Jenna. *Singing in my Soul: Black Gospel Music in a Secular Age*. Chapel Hill: University of North Carolina Press, 2004.

Jacobson, Marion. "From Communism to Yiddishism: The Reinvention of the Jewish People's Philharmonic." In *Chorus and Community*, edited by Karen Ahlquist, 202-220. Champaign: University of Illinois Press, 2006.

—. "With Song to the Struggle: An Ethnographic and Historical Study of the Yiddish Folk Chorus." Ph.D. diss., New York University, 2004. ProQuest [2004. 3114198].

James, S.E., J.L. Herman, S. Rankin, M. Keisling, L. Mottet, and M. Anafi. "The Report of the 2015 U.S. Transgender Survey." Washington, DC: National Center for Transgender Equality, 2106. Accessed July 11, 2018. http://www.transequality.org.

Janovy, C.J. "Transgender Choruses Harness the (Changing) Power of Voices." NPR Weekend Edition broadcast Saturday, May 21, 2016. Accessed July 11, 2108. http://www.npr.org/sections/deceptivecadence/2016/05/21/478863157/transgender-choruses-harness-the-changing-power-of-voices.

Jay, Karla. *Tales of the Lavender Menace*. New York: Basic Books, 2000.

Jesudason, Melba and Sally Drew, "Feminist Music and WOMONSONG Choir of Madison, Wisconsin." *Studies in Popular Culture* 15, no. 1 (1992): 61-74. Accessed July 11, 2018. http://www.jstor.org/stable/23414480.

Johnson, Katie and Julie Lessard. "Earth, Water, Fire and Love Stories from the Dominican Republic." *MUSE Choir*. Writings: Activism, March 29, 2009. http://www.musechoir.org/writings/activism/428. (Site discontinued. Used by permission.)

Johnston, Jill. *Lesbian Nation: The Feminist Solution*. New York: Simon and Schuster, 1973.

"Join Us." Common Woman Chorus website. Accessed August 27, 2018. http://www.commonwomanchorus.net/join.

"JPPC Milestones 1922-2013." Jewish People's Philharmonic Chorus website. Accessed July 11, 2018. http://www.thejppc.org/id16.html.

Karkabi, Barbara. "Songs from the heart: For 50 women, amateur choral group HeartSong is a refuge from Houston's hectic pace." *The Houston Chronicle*, April 14, 1991, 3G. Posted in "HeartSong: Clippings and Miscellaneous," Houston LGBT History, collected by JD Doyle. Accessed July 11, 2018. http://www.houstonlgbthistory.org/heartsong-clippings.html.

Katz, Judith H. *White Awareness: Handbook for Anti-Racism Training*. Norman: University of Oklahoma Press, 1978.

Katz, Nancy. "Union Maid." In *Songs of the Workers To Fan the Flames of Discontent*, 34th ed., 46. Chicago, IL.: Industrial Workers of the World, 1973.

Keener, Mardy. "Letter to Chorus Mailing List, June 9, 1980." Sister Singers Network Archive, 1981-2003, Sophia Smith Collection, Smith College, Northampton, Massachusetts.

Kendall, Laurie J. "From the Liminal to the Land: Building Amazon Culture at the Michigan Womyn's Music Festival." Ph.D. diss., University of Maryland, 2006. Accessed August 28, 2018. https://drum.lib.umd.edu/bitstream/handle/1903/3499/umi-umd-3329.pdf?sequence=1&isAllowed=y. ProQuest [3212615].

Keogh, Tom. "Leader, Advocate, Legend." Seattle Choruses Blog, June 6, 2016, Accessed July 12, 2018. http://www.seattlechoruses.org/blog/leader-advocate-legend/#sthash.2iLmvDQ4.dpuf.

Kessler-Harris, Alice. "Labor Movement in the United States." Jewish Women's Archive website. Accessed July 11, 20018. https://jwa.org/encyclopedia/article/labor-movement-in-united-states.

Kinney, Janice. "'Making Church': The Experience of Spirituality in Women's Choruses." PhD. diss., University of Washington, 2010. Accessed August 28, 2018. https://gwss.washington.edu/research/graduate/making-church-experience-spirituality-womens-choruses. ProQuest [3445507].

Knapp, James. Interview with the author, September 18, 2014.

Kohler, Will. "Today in Gay History—June 19, 1983: Founder of the Moral Majority Jerry Falwell: 'Aids is God's Punishment for Homosexuals.'" *Back2Stonewall*. Accessed July 11, 2018. http://www.back2stonewall.com/2018/06/june-19-1983-founder-moral-majority-jerry-falwell-aids-gods-punishment-homosexuals.html.

Kort, Michelle. "Portrait of the Feminist As an Old Woman: Betty Friedan Has Survived Fame, Bitter Feuds and Heart Surgery. Now, in a New Book, She Celebrates Life, Aging and Family." *Los Angeles Times Magazine*, October 10, 1993. Accessed July 11, 2018. http://articles.latimes.com/1993-10-10/magazine/tm-44091_1_betty-friedan/7.

Koskoff, Ellen. "The Sound of a Woman's Voice: Gender in a New York Hassidic Community." In *Women and Music: A Cross-Cultural Perspective*, edited by Ellen Koskoff, 213-223. Champaign: University of Illinois Press, 1989.

Kosse, Roberta. "Chronicle of a Feminist Composer." *Paid My Dues* 2, no. 3 (Spring 1978): 6-7, 39.

Koyama, Emi. "A Handbook on Discussing the Michigan Womyn's Music Festival for Trans Activists and Allies." Accessed July 11, 2018. http://www.confluere.com/store/pdf-zn/mich-handbook.pdf.

Koza, Julia E. "Getting a Word in Edgewise: A Feminist Critique of Choral Methods Texts." *The Quarterly* 5, no. 3 (Fall, 1994). Reprinted in *Visions of Research in Music Education,* 16, no. 5 (Autumn, 2010): 68-77. Accessed July 11, 2018. http://www-usr.rider.edu/~vrme/v16n1/volume5/visions/fall8.

Krasovic, Mark. "Ex-Slave Interviews in the Depression Cultural Context." In *Been Here So Long: Selections from the WPA American Slave Narratives.* Accessed February 1, 2017. http://newdeal.feri.org/asn/hist02.htm. (Site discontinued.)

Krehbiel, Henry Edward. "Concert of the Rubenstein Club." *New York Tribune,* April 18, 1890, quoted in Horn, 42, 43.

Lacour, Greg. "How North Carolina Got Here (updated)." *Charlotte Magazine*, March 2017. http://www.charlottemagazine.com/Charlotte-Magazine/April-2016/HB2-How-North-Carolina-Got-Here.

Ladyslipper Music Women's Music Aural Herstory Interviews. Accessed August 28, 2018. https://archive.org/search.php?query=Ladyslipper%20Music.

Lambert, Bruce. "In Texas, AIDS Struggle Is Also Matter of Money." *The New York Times*, January 5, 1990. Accessed July 11, 2018. http://www. nytimes.com/1990/01/05/us/in-texas-aids-struggle-is-also-matter-of-money.html?pagewanted=all.

"Land of Our Dreams." Central Pennsylvania Womyn's Chorus website. Accessed July 9, 2018. http://www.cpwchorus.org/programs/ landofourdreams.pdf.

Lankford, Ronald D., Jr. *Folk Music U.S.A.: The Changing Voice of Protest.* New York: Schirmer Trade Books, 2005.

Lapis, Diane. "Nitgedaiget: A Vanished Utopia." *Dutchess County Historical Society 2015 Yearbook,* Volume 94, 131-145.

Lardinois André. "The parrhesia of young female choruses in Ancient Greece." In *Archaic and Classical Choral Song*, edited by Evan Bowie and Lycia Athanassaki, 161-172. Berlin: Walter deGruyter, 2011.

Larson, Libby. "I Lift My Eyes to the Mountains—Psalm 121: In Memoriam Patty Hennings." in *Take Up the Song*, 18-22.

Larson, Peggy. E-mail message to the author, July 27, 2010.

Latour, Kathy. "Sing for the Cure." *CURE*, May 6, 2010. Accessed July 11, 2018. http://www.curetoday.com/articles/sing-for-the-cure.

LeDonne, Rob. "Inside 'Shut Up and Dance,' WALK THE MOON's number one hit." *American Songwriter*, March 5, 2015. Accessed July 11, 2018. https://americansongwriter.com/2015/03/inside-shut-up-and-dance-walk-the-moons-number-one-hit.

Lee, Anna. "For the Love of Separatism." *Lesbian Ethics* 3, no. 2 (Fall, 1988). Accessed July 11, 2018. http://www.feminist-reprise.org/docs/ leelovesep.htm.

Lee, Don. "The Evolution of GLBT Choruses." Chorus America website, June 20, 2013. Accessed July 11, 2018. https://www.chorusamerica.org/ singers/evolution-glbt-choruses.

—. "Choruses and Community Wellness." Chorus America website, April 2, 2013. Accessed July 11, 2018. https://www.chorusamerica.org/ singers/choruses-and-community-wellness.

Lee, Trymaine. "Singing with the Freedom Riders: The Music of the Movement." *Huffington Post*, May 30, 2011. Accessed July 11, 2018. https://www.huffingtonpost.com/2011/05/30/gospel-and-the-freedom-ri_n_868299.html.

Levine Iris and Shelbie Wahl. "Women's Choirs: Model Repertoire Repertoire as Model." *The Choral Journal* 51, no. 11 (June-July, 2011): 55-57. Accessed July 11, 2015. http://www.jstor.org/ stable/23561627.

Lewis, Grace Ross. *1001 Chemicals in Everyday Products*. New York: John Wiley & Sons, 1999.

Lieberman, Robbie. *My Song is My Weapon: People's Songs, American Communism, and the Politics of Culture, 1930-50*. Champaign: University of Illinois Press, 1995.

Linder, Doug. "The Gay Rights Controversy." *Exploring Constitutional Conflicts*. Accessed July 11, 2018. http://law2.umkc.edu/faculty/projects/ftrials/conlaw/gayrights.htm.

Lomax, John A. *Our Singing Country*. New York: Macmillan 1941. Reprint, New York: Dover, 2000. Accessed July 11, 2018. http://www.traditionalmusic.co.uk/our-singing-country/our-singing-country%20-%200013.htm.

Lynskey, Dorian. *33 Revolutions Per Minute: A History of Protest Songs, from Billie Holiday to Green Day*. New York: Harper Collins, 2011.

MacNeela, Janie. Interview with the author, December 17, 2010.

Macy, Laura W. "Women's History and Early Music." In *Companion to Medieval and Renaissance Music*, edited by Tess Knighton and David Fallows, 93-98. Berkeley and Los Angeles: University of California Press, 1997.

Maddocks, Fiona. "Women Composers: Notes from the Musical Margins." *Guardian UK Observer*, March 13, 2011. Accessed July 11, 2018. https://www.theguardian.com/music/2011/mar/13/london-oriana-choir-women-composers.

—. *Hildegard of Bingen: The Woman of Her Age*. New York: Doubleday Image Books, 2001, 2003.

Menahan, Kelsey. "The Butterfly Music Transgender Chorus: A Safe Space for Transgender Singers." In "Beyond Outreach: Four Community Engagement Stories." Chorus America website, May 3, 2016. Accessed July 11, 2018. https://www.chorusamerica.org/education-training/beyond-outreach-four-community-engagement-stories.

—. "With Access and Accommodation for All." Chorus America website, December 2008. Accessed July 11, 2108. https://www.chorusamerica.org/management-governance/access-and-accommodation-all, reposted at http://www.performingartsconvention.org/file/Vol32No2%2008-09%20Accessibility.pdf.

Manalansan, Martin F. IV, Chantal Nadeau, Richard T. Rodriguez, and Siobhan B. Somerville, eds. *Queering the Middle: Race, Region, and a Queer Midwest: A Special Issue of the Journal of Lesbian and Gay Studies* 20, no.1-2 (2014). https://read.dukeupress.edu/glq/article/20/1-2/1/34879/Queering-the-MiddleRace-Region-and-a-Queer-Midwest. Accessed September 30, 2018.

Marech, Rona. "Singing the gospel of Transcendence: Nation's first all-transgender gospel choir raises its voices to praise God and lift their own feelings of self-love and dignity." *San Francisco Chronicle*, April 18, 2004. Accessed July 11, 2018. http://www.sfgate.com/bayarea/article/SAN-FRANCISCO-Singing-the-gospel-of-2791956.php.

Margolick, David. *Strange Fruit: Billie Holiday, Café Society, and an Early Cry for Civil Rights*. Philadelphia: Running Press, 2000.

Marigold, Margaret. "National Women's Music Festival." *Paid My Dues* 1, no. 3 (October, 1974): 15-16.

Marsh, Charles. *God's Long Summer: Stories of Faith and Civil Rights*. Princeton: Princeton University Press, 2008.

Martin, Susan F. *A Nation of Immigrants*. New York: Cambridge University Press, 2010.

Mase, Sheryl. Interview with the author, July 23, 2011.

Matthews, Susan. Interview with the Author, May 3, 2006.

Matthews Carol. Interview with the author, May 20, 2016.

May, Meredith. "Gay Men's Chorus Carries On." *SFGate*, June 4, 2006. Accessed July 11, 2018. http://www.sfgate.com/health/article/Gay-Men-s-Chorus-carries-on-A-quarter-century-2533823.php.

McClary, Susan. *Feminine Endings: Music, Gender, & Sexuality*. 2nd. ed. Minneapolis: University of Minnesota Press, 2002.

"Meet Our Youth." GALA Choruses website. Accessed July 10, 2018. http://galachoruses.org/resource-center/youth/meet-our-youth.

Meier, Kenneth J. *The Politics of Sin*. New York: Routledge, 2015. First published 1994 by Taylor and Francis.

Meixelsperger, Jennifer. "The Struggle is Real: Propaganda and Workers Songbooks Published by the Workers Music League, 1934-35." Ph.D. diss., University of Wisconsin, 2015. https://dc.uwm.edu/etd/820.

Melin, Nancy. Interview with the author, July 21, 2013.

Menk, Nancy. "Writing for Women's Voices: A Conversation with Composers." In *Conducting Women's Choirs: Strategies for Success*, edited and compiled by Debra Spurgeon, 167-188. Chicago: GIA Publications, 2012.

Meredith, Victoria. "The Pivotal Role of Brahms and Schubert in the Development of the Women's Choir." *The Choral Journal* 37, no. 7 (February, 1997): 7-12. Accessed July 11, 2018. http://www.jstor.org/stable/23551511.

Meyers Carol. "Miriam, Music, and Miracles." In *Miriam, the Magdalen, and the Mother*, edited by Deirdre Good, 27-48. Bloomington: University of Indiana Press, 2005.

"Mission and Vision." Fortissima: DC's Feminist Singers website. Accessed July 10, 2018. http://www.fortissima.org/mission_vision.shtml#. WQpTZ1Pyul

Militante, Faye. E-mail message to the author April 15, 2017.

Miller, Jamie. Interview with the author, September 12, 2014.

Miller, Jane Ramseyer. "Jane Ramseyer Miller— Interview." GALA Choruses Blog, October 11, 2013.Accessed July 11, 2018. http://galachoruses. org/blog/jane-ramseyer-miller-interview.

Miller, Jane Ramseyer. "Creating Choirs That Welcome Trans Singers." GALA Choruses Blog, February 8, 2016. Accessed July 11, 2018. http:// galachoruses.org/blog/creating-choirs-that-welcome-trans-singers.

Miller, Zamani. "Legacy of Four the Moment: Interview with Delvina Bernard," October 27, 2017. Africentric TV. Accessed July 11, 2018. https://www.youtube.com/watch?v=owFGw290R5I.

"Minutes of 1988 Meeting." Sister Singers Archive 1981-2003, Sophia Smith Collection, Smith College, Northampton, Massachusetts.

Mora, Pat. "Ode to Women." In *Adobe Odes,* 92-93. Tucson: University of Arizona Press 2006.

Morgan, Joe. "Survivors of 1980s AIDS Crisis Reveal What Happened to Them." *Gay Star News*, February 2, 2015. Accessed July 11, 2018. http://www.gaystarnews.com/article/survivors-1980s-aids-crisis-reveal-what-happened-them020215.

Morris, Bonnie. "Olivia Records: The Production of a Movement." *Journal of Lesbian Studies* 19 (2015): 290-304. Accessed July 11, 2018. DOI: 10.1080/10894160.2015.1026699.

—. *Eden Built by Eves: The Culture of Women's Music Festivals*. Los Angeles: Alyson Books, 1999.

Morris, Kelly. "Sara Bareilles: 'Brave' Was inspired by Close Friend's Coming Out." *The Seattle Lesbian*, February 3, 2014. Accessed July 11, 2018. http://theseattlelesbian.com/sara-bareilles-brave-was-inspired-by-close-friends-coming-out.

Moy, Wendy K. "Come Together: An Ethnography of the Seattle Men's Chorus Family." Ph.D. diss., University of Washington, 2015. Accessed August 23, 2018. https://digital.lib.washington.edu/researchworks/bitstream/handle/1773/33215/Moy_washington_0250E_14101.pdf?sequence=1. ProQuest [3688950].

Mumford, Marilyn. "A Feminist Prolegomenon for the Study of Hildegard of Bingen." In *Gender, Culture and The Arts: Women, the Arts, and Society,* edited by Ronald Dotterer and Susan Bowers, 44-53. Selinsgrove, Pennsylvania: Susquehanna University Press, 1993.

Murray, Gail. *Throwing Off the Cloak of Privilege: White Southern Women in the Civil Rights Era.* Gainesville: University Press of Florida, 2004.

"National Women's Choral Festival 2." 1985 Program Book. Sister Singers Network Archive, 1981-2003, Sophia Smith Collection, Smith College, Northampton, Massachusetts.

Near, Holly. *Fire in the Rain...Singer in the Storm: An Autobiography.* New York: William Morrow, 1990.

New Harmony Sisterhood Band. *"And Ain't I a Woman?"* Liner Notes. Accessed July 11, 2018. http://media.smithsonianfolkways.org/liner_notes/paredon/PAR01038.pdf.

New York City Gay Men's Chorus. 25th Anniversary Journal. Accessed July 11, 2018. https://issuu.com/jimvivyan/docs/nycgmc25/61.

Newman, Barbara. "Sybil of the Rhine." In *Voice of the Living Light: Hildegard of Bingen and Her World,*" edited by Barbara Newman, 1-29. Los Angeles: University of California Press, 1998.

—. *Sister of Wisdom: S. Hildegard's Theology of the Feminine.* Berkeley and Los Angeles: University of California Press, 1987.

"News." Southern Arizona Women's Chorus website. Accessed July 12, 2018. http://www.southernarizonawomenschorus.org/news.html.

Nicola, George T. "Oregon Anti-Gay Ballot Measures." *Gay and Lesbian Archives of the Northwest.* Accessed July 11, 2018. https://www.glapn.org/6013OregonAntiGayMeasures.html.

"No Whining, No Flowers." Cornell Chorus Commissioning Project. Cornell University Chorus website. Accessed July 11, 2018. http://cuchorus.com/commissioning-project.

Nordeen, Debbie. Interview with the author, November 7, 2009.

North, Connie. Interview with the author, March 15, 2015.

O'Brien, Lynn. Interview with the author, July 26, 2015.

O'Connor, Karyn. "The Anatomy of the Voice." *Singwise.* Accessed July 11, 2018. http://www.singwise.com/cgi-bin/main.pl?section=articles&doc=AnatomyOfVoice.

O'Dair, Barbara. *Trouble Girls: The Rolling Stone Book of Women in Rock.* New York: Random House, 1997.

O'Pry, Kay. "Social and Political Roles of Women in Athens and Sparta." *Saber and Scroll* 1, no. 2 (Summer 2012): 7-14. Edited and Revised April 2015. Accessed August 18, 2018. https://pa02217736.schoolwires.net/site/handlers/filedownload.ashx?moduleinstanceid=23317&dataid=29076&FileName=Social%20and%20Political%20Roles%20of%20Women%20in%20Athens%20and%20Sparta.pdf.

Obama, Barack. "Remarks by the President in State of the Union Address, January 20, 2015." Accessed July 11, 2018. https://obamawhitehouse.archives.gov/the-press-office/2015/01/20/remarks-president-state-union-address-january-20-2015.

Obergefell v. Hodges. Accessed July 11, 2018. https://www.supremecourt.gov/opinions/14pdf/14-556_3204.pdf.

Ode Kim. "Calliope Sings of Women's Health." *Minneapolis StarTribune*, May 13 2009. Accessed August 24, 2018. https://www.highbeam.com/doc/1G1-199872467.html.

Omega Institute. "Sing Your Prayers: an Interview with Bobby McFerrin." *HuffPost*, 6/11/2016. Accessed July 11, 2018. https://www.huffingtonpost.com/omega-institute-for-holistic-studies/bobby-mcferrin_b_1582043.html.

"Open Letter to Olivia." Reprinted in Matt Abernathy, "Transphobic Radical Hate Didn't Start with Brennan: The Sandy Stone-Olivia Records Controversy." *The Trans-Advocate*, n.d. Accessed July 11, 2018. http://transadvocate.com/transphobic-radical-hate-didnt-start-with-brennan-the-sandy-stone-olivia-records-controversy_n_4112.htm.

"Orange County Women's Chorus Presents 'You Can't Sing That!'" Press release, April 20, 2009. http://www.ocwomenschorus.org/sites/default/files/OCWC-PR-You-Can't-Sing-That.pdf. (Site discontinued.)

Orr, N. Lee. "The United States." In *Nineteenth Century Choral Singing*, edited by Donna M. DiGrazia, 475-499. New York: Taylor and Francis, 2013.

Osborne, Karen Lee and William J. Spurlin, eds. *Reclaiming the Heartland: Lesbian and Gay Voices from the Midwest*. Minneapolis: University of Minnesota Press, 1996.

"Our Herstory." Artemis Singers website. Accessed July 9, 2018. https://artemissingers.org/herstory.

"Our Herstory." Voices Rising website. Accessed July 12, 2018. http://www.voicesrising.org/about-voices-rising/our-herstory.

"Our Music." Fisk Jubilee Singers website. Accessed August 29, 2018. http://fiskjubileesingers.org/the-music/.

"Our Vision." Voices Rising website. Accessed July 12, 2018. http://www. voicesrising.org/about-voices-rising.

Packer, William. "Vivaldi and the Chorus of Unwanted Children." *Financial Times.Com*, August 29, 2005.Accessed July 11, 2018. http://www. toddtarantino.com/hum/vivaldiarticle.html.

Page, Christopher. *The Owl and the Nightingale: Instrumental Practice and Songs in France, 1100-1300.* Berkeley & Los Angeles: University of California Press, 1989.

Palmer, Pamela. "Lucie E. Campbell-Williams: A Legacy of Leadership through the Gospel." 2008 Rhodes Institute for Regional Studies, 15. Accessed July 12, 2018. https://dlynx.rhodes.edu/jspui/ bitstream/10267/23978/1/2008-Pamela_Palmer-Lucie_E_Campbell_ Williams-Blankenship.pdf.

Parham, Marte. Interview with the author, September 12, 2014.

Park, Haeyoun and Iaryna Mykhyalyshyn. "L.G.B.T. People Are More Likely to Be Targets of Hate Cries Than Any Other Minority Group." *The New York Times*, June 16, 2016. Accessed July 12, 2018. https://www. nytimes.com/interactive/2016/06/16/us/hate-crimes-against-lgbt. html?_r=0.

Parsons, Betsy. Interview with the author, September 5, 2008.

Patterson, Laura. "The Late 20th Century Commercial Revival of Hildegard of Bingen." Master's thesis, Washington University in St. Louis, 2010. Accessed August 18, 2018. https://openscholarship.wustl.edu/cgi/ viewcontent.cgi?article=1476&context=etd.

Pereclay, Rachel. "Seventeen School Districts Debunk Right-Wing Lies About Protections for Transgender Students." *Media Matters for America*, June 3, 2015. Accessed July 12, 2018. https://mediamatters. org/research/2015/06/03/17-school-districts-debunk-right-wing- lies-abou/203867.

Petersen, Karen E. "An Investigation into Women Identified Music in the United States." In *Women and Music in Cross-Cultural Perspective*, edited by Ellen Koskoff, 203-212. Champaign: University of Illinois Press, 1987.

"Past Performances." Resonance Women's Chorus website. Accessed July 12, 2018. .http://www.resonancechorus.org/past-performances.html

Petricca, Nicholas, Kevin Ray, Sean Waugaman, Eli Maiman, Ryan Mcmahon, and Ben Burger. "Shut Up and Dance." Warner/Chappell Music, Inc.

Philbrook, Erik with Brianne Galli. "Pihcintu, A Unique Multicultural Chorus from Maine, Gives Children from War-torn Countries Hope and a Voice." Accessed July 12, 2018. ASCAP website. https://www.ascap.com/playback/2012/02/radar-report/pihcintu.aspx.

Phillips, Estelle. Interview with the author, July 3, 2010.

Phillips, Scoop. "The Churches: Not Always the Enemy." In "Excavating Our Pride," Feature Supplement, *Kansas City News-Telegraph*, March 1992. Accessed July 12, 2018. https://library2.umkc.edu/spec-col/glama/pdfs/history/article-phillips2.pdf.

—. "The Making of a Community." In "Excavating Our Pride." https://library2.umkc.edu/spec-col/glama/pdfs/history/article-phillips1.pdf.

Phoenix Women's Chorus. Group interview with the author, March 8, 2011.

"Planning/Invitational Letter." Sister Singers Archive 1981-2003, Sophia Smith Collection, Smith College, Northampton, Massachusetts.

Pomeroy, Sarah. *Goddesses, Whores, Wives, and Slaves: Women in Classical Antiquity.* New York: Schocken Books, 1975, 1995.

"Portland to Host 8th Festival." *Across the Lines: The Sister Singers Newsletter* (May, 1996), 1,3. Sister Singers Archive 1981-2003, Sophia Smith Collection, Smith College, Northampton, Massachusetts.

Pride. Directed by Matthew Warchus. Pathé, BBC films, 2014. DVD. Available for rental at https://www.youtube.com/watch?v=Jv4XKNUAzCM.

"Protecting Youth and Your Chorus." GALA Choruses Resource Center. GLA Choruses website. Accessed July 10, 2018. http://galachoruses.org/resource-center/youth/protecting-youth-and-chorus.

Quin-Easter Erica. "Singing in Another Voice: Exploring the Mystery of Multiculturalism with American Slavic Choirs." Master's essay, University of Southern Maine, 2006.

—. Program Notes, "Women in Harmony: Moving On: Immigration In Song," Portland, Maine, May 14-14, 2011. In possession of the author.

Quinn, John. "Local Businessman to Wrestle in Gay Games VI." *Between the Lines,* July 13, 2006. Accessed August 23, 2018. https://pridesource.com/article/19498; https://galachoruses.org/about/history.

Radical Harmonies. Directed by Dee Mosbacher. San Francisco: Woman Vision, 2002. DVD.

Ramirez, Marc. "Lon Mabon Sets 'Em Straight." *Seattle Times*, October 3, 1993. Accessed July 12, 2018. http://community.seattletimes.nwsource.com/archive/?date=19931003&slug=1724056.

Rapp, Linda, "Christian, Meg." *GLBTQ Encyclopedia.* Accessed July 12, 2018. http://www.glbtqarchive.com/arts/christian_m_A.pdf.

Ray, Linda (Echo). Interview with the author, July 5, 2010.

Ray, Linda and Linda Small. "Letter to Sister Singers, January 2, 1981." Sister Singers Network Archive, 1981-2003, Sophia Smith Collection, Smith College, Northampton, Massachusetts.

Raymond, Janice. *The Transsexual Empire: The Making of the She-Male.* New York: Teachers College Press, 1994. First published 1979.

Rayor, Diane J. "Competition and Eroticism in Alcman's Parthenaion [1PMG]." *American Philological Society Association Annual Meeting Abstracts.* Decatur, Illinois, 1987.

Reagon, Bernice Johnson. "Foreword." In *Reimaging America: The Arts of Social Change*, edited by Mark Obrien and Craig Little, 1-8. Philadelphia: New Society Publishers, 1990.

—. *Compositions One.* Washington, D.C.: Songtalk, 1986.

—. "In Our Hands: Thoughts on Black Music." *Sing Out!* 24 (January/February 1976): 1–2, 5.

—. "Let Your Light Shine—Historical Notes," in *We Who Believe in Freedom: Sweet Honey in the Rock...Still on the Journey* 13-69.

—. "Singing for my Life." In *We Who Believe in Freedom: Sweet Honey in the Rock...Still on the Journey*, 133-168.

Redmond, Layne. *When the Drummers Were Women: A Spiritual History of Rhythm.* New York: Three Rivers Press, 1997.

Regner, Julie. Interview with the author, July 1, 2010.

Reid, Erin. Interview with the author, August 27, 2015.

Reuss, Richard with Joanne Reuss. *American Folk Music and Left-Wing Politics, 1927-1957.* Lanham, Maryland: Scarecrow Press, 2000.

Robertson, Mary. E-mail message to the author, Aug. 5, 2014.

Robinson, Joe. "Is Your Work Ethic Keeping You from Living Your Life?" *Huffington Post* Blog, December 7, 2010, updated November 17, 2011. Accessed July 12, 2018. http://www.huffingtonpost.com/joe-robinson/why-the-work-mind-leaves_b_790703.html.

Rockwell, John. "The Pop Life Deadly Nightshade Trio Speaks Well of Women." *The New York Times*, Sept. 13, 1974. Accessed August 20, 2018. http://www.nytimes.com/1974/09/13/archives/deadly-nightshade-trio-speaks-well-of-women-the-pop-life.html.

Roma Catherine. Interviewed by Jane Ramseyer Miller. Gala Choruses Blog, July 28, 2014. Accessed July 12, 2018. https://galachoruses.org/blog/cathy-roma-and-jane-ramseyer-miller.

—. "Women's Choral Literature: Finding Depth." *The Choral Journal* 44, no. 10 (May, 2004): 29-37. Accessed July 12, 2018. http://www.jstor.org/stable/23555441.

—. Interview by Joyce Follet, June 19 and 20, 2005. Voices of Feminism Oral History Project, Sophia Smith Collection, Smith College, Northampton, Massachusetts.

—. Interview with the author, April 7, 2010.

Roma, Catherine and Marilyn Ebertz. "The Seventh National Women's Choral Festival: A Feminist Fourth." *Hot Wire* 10, no. 1 (January 1994): 22-23, 57.

Roth, Benita. *Separate Roads to Feminism: Black, Chicana, and White Feminist Movements in America's Second Wave*. Cambridge, UK: Cambridge University Press, 2004.

Rothstein, Edward. "CONCERT: 'FIRST GAY CHORAL FESTIVAL." *The New York Times*, September. 9, 1983. Accessed August 23, 2018. https://www.nytimes.com/1983/09/13/arts/concert-first-gay-choral-festival.html

"Rubenstein Club." *The Encyclopedia of Cleveland History*. Accessed July 12, 2018. http://ech.case.edu/cgi/article.pl?id=RC3.

Rubin-Rabson, Grace. "Why Haven't Women Become Great Composers?" *High Fidelity* 23, no.2 (February, 1973): 46-53.

Rufo, Robert. "34 Years Later, Harvey Milk's Legacy Lives On." Accessed July 12, 2018. https://www.youtube.com/watch?v=AT1TO075xwk.

Saint Louis Coordinating Committee. "Letter to Sister Singers, June 12, 1984." Sister Singers Network Archive, 1981-2003, Sophia Smith Collection, Smith College, Northampton, Massachusetts.

Sanday, Peggy R. "Female Status in the Public Domain." In *Woman, Culture, and Society*, edited by Michelle Zimbalist Rosaldo and Louise Lamphere, 189-206. Stanford: Stanford University Press, 1973.

Sandstrom, Boden. "Performance, Ritual and Negotiation of Identity in the Michigan Womyn's Music Festival." Ph.D. diss., University of Maryland, 2002. Accessed August 22, 2018. ProQuest [3080281].

—. "Women's Music, Passing the Legacy." In *Women's Culture: The Women's Renaissance of the Seventies*, edited by Gayle Kimball, 99-134. London: Scarecrow Press, 1981.

Sargent, Mary Lee. Interview with the author, August 18, 2011.

Say Amen, Somebody. Directed by George T Nirenberg. GTN Productions, 1982. DVD.

Scalza Janice. Interview with the author, July 23, 2011.

—. Letter to Lucille Clifton, reprinted in Gwyneth Walker, "Lucille Clifton Writes on Experiencing Her Poetry." Gwynth Walker's website. Accessed July 12, 2018. https://www.gwynethwalker.com/clifton.html.

Schaefer, Jacob. *Mit Gesang Tzum Kampf.* New York: International Workers Order, 1932.

Schneir, Miriam, ed. *Feminism in Our Time: The Essential Writings, World War II to the Present.* New York: Vintage Books, 1994.

Schultz, Debra. *Going South: Jewish Women in The Civil Rights Movement.* New York: New York University Press, 2001.

"Seattle Men's Chorus & Seattle Women's Chorus Celebrate Marriage Equality in Washington State." Accessed August 24, 2018. https://www.youtube.com/watch?v=YueVSEOSXe8.

Seeger, Nancy. "Sisterfire '88." *Hot Wire* 5, no. 1 (January, 1989): 30-31.

—. "Welcome Back Sisterfire 1987." *Hot Wire* 4, no. 1 (November, 1987): 38-40.

Seeger, Pete. *Talking Union and other Union Songs.* The Almanac Singers. Washington DC: Folkways Records, 1955. Liner notes.

Seeger, Pete and Bob Reiser. *Carry It On.* New York: Simon and Schuster, 1985.

Seelig, Tim. Interview by JD Doyle. "Gay & Lesbian Choruses: The History & Music of the Gay & Lesbian Choral Movement." Queer Music Heritage, November 2010. http://queermusicheritage.com/nov2010.html.

—. Interviewed by Kris Schindler. "An Interview with the Conductor of Sing for the Cure: Dr. Timothy Seelig." Accessed July 12, 2018. https://www.youtube.com/watch?v=9B4tLzLruvQ.

Setoodeh, Ramin. "Young, Gay and Murdered in Junior High." *Newsweek,* July 18, 2008. Accessed August 28, 2018. https://www.newsweek.com/young-gay-and-murdered-junior-high-92787.

Seyforth Scott C. and Nichole Barnes. "'In People's Faces for Lesbian and Gay Rights': Stories of Activism in Madison, Wisconsin, 1970 to 1990." *The Oral History Review* 43, no. 1 (Spring, 2016): 81–97. Advance Access publication 17 March 2016.

Shaw Kim. Interview with the author, July 1, 2010.

Shelton, Robert. "Songs a New Weapon Civil Rights Battle. *The New York Times,* August 20, 1962. Accessed July 12, 2018. http://www.nytimes.com/learning/teachers/archival/19620820songsweapon.pdf.

Siciliani, Teri. Interview with the author, May 29, 2011.

"Sisterfire Music festival to ignite next weekend." *The Washington Blade*, June 24, 1988: 3. Accessed July 12, 2018. http://digdc.dclibrary.org/cdm/ref/collection/p16808coll24/id/14766.

Small, Christopher. *Musicking: The Meanings of Performing and Listening.* Middletown, Connecticut: Wesleyan University Press, 1998.

Small, Linda. "How to Share Music Without Getting Arrested for being Politically Incorrect." Sister Singers Network Archive, 1981-2003, Sophia Smith Collection, Smith College, Northampton, Massachusetts.

Small Linda and Linda Ray. "Letter to Chorus Mailing List, October 28, 1980." Sister Singers Network Archive, 1981-2003, Sophia Smith Collection, Smith College, Northampton, Massachusetts.

Smith, James William. "Political Parthenoi: The Social and Political Significance of Female Performance in Archaic Greece." Ph.D. diss., University of Exeter, 2013. Accessed July 12, 2018. http://hdl.handle.net/10871/10901.

Smothers, Ronald. "Newark Preaches Tolerance of Gays Year After Killing." *The New York Times*, May 12, 2004.Accessed July 12, 2018. http://www.nytimes.com/2004/05/12/nyregion/newark-preaches-tolerance-of-gays-year-after-killing.html.

Snyder, Robert. "The Paterson Jewish Folk Chorus: Politics, Ethnicity and Musical Culture. *American Jewish History* 74, no. 1 (September, 1964): 27-44. Accessed July 12 2018. http://www.jstor.org/stable/23882496.

Snow, Jan C. Interview with the author, July 25, 2015.

Solie Ruth. "Afterword." In Drinker, *Music & Women*, 325-368.

"Something Inside So Strong." BBC Soul Music. Series 18, Episode 3. Accessed July 9, 2018. http://www.bbc.co.uk/programmes/b040hx6j.

Southern Poverty Law Center. *SPLC Intelligence Report.* 2010 Winter Issue (February 27, 2011). Accessed July 12, 2018. https://www.splcenter.org/fighting-hate/intelligence-report/2011/anti-gay-hate-crimes-doing-math.

Spegal, Kathie. Interview with the author, July 21, 2013.

Stebbins, Lucy Poate & Richard Poate Stebbins. *Frank Damrosch: Let The People Sing.* Durham: Duke University Press, 1945.

Stehle Eva. *Performance and Gender in Ancient Greece: Nondramatic Poetry in its Setting.* Princeton: Princeton University Press, 1979.

Stein, Marc. "Memories of the 1987 March on Washington." *OutHistory.org.* Accessed July 12, 2018. http://outhistory.org/exhibits/show/march-on-washington/exhibit/by-marc-stein.

Steinbeck, John. "Foreword." In *Hard Hitting Songs for Hard-Hit People*, edited by Alan Lomax, Woody Guthrie, and Pete Seeger, 8-14. New York: Oak Publications, 1967.

Steiner, Jody and Laurie Rothfeld. "ASL Interpreting for Concerts: An Interpreter's Voice." *Hot Wire* 2, no. 1 (November 1985): 8-9, 61.

Stephan, Naomi. "Is it Just (,) You Girls? A Plea for Women's Choral Music." *IAWM Journal* 11, no. 2 (2005):1-9.

Stocker, Midge. "Self-Directed Chorus." Sister Singers website. Accessed July 12, 2018. http://www.sistersingers.net/Tools/SelfDirectedChorus. shtml#.WQpUAFMrKlM

—. Interview with the author, May 29, 2011.

Stone, Amy L. *Gay Rights at the Ballot Box*. Minneapolis; University of Minnesota Press, 2012.

Stone, Merlin. *When God Was a Woman*. New York: Houghton Mifflin, 1976.

Stone, Sandy. "The Empire Strikes Back: A Posttransexual Manifesto." Accessed July 12, 2018. https://sandystone.com/empire-strikes-back. pdf.

"Student Life and Culture." University of Illinois at Urbana-Champaign Archives. Accessed July 12, 2018. http://archives.library.illinois.edu/ slc/research-education/timeline/1970-1979.

Sturgis Susanna J. "Ladyslipper: Meeting the Challenge of Feminist Business." *Hot Wire*, 1, no. 2 (March, 1985): 36-38.

—."The D.C. Area Feminist Chorus." *Hot Wire*, 2, no. 1 (November 1985): 48-49.

Sulik, Gayle. *Pink Ribbon Blues: How Breast Cancer Culture Undermines Women's Health*. New York: Oxford University Press, 2011.

Swafford, Jan. *Johannes Brahms: A Biography*. New York: Alfred A Knopf, 1997.

Swan Philip A. "The Y Factor in an X Chromosome World." In *Conducting Women's Choirs,* 133-143.

Sydney Women's Vocal Orchestra website. Accessed July 12, 2018. https:// swvo.wordpress.com/about.

Szymko, Joan. Interview with author, August 31, 2010.

—. "*Viriditas*: The Breeze That Nurtures All Things Green." In *Take Up the Song*, 24-25.

Takai, George. "It's Not About Bathrooms." Twitter Post, February 23, 2017. Accessed July 12, 20187. https://twitter.com/georgetakei/ status/834907705349386240?lang=en.

Talbot, Michael. ""Tenors and Basses at the Venetian 'Ospedali.'" *Acta Musicologica* 66, no. 2 (July - December, 1994): 123-138. Accessed August 29, 2018. DOI: 10.2307/932767. https://www.jstor.org/stable/932767.

Tallen, Bette S. "How Inclusive Is Feminist Political Theory? Questions for Lesbians." In *Just Methods: An Interdisciplinary Feminist Reader*, edited by Alison M. Jaeger. Updated ed., 205-212. New York: Routledge, 2016.

Tan, Avianne. "Boston Chorus Empowers Transgender Singers by Helping Them Find Their Voices." *ABC News*, December 10, 2015. Accessed July 12, 2018. http://abcnews.go.com/US/boston-chorus-empowers-transgender-singers-helping-find-voices/story?id=35699949.

"Tenth National Choral Festival Program." Sister Singers Network. In the author's possession.

Terkel, Studs. "Louis Armstrong, 1962." In *And They All Sang: Great Musicians Talk About Their Music*, 145-148. London: Granta Books, 2007.

The American Future: A History. Presented by Simon Schama. BBC Two, 2008. DVD.

"The Chorus Impact Study: How Children, Adults, and Communities Benefit from Choruses." Chorus America website, 2009. Accessed October 3, 2018. https://www.chorusamerica.org/publications/research-reports/chorus-impact-study.

The Combahee River Collective: "The Combahee River Collective Statement," copyright © 1978 by Zillah Eisenstein. Accessed July 12, 2018. http://americanstudies.yale.edu/sites/default/files/files/Keyword%20Coalition_Readings.pdf.

"The History of Coming Out." The Human Rights Campaign website. Accessed July 12, 2018. http://www.hrc.org/resources/the-history-of-coming-out.

The Military Wives. *Wherever You Are*. London: HarperCollins, 2013.

"The Red Ribbon Project." Visual Aids website. Accessed July 12, 2018. https://www.visualaids.org/projects/detail/the-red-ribbon-project.

"Think Before You Pink, a Project of Breast Cancer Action." Accessed July 12, 2018. http://thinkbeforeyoupink.org.

Tick Judith. *Ruth Crawford Seeger: A Composer's Search for American Music*. New York: Oxford University Press., 2000.

"Transcendence Gospel Choir." Transfaith website. Accessed July 12, 2018. http://www.transfaithonline.org/explore/christian/traditions/black/transcendence_gospel_choir.

Trible, Phyllis. "Bringing Miriam Out of the Shadows," in *A Feminist Companion to Exodus-Deuteronomy*, edited by Athalya Brenner, 166-186. Sheffield England: Sheffield Academic Press, Ltd. 1994.

Trumbore, Dale. "Composing While Female." Center for New Music website, August 17, 2015. Accessed July 12 2018. http://centerfornewmusic.com/composing-while-female.

"Upcoming Performance: Performance: Marriage Equality Open House." Calliope Women's Chorus website. Accessed July 9, 2018. https://calliopewomenschorus.org/2012/09/18/upcoming-performance-marriage-equality-open-house.

Van Ausdall, Aimee. Facebook post. January 31, 2017. Used by permission.

van Dijk-Hemmes, Fokkelien. "Traces of Women's Texts in the Hebrew Bible." In *On Gendering Texts: Female and Male Voices in the Hebrew Bible*, edited by Athalya Brenner and Fokkelien van Dijk-Hemmes, 17-112. Leiden, The Netherlands, E.J. Brill, 1996.

Van Engen, John. "Abbess: 'Mother and Teacher.'" In *Voice of the Living Light: Hildegard von Bingen and Her World*, edited by Barbara Newman, 30-51. Los Angeles: University of California Press, 1998.

Vasilakes, Argerie. Interview with the author, July 26, 2015.

Vickhoff Björn, Helge Malmgren, Rickard Åström, Gunnar Nyberg, Seth-Reino Ekström, Mathias Engwall, Johan Snygg, Michael Nilsson, and Rebecka Jörnsten. "Music Structure Determines Heart Rate Variability of Singers." *Frontiers in Psychology* 9 (July, 2013). Accessed August 26, 2018. https://doi.org/10.3389/fpsyg.2013.00334

Vivaldi's Women Facebook Page. https://www.facebook.com/Vivaldis-Women-191192901080329.

Vivaldi's Women. Directed by Rupert Edwards. BBC Wales, 2006. DVD. Courtesy of Richard Vendome. Used by permission.

Voices from the Heart website. Accessed July 12, 2018. http://www.voicesfromtheheart.org.

Wachspress, Debbie. E-mail message to the author, June 18, 2015.

—. "A Reflection from Rochester." *Across the Lines: The Sister Singers Newsletter*, no. 4 (1993). Sister Singers Archive, 1981-2003, Sophia Smith Collection, Smith College, Northampton, Massachusetts.

Wadler, Joyce. "A Baton Is Passed, but the Chorus Sings On." *The New York Times*, June 25, 1998. Accessed July 12, 2018. http://www.nytimes.com/1998/06/25/nyregion/public-lives-a-baton-is-passed-but-the-chorus-sings-on.html.

Wahl, Shelbie. "By Women, For Women: Choral Works for Women's Voices." In *Conducting Women's Choirs*, 144-166.

Walker, Alice. "Sweet Honey in the Rock—The Sound of Our Own Culture." In *We Who Believe in Freedom: Sweet Honey in the Rock...Still on the Journey*, 7-10.

Walker, Steve. "Women's chorus sets issues to music." *The KC View*, October 18-31, 1989. Sister Singers Archive 1981-2003, Sophia Smith Collection, Smith College, Northampton, Massachusetts.

Wallner, Joan. "Founding Mothers: Twenty-five years at Amazon." *Minnesota Women's Press*, January 25, 1995, 19, 27.

Ward Michael and Mark Freeman. "Defending Gay Rights: The Campaign Against the Briggs Amendment in California." *Radical America* 13, no. 4 (July-Aug.1979): 11-26. Accessed August 23, 2018. https://library. brown.edu/pdfs/1125404303746164.pdf.

"We Make the Music: 1987 Program Book." Sister Singers Archive 1981-2003, Sophia Smith Collection, Smith College, Northampton, Massachusetts.

Weber, Deanna F. "The SNCC Freedom Singers: Ambassadors for Justice." In *We Shall Overcome: Essays on A Great American Song*, edited by Victor V. Bobetsky, 27-42. Lanham, Maryland: Rowman and Littlefield, 2015.

Weinert, Naomi. Interview with the author, July 2, 2010.

Weisstein, Naomi. "Days of Celebration and Resistance: The Chicago Women's Liberation Rock Band, 1970-1973." In *The Feminist Memoir Project: Voices from Women's Liberation*, edited by Rachel Blau DePlessis and Ann Snitow, 350-361. New Brunswick, New Jersey: Rutgers University Press, 2007.

Welter, Barbara. "The Cult of True Womanhood: 1820-1860." *American Quarterly* 18, no. 2, Part 1 (Summer, 1966): 151-174.

Wexler, Sanford. *The Civil Rights Movement: An Eyewitness History*. New York: Facts on File, 1993.

"What She Wants." *The Encyclopedia of Cleveland History*. Case Western Reserve University. Accessed July 12, 2018 http://ech.case.edu/cgi/ article.pl?id=WSW.

Wheeler, Carol. Interview with the author, August 10, 2014.

White, Carol. Keynote speech presented at the Denver Women's Chorus 30th Anniversary Dinner, Denver, Colorado, May 17, 2014.

White, Micky. "Vivaldi and the Pietà." Accessed August 18, 2018. http://www. excellence-earlychildhood.ca/documents/Micky_White.pdf.

White, Wendy. Interview with the author, October 8, 2015.

Whitesitt, Linda. "Women as 'Keepers of Culture': Music Clubs, Community Concert Series, and Symphony Orchestras." In *Cultivating Music in America: Women Patrons and Activists since 1860*, edited by Ralph P. Locke & Cyrilla Barr, 65-86. Berkeley & Los Angeles: University of California Press 1997.

Weigand, Kate. *Red Feminism: American Communism and the Making of Women's Liberation*. Baltimore: The Johns Hopkins University Press, 2001.

Williams, Cristan. "Michigan Womyn's Music Festival." *The TransAdvocate*, April 9, 2013. Accessed July 12, 2018. http://transadvocate.com/ michigan-womyns-music-festival_n_8943.htm.

Windsong: Cleveland's Feminist Chorus website. Accessed July 12, 2018. http://windsongcleveland.org.

Wolensky, Kenneth C. "'We're Singing for the Union': The ILGWU Chorus in Pennsylvania Coal Country, 1947-2000." In *Chorus and Community*, 223-247.

Wolff, Francie. *Give the Ballot to the Mothers: Songs of the Suffragists - A History in Song*. Springfield, MO: Delinger's, 1988.

Womack, Catherine. "LA's First Trans Chorus is Drowning Out the Nasty Rhetoric." *LA Weekly*, May 5, 2016. Accessed July 12, 2018. http:// www.laweekly.com/arts/las-first-trans-chorus-is-drowning-out-the-nasty-rhetoric-6899760.

Womack, Jennifer. "Singing for Our Lives." Master's thesis, The University of North Carolina at Chapel Hill, 2009. ProQuest [1467319].

"Women's Choir Repertoire & Standards Leadership." American Choral Directors Association website. Accessed July 9, 2018. https://acda. org/ACDA/Repertoire_and_Resources/Repertoire_specific/womens_ choir_History.aspx.

"Year on Twitter: #LoveWins in the United States," posted December 14, 2015. Accessed July 12, 2018. https://twitter.com/i/ moments/672083334550446080?lang=en.

Yount, Rena. "Sisterfire." *Hotwire* 1, no. 1 (November 1984): 28-29, 61-62.

Zamansky, Stephen. "Colorado's Amendment 2 and Homosexuals' Right to Equal Protection of the Law." *Boston College Law Review* 35, no. 1 (1993): 221-258. Accessed July 12, 2018. http://lawdigitalcommons. bc.edu/bclr/vol35/iss1/6.

Zezima, Katie. "'Not about bathrooms': Critics decry North Carolina law's lesser-known elements." *The Washington Post*, May 14, 2016. Accessed July 12, 2018. https://www.washingtonpost.com/national/not-about-bathrooms-critics-decry-north-carolina-laws-lesser-known-elements/2016/05/14/387946ec-186b-11e6-924d-838753295f9a_ story.html?utm_term=.84316dd69349.

Index

M

Mabon, Lon 187, 328

Madison, Wisconsin 107-10, 112, 136, 149, 168, 176, 319, 331

Maines, Nicole 251

male directors 195-98, 235

March on Washington (1987) 120, 169, 188, 307, 332

marriage equality 199, 237-241, 312, 317

Mase, Sheryl 233-35, 323

Matheson, Min and Bill 62

Matthews, Carol 222-24, 323

McFerrin, Bobby 167, 216-17, 326

McLauren, Charles 65

Measure 8 *See Oregon Citizen's Alliance*

Meier, Camilla 30-31

Meier, Franziska 24-31

Melin, Nancy 120-21, 135, 323

Mellaart, James 1-2

Menahan, Kelsey 161, 322

Mendocino Women's Choir 160

Merriam, Eve 53

Metzner, Linda 150, 151

Meyers, Carol 4-5, 324

Michigan 49, 81, 92-93, 99, 113, 119, 122-125, 127, 132, 133-34, 155-56, 210, 233-35, 240, 253, 330, 337

Michigan Womyn's Music Festival 81, 93, 99, 113, 119, 122-25, 127-28, 132-34, 253, 319, 320, 330, 337

Midwest, stereotypes and culture 44, 76, 119, 133-37, 170, 326

Milk, Harvey 120, 175-76, 256, 330

Miller, Gary *vi*, 183

Miller, Jane Ramseyer 185, 214, 254-255, 257, 324, 329

Millett, Kate 119

Millington, June and Jean 78

Miriam (Hebrew Bible) *viii*, 3-5, 305, 308, 310, 324, 335

Morality Politics 186-87

Morris, Bonnie 89, 134, 324

Moses, Bob 65

Mothersingers 39

Moy, Wendy 194, 324

MUSE Cincinnati Women's Choir 112, 117, 152, 153, 163, 164-67, 171, 179, 202, 204-05, 214, 215, 232, 248, 261, 319

Music & Women 2-3, 312

Musicking (Christopher Small) 100, 138, 221, 332

N

National Association of Colored Women 36

National Convention of Gospel Choirs and Choruses 42

National Organization for Women (NOW) 72, 313

National Women's Music Festival 81, 94, 119-22, 126, 132-35, 232, 263, 305, 312, 323

Near, Holly 81, 83, 86-88, 90, 93, 95, 99, 124, 129, 155, 167, 190-91, 211, 325

New Harmony Sisterhood Band 79-80, 306, 325

New Spirituals Project 167, 171, 215, 318

New York City *vi*, 33-35, 38-39, 44-45, 47, 55, 57-58, 61, 62, 72, 75, 81, 100-02, 103, 119, 156, 176, 177, 183, 190, 212, 242, 260

New York City Gay Men's Chorus *vi*, 176, 177, 183, 190-91, 242, 325

Nordeen, Debbie 149-50, 159, 325

O

O'Brien, Lynn *iii*, 325

O'Toole, Patricia 21-22

Obergefell v. Hodges 199, 237, 240-41, 326

Off Our Backs 125, 317

Olivia Collective 88-92, 252

Olivia Records 88-92, 99, 103, 104, 252, 324

About the Author

A former Professor of Teacher Education and Women's Studies at the University of Southern Maine until her retirement in 2010, Rita Kissen also taught high school and college in Massachusetts, Nebraska, and Michigan. She is the author of *The Last Closet: The Real Lives of Lesbian and Gay Teachers* and the editor of *Getting Ready for Benjamin: Preparing Teachers for Social Diversity in the Classroom*. Rita was a founding member of the Portland, Maine chapter of PFLAG (Parents, Families and Friends of Lesbians and Gays) and of the Southern Maine Chapter of GLSEN (the Gay, Lesbian and Straight Education Network). She and her husband, Norm Rasulis, lived on Peaks Island, Maine for 20 years before moving to Fort Collins, Colorado in 2013. She is a proud alumna of Women in Harmony of Portland, Maine, and now spends her time singing with the Silvertones Senior Chorus of Fort Collins, volunteering with like-minded activists, traveling with Norm, and enjoying her five grandchildren.

Rita and Conrad, 2009

Made in the USA
Middletown, DE
29 July 2019